IMPERIAL
FOOTPRINTS

ALSO BY JAMES L. NEWMAN

The Peopling of Africa: A Geographical Interpretation

Eliminating Hunger in Africa: Technical and Human Perspectives
With Daniel Griffith

Population: Patterns, Dynamics, and Prospects
With Gordon Matzke

Contemporary Africa: Geography and Change
With C. Gregory Knight

*The Ecological Basis for Subsistence Change among
the Sandawe of Tanzania*

Editor of Drought, Famine and Population Movements in Africa

IMPERIAL
FOOTPRINTS

Henry Morton Stanley's African Journeys

JAMES L. NEWMAN

Brassey's, Inc.
Washington, D.C.

Library of Congress Cataloging-in-Publication Data

Newman, James L.
  Imperial footprints : Henry Morton Stanley's African journeys / James L. Newman.—1st ed.
      p. cm.
    Includes bibliographical references (p.   ) and index.
    ISBN 1-57488-597-9 (alk. paper)
    1. Stanley, Henry Morton, Sir, 1841–1904. 2. Explorers—Africa, Sub-Saharan—Biography. 3. Explorers—Great Britain—Biography. 4. Africa, Sub-Saharan—Description and travel. 5. Africa, Sub-Saharan—Discovery and exploration—British. I. Title.
  DT363.2.S755N47   2004
  916.704'23'092—dc22
  [B]   2004051838

ISBN 1-57488-597-9

(alk. paper)

Printed in the United States of America on acid-free paper that meets the American National Standards Institute Z39-48 Standard.

Brassey's, Inc.
22841 Quicksilver Drive
Dulles, Virginia 20166

First Edition

10 9 8 7 6 5 4 3 2 1

To Philip W. Porter
and
Ward J. Barrett,
teachers, advisors, mentors,
and friends

Contents

List of Maps

List of Illustrations

Acknowledgments

AUTHORS of biographies inevitably owe many people for an array of things. Some are anonymous, such as those in the library at University College London's School of Oriental and African Studies who helped me with the Mackinnon Papers that are so important to the chapter on the Emin Pasha expedition. Also included in the ranks of the anonymous are the employees of the British Library's newspaper collection, whose courteous efficiency always made the train ride from London to Colindale a fruitful one. And I can't forget to mention Syracuse University's interlibrary loan staff, who quickly located many hard-to-find books and articles that I needed.

As for identifiable people, I must start with the History of the Belgian Presence Overseas division of the Musée Royal de l'Afrique Centrale, or Koninklijk Museum voor Midden-Afrika, depending on one's Belgian language preference, where I went every summer from 1997 to 2002 to consult the Stanley Archive. Without access and assistance I could not have written this book. My first contact was department head Philippe Marechal, whose kindly response to a request to consult the archive portended things to come. When I showed up at the door of the Stanley Pavilion for the first time on a rare warm early-May morning, Patricia Van Schuylenbergh welcomed me with a smile. At that time the papers were still cataloged under a cumbersome system designed by Christie's that made locating items difficult, if not impossible. But she handled each request cheerfully and in all instances emerged from the basement vault having miraculously found the item. This pattern continued the next year, when toward the end of my stay I was introduced to Maurits Wynants. An expert on Tervuren history, he'd been hired to recatalog the papers into a more usable system. What a godsend! He eased my task in so many ways that it would take pages to enumerate them. Over the years since that first meeting, we've become both colleagues and friends. Others at the Pavilion to whom I owe a lot, including being made to feel part of the family, are Sabine Cornelis, Nancy Vanderlinden, Anne Welschen, Jos Libotten, and Peter Daerden.

The list of people in Tervuren who are essential parts of this book includes several outside the museum. For sheer enthusiasm, no one beats Ramón Jiménez Fraile. He researched Stanley's times in Spain as a newspaper reporter, and discussions with him invariably led to new insights about the man and his exploits. On top of this, he ranks among the warmest, most gracious people one could ever have the pleasure to know. Another is Mat Leduc, a Ph.D. candidate from France, interested in Stanley's photographic record. She, too, sparkles with enthusiasm, and we've engaged in some good, friendly arguments about subjects related and unrelated to Stanley. Not a Stanley person, but definitely one who has made Tervuren special for me, is Els Cornelissen. One of us always owes the other a dinner. In a classic instance of serendipity, we met at an archaeological conference in Syracuse.

Then there's Marc Leo Felix, from whom I received a letter in 1996 about two possible errors on a map of the Congo in my book *The Peopling of Africa*. Sure enough, he was right, and this started a friendship that I greatly cherish. He put me up at his house in Brussels during my first visit and in other ways eased my introduction to the city and its environs. Each time I have visited since, we've gotten together for a meal at one of the special restaurants he knows. The trip is usually in a yellow Mercedes convertible once owned by Tony Curtis. And I always know that if I need anything, Marc will be there to help, despite his busy schedule. Beyond this, he's been a constant stimulus for me. If he thinks I've done something less well than it could be done, he tells me. Similarly, he'll let me know if he likes what I've done. Authors can't ask for anything more than this.

Two people in England deserve special mention. Christopher Hilton provided assistance in locating documents in the Western manuscripts section in the Wellcome Library for the History and Understanding of Medicine, and Andrew Tatham kindly took time away from his normal duties as "keeper" to make the Stanley files at the Royal Geographical Society available to me.

I owe Richard Curtis thanks for two things—his diligent search for a publisher and his constant encouragement that I had a story worth telling.

Joe Stoll is the creative force behind the cartography. I'd give him base maps, which had to be scanned and merged. All I'd do after this was tell him what I'd like shown, and—voilà!—maps would appear.

By being tough readers of early drafts, Rich Symanski and Judy Walton helped bring the book's story into better focus. They might not have had the chance without Donna Woolfolk Cross's enthusiastic response to a very early draft. She saw possibilities I hadn't. Once in Brassey's hands, an anonymous reader did what an author hopes for—give a critical, helpful review. I thank her or him for the time taken to produce such a thorough job.

I also want to extend my thanks to the Maxwell School and Department of Geography at Syracuse University for providing much needed financial support to help offset the costs of making annual trips across the Atlantic.

On the home front, Carole has served as a constant source of support and encouragement. And after a while, Friday, a big—and I mean big—domestic shorthair cat, eventually forgives my absences.

Preface

STANLEY AND AFRICA

WHEN I mention the name Henry Morton Stanley to people, the usual reaction is a quizzical look, followed by "who was he?" Once in a while, an intrepid soul will venture "didn't he find Livingstone or some such thing?" That's about as far as it tends to go. Yet not too long ago, Stanley was known far and wide. Many people considered him a hero for having survived one perilous African journey after another in the names of commerce, exploration, and Christianity.[1] Comparisons with Christopher Columbus (then a mostly admired figure) seemed apt.[2] According to a contemporary, "He [Stanley] has helped to make the history of the century, created a New State, and secured for himself a front place amongst the noblest pioneers of civilization and the truest friends of humanity in our time."[3] Mark Twain concurred, going so far as to proclaim that "when you compare these achievements of his with the achievements of really great men who exist in history, the comparison I believe is in his favor."[4]

Others reacted differently. Milder critics dismissed Stanley as a mere journalistic "sensationalist," whereas harsher ones said he marched at the head of buccaneer-like expeditions that used the latest weapons to run roughshod over Africans whenever they got in the way. Instead of representing noble interests, he was accused of fronting for a "shoddy commercialism," with little more in mind than making the largest profits possible for investors.[5]

At the time of Stanley's death, in 1904, the former view outweighed the latter by quite some margin. He'd been knighted, and in an obituary, Sir Harry H. Johnston put him at the "top of the role of African explorers," expressing puzzlement as to how he could ever have become known as "a blood thirsty, unscrupulous conqueror."[6] The 1939 Hollywood epic *Stanley and Livingstone,* with Spencer Tracey as Stanley, fit the heroic mold, and from time to time, would-be explorers have tried to follow his paths and thereby share in the heroism.[7] This assessment reflects the ascendant imperi-

alism of the time, which stayed in place until after the middle of the twentieth century. Even such a latter-day anti-imperialist as Patrice Lumumba once
hailed Stanley as *"un explorateur incomparable"* and *"le précurseur de la civilis-
ation"* in the Congo.[8] But the world's political map had by then begun to
change, and the positive view of Stanley's accomplishments gave way to the
negative. In many minds, he came to personify all the wrongs inflicted on
Africa and Africans by European colonialism; he was a veritable "horror" of
a man in some minds.[9]

This about-face in opinion happened without anything substantially new
about Stanley having been revealed. One might have expected modern historians to deem him a person worthy of detailed study, but only two, Norman
Bennett and Francois Bontinck, have devoted much space to Stanley. Neither, however, has produced a synthesis of his life and activities. This lack of
attention is revealed in recent histories of Africa, where Stanley is pretty
much a forgotten figure, worthy, at best, of a comment or a footnote. You'd
hardly know he'd once been compared with Columbus and was one of the
late nineteenth century's most newsworthy figures.

Biographers have been less shy. One wrote as early as 1872, just as Stanley
became a celebrity.[10] Additional biographies came out during his lifetime,
although they were largely insubstantial works based on already published
materials, mostly Stanley's own, and some conjecture.[11] In 1933 Jacob Was-
sermann published *Bula Matari: Stanley Conqueror of a Continent,* but the
book added little to what had already been said. Two years later, Frank Hird
broke the mold. Called *H. M. Stanley: The Authorized Life,* his book
included entries from some of Stanley's journals and letters then stored at
the family estate of Furze Hill in Pirbright, Surrey, England. Although a
significant improvement on what came before, the book reads as an apologia.
It took forty years before a more evenhanded interpretation, Richard Hall's
Stanley: An Adventurer Explored, reached bookstore shelves. Hall also consulted materials at Furze Hill, and in doing so helped clarify some of the
mysteries surrounding Stanley, which the man himself often created.

The year 1989 saw the appearance of two new efforts. Emir Wynn Jones
examined previously unused sources from Stanley's birthplace in Wales to
write a psychoanalytic study titled *Sir Henry M. Stanley: The Enigma
Review of the Early Years,* and Frank McLynn released *Stanley: The Making
of an African Explorer,* the first of a two-volume biography. The second,
Stanley: Sorcerer's Apprentice, came out in 1991. In between was John Bierman's *Dark Safari: The Life Behind the Legend of Henry Morton Stanley.* Like
Jones, Bierman and McLynn probed Stanley's persona, emphasizing, as is
often the case with the psychobiography genre, the "dark side." For example,

Bierman portrayed him as having been a "swaggering, assertive little man" marked by "suspicion and paranoia" and "decided sexual ambivalence," who although "steadfast, brave, enduring, resourceful, and an inspired leader" was also a "bully, a braggart, a hypocrite, and a liar."[12] McLynn went even farther, seeing Stanley as having been motivated by "a desire for revenge on life and mankind for his unhappy childhood." Purportedly, this led him to develop a "generalised misanthropism" and distrust of strangers that resulted in a "wounded, paranoid, hyper-suspicious personality," manifesting such traits as repressed homosexuality, sadomasochistic tendencies, self-righteousness, callousness, and brutality.[13] Repeated attempts to prove their points make it hard not to believe that each author found what he set out to find. Suspicion is heightened by numerous incidents of stretching the truth to fit characterizations and leaving out information that doesn't fit.

No matter the focus, the biographies tell us little about the most important aspect of Stanley's life—his relationship with Africa. Given the inattention by historians, our understanding of the Stanley and Africa theme isn't much further advanced than it was a hundred years ago. A revisiting thus seems in order. To do this in a meaningful way requires focusing on his journeys. Everything ultimately revolved around them. In the pages that follow, each is re-created, with attention paid to why Stanley made it, what transpired along the way, and what happened afterward as a result. Such an approach makes history and geography essential parts of the chronicle.

Leaving aside a couple of short stays in Egypt, Stanley made seven African journeys, the first four taken while working as a newspaper reporter. In 1868 he accompanied a British expeditionary force seeking to gain the release of prisoners held by Abyssinia's (Ethiopia) Emperor Theodore. Then came the search for Dr. David Livingstone in 1871–1872, which propelled Stanley into the public limelight and pointed him toward an Africa-centered career he'd never before envisioned. A four-month-long sojourn to the Gold Coast (Ghana) to report on another British military action, this one designed to check the Asante kingdom's regional aspirations, followed in 1873–1874. From late 1874 to August 1877, Stanley made an east-to-west crossing of the continent that is often called the single greatest feat of African exploration ever. Among other things, he circumnavigated Lake Victoria, proved that Lake Tanganyika was not the source of the Nile, and showed the Lualaba and Congo rivers to be one waterway. The journey also involved a new dimension to African exploration introduced by Samuel Baker just a few years earlier, the show and sometimes use of military-like force to counteract local opposition. As an adventure, it has few equals.

The feat of following the Congo to its mouth caught the attention of Leopold II of Belgium, for whom Stanley made two trips between 1879 and 1884 in order to lay the foundation for what eventually became the king's Congo Free State fiefdom. Less newsworthy than either the Livingstone or the 1874–1877 journey, in many ways they rank as his most significant journeys in terms of both short- and long-term outcomes. Finally, during 1887–1889, Stanley crossed the continent from west to east as the leader of an expedition to rescue a relatively obscure man named Emin Pasha from presumed disaster in Equatoria, a cutoff province of Egypt in the southern Sudan. In the process of bringing Emin out, Stanley produced the first descriptions of the Ituri rain forest, put the Ruwenzori mountain range on the map, and added the final pieces to the Nile River puzzle. The costs to both the expedition and equatorial Africa, however, were considerable. When totaled, the events constituted a true horror story. Some of them may have inspired portions of Joseph Conrad's *Heart of Darkness.* Although the Emin Pasha expedition ended Stanley's career of following armies or leading men in search of someone or something, it didn't end his involvement with Africa. He continued to advise and speak out on a number of related issues almost to the end.

Stanley entered Africa at a time of crucial change. The first four journeys came toward the end of a roughly fifty-year period often described as the "prelude to imperialism."[14] Its essential features were an extension of contacts from Africa's coasts to the interior and a consequent filling in of the blank spots on maps. Desires to spread Christianity; to resolve geographic mysteries, most notably those associated with the Nile and Niger Rivers; and to seek adventures in exotic, faraway places seem to have been the main motivations for most of those who did the documentary work. Few appear to have been activated solely by a quest for personal fortune, although seeking fame and validating self-worth came into play in some instances. They certainly did for Stanley. The prelude also involved the first true wars between Europeans and Africans, though without territorial conquest in mind. In essence, these served more as testing grounds for newly flexed military muscles linked to growing efforts to control world commerce.

Stanley's 1874–1877 journey basically signaled the prelude's end, for when he completed it, only a few blank spots remained on the map. The full-fledged colonial era then began. Often cloaked behind lofty philanthropic goals, colonialism's land grab known as the "scramble for Africa" actually had much more to do with power plays in Europe, Africa being the last substantial bit of foreign soil where this could happen.[15] And in the vanguard of the scramble was Stanley.

Significantly affecting Stanley's activities in Africa were ties to other people. The list of those he depended upon or served includes Africans, Arabs, and Europeans. On many occasions this meant juggling multiple demands, which essentially put him in the position of being a broker. His choices were often competing and difficult, and on a few occasions, events definitely got the better of him, producing behaviors that provided fuel for his critics, both at the time and afterward.

Each journey had its effects on Stanley, and thus influenced his actions during subsequent ones. And, cumulatively, they produced a person in many ways quite different from the one prior to 1868. The evolution of Stanley is thus a necessary part of the relationship story, and this, of course, requires that I deal with his life before Africa. I won't, however, present every detail I've found. Instead, I'll concentrate on those events that seem most pertinent to the Stanley and Africa theme and that best explain his motivations and behaviors. Nor will I attempt to psychoanalyze him. That is something for professionals in the field to do, and I'm not one of them.

Stanley left behind an almost unparalleled wealth of writings for investigators to examine. There are his books. The first and most famous was *How I Found Livingstone,* published at the end of 1872. Next came *Coomassie and Magdala: The Story of Two British Campaigns in Africa* in 1874, followed by the two-volume *Through the Dark Continent* in 1878, depicting the events of 1874–1877. Two volumes were also necessary for *The Congo and the Founding of Its Free State,* published in 1885, and *In Darkest Africa, or the Quest, Rescue, and Retreat of Emin, Governor of Equatoria,* released in 1890. These are invaluable sources for establishing itineraries and chronologies, and also for examining Stanley's imperial motives and recommendations. They are less valuable when it comes to determining exactly what took place during the journeys. Some incidents he clearly altered to make them seem more dramatic and harrowing, whereas others were modified or left out altogether in order to mute criticism. Affecting the Congo narrative was the fact that King Leopold insisted on approving the text before publication. The books come in a variety of versions, and availability determined which ones I used.

The Autobiography of Sir H. M. Stanley doesn't qualify as an autobiography in the usual sense. Stanley did start writing one but gave up after getting no further than 1862. His wife, Dorothy, put this part together with later sections she crafted for the book, which came out in 1909, five years after Stanley's death. What he wrote was full of distortions and untruths about his early life, while Dorothy chose to include only those journal and notebook entries that cast him in the most positive light. Had the *Autobiography* never been released—and his giving up on it suggests he didn't want it to be—Stanley's personal critics would have had far less ammunition to support their cases. Still, there are passages in the book that provide useful information.

Fortunately, there are a variety of supplementary sources that can be used to check facts and fill gaps. Included are Stanley's newspaper dispatches for the *New York Herald,* with those of the Livingstone expedition and the 1874–1877 journey, assembled into one volume by Norman Bennett.[16] The British Library newspaper collection in Colindale, England, contains a wealth of stories and editorials by and about Stanley from 1872 onward.

Some of Stanley's voluminous private writings can be found in the 'H. M. Stanley Collection,' at the Royal Geographical Society, and the Wellcome Library for the History and Understanding of Medicine has a small number of letters and other documents of interest. In the library of the University of London's School of Oriental and African Studies are the papers of Sir William Mackinnon, with whom Stanley had many dealings. Of particular importance are letters that relate to the Emin Pasha expedition and Stanley's later years.

By far the richest source of information is the 'Stanley Archive,' housed in the Stanley Pavilion at the Royal Museum of Central Africa in Tervuren, Belgium. Purchased from the Stanley family in 1982, the 'archive' contains many of his journals and notebooks, thousands of letters, newspaper clippings, and an array of memorabilia. Dorothy's diaries and correspondence are also part of the collection. Cataloged by Christie's for the sale, everything has been recataloged according to a simpler time of production and type of document. A second, smaller batch of materials came into the museum's possession in 2000. Through the good graces of the museum, I was given free access to the entire archive, and I've relied on it extensively to inform my narrative.

Several of the journals require a little commentary. Numbers 34, 35, and 36 cover the Congo years. They were compiled later, probably in the mid-1890s, and were meant to tell an alternative story from that presented in the book. Of special note are copies of letters written to and by Stanley. Number 64 consists of two volumes dealing with the Emin Pasha expedition and also adds significantly to the book. It, too, seems to have been compiled in the mid-1890s. Only a few of the notebooks from which they were produced have survived. Number 73 has mostly short entries for scattered dates covering 1841–1879. It was clearly put together from other sources, apparently to

Dear Major -
I send this on to you -
the former attempt was a failure.

Camp on S bank Aruwimi River
Opposite Arab Settlement.
September 18ᵗʰ 1887.

My dear Major Wᵐ Lewis

You will I am certain be as glad
to get news – definite & clear of our movements, as I am
to feel that I have at last an opportunity of presenting
them to you, As they will be of immense comfort to you &
your assistants & followers. I shall confine myself to
give you the needful details. And first here is a small
chart for your guidance : —

The little dots along the course are villages.

We have travelled 340 English miles to make only 192 Geog miles of our
Easterly course. This has been performed in 83 days which gives us a rate
of 4¹⁰/₁₀ miles per day. We have yet to make 130 geog miles, or a winding
course perhaps of 230 English miles which at the same rate of march
as hitherto we may make in 55 days. We started from Yambuya
389 souls – Whites + blacks. we have now 333 of whom there are 20

An excerpt from Stanley's journal. *Stanley Papers at the Royal Museum of Central Africa, Tervuren, Belgium.*

serve as a reminder of places visited and people met. Curiously, the first dozen entries are written in Kiswahili. Stanley's reasons for using it remain one of the many mysteries he left behind.

Portions of what now constitutes the archive have been published. Albert Maurice assembled letters from 1881–1882 pertaining to Stanley's first stint for Leopold in the Congo. The initial edition in French contained some crucial translation errors, but fortunately an English version appeared shortly afterward that remedied the problem.[17] In addition, Stanley's grandsons Richard and Alan Neame put together an edited collection of diary entries covering 1874–1877.[18] Because of greater ease of access, I've cited both these publications in the notes in preference to the archive sources when they correspond.

Of all the journeys, the Emin Pasha expedition has received the most attention. Books, some posthumous, were produced from the diaries and journals of other Europeans involved in one way or another, newspapers carried story after story, and analyses have been attempted from time to time.[19] During the 1950s and 1960s, Belgian scholars produced an array of articles and monographs that help us better understand Stanley's Congo days from 1879 to 1884. In each case, these sources will be noted when appropriate.

I'm a geographer by training, and as is usual with the breed I love maps. It's hard, in fact, for me to think without them. For others so inclined, I've made maps for each of the journeys. Stanley drew his own, and though useful to me in the drafting process, they often contain inaccuracies. This is especially the case for those covering the Livingstone expedition and the 1874–1877 crossing, when he sometimes didn't quite know where he was. In addition, many of the place names mentioned no longer exist. But perseverance has its rewards, and by using such things as Stanley's landscape descriptions and directions and distances traveled, I believe my portrayals are pretty accurate. So as not to overwhelm readers, I've limited place names in the text and on the maps to those where something important happened and to provide points of reference. Today's generally accepted spellings are given whenever possible. In instances where Stanley's renderings are noticeably different, I've put them in parentheses for readers who are familiar with or wish to consult his books. Perforce, I have had to use Stanley's names when modern counterparts couldn't be found. I have, however, tried to keep these to a minimum.

Names of individuals and peoples also present difficulties. Both are almost overwhelming in number, and I've sought to include only those people who were key players in one way or another. As with place names, I use the most widely accepted modern terms to refer to African peoples. In instances where Stanley got the names wrong, I make the correction. I don't, however, use *sic* to indicate misspellings of general vocabulary. Allowing Stanley to speak for himself is necessary for conveying the full flavor of what he did and meant, and since many of the quotes come from notebooks and journals, corrections would be numerous and distracting. In addition, some words are spelled differently in British and American English, and in other instances spellings have changed since the late nineteenth century. In another attempt to simplify and stay with the tenor of the times, I retain Stanley's use of the U.S. customary and imperial weights and measures rather than converting them to the metric system. The same holds for height and distance, which Stanley always recorded in feet and miles, as opposed to meters and kilometers.

Dates are occasionally problematic. I've done considerable cross-checking of sources and feel confident that most are accurate. Still, a future researcher might find additional sources to correct some of my deductions.

One last note for now: I haven't examined every possible source of information about Stanley, even those known to exist. James Casada's 1976 annotated bibliography contained more than a thousand published works, and others have been added since.[20] Trying to track them all would be virtually impossible for one person, especially since many are difficult to find. Mine is a particular study of Stanley, both in focus and in sources used. Plenty of room exists for others to offer different interpretations.

CHAPTER 1

The Making of Henry Morton Stanley

AN IDENTITY CREATED

On January 28, 1841, Elizabeth (Betsy) Parry, an unwed 19-year-old, gave birth to a son in Denbigh, a small town situated in the scenic Clwyd valley of northeastern Wales. At the christening three weeks later, the infant officially became John Rowlands, after his reputed father, a farm laborer and son of John Rolant from nearby Llys. It's more likely, however, that John's biological father was James Vaughn Horne, a married solicitor from a prominent Denbigh family.[1] The revelation of an affair with Betsy, much less his getting her pregnant, would have ruined Horne, and it appears a colleague convinced Rowlands to take responsibility instead. Given his poverty and fondness for liquor, some money undoubtedly changed hands. No one knows whether Rowlands had also been intimate with Betsy, but she obviously agreed to go along with the story, making it hard not to believe that something from Horne passed into her hands as well.

Stanley accepted this version of his origin. He said so in a 1869 letter, noting, "I am an illegitimate child of Elizabeth Parry & John Rowlands of the Lys."[2] And many years later he claimed to have visited his grandfather, "old J. R. of Lys," describing him as "A terrible old man truly."[3] If such a visit ever occurred, it had to be before Rolant's death in July 1856. His son had passed on two years earlier, a victim of alcohol abuse. In Stanley's version, Rowlands died within a few weeks of his birth. It's not possible to say for certain whether this is what others told him or he made it up. Of Horne,

Stanley knew nothing, the secret having been kept within a small circle of family and friends for many years. Horne died in 1848 after a long illness.[4]

Shortly after the christening, Betsy went to London, hoping to find employment as a domestic. She left John with her elderly father, Moses, a butcher by trade and a widower since 1823, who did what he could to provide for the boy in a humble neighborhood just outside Denbigh Castle. Betsy returned the next year and on April 2, 1843, gave birth to an illegitimate daughter, Emma, with John Evans of Liverpool listed as her father.

On June 22, 1846, Moses collapsed and died, and after the funeral John's uncles arranged for a neighbor couple to take in the boy. Many years later, Stanley attributed a long-held fear of the night to being left in the care of a daughter named Sarah. As he put it,

> It is the fate of poor children to be left to the care of poor people who are not only illiterate, but are careless of speech, & heedless in their acts, and altogether ill-judges. Sarah, though a good-hearted, & honest wench and a model of female propriety had the vice of unquestioning belief in spooks, and she spent most of her evenings in the company of other females of her class and insisted on taking me to those soirees. I gradually imbibed an idea that the world which seemed so fair by day was peopled by night with a multitude of ghosts which made the darkness hideous & painful to all people.[5]

The half crown per week subsidy provided by the uncles soon proved inadequate for his upkeep, and thus on February 20, 1847, John was handed over to the Board of Guardians at St. Asaph Union Workhouse (now the H. M. Stanley Hospital) for the "cause of desertion."[6] About five miles north of Denbigh, St. Asaph served as a place of last resort for orphans, the elderly, and other indigents. John remained there for more than nine years and later described the period as one of almost unrelenting hardship and misery, laying most of the blame on the schoolmaster, James Francis. Although life at St. Asaph was hardly idyllic, even by mid-nineteenth-century standards, many of his accusations against Francis have been shown to be distorted and occasionally even false.[7] Why did Stanley lie about this and other matters pertaining to his early life? It's hard to say for sure, but when the instances are put together a pattern emerges suggestive of a strong desire to impress people with an ability to overcome any obstacle as the primary motive. A flair for the dramatic, something Stanley certainly exhibited many times later in life, could also have been a cause.

In an ironic twist, Betsy became a ward of St. Asaph's on June 14, 1851, bringing along Emma and illegitimate child number three, Robert. Although

Betsy and Robert didn't stay long, Emma remained under guardian care until 1857.[8]

John left the workhouse on May 13, 1856, and, maintaining the drama, portrayed it as a hair-raising escape brought on by knocking Francis cold during an attempt to ward off a beating. The facts suggest a voluntary and mutually agreed upon separation. After failing several times to gain assistance from relatives in Denbigh, John went to see his cousin Moses Owen, who headed a National School for poor children in the hamlet of Brynford. Everything considered, the education provided by St. Asaph was quite good, better than available to most children in Wales at the time. By all accounts, John excelled in the classroom, displaying special gifts in mathematics, geography, drawing, and English. A Bible, representing the institution's strong Calvinist flavor, given to him in early 1855 carried the inscription "for diligent application to his studies and for general good conduct."[9] Because of these skills, Moses hired him as a combined pupil-teacher for room and board. At first John seemed to have enjoyed the job, and the substantial library on the premises allowed his education to continue. Moses helped him along, but John also possessed a highly developed ability to self-educate, and henceforth, it would be how he learned most things.

The cousins, however, soon began squabbling, which prompted John to leave and take up residence with Moses's mother, Mary, Betsy's elder sister, who ran a farm and inn called Ffynnon Beuno (St. Beuno's Well) in nearby Tremeirchion. Powerfully built and already at his adult height of five feet, five inches, the teenager could handle the tasks she assigned with little difficulty. Both looked on the arrangement as temporary, hoping a better job would materialize. When one didn't, John set off for Liverpool in August 1858, destined for the home of Tom and Maria Morris, the third of the Parry sisters. When a hoped-for clerk's position with an insurance company fell through, John spent many long days on the streets looking for other means of support. A haberdasher hired him part-time to do odd jobs, a position he lost when illness kept him away for a week. A nearly monthlong search afterward turned up nothing better than becoming a butcher's delivery boy. Desperate for money, he took the position even though the foreman struck him as "a twin brother of spleen."[10]

Unhappy with both his living arrangements and his prospects for advancement in Liverpool, John made a quick decision and signed up, possibly using Rollins instead of Rowlands, to be a cabin boy aboard the packet ship *Windermere*, out of Boston and bound for New Orleans. Struck down by seasickness just after weighing anchor on December 20, John recovered sufficiently to begin duties and learned the captain had hoodwinked him:

John Rowlands at age 15. *Courtesy of the Royal Museum of Central Africa*

The job turned out to be the grueling one of deckhand. As on virtually all such ships at the time, conditions for the crew were rough, language salty, and discipline maintained by lashings and floggings. Exhausted after fifty-two days of hard work, and reeling from a confrontation with the second mate, John decided to jump ship while it lay at anchor in New Orleans. With willing boys a dime a dozen, ships' captains and officers often made life miserable for the youngest members of the crew, hoping they'd abscond before collecting their pay. The *Windermere* was no exception.

New Orleans marks the beginning of Stanley's American years, the details of which are often missing or obscured by his remembrances of things past. Nevertheless, enough facts exist to allow at least a sketch to be made of those events that relate to his career in Africa. Among them is how he came to change his name. As Stanley later told it, on his first day in town, and with nary a penny in his pocket, he approached a man and asked, "Do you want a boy, sir?"[11] Impressed by John's reading ability, the man reportedly took him in tow and after several months became his legal father by adoption. To reinforce the point, Stanley titled a chapter of his intended autobiography "I Find a Father." No formal adoption papers have been discovered, and it's unlikely one ever occurred, as John lived in a boarding house at the time. The man in question, Henry Hope Stanley, was real enough, however. Born in Stockport, England, in 1811, Henry Hope moved to New Orleans in 1838 and by the 1850s had become an affluent cotton broker and highly respected member of the community. He also owned a plantation in nearby Arcola. More than likely, John simply appropriated Henry and Stanley, rather than having been given them. Morton came much later, after he experimented with several other middle names, including Morelake and Moreland.

After providing him a meal and a haircut, Henry Hope arranged a job for his new charge at a wholesale/commission store and warehouse run by an acquaintance, and within a week John received a promotion to junior clerk at what seemed a princely salary of twenty-five dollars per month. Always frugal, he saved money for books to continue his education. Later that summer the owner died, and although initially retained by the new firm, John was let go for, according to the adult Stanley, spiritedly challenging a refusal by the boss to grant him a few days off.[12] A variety of jobs took him upriver as far as St. Louis, and toward the end of 1859 John returned to New Orleans to work for Henry Hope. Uncertainty exists about what happened after that, although this does seem to be when the name change, at least the Stanley part, took place, for sometime during early or midsummer of 1860 he showed up in Cypress Bend, Arkansas, as William H. Stanley.[13] Henry Hope apparently sent him there after a falling out, one serious enough for Stanley to record that his "father" died suddenly while on a business trip to Cuba in 1861. He also described an earlier tragic death from yellow fever of Mrs. Stanley, whom John greatly adored, claiming she demonstrated through dress, speech, and manners "the immense difference between a lady and a mere woman."[14] In fact, both lived until 1878.

Situated in the midst of swamplands, Cypress Bend introduced Stanley to something he would experience many times while in Africa; attacks of malaria. And he learned how to shoot a rifle, a highly valuable skill that he would shortly put to use. That was because Cypress Bend also got him caught up in the excitement about southern secession and the imminent prospect of going to war over it. Stanley had no intention of joining the cause—he was an outsider and didn't think slaves worth a war—but claimed a young woman shamed him by sending a box with a chemise inside, a sign of cowardice, like a white feather.[15] He enlisted with the local Dixie Grays that same afternoon, still using William H. instead of Henry. Stanley later called this impulsive act a "grave blunder."[16]

In early July 1861, the Grays marched to Little Rock to join the Sixth Arkansas Regiment of Volunteers. They received only cursory training before heading east, and along the way many of the men became sick, with some dying from an array of maladies including typhus. Stanley managed to avoid being among the stricken. In August the Grays were at the Battle of Belmont near Columbus, Kentucky, but as observers, not participants. A couple of months at a camp in nearby Cave City came next, and from mid-February through March, Stanley and his colleagues found themselves either being shuttled by trains or marching through parts of Georgia and Tennessee.

The Grays' first action came at Shiloh.[17] The historic battle began on April 6, 1862, with intense dawn-to-dusk fighting that initially went the Confederate way. As Stanley later recalled,

> Within 30 minutes all thoughts of God & religion were drowned by the savage passions aroused by the tempest of war. We were wholly brutal, a troop of lions after a herd of antelope, could they have spoken, would have been mild compared to the demonic hate we breathed.[18]

In spite of taking heavy casualties, the Grays marched with the advance the next morning. Shortly after getting under way, Stanley found a hollow about eighteen inches deep that provided a "capital place" from which to fire upon a line of advancing Union troops. Absorbed by the task, he claimed not to have noticed the other Grays withdraw and within minutes found himself surrounded by Blues. Ordered to drop his rifle, he did so instantly on fear of being shot. Shipped first to St. Louis, he eventually wound up in Camp Douglas, a makeshift and overcrowded prisoner-of-war camp near Chicago. The camp was pestilential in the extreme, and inmates died daily from typhus and dysentery. Stanley said he remembered one man calling out "Great God, let me die. Good God, why don't I die & be done with this—sickness."[19] Despite having an explosive temper, he seldom cursed, and never in writing, including the pages of private notebooks.

Able-bodied captives had a way out of prison: They could enlist in the Union Army. Stanley took the opportunity and signed for a three-year stint with the First Illinois Light Artillery in early June. But before he fought with the unit, army records show him as "not heard from," which in due course became "deserter."[20] Apparently, he simply walked away after being hospitalized at Harper's Ferry, (then) Virginia, on June 22, 1862, for a recurrence of dysentery contracted in Camp Douglas. Perhaps this was when he decided to go by Henry instead of William. More than two decades later, Stanley sent an affidavit to the American Secretary of War requesting that the charge of desertion be dropped from his service record. As he explained,

> I, Henry M. Stanley, do solemnly declare and affirm as follow, to wit: when I enrolled at Chicago I was a boy 18 years of age, my condition physically very much reduced by prison life, I then served with my company, doing honorable duty until I was prostrated by a wasting disease from which I suffered for two months, after which I was discharged from the hospital having received a certificate the contents of which I at this day forget, but I well remember that I was so feeble as to be incapable of service. I understood and believed that the certificate was an honorable discharge and acted upon that understanding and belief. My weight at the time was about 95 lbs. and I did not recover my health and strength until six months had elapsed. After my enlistment and to this day, I was and have been loyal to the Union and the American flag. To the best of my recollection I entered the hospital in the early months of 1863, and was discharged about March or April, 1863. Owing to disease from which I suffered my memory of those events is exceedingly imperfect.[21]

With regard to his age and time in the hospital, Stanley's memory clearly failed him, whether intentionally or not. Given a lack of evidence one way or other, the Secretary of War ordered the change to an honorable discharge dated June 22, 1862, under the name Henry M. Stanley.[22] From Harper's Ferry, Stanley crossed into Maryland and luckily found a place of refuge on a farm just outside Sharpsburg. Restored to health by the family's care, in mid-August he set off for Baltimore to take another crack at a sailor's life.

After working on an oyster boat for a month or so, Stanley joined the crew of the schooner *E. Sherman*, and in November he returned to Great Britain. While there he paid a brief visit to his mother, now married to Robert Jones and living in Glascoed, along with Emma, Robert, and another son James. The previous James had died from meningitis at age six. His mother did little to make him feel welcome, saying that he needn't bother to come back unless "better dressed and in far better circumstances."[23] That he hoped for something more is evident from a musing jotted on a small scrap of paper titled "Mother," which proclaims, "It was with certain pride that I knocked at the door buoyed up by a hope of being able to show what manliness I had acquired. . . . I had arrayed my story to please what I hoped would be a doting mother."[24]

December found Stanley working on the *Ernestine*, headed for New York, his first of many encounters with the great city. A succession of seafaring jobs lasting until October followed, until his ultraneat handwriting landed him a clerk's position in a Brooklyn legal office. One day, seemingly on a whim, Stanley decided to resign and sign up for a three-year stint with the Federal Navy. Records show an enlistment date of July 19, 1864, under the name Henry Stanley, with England as his country of birth.[25] Given the state of recordkeeping at the time, the chances of finding out about his disappearance from the army under a different first name were slim. First assigned to the *North Carolina* as a landsman (nonsailor), several weeks later he joined the crew of the frigate *Minnesota,* being assigned the additional role of "ship's writer." The tour of duty allowed him to record two bombardments of the Confederacy's last Atlantic coast stronghold, Fort Fisher, North Carolina. The experience could well have been the defining one for his decision to become a journalist and the impetus to jump from the *Minnesota* on February 10, 1865, during a call at Portsmouth, New Hampshire. According to Lewis Noe, an impressionable fifteen-year-old who went along with him, Stanley forged the commodore's signature on a shore-leave pass to get them by the guards.[26]

When the duo reached New York City, Noe opted to go home to Sayville on Long Island, where his parents urged him to return to the ship right away. Instead, he joined the Eighth New York Mounted Volunteers, using the name Lewis Morton. As for Stanley, when attempts to sell stories about the Civil War failed to pan out, with help from Lewis Stegman, he found a job with a law firm. The two had met during Stanley's previous stay in the city, and upon reuniting they talked about going to Australia or South America to look for gold.[27] That came to naught, and in mid-May 1865, Stanley set off for the West, probably intent on finding a newspaper job somewhere.

During a stop in St. Louis, he signed on as an "occasional," a kind of glorified freelance reporter, with the *Missouri Democrat*. Little is known of his activities during the coming months between June 1865, and May of 1866, except that he continued to journey westward searching for stories and jobs in, among other places, Denver, Salt Lake City, and San Francisco. Stanley worked for a while as a day laborer at a smelter in Black Hawk City, Colorado, and, to keep in practice, wrote some letters for the local paper. He also struck up a friendship with William Harlow Cook, another budding journalist, and the two of them started planning a trip to Asia, hoping it would yield the fame and fortune the American West hadn't.

As a way to get in shape for their adventure, they decided to navigate the Platte River in a homemade flat-bottomed boat. The journey began on May 17, 1866, and nearly ended in disaster when the boat capsized. They survived the mishap, but soldiers took them into custody as possible deserters from Ft. Laramie, Wyoming. Faced with being detained for questioning, and maybe even looking at time in jail, Stanley, according to Cook, "in all the fiery blood of his naturally impetuous nature" picked up his belongings and moved toward the door. When asked by the captain in charge if he wished to be arrested, Cook said, Stanley brandished a revolver and replied, "Yes, if you have enough men to do it," and they walked away.[28] Many years later Cook told a less dramatic version, saying the officer in charge probably recognized that they "were above common deserters."[29] A second capsizing then occurred, and the two became separated for several days. They met in St. Louis, and then Stanley went to Chicago and New York City, being joined by Cook en route. Since parting, Noe and Stanley had kept in touch by mail, and with a little convincing, Lewis's parents agreed to let their son go along on the Asia trip. The search for affordable passage led to Boston, and a departure date of July 11, 1866, aboard the *E. H. Yarrington* headed for Smyrna (Izmir), Turkey. Calm winds made for slow going, and the ship didn't reach port until the last day of August.

Their trek inland from Smyrna covered only about three hundred miles before it had to be aborted. The stories told by Stanley and Cook differ substantially from Noe's, but they agree about running afoul of locals near a village called Chihissar on September 18. Sensing an imminent robbery, the three fled, only to be overtaken after a nearly four-hour chase across the hilly countryside. Blindfolded and bound together by neck ropes, they were dragged to a nearby encampment, where later that night, several of their captors sexually assaulted Noe. The next day, the trio was taken to the jail at Karahissar, a five-hour ride away. Word of what happened reached the provincial governor, and after speaking with the Americans through an Imperial

Ottoman Bank employee named L. E. Peloso who knew some English, he ordered them released and the abductors jailed instead.[30]

Stanley wrote a brief account of the experience that appeared in the October 17, 1865, edition of the *Levant Herald*. It caught the attention of Edward Joy Morris, the resident U. S. Minister in Constantinople, who promptly provided a loan of 150 pounds sterling to cover their losses. Stanley parceled out fifty-nine pounds each to himself and Cook, and Noe got the remaining thirty-two pounds.[31] On November 14, Stanley and Noe boarded a ship bound for Marseilles and from there took a train to Paris on the way to England. Cook stayed behind to await the conclusion of the on again and off again trial. Finally in mid-January the court finished its work and awarded them the Turkish equivalent of $1848.88. A few years later, a question arose as to whether Stanley ever repaid the loan. Morris said the 150 pounds were deducted from the settlement and certified that "The debt of Mr. Stanley has been thus discharged and I have no claim whatsoever against him or any cause of complaint."[32]

Stanley deposited Noe in Liverpool with the Morris family and headed for Denbigh and St. Asaph. In an attempt to make a more favorable impression than last time, he passed himself off as an ensign on the USS *Ticonderoga*. A kind of officer's uniform purchased in Constantinople seems to have done the job, even though its buttons bore the Turkish crescent and star emblem. As a signed statement in the entry book to Denbigh Castle indicates, Stanley reverted to being John Rowlands for the trip. According to his account, all went well, including visits with Betsy and Emma, who'd become a favorite. Nonetheless, Stanley didn't plan on staying long, believing Denbigh a rather loathsome place. As he put in a letter not too long after,

It makes me sick in the stomach every time I think of the life I lead when I come to Denbigh. From morning till night from night till morning nothing is heard but slanderous gossip, fouling everybody's character, contaminating every ear and sense. Denbigh is a den of petty cunning, petty malice, filthy mischief, such are my impressions of it.[33]

By January 7, 1867, Stanley was back in Liverpool, and less than a week later he boarded ship for New York. Noe caught a later sailing. Stanley didn't dally long in the city and once again set off for St. Louis, where the *Missouri Democrat* rehired him to cover the state legislature in Jefferson City at a salary of fifteen dollars per week, plus expenses.[34] He also tried the lecture circuit, passing himself off as a recently returned expert on the Near East. The promotional handbill proclaimed:

The American Traveler,
HENRY STANLEY,
who was cruelly robbed by the Turks on September 18,
1866, and stripped, by overwhelming numbers, of his
arms, passports, letter of credit, and over $4000 in cash,
will lecture on his

TRAVELS AND ADVENTURES IN TURKEY
AND
LIFE IN THE ORIENT!![35]

Disgusted by the small turnout for the first performance on a "cold, bleak February night," Stanley gave up on the idea of a lecture tour.[36]

On the other hand, Stanley's reporting did produce results, for on March 28, 1867, he left St. Louis as the *Democrat*'s "special" correspondent to a newly formed Indian expedition under Major General Winfield Scott Hancock, a hero of Gettysburg. Designed to clear the way for westward expansion via negotiated settlements or, if need be, war, the expedition accomplished little during its several months of marching through Nebraska and Kansas. Nevertheless, the assignment proved crucial for Stanley's future—it gave him a firsthand look at the plight of indigenous peoples coming face-to-face with an imperial power bent on territorial expansion and he sold some stories to other newspapers, including a future employer, the *New York Herald*. Told in letter format, the stories mostly related what Stanley heard and saw each day, including colorful personalities like "Wild Bill" Hickok and "Big Goat." From the outset, he had mixed feelings about Indians. For certain, they'd "been used and abused by the military civil authorities," but they also murdered and tortured settlers. Perhaps, he speculated, "There ought to be a large tract of land given them, where they may hunt the buffalo, the antelope, and other game, as of old." Certainly "a great nation" shouldn't be involved in an extermination campaign.[37] But on occasion Stanley indulged in opinions that supported the American land grab. In one dispatch, for example, he noted that "Morality is hardly known amongst the Indians; but it frequently happens that when a squaw is unfaithful to her spouse *her nose is cut off* [!], which, surely, does not add to the beauty of her countenance. As a mother, the squaw ranks little above the lower animals."[38]

A "powwow" at Fort Hays, Kansas, in early May brought the Hancock expedition to an end, but not Stanley's reporting assignment, and he continued to forward dispatches to the *Democrat* about the conflict between settlers and Indians. The more Stanley learned, the more he became convinced that United States policy in the West was wrong. It amounted to "suicide," for, according to him, it left the settlers with only two options. They could "either succumb to the unequal conflict, or unite in bands to carry on the war after the manner of the Indians, which means to kill, burn, destroy Indian villages, innocent papooses and squaws, scalp the warriors, and mutilate the dead."[39]

A Peace Commission to stop the wars and settle the Indians had been authorized by Congress, and Stanley was assigned to cover it. Omaha had been selected as the meeting place for the commissioners, with Gen. William Tecumseh Sherman in charge of operations. Stanley hurried to beat them there. He needn't have rushed because it took a while for everyone to arrive and get organized. During the wait, he fell in love with actress Annie Ward, only to discover after proposing marriage that she already had a husband.[40] One night Stanley drank a little bit too much and got into a fight with the editor of a local newspaper who poked fun at their relationship. Charged with assault and battery, a jury found him not guilty based on "justifiable cause."[41]

Stanley did more than play during the interlude, and on August 21 he wrote an impassioned letter about the plight of the Indians and what the country should do to solve the continuing conflicts.

> Now the great cause of all these troubles—these blazing farms, these mutilated corpses, these scalped and wounded men—will be found in this: that the Indian was an outlaw ranked with the wild beasts. If a white man shot an Indian, what law touched him—what power tried him for the offense and made him pay the penalty of his murderous deeds? It was as if he had shot a buffalo. Nothing was done, nothing was thought of it. And the red man, to make matters straight killed the first white man he came across, took interest in the shape of stock, and called the account settled. Immediately a cry went up to heaven; outrages by the Indians filled the papers, and the Western men and the frontier men, and all who had money to make by an Indian war, and all who had property at stake by an Indian invasion, raised the cry of extermination. . . . The Western world shrieked out that the Indian opposed himself to civilization, and that the railroads would be destroyed, and that emigrants would be massacred, because the Indians of the plains were being driven to meet the Indians of the mountains; and civilization advanced like a mighty wave of the ocean, and the Indian had to force it back, or die. Poetical, plausible, yet untrue. The Indian will accept civilization, if it is offered to him with conditions that will make it worth his while to accept. Make him one of ourselves, bound by the same desires, possessing the same rights, and he will,

in time, forget the savage pleasures of the past in the happiness of an assured future, and the comfort of a well-filled belly.[42]

As August drew to a close with still no sign of Peace Commission activity, Stanley decided to go to Colorado for stories. He sent three dispatches from there before heading back to Omaha to join the commissioners for negotiations with the Brule, Ogallala Sioux, and Cheyenne in North Platte. Next he followed them to Medicine Lodge Creek, Kansas, for discussions with the Osage, Apache, Arapaho, Commanche, and Kiowa, and from there they all proceeded to Fort Laramie to meet with Black Foot representatives. By this time Sherman had been recalled to Washington. A second stop at North Platte on November 25 to finalize the treaties made earlier constituted the commission's last official item of business.

Nothing of great excitement took place at the meetings or along the way, and Stanley's reporting generally focused on the people present and the speeches given. The *Democrat* never published his final dispatch, dated November 24 and 25, probably because it was a summary of what Stanley had learned about Indian history and customs, rather than a story about the commission. Although he still thought the Indians were savages, they had at least become somewhat "noble" in his eyes and worthy of sharing in America's bounty. As for the Peace Commission's efforts, he considered them mostly successful.[43] He was, of course, wrong, as the conflicts continued for another twenty years.

On December 9 Stanley departed St. Louis, bringing the American West phase of his life to an end. During it, he'd found a new career as a journalist and forged a new identity. The time had come to move on to bigger and better assignments. With some three thousand dollars in pocket from saving much of his salary and collecting fees from newspapers in Cincinnati and Chicago, Stanley decided to look for a foreign-correspondent job in New York City. He first stopped at the *Tribune,* another buyer of his western stories, and was told no current openings existed. A visit to the *Herald* resulted in a more positive response. The paper was known for its no-holds-barred journalistic style and proclaimed to be the "Greatest Newspaper of the Age." Stanley secured an interview on December 17 with owner, James Gordon Bennett, Jr. Almost impossible to see, even by staff, Bennett probably recognized Stanley's name from some of the Hancock expedition and Peace Commission articles the *Herald* had carried. Whatever the reason, they got into a discussion in which events in Abyssinia came up. A war involving Great Britain seemed imminent, and, Stanley claimed, he brought up the idea of covering it. This is plausible, given his thirst for a foreign posting and familiarity with the news of the day. Bennett reportedly said that the war wouldn't be of much interest to Americans but agreed to send him to Abyssinia on the condition that Stanley foot his own expenses and work exclusively for the *Herald*.[44] If the stories proved to be satisfactory, he would be paid at the same rate as other special correspondents, and a permanent position might be possible when the assignment came to an end. The gamble appealed to Stanley, who later recorded, "and thus I became what had been the object of my ambition, a regular, I hope, correspondent of the New York Herald."[45] As for Bennett, he had nothing to lose and maybe something of value to gain.

CHAPTER 2

Abyssinia and Aftermath

A STAR REPORTER IS BORN

Impatient as usual, Stanley took the first available ship to England and reached Liverpool in time to ring in the New Year. After a brief stay in London, he went to Paris and on January 10, 1868, left for Suez, the British army's command center. Arriving ten days later, he discovered that all reporters would be required to obtain official permission before proceeding to Zula on Annesley Bay (now the Gulf of Zula) in Eritrea, the gathering place for the force destined to move against Abyssinian Emperor Theodore (Téwôdros II). Led by Lt. Gen. Robert Napier, the number of troops eventually surpassed thirteen thousand. The global division of labor at the time placed the country under India office jurisdiction and thus most of the troops came from the sub-continent. To transport men and supplies over nearly four hundred miles to Theodore's heavily fortified mountain stronghold at Magdala, the expedition required thousands of animals, including Indian elephants. Parliament had allocated two million pounds sterling to cover costs. The final tab amounted to more than four times as much.

Hindsight makes the reasons why an expeditionary force, much less one of this size, was ever sent to Abyssinia look preposterous, but these were times of intense imperial competition. For Britain, the issue centered on maintaining hegemony in the Red Sea region, while Theodore worried about Egyptian advances southward and secessionist movements that threatened to tear apart his newly created state.[1] Honor as a national priority also came into play with both parties. In this particular instance, the problem started with a letter Theodore wrote to Queen Victoria in October 1862. He wanted assistance in his struggles with the Ottoman rulers of Egypt and a guarantee that his ambassadors could reach Britain safely.[2] Charles Cameron, the British consul stationed in Massawa, forwarded the letter to London, along with one of his own telling of Theodore's desire for European engineers and doctors to assist in the country's efforts to modernize. Unfortunately, the letters were set aside due to a bureaucratic snafu involving the Foreign Office and India Office—each thought the other responsible for drafting a reply.[3] As months went by without an answer, Theodore grew increasingly frustrated. Frustration turned to anger when events suggested to him that Britain might be abandoning Abyssinia as an ally in favor of the hated Ottomans. He reacted by having Cameron and five other Europeans arrested in January 1864 on charges of spying. The unpleasant and sometimes brutal prison conditions they experienced are revealed in what Cameron said happened to him on one occasion:

> Twenty Abyssinians tugging lustily on ropes tied to each limb until I faint. My shoulder blades were made to meet each other. I was doubled up until my head appeared under my thighs, and while in this painful posture, I was beaten with a whip of hippopotamus hide on my bare back, until I was covered with weals, and while the blood dripped from my reeking back, I was rolled in the sand.[4]

When news of the imprisonment reached London, Theodore's letter miraculously reappeared and the government immediately sent a reply via the British assistant resident in Aden, Hormuzd Rassam. Seemingly satisfied by the turn of events, Theodore ordered the prisoners released. Within two days, however, Cameron was back under lock and key, along with Rassam and several missionary families and their servants. Two matters seemed to have triggered this sudden about-face: the emperor's growing concern that the European workers he wanted would never be sent and rumors of a British firm agreeing to build a railway into Abyssinia from the Sudan in order to facilitate an Egyptian invasion.[5] Kept at first near the royal palace at Debra Tabor, just east of Lake Tana, the prisoners were later transferred to Magdala. They wouldn't be freed, he said, until the British met his demands and provided assurances of continued support.

Anxious to avoid a costly military confrontation, and believing the prisoners to be safe and reasonably well cared for, the British continued with their efforts to achieve a negotiated settlement. The Foreign Office even sent a civil engineer and seven craftsmen to Abyssinia as a goodwill gesture; because of safety concerns, they sat around Massawa for six months before going home.[6] Eventually those in Britain advocating a more forceful response gained the upper hand by arguing that should Theodore's defiance go unpunished the country would lose face and invite challenges to its preeminence in the Red Sea.[7] To avoid such eventualities, a letter from Her Majesty's Government dated May 17, 1867, presented the emperor with two options—either free the prisoners within three months or face the consequences. By not responding, Theodore, in effect, chose to call Britain's bluff.

Stanley reached Zula on January 28, 1868, accompanied by Ali, a young Arab engaged at Suez to be his general-purpose servant. Two things immediately struck him: the "sweltering heat," which made the sands so hot "that the boots become baked" and mounds of seemingly never ending supplies.[8] When told that a pioneer brigade had already advanced some forty miles inland, Stanley purchased two mules and hurried to the army post at Kumayli, at the head of the pass into the mountains. The higher elevation provided much needed relief to men and animals, plus newly installed American-made pumps brought an abundance of pure drinking water to the surface. To make life even more congenial, a bazaar supplied everything the troops could ask for. According to Stanley,

> Nets of onions, tobacco in leaf, and brown heaps of fragrant weed grown in Latakiah and imported from far Stamboul, were temptingly arrayed on wooden trays, in vari-coloured paper; figs strung together on rushes, and figs in round cases; pipes with amber mouth-pieces, pipe-bowls with quaintest figures engraved on them; common English clay pipes, narghilehs from Grand Cairo, and hubble-bubbles from Persia and Delhi; jars full of black olives, pocket glasses, in red pasteboard cases; pickles, gherkins, sweets, jellies, cognac, claret, soda-water and innumerable other things from Paris and London.[9]

Beyond Kumayli a rough road climbed steadily upward through a desolate yet spectacular countryside. Along some stretches, steep, nearly perpendicular cliffs rose up on each side, and another section Stanley described as "masses of ribbed rock and earth lying diagonally along the bottom of the defile, looking as if they were cast down purposely by some mighty power." With few if any people to observe, the scenery had to do as story line. Fortunately, it continued to impress Stanley. At Senafe, for example, he heard that a spectacular view of a sunset could be had from a nearby peak. As he told readers,

> When I actually had surmounted the summit of the peak, and prepared myself to behold the scene, I looked toward the east, and beheld such a one as painter never sketched.

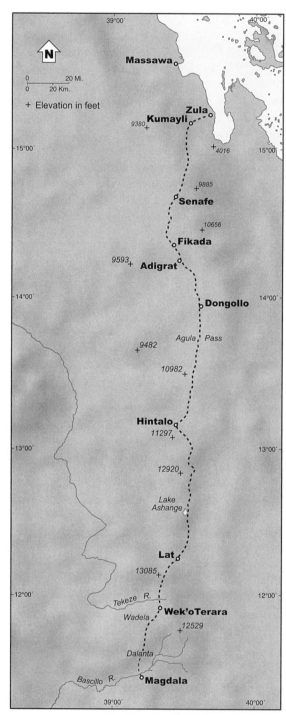

Map 2.1   The Route to Magdala, 1868

Those who saw it will be for ever haunted by that one moment when the flashing glare of departing day lighted up the Adowa peaks, and bathed the endless chain of rising hills in a sea of light, before the sun dipped beyond them to shine in other worlds.

Stanley's other major subject for the moment involved military personalities. One, called Captain Smelfungus, after a character in Laurence Sterne's amusing tale *Sentimental Journey through France and Italy,* served as a foil for commenting on the pretentious behavior of some officers. Although for the most part they treated him kindly, their comportment suggested that they considered him "an unsophisticated kind of Yankee" who'd become the "object of a good deal of chaff." The attitude of many English journalists rankled Stanley even more. They made him feel that as an American, he hadn't been fashioned from "such fine clay" as they.[10] Stanley thought United States citizenship came automatically with the oath of allegiance required to enlist in the Union Army and had since then considered himself American rather than British. That others did as well indicates how much his accent had changed in less than a decade.

At Senafe he and Ali joined part of the army for a while. After camping at a place that struck him as being located "in one of the most lovable, delightful little vales that could possibly be found," they pushed on to Fikada, where the column planned to pause for several days. The downtime allowed Stanley an opportunity to visit a church and thereby report on something Abyssinian besides scenery.

On February 8 he and Ali left the army for the next station at Adigrat, some ten miles away. People became more prominent, with some "nut-brown girls with cunning chignons at the back of their heads" providing a moment of enjoyment by crowding around the "pale-faced strangers" in a welcoming fashion. One, in particular, caught Stanley's eye. He described her as being "graceful as a Hebe" when she brought some milk to quench his thirst. An imposing castle marked Adigrat, and nearby stood a church Stanley felt to be the finest one seen so far. He stopped to see it and visit with the priests. Two days later they began following the army again as it passed through country dotted by fortified towns perched on top of conical hills known as ambas on the way to the station at Dongollo. A hot full day's march from there brought them to Agula Pass and a chance meeting with Lt. Col. W. L. Merewether, the officer in charge of the army's logistical arrangements. With him was the expedition's official geographer Clements Markham, a man Stanley would subsequently encounter in very different circumstances. Hintalo had been selected as the final supply depot for the

remaining 170-mile march to Magdala. When Stanley got there, he found
that from this point on, all reporters would have to stay with the army.

General Napier arrived on March 2 to oversee final preparations. Following a brief audience with him, Stanley remarked, "What a charming old
gentleman he is! Nothing could have been kinder than his reception of
me."[11] Time on the trail seems to have lessened somewhat his sense of insecurity in the face of British upbringing and all its class connotations.

To date, everything had gone far more smoothly than expected. Because
the country was largely controlled by Theodore's enemies, no one offered
any resistance, and Napier's diplomatic skills ensured the cooperation, or at
least neutrality, of local leaders. Furthermore, contrary to dire predictions
made by those in Britain who opposed the expedition, neither disease nor
marauding wildlife had caused any serious problems. Poking fun at them,
Stanley proclaimed, "Lo! it was miraculous! All England stood amazed; the
false prophets, with their false vaticinations, must need hush their everlasting
moan."

The army finally moved out on March 10 in a train of soldiers, animals,

General Napier and his staff en route to Magdala in 1868. *Courtesy of the Royal
Museum of Central Africa*

and camp followers that stretched over many miles. Four more days passed before Stanley was able to leave. He hated this portion of the journey because the slow pace meant being on the road for up to fifteen hours, which left only about three hours of sleep after writing up the events of the day. Napier resisted urgings to adopt a "flying column or columns" approach to secure a quick victory.[12] A cautious man by nature, Napier cared more about logistical details and reducing the possibilities for error than speed. For greater comfort and ease of travel, Stanley purchased an Arabian horse, Said.

The first ripple of concern came when a large contingent of Oromo (often incorrectly called Galla) warriors suddenly made an appearance near Lake Ashange on March 19. Since they were known for being none-too-welcoming of strangers, the army went to full alert in case they showed any hostile intent. Instead, the encounter proved to be an amiable one, and the expedition resumed its journey to Lat, where Napier made final campaign preparations. Much to the disgruntlement of the troops, these included the prospect of longer and quicker marches. The road led to the Tekeze River, which Stanley misidentified as the Blue Nile. On the other side a huge wall of rock stood in the way. It would have to be surmounted to reach the vast Wadela plateau, some 11,000 feet above sea level. Once up and over, Stanley described what he saw in the distance as looking

> like another Laramie region, undulating as far as vision of man can reach, in nude dunes, bereft of the least sign of shrub, rolling like a vitrified sea—such was the Wadela plateau rising above the nether world: strangest freak of nature this! A country combining all temperature!

The army finally caught up with the pioneer brigade at Wek'o Terara (Santarai). Targets of repeated raids by Theodore's forces, the villagers on the Wadela were now under the protection of one of the emperor's rivals, Wagshum Gobazie, ruler of Lasta. Gobazie sent his leading commander, Gen. Mashesha, whom Stanley described as a "Medium-sized man, about five-and-thirty years old, with a kindly good-humored face, full of lively intelligence," to meet with Napier. Cordial negotiations produced an agreement between the two sides, and the march to Magdala resumed free of concerns about local opposition. Considerable uncertainty existed, however, about a number of other things. How long would it take to reach the fort? Maybe six or seven days, or possibly as many as twelve? How large would the opposing force be? What weapons would they have? Was Theodore even at Magdala? The reports that filtered in all seemed to contain different information.

Another problem involved food. The supply line couldn't keep pace, forcing the troops to live pretty much off the land. According to Stanley, the situation had reached the danger point:

For a week before we had no coffee, sugar, potatoes, rum, vegetables, or ghee. We were living on the toughest of beef—one pound per day, sugarless tea, ten ounces of flour, four ounces of rice, and half an ounce of rock salt, while our servants got but half of the soldiers' ration. Our horses were living on eight pounds of grass, and four pounds of barley grain, and the mules on four pounds of grass and three pounds of grain. Ahead the prospect was still darker. Two days at the furthest would consume all our stores. If our Commissariat Department was not replenished daily, starvation would certainly ensue, unless we killed our animals. Yes, by that method we might be able to live another month, until further supplies could be brought from Antalo. The idea was, however, anything but pleasant.

When hearing that Capt. Charles Speedy intended to visit nearby villages to see what he could find in the way of food and other supplies, Stanley asked to go along. Speedy, one of those remarkable nineteenth-century soldier-of-fortune types who always seemed to be in the thick of the action, spoke the local language of Amharic fluently, and it helped them stock up on grain, flour, bread, cakes, and even mules and horses. At one village they were given a royal-like reception. Once again, the young women caught Stanley's attention. He said they "skipped and danced" around him and brought "Pitchers and jars full of the richest cream" to drink, with a "damsel as rich in graces as Cleopatra could boast" catering to his needs.

Although the army was now better supplied, a major physical obstacle, a ravine nearly four thousand feet deep and two miles wide separated the Wadela plateau from the equally high Dalanta on the other side. Despite being able to follow a road constructed several years earlier by Theodore's engineers, an army of 5,500—the rest of the troops guarded the supply line—required more than a day to make the treacherous descent and ascent. Along the way, many pack animals died. But once on the Dalanta, prospects brightened: the local chiefs provided ample food, and Magdala and its two flanking fortresses, Fahla and Selasse, could be seen in the distance. More important, all signs pointed to Theodore being in residence.

On Thursday, April 9, the army crossed the Dalanta to its precipice four thousand feet above the Bascillo River. The next day, Good Friday, it advanced, encountering no opposition, even though conditions seemed perfect for an ambush. Stanley pointed out that "There were many available places where the enemy could have hidden and taken us at a disadvantage . . . . From prominent points in front, in rear, and flanks, we might have been subjected to enfilade, slant, and reverse fires." Theodore's troops waited until the army began setting up camp on the opposite summit before opening up with cannons to cover the charge of some five thousand men. Stanley said,

They all appeared confident of the issue. Their war songs came pealing toward us. We could see their cavalry caracoling and bounding joyously along; the foot soldiers leaping and brandishing long spears and swinging their black shields. With loud chorus all sang the death-doom of the invaders.

Despite not yet being fully assembled, much less deployed, Napier's artillery batteries and riflemen had a field day against the badly outgunned Abyssinians, and just three hours after beginning, the Battle of Arogi ended in a complete rout. British casualties numbered thirty-two wounded, two of whom later died, whereas some seven to eight hundred Abyssinians lost their lives, with at least twice that number seriously wounded.[13]

Napier sent a message to Theodore demanding that he release the prisoners and submit to the queen. The emperor agreed to do the former, and over the next two days all the captives, save one too sick to travel, made it safely into British hands. He would not, however, submit, and to make the point ordered his men to shoot at anyone who came within range of Magdala. Theodore also agreed to turn over a thousand head of cattle and five hundred sheep as a gesture of peace.[14] Napier refused the offer and at 8:30 A.M. on Easter Monday ordered his troops to begin the assault. The commanders at Fahla and Selasse quickly capitulated, but it required a two-hour artillery bombardment of Magdala to clear the way for the infantry. Stanley accompanied a Yorkshire regiment, and upon entering the fort said he beheld "the remains of him whom men called THEODORUS, EMPEROR OF ABYSSINIA, THE DESCENDENT OF MENELIK; SON OF SOLOMON, KING OF KINGS, LORD OF EARTH, CONQUEROR OF ETHIOPIA, REGENERATOR OF AFRICA, AND SAVIOUR OF JERUSALEM." In point of fact, Theodore could not claim dynastic legitimacy. He'd usurped the throne, which proved to be a vital weakness. His death came by using one of a pair of pistols Queen Victoria sent him in 1854 to commit suicide. According to Stanley, the weapon lay beside him, bearing the inscription

PRESENTED
BY
VICTORIA
QUEEN OF GREAT BRITAIN AND IRELAND
TO
THEODORUS
EMPEROR OF ABYSSINIA
AS A SLIGHT TOKEN OF HER GRATITUDE FOR HIS
KINDNESS TO HER SERVANT PLOWDEN 1854

Stanley puzzled over Theodore. In many ways, he seemed more akin to an Oriental potentate than an African chief. But then he was also a Christian, if a Coptic one. Stanley described him as both hero and villain, with language befitting one in the employ of the *Herald:*

> We left him in our introduction struggling manfully against a cursed fate; beating back his Briarean-handed foes which beset him round about. His vast empire was dissolving like the waxen wings of Icarus before the fierce light of revolution. The lurid fires of towns and hamlets burning flashed their portentous blaze athwart the midnight sky; the wails of widowed women and fatherless children rent the air; the groans of dying warriors murdered by cruel hands called loudly to Heaven for vengeance.
>
> It is said that 30,000 men, women, and children were destroyed by crucifixion, the relentless courbach [whip], or by shooting, stabbing, or decapitation, within three months. At such times he appeared like a demon. He was crazed with drunkenness and despair. He slew his best friends and councilors, and condemned to death tried and trusted warriors. Truly is it 'whom God purposeth to destroy, He taketh away his understanding.' Unhappy Theodore! None was more wretched than he!

After rounding up all portable valuables, probably better described as a plundering, and seeing to its evacuation, Napier ordered Magdala torched on April 17. As Stanley described it:

> The easterly wind gradually grew stronger, fanning the incipient tongues of flame visible on the roofs of houses until they grew larger under the skillful nursing, and finally sprang aloft in crimson jets, darting upward and then circling round on their own centres as the breeze played with them. A steady puff of wind levelled the flaming tongues in a red wave, and the jets became united in an igneous lake! The heat became more and more intense; loaded pistols and guns, and shells thrown in by the British batteries, but which had not been discharged, exploded with deafening reports, and projectiles whistled ominously near us. Three thousand houses, and a million of combustible things, were burning. Not one house could have escaped the destruction in the mighty ebb and flow of that deluge of fire.

The message conveyed by the stories was a simple one—those who dare mess with British citizens and then refuse to make amends had better beware.

The army broke camp for the march back to Zula a week later. The British had no intention of occupying the country, and at the expedition's end, Napier handed over the remaining supplies to Prince Karsa of Tigre, who became Emperor Johannis in 1872. By the time the army reached the halfway point at Hintalo on May 12, the grueling journey had exacted an enormous toll on the animals. "In a proportionate sense the retreat from Moscow," Stanley opined, "could not have proved more adverse to animal life than this march. Hundreds of mules died daily. Camels succumbed the most readily, and even the elephants suffered. The cavalry horses died by the dozens." Eager to reach Zula as soon as possible, Stanley and his party left the main body of the army at Senafe. The few officers who decided to come along turned back when they heard about floods making the road ahead impassable. In spite of pouring rain, Stanley pushed on in hopes of catching the next boat for Suez. About thirty miles from Zula, a raging torrent of water blocked the way. "To add to the horrors of the scene," Stanley said,

> corpses of men rolled by with outstretched arms appearing above the turbid waves, and carcasses of oxen, horses, and mules tumbled headlong, colliding heavily with rocky obstructions; telegraph poles shot past with lightening speed, dragging long lines of wire after them; carts and wheels crushed against our granite islet; bales of hay and yellow straw, clumps of bushes, and again corpses of men, all commingling in the turbid stream.

Just when it looked as though they too were about to become part of the water's flotsam and jetsam, the rain stopped and the sun came out. Still, an eight-foot-deep span of water blocked the way. From all indications, it would not be subsiding anytime soon, and so after offloading unnecessary baggage, they plunged in. Miraculously all, animals included, made it safely to the other side. Stanley credited Ali and his horse, Said, for saving him during the crossing.[15] How much of the story is true is anybody's guess.

Stopping just long enough to catch their breaths, Stanley and Ali hurried on in order to reach Zula by noon the next day. This would allow enough time to settle details and catch the steamer *Indore* for Suez the following morning. A particular concern was making arrangements for Said to come along. Stanley had a great fondness for animals and hated losing them. On board he met a colonel carrying Napier's letters to Queen Victoria, along with many of the stories about the campaign from British reporters, who were still on the road with the army.

Mishaps marred the way. First, the *Indore* hit a reef and remained stuck for several days, which delayed reaching Suez until June 1. Once there, officials put the ship under quarantine for five days, suspecting cholera aboard. Stanley, however, managed to slip several dispatches through the guards and have them delivered to William Warren, the telegraph operator. Just before leaving for Zula, Stanley struck a deal with him to send his stories first. By the time the quarantine was lifted and Warren got around to sending those of the other reporters, the cable had snapped somewhere under the Mediterranean, necessitating the routing of all messages via ship to the next working telegraph station in Malta. Stanley had scored a major coup for himself and Bennett; such a major one, in fact, that many people considered the first stories published by the *Herald* to be forgeries. Readers eagerly consumed them anyway, especially the ones about the Battle of Arogi and the fall of Magdala, for, as his publicist-to-be Edward Marston later put it, the "vividness of description of scenes and events, and the careful adherence to facts," an ideal combination by reporting standards.[16] Satisfied with the job he'd done and fairly certain of having wrapped up a permanent position with the *Herald,* Stanley headed to Cairo in high spirits. But he couldn't rest on the laurels and needed another coup to make sure. The key questions were where he would be sent next and when.[17] The short-term answers turned out to be nowhere in particular and not for a while.

Stanley cooled his heels in Egypt, spending most days in Alexandria. The only noteworthy exception involved a side trip from July 9 to 14 to report on progress building the Suez Canal. A recreational dip in the Mediterranean later that month nearly proved fatal. Weakened by an attack of fever the day before, Stanley called out for help to get back to shore. A Reuters employee named Edward Virnard came to the rescue. Without his aid, Stanley remarked, "I should have been carried out by the tide, and drowned."[18] The price would be putting up with years of requests by Virnard about doing him favors of one kind or another.

Word of a new *Herald* assignment finally arrived on August 7: Stanley was to cover the conflict between Greeks and Turks on Crete. On the way, he stopped in Smyrna and from there went to the "place of trouble" with Lewis Noe in 1866.[19] A visit to the island of Sira followed. Here Stanley met Christo Evangelides, who advised him to marry a Greek girl. Stanley was initially concerned about having the means to take a wife, but further thought made the prospect more appealing. This is revealed in a journal entry, which reads,

> A wife! *My* Wife! How grand. . . . To be loved with heart & soul above all else, forever united in thought & sympathy with a fair & virtuous being whose very touch gave strength & courage & confidence.[20]

Evangelides suggested his daughter, but finding her unattractive, Stanley politely refused. A meeting with a pretty sixteen-year-old named Virginie

Ambella produced a different response, and within a few days they agreed to marry after he completed the Crete assignment.

The island proved disappointing. Nothing much seemed to be happening, so Stanley wrote a story for the *Herald* about being with a Greek force during a victorious battle deep in the mountainous interior.[21] He did this while enjoying the sights of Athens, a fact that didn't come out until many years later.

Stanley went back to Sira to see about setting a wedding date. The Ambella family wanted more information about his worthiness to marry Virginie and when Stanley left September 14 on another journey the matter remained unresolved. His itinerary included a second pilgrimage to the 1866 "place of troubles," plus sightseeing in Rhodes, Tripoli, Beirut, Jaffa, and Port Said. During a call at Alexandria on September 25, Stanley opened a wire from the *Herald*'s European bureau chief, Finlay Anderson, containing instructions to go cover the revolution in Spain without further delay. Hurrying to Madrid, he found another telegram instructing him to proceed immediately to London for a meeting with Bennett.[22] By this time, the marriage had been called off and Stanley never saw Virginie again. Some years later she wrote him several times, sending pictures as reminders of their former relationship.[23] He seems to have ignored the overtures.

On October 17, Bennett gave Stanley a potentially more rewarding assignment—to find out what he could about the revered missionary cum explorer Dr. David Livingstone's supposed homeward journey from Central Africa. Having heard nothing from him for several years, many in Britain assumed Livingstone to be "lost," and a large outcry had arisen to do something. It's unlikely that any other person could have generated a similar level of concern. He'd achieved a saintlike stature among the public, and stories about him reached a wide, expectant audience. The doctor also served as a roving consul for the Foreign Office and had Royal Geographical Society backing. Stanley first learned of him while in New Orleans in 1859 and had his interest piqued enough to buy a copy of Livingstone's *Missionary Travels and Researches in South Africa*. He remembered being impressed by the account, but hadn't thought about the book or him since then.[24]

Before setting off, Stanley went to see his mother and Emma. He'd written them from time to time from the United States and Abyssinia and brought along some small gifts for both. Whatever past reservations she may have harbored about him, Betsy by now had warmed to her eldest son, and they spent a happy time together. Afterward Stanley returned to London to catch a train to Marseilles and a sea voyage to an unknown final destination.

A letter from Anderson awaited him in Alexandria with news about Livingstone coming home via Zanzibar. Stanley should try to meet him there or at Suez if he'd already left and get a report on his recent journey and discoveries.[25]

When Suez yielded nothing new, Stanley went to Aden. Still in the dark, he decided to stay until some concrete evidence about Livingstone or further instructions from the *Herald* reached him. To pass the time he read voraciously including works by Ben Jonson, Shakespeare, and Milton. In between, he finished the manuscript for an intended book on Abyssinia, but noted, "It cannot be published for many a long day."[26] He was right. The story in book form would be delayed a few more years.

Aden struck Stanley as bleak and uncomfortable. "The whole mass," he wrote, "appears as scorched as though a devouring fire had lately destroyed every vestige of a combustible thing;" and the heat made "clothes except for decency . . . entirely superfluous." The many Somalis living there generated a more favorable response. Given their "intelligence, aptitude, & manly bearing," he felt they should "constitute the garrison, & so relieve the parboiled British soldiers of their distress."[27] The future would bring several opportunities for Stanley to employ Somalis.

As 1868 turned into 1869, Zanzibar remained mute concerning Livingstone's whereabouts and plans. Concluding that prospects of the doctor leaving Africa anytime soon, at least via the east coast, seemed slim, Stanley departed Aden for Cairo on February 2. As a journal entry shows, the current circumstances left him feeling a bit anxious:

> It is a most miserable life in Cairo when one has nothing whatever to do but to pursue an aimless life almost or pursue some ideal that has no tangible component part. But I always feel out of place in any town or country that has in it the least of anything approaching French tastes. Such is the way I feel in Cairo.

Time seemed to be slipping away and he began to have second thoughts about having left Aden. "What the devil am I to do?" he pondered.[28]

On February 17 a telegram from Anderson instructed Stanley "to come home." He left two days later, fretting that the telegram's brevity might mean the *Herald* "is disappointed with me."[29] Despite feelings about "French tastes," Stanley made a short stopover in Paris. During the stay a young American lad named Edwin Swift Balch gave him a tour of the city. He'd met the senior Balch in Cairo, who'd provided him a letter of introduction to the family. Several things are interesting about the meeting with Edwin. One is Stanley's continuing penchant for telling "tall tales," this time about having been a reporter during the American Civil War and jumping from a Spanish ship. He also gave Edwin two books, Livingstone's *Missionary Travels* and E. D. Young's *The Search for Livingstone,* thinking he'd no longer need them. An inscription on the former bears the signature Henry Morelake Stanley, and the latter contained a series of questions Stanley planned to ask the doctor when they met.[30]

Back in London, Stanley learned his worries were groundless, as he'd be returning to Spain under the title "special correspondent" at a salary of four hundred pounds per year. With no need to get there right away, he decided to take his mother and Emma on a grand tour of Paris. Once again, they all seemed to have had a great time.

Just prior to this, Stanley recorded running into a solicitor from Denbigh named Roberts who suggested that his daughter Katie would make a good wife. She'd come to a marriage with a dowry of a thousand pounds. Stanley said he'd consider it, noting that nothing could happen without "mutual consent."[31] Katie apparently wasn't present at the time, for, Stanley remarked, that while having a vague recollection of her, "I should have seen the daughter first." They must have met shortly thereafter because he described Katie as "plump, good looking," and from all indications proposed marriage the same day.[32] To win her heart, Stanley wrote a long letter telling of his trials, tribulations, and triumphs. Using a little flattery as well, he remarked, "Had any person informed me that I could have been so moved at the sight of any lady from Denbigh, I should not certainly have denied *in toto coela* such unwarranted imputation."[33] Despite the stiffness, Katie agreed to become Mrs. Stanley when he returned from Spain.

Bennett gave final confirmation to the posting on March 25, and six days later Stanley reached Madrid to cover events on the Republican side. He did the job with great aplomb, learning Spanish and crisscrossing the country for more than five months to find stories. The motivation came from a desire to impress Bennett so that he could one day become "his own master & that of others."[34] All the dispatches were published unsigned, but as Stanley was the only *Herald* correspondent on the scene, it's clear he wrote them.[35] One from Vittoria in Basque country typifies his style of blending descriptions of people and editorial commentary with scenes of action:

> The peasants all wear either red or blue-skull caps of coarse wool, and their wives glory in red handkerchiefs and two long tresses of hair hanging adown their backs (the longer the better; the vainest are thise who have then dangling

on the protuberances behind). The men are very handsome, cherry-cheeked, straight and well formed; the women are beautiful.

It is indeed a curious sight to behold a family of fine boys and beautiful girls bent down in a row with mattock in hand vigorously working the fallow ground; far better than to see another family of dandies and coquetes dangling canes and silk parasols in a stroll: for one sees humanity at work, feeling themselves ennobled by it, on the one hand, and on the other shiftless humanity feeling its way by degrees to the grave without the power of human nature having been exercised.

On Thursday evening the hitherto quiet town was disturbed by hundreds of excited men rushing into the streets shouting "Viva Cabrera" "Viva Don Carlos VII, King of Spain; Down with the Liberals, Down with the Government." They were armed with stakes of wood, scythes, pitchforks, and many of them had revolvers, which they kept firing into the air, stopping every passer-by and making him shout "Long live Don Carlos and death to the liberals.[36]

Journal entries show interludes filled with introspection. They contain long extracts, many of them cutouts, from the Scriptures and the classical poets Ovid and Virgil, plus ruminations about a host of topics such as Foliage, Storms, Sunsets, Love, Women, Melancholy, and Conscience.[37] None, however, indicate Africa being on Stanley's mind. The same holds true for the numerous letters he wrote to Katie. Two are worth quoting at length. The first speaks to his deep-seated insecurity. Telling her about becoming "unhinged," he goes on to say,

My usual thoughts, ambitions, hopes, aspirations have utterly left me, eclipsed by constant unrepressed thoughts of you. Were this state of affairs long to continue, without a decided effort on my part to check the effeminate and very unusual luxury to me of thinking of any woman, I believe I would dwindle down shortly into an imbecile. I almost despise myself that I have lain helpless, aimless, driftless. . . . This prevailing passion for you which has robbed me of six weeks enjoyment of intellectual labor, has so pained my thoughts to one set of confined space that I have not been able to think reasonably of ordinary affairs, nor talk intelligently to acquaintances, nor amuse myself in any way, save by letting myself mope away valuable hours, upon one solitary subject. My other intended book I have not touched. My newspaper correspondence is sadly dull, incondite, empty matter, and did I not know the primary cause of this awful state I am in I should have just cause to believe that I was getting to be an eligible candidate for a lunatic asylum.[38]

The second illustrates his method of dealing with the problem. It's full of puffery in an attempt to show Katie how valuable marriage to him would be for her two brothers.

I have been to every state in America and have visited every country in Europe, can write or speak upon the politics of any country, can draw a map of every country in the four continents; have lectured upon the prospects of Kingdoms and Commonwealth, and lastly have acquired knowledge of six languages. I have studied the classics in Greece, roman History in Rome, English History in 10 years of schooling in St. Asaph—American history during 9 years in America, the world's History in respective countries, besides having the acquaintance of eminent people in their own countries. Now, if I were to devote one year to studying law, by the time I was 30, which will be in 18 months from now, I would be a lawyer in excellent practise. . . . In two years from my admission to the bar I would be a member of the American Parliament, or Congress.[39]

To complicate matters between them, the *Herald* now wanted Stanley to go to Egypt and then Rome after finishing the Spain assignment.

A telegram from Bennett dated September 15 instructed Stanley to come to Paris "unless something very startling will take place within the next 20 days." Indeed, two "startling" things did happen, the battles at Zaragosa and Valencia. While covering the latter, Stanley came under heavy fire repeatedly, with a bullet reportedly grazing his hair during one episode.[40] Both stories he told with all the drama of Magdala.[41]

Then, according to Stanley,

On the sixteenth day of October, in the year of our Lord one thousand eight hundred and sixty-nine, I am in Madrid, fresh from the carnage at Valencia. At 10 A.M. Jacopo, at No. — Calle de la Cruz, hands me a telegram: on opening it I find it reads, "come to Paris on important business." The telegram is from Jas. Gordon Bennett, jun., the young manager of the "New York Herald."

Down come my pictures from the walls of my apartment on the second floor; into my trunks go my books and souvenirs, my clothes are hastily collected, some half washed, some from the clothes-line half dry, and after a couple of hours of hasty hard work my portmanteaus are strapped up labelled for "Paris."[42]

Following a series of good-byes to friends, he said he caught the 3:00 P.M. train, intending to reach Paris the next day. Despite not arriving until after sunset because of a four-hour delay in Bayonne, he decided to head straight for the Grand Hotel to see Bennett. The following exchange then purportedly took place:

David Livingstone. *Courtesy of the Royal Museum of Central Africa*

Bennett:	Where do you think Livingstone is?
Stanley:	I really don't know, sir!
Bennett:	Do you think he is alive?
Stanley:	He may be, and he may not be.
Bennett:	Well, I think he is alive, and that he can be found, and I am going to send you to find him.
Stanley:	What . . . do you really think I can find Dr. Livingstone? Do you mean me to go to Central Africa?
Bennett:	Yes; I mean that you shall go, and find him wherever you may hear that he is, and to get what news you can of him. . . . Of course you will act according to your own plans, and do what you think best— BUT FIND LIVINGSTONE![43]

They then discussed costs. Stanley said Bennett remarked, "Well, I will tell you what you will do. Draw a thousand pounds now; and when you have gone through that, draw another thousand, and when that is spent, draw another thousand, and when you have finished that, draw another thousand, and so on; but, FIND LIVINGSTONE."[44] In response to whether he should go "straight on to Africa." Bennett answered, "No!" Other tasks needed attending to beforehand. These included going to Egypt to cover the opening of the Suez Canal, finding out about Samuel Baker's plans for an expedition to the upper Nile basin, and producing a useful tourist guide of the country. Afterward Stanley was to write about Jerusalem and Constantinople, visit the Crimea, cross the Caucasus Mountains to the Caspian Sea, and cover various stories in Persia and India. If by this time Livingstone still hadn't made an appearance, he could then "go into the interior and find him, if alive."[45]

Questions have been raised about the meeting. Did it really take place, and if it did, why such a baffling itinerary? Why not seek out Livingstone right away? After all, this had been the intent the year before. A letter from Bennett's agent Douglas Levien shows that while Stanley may have embellished the conversation for dramatic effect, he didn't concoct the assignment. The key portion reads:

I enclose you a letter of credit for £600 and with it my best wishes for your signal success in your great undertaking. I have no doubt you will carry it through in perfect style. The latest news from Livingstone seems to render it certain that he is alive, and that after all is the most important feature of your commission. I talked the matter over with Mr. Bennett, and his idea is decidedly Napoleonic.

Write as often as you can & always let me know personally how you are getting along. You may fully rely on my sending you supplies of money promptly. I make the present letter £100 more than you asked because I am sure you will be careful as you always have been in regard to expenditures.[46]

The date for the meeting is wrong, however. As noted by Stanley in two other places, it took place October 28, not 17, when he was actually in Valencia.[47] Why the inconsistency? Did Stanley have something to hide in Spain? Without further information, nothing productive of insight can be offered. Maybe he just erred.

Whatever the case may have been, Stanley had a frantic next couple of days. First came a quick trip to London, where efforts to set a wedding date with Katie fell through. Then it was back to Paris. He'd written a letter to Edwin Balch about going with him on the upcoming assignment, but his parents refused to grant permission.[48] On November 1, the grand journey got under way. He told a friend who saw him off from Paris, "I may not be back for many years . . . but I will be back."[49]

Stanley reached Suez just in time for the beginning of the canal opening ceremonies. They started at sunrise on November 16 with "thundering salutes" and continued through the next day when more than forty steamers from an array of countries officially opened the canal to traffic.[50] Stanley wrote up the stories immediately, and their quick arrival gave the *Herald* another scoop.

The task of writing about the Nile kept Stanley in Egypt until January 7, 1870, when he left to seek out stories in Jerusalem and Jaffa. After that he went on to report about Turkey and the Black Sea, staying until late April. The "place of trouble" again beckoned him. Was it guilt, morbid fascination, or something else that motivated these pilgrimages? Stanley's surviving journals and notebooks only record his having made the visits.[51]

On April 11, Stanley sent a "private letter" to Levien about Livingstone, telling him that he would write later from Zanzibar concerning the amount of money needed and that the British Consul should be used as a mailing address.[52] The letter indicates Stanley had some kind of plan in mind.

The route from Turkey led through Georgia, to the Caspian, and on to various stops in Persia, a country Stanley found disappointing. "Instead of being one of the happiest countries under the sun, 'the garden of verdure and fruit trees, and rose bushes haunted by nightingales,'" he described it as "the worst-governed, the worst-cultivated, and the most ill-watered country in the world!"[53]

On August 1 Stanley reached Bombay, which turned out to be his final Asian destination. The many months and places he visited allowed him to write up dispatches describing a diverse array of cultures, landscapes varying from desert to snow-covered mountains, colorful markets, differing religions, history in abundance, fascinating people, and a Stanley favorite, the appearance of women. One can see his eye for detail getting sharper and his writing skills improving. Lacking, however, were dramatic events—no great battles and no harrowing escapes from danger with which to regale readers. In the end, only a few of the letters were published. Some apparently never reached the *Herald* and other more pressing news claimed paper space.

Stanley found Bombay particularly dull and said little about it, even in journals. When not finishing the stories about Persia, time was whiled away reading travel books about Africa. He also wrote a final letter to Katie, not knowing that she'd recently become Mrs. Rufus Bradshaw.[54]

As days turned into weeks and boredom mounted, Stanley finally decided to seek out Livingstone. Uncertainties, though, filled his mind. Maybe it would be better to go straight to the east coast rather than stopping first at Zanzibar? And how to organize a trip to find the doctor appeared no clearer now than a year ago. Even worse, Livingstone might already be on his way home. "Ah, then in that case," he jotted in his journal, "I had better go home too or continue on my voyages to China as ordered by Mr. J. G. Bennett, Jr.," a possibility he left out of his account of their meeting. Given the lack of a direct route to Africa, Stanley boarded the *Polly,* headed for Mauritius on October 12. With him was Selim Heshmy, a young Christian boy from Jerusalem, whom he'd hired as an Arabic interpreter and personal servant the previous January. As would be the case on other journeys, he also took along a dog, Omar. At Mauritius, they caught the schooner *Ronfi* for Mahé in the Seychelles, and from there began the last leg of the journey to Zanzibar on the American whaler *Falcon.* Its destination made the decision of where to start for him. When he disembarked on January 6, 1871, Stanley knew nary a soul personally, carried no letters of introduction, and had only a few ten-pound notes to cover immediate expenses.[55]

CHAPTER 3

Finding Dr. Livingstone

THE EVOLUTION FROM REPORTER
TO AFRICAN EXPLORER

Z anzibar surprised Stanley. Expecting to find it "but a little better than a great sandbar, or a patch of Sahara, with a limited oasis or two, surrounded by the sea," he instead discovered a verdant island home to a bustling international city.[1] For many centuries a relatively minor port in the Indian Ocean monsoon wind-driven trade network, Zanzibar's rise to prominence started during the last years of the eighteenth century with the expansion of activities by Omani Arabs from Muscat. It then literally "took off" when Muscat's ruler Said bin Sultan, or Seyyid Said, relocated the capital there in 1832 and shortly thereafter proclaimed himself suzerain over a long stretch of mainland coast extending southward from the vicinity of Mogadishu to beyond Cape Delgado. Two factors seem to have influenced Said's decisions—his desire to get away from the internal politics plaguing Muscat and a wish to be closer to and have more control over the major sources of wealth on which its prosperity had come to depend. Ivory was the primary lure. The demand for piano keys, billiard balls, and other luxury items to decorate the lives of the wealthy in the Far East, Europe, and the Americas, regularly outpaced supply. Gum copal from the adjacent mainland provided another valuable source of income, as did cloves, mostly from plantations on nearby Pemba Island. Later, both sugar and coconuts added to export revenues.[2] More and more, though, slaves came to predominate. By the time of Stanley's arrival as many as twenty thousand per year passed through the city's mart destined for southwest Asia or, more important, to work on plantations located on the two islands and adjacent mainland. The combination of low birth and high death rates among the laborers kept demand high.

Zanzibar's economic boom produced a highly diverse population that may have numbered close to one hundred thousand in 1871. Arabs dominated the political arena and ran shops. Whereas some could claim direct Omani descent, the majority came from unions of Arab men with African women. Although this meant a diminution with time of the Arab biological contribution, the number of people calling themselves Arabs rose because the father determined one's identity. Indians controlled the purse strings. Commonly called Banyans after the Hindu trader caste, most were, in fact, Muslims. The richest among them had links to commercial houses in Bombay.

Growth in prosperity led to an increase in the numbers of Waswahili.[3] Derived from Bantu-speaking communities resident along the Kenya coast, they'd developed a distinctive town-based mercantile culture, with Islam as an important component. The ever greater profitability of inland trade made Zanzibar an important place for them to be. Prosperity also attracted Wanyamwezi, whose homeland lay directly on the lucrative route leading to Lake Tanganyika and thence the Congo. They eagerly took jobs as porters on caravans, and with the money earned some became traders and caravan leaders themselves. A small number of indigenous inhabitants called Hadimu and Tumbatu made up the rest of the "free" Africans, commonly grouped together as Wangwana, a name connoting civilized as contrasted with Washenzi, or uncivilized. In general, the distinction rested on whether or not one practiced Islam. Numerically, however, slaves from an array of peoples located as far away as the Congo and Zambezi river basins predominated. Around one hundred Europeans and Americans, playing mostly diplomatic and commercial roles, rounded out the island's diversity.

Stanley was relieved to learn that Livingstone's whereabouts remained a mystery. So, too, did the organization of an expedition. He had little idea of what would be needed, and like other would-be travelers turned to the Arabs for advice. They told him that in addition to firearms, ammunition, and everyday items, a caravan would have to carry large quantities of cloth (in four-yard measures called *doti),* beads, and copper wire for paying the *honga,* or tribute, demanded by many groups for right of territorial passage. Since color and shape preferences varied, the lots couldn't all be of one style. Among the cottons the American variety called *merikani* was the most popular, although *kanki* made in India also had value. Stanley liked creature comforts, such as champagne, a bathtub, and Persian carpets to line the floor of his extra-large tent. Conveniently, the shopkeepers could supply all his needs.

Fearful that Livingstone might try to hide or come home by another route if word of the true purpose of the expedition ever reached him, Stanley told people that he had come to Zanzibar to explore along the little-known Rufiji River. This wasn't a complete ruse, for he did wish to see if it could be followed at least part of the way to Lake Tanganyika. Remarks made by the British political agent in Zanzibar, Dr. John Kirk, only served to heighten Stanley's fears about finding Livingstone. Kirk knew him as well as anybody, having served as botanist, medical officer, and eventually second-in-command on the 1858–1863 Zambezi expedition Livingstone led in an attempt to spread commerce and Christianity into the continent's interior. At the cost of many lives, including that of Livingstone's wife, Mary, the expedition accomplished little beyond adding the Shiré Highlands and Lake Nyasa (Malawi) to the cartographer's maps. Kirk called the doctor "a very difficult man to deal with" and said he would likely flee the approach of unwanted visitors.[4] Ever since their Zambezi days, the two men had had a shaky relationship due to personality and responsibility conflicts. Still, it is true that Livingstone preferred solitude and disliked others intruding on his plans. He also chafed at so-called admirers, who used his name whenever it happened to suit their purposes.[5]

But a more immediate problem existed—no deposit from the *Herald* to cover expenses was waiting for him. A journal entry from the day before he reached Zanzibar shows Stanley worrying that this very thing might happen. If it did, he felt,

> the Expedition will be a failure. In that case my long voyage and great expenditure I have already risked will have been for naught. In that case I shall believe myself truly unfortunate, and not only I, but also the 'Herald' in having such a careless man [Douglas A. Levien] as agent in London.[6]

Why he should have expected money to be available is unclear, given his April letter to Levien. There's no indication of a subsequent letter telling of a change of plans. As luck would have it, the American consul in Zanzibar, Francis Webb, agreed to guarantee all purchases and to store the goods at his home until the expedition left the island. Webb had been Stanley's Zanzibar contact while in Aden and thus knew of the *Herald* connection. In addition, canceled letters of credit from the J. P. Morgan company indicated Stanley had financial backing.[7] Did Webb also know about the Livingstone mission? The one bit of relevant evidence is found in a letter to the State Department, and it can be read either way:

> His intention is to carefully explore the Lake regions of Central Africa and either return to this point or to return to Europe down the Nile, and well probably be absent about a year. He may possibly meet with Dr. Livingtone.[8]

Webb's largesse could have been motivated by personal reasons. Before the Civil War and the opening of the Suez Canal, no nation traded as much with Zanzibar as the United States. Now ships carrying the flags of Germany and Great Britain predominated. A successful mission by Stanley might re-energize American interest in the region, and should that happen, Webb, who worked for Salem, Massachusetts–based John Bertram & Co., stood to profit handsomely.

With the money problem solved, Stanley set about putting his team together. Aboard the *Polly* he convinced its Scottish first mate, William Farquhar, to join as "superintendent of porters," and in Zanzibar another willing participant, John Shaw, a Cockney, agreed to become a member. Recently released from serving on the USS *Nevada,* Shaw spent most of his time lolling around the city's drinking establishments and houses of ill repute. An American named John Smith also signed a contract but never went along.[9] He remains a phantom figure. In addition, Stanley hired six so-called faithfuls who'd accompanied Speke on his last journey and some of Burton's former *askari,* the Kiswahili word for soldiers. Mubarak Mombai (better known as Bombay), who'd served both men, joined as the caravan's captain. That Stanley's employees, too, remained in the dark about the purpose of the expedition is revealed in a letter Farquhar wrote to his sister. He told her, "I have been engaged with this gentleman, and agreed to accompany him and assist in "discovering the sources of the Nile, and different parts where no white has been."[10]

The day prior to leaving the island, Stanley paid a courtesy call on Sultan Barghash bin Said, who, in return, provided invaluable letters of introduction to officials and traders on the mainland. He also presented Stanley with a prize Arabian horse. On February 5, 1871, four dhows (the Arab sailing vessel) loaded with men, eight thousand dollars' worth of supplies, two horses, twenty-five donkeys, and two small disassembled boats crossed the channel to Bagamoyo, the principal port connecting Zanzibar with the interior and the place to hire *wapagazi,* or porters. Stanley intended to get this task over quickly to avoid traveling during the *masika* (great rains). Few candidates could be found, however. Cholera had devastated the coast the year before, and only now were men in search of work beginning to reappear. The slow process of negotiating to obtain them proved frustrating and resulted in Stanley describing the time spent in Bagamoyo as something a "convict at Sing Sing would not have envied. It was work all day, thinking all night; not an hour could I call my own. It was a steady grind on body and brain this work of starting."[11] On the other hand, he enjoyed sleeping out under cool breezes and starting each day with a refreshing dip in the ocean, pleasures denied by sultry Zanzibar. Another luxury involved partaking of an elegant meal, champagne included, put on by French priests at Bagamoyo's Holy Ghost mission station.

During the protracted stay, Stanley learned a valuable piece of information, namely that he should outfit several caravans instead of one large one in order to lessen the amount of *honga* demanded and cut down on the chances of losing everything to an attack. Ultimately, he put together six of them containing a total of 192 men. The first caravan left Bagamoyo on February 18; the second three days later; the third, with Farquhar in command, on the 25th; the fourth on the 28th; the fifth on March 11; and the sixth, which included Stanley and Shaw, on March 22.[12] A small contingent of *askari* armed with flintlocks, pistols, and a few Winchester repeating rifles went with each to provide defense. Stanley's, for example, contained nine armed guards. Sporting such limited numbers and weapons, the caravans hardly constituted forces capable of overcoming serious local opposition, much less imposing their wills on communities guarded by warriors as many were. Each caravan had instructions to head for Tabora in the Unyanyembe chiefdom of Unyamwezi. A place where trade routes converged, Tabora was the Arabs' most important commercial center in the interior. From there Stanley intended to go to Ujiji on Lake Tanganyika, hoping to find Livingstone, or, at the very least, get more accurate information concerning his whereabouts. The doctor had chosen the town as his base of operations because it was being far enough away to discourage unwanted visitors yet well enough connected via trade routes to the east coast to allow for regular provisioning. Ujiji also provided access to lands on the other side of the lake that he felt held the key to the source of the Nile.

Marked by flat terrain of dull sameness and having few people due to generally infertile soil and diseases like sleeping sickness and malaria, the *mrima,* or coastal plain, immediately inland from Bagamoyo contained little of interest for a reporter to write about. Furthermore, at this point, Stanley evinced little desire to do much in the way of exploration, proclaiming that "I was sent out on an errand, not as a discoverer, and the quickest and shortest method of fulfilling my duty was to be my study."[13] Still, he initially chose to follow a route that went somewhat north of the one taken by his predecessors Burton, Grant, and Speke, so as to cover slightly different ground.

Portents of things to come began almost immediately. Trees had to be cut to build a crude bridge to get the animals across the muddy Kingani River, the name for the Ruvu in its lower portions, and stretches covered with "wait-a-bit" thornbushes Stanley called *acacia horrida* tore clothing and skin.

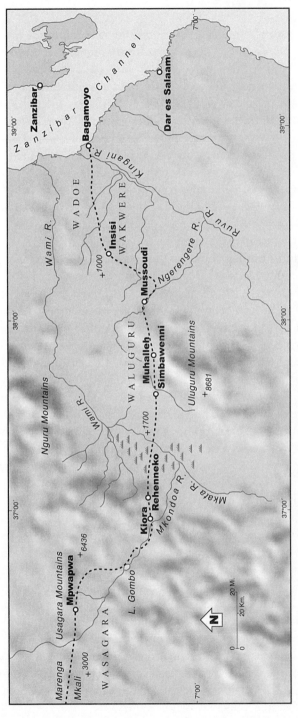

Map 3.1   The Journey to Find Livingstone, March–May 1871

Various illnesses plagued the men, and before the end of the first week both of Stanley's horses died. The Arabian from Barghash went down first, and curious as to why, Stanley opened his stomach and found the intestines crawling with worms. The second death he attributed to cancer, although the symptoms presented and postmortem findings better describe African horse sickness, a virus spread by midges or gnats (*Culicoides*). Death can ensue within a few days of infection.

By now the *masika* had also started, and a fifteen-mile march to a place called Insisi proved to be more than many of the men could handle. Stanley thus let them rest for a day. From Insisi they veered to the south instead of continuing westward, as noted on the map Stanley drew. With only a compass and the sun and stars as guides, he often didn't know their exact heading. Stanley described the country as a jungle, and because the "odour emitted from its fell plants was so rank, so pungently acrid, and the miasma from its decayed vegetation so dense," he feared everyone might "drop down in paroxysms of acute fever."[14] The role of the anopheles mosquito in spreading malaria hadn't yet been discovered, and he, like most people, accepted the miasma, or bad air, theory of its causation. And while no one "dropped down," some carriers chose to drop out by deserting.

Travel conditions improved as they neared the valley of the Ngerengere River. Now that they were back on the main trade route, the first of what would be many slave caravans passed in view. Stanley said little about it other than to note that "Were it not for their chains, it would have been difficult to discover master from slave; the physiognomic traits were alike—the mild benignity with which we were regarded was equally visible on all faces."[15] It would take a while longer before he saw ending slavery as a cause worth embracing.

On April 14 they crossed the Ngerengere at Mussoudi and headed west. Upstream, the river makes a loop, and upon nearing its valley again, Stanley described a scene of "wonderful fertility," with fields rivaling the best he'd seen growing on the rich alluvial soils of Arkansas. At the village of Muhalleh, he came across one of the caravans stopped for a second time because of illness. As before, the leader decided to wait for Stanley to bring medicines. During the interlude, an Arab leading an ivory caravan to the coast provided the first news about Livingstone in a long while. He described the doctor as "looking old" and "very wan" because of a recent illness. Nonetheless, he still planned to make a trip to Umanyema, a Kiswahili name for the Congo basin west of the Lualaba River that had recently been opened to slave and ivory trading.[16] In keeping with standard Kiswahili nomenclature, its Bakusu inhabitants became known as Wamanyema.

Within two hours of leaving Muhalleh, the caravan passed the walled town of Simbawenni at the base of the Uluguru Mountains. Stanley estimated its population at three to five thousand and compared the fortifications favorably with cities in Persia. Discomforted by stares from large groups of Waluguru lining the way, he decided to push ahead a few more miles before pitching camp for an intended two-day stop. The baggage needed to be repacked, repairs made, the donkeys rested, and the other caravan sent on its separate way. During the stop, Stanley came down with his first attack of African malaria, but thanks to a quinine treatment regime he had learned in Arkansas, the symptoms were kept under control. The *masika* proved a greater cause of concern. Stanley described it as "such a rain as shuts people in-doors and renders them miserable and unamiable—a real London rain—an eternal drizzle accompanied with mist and fog."[17] An array of ants, centipedes, wasps, and beetles infesting tents added to the misery of the season.

Besides their penchant for staring, Stanley didn't care for the way the Waluguru bartered, claiming that if remonstrated about the price asked, they grew angry and "were glib in their threats."[18] This differed markedly from the "civility" previously demonstrated by the Wadoe and Wakwere. Because of fear or, more probably, disinterest, they kept their distance.

On April 23 the rain let up enough to attempt crossing the swollen Ngerengere. A morning of hard work left the men exhausted, and the caravan managed to go only a little ways before having to halt. The need to search for a cook who'd fled from camp after being punished for stealing resulted in a longer stay than intended. No one really wanted to start up again, for ahead lay the virtually uninhabited plain surrounding the Mkata River, at this time of year a vast swamp. Once they were into it, the water and thick mud slowed travel to such an extent that it required six days of short marches to reach Rehenneko on the other side. By then the *masika* had come to an end, only one day shy of the forty people in Bagamoyo said it normally lasted.

Down more than thirty pounds in weight since leaving Bagamoyo, and with the men weakened by fatigue, malaria, smallpox, and dysentery, Stanley opted to remain at Rehenneko for a few days. Although the higher elevations beyond there provided a pleasant change from slogging through swamps, it didn't help much and the first days' march lasted only a few hours. After another day of tough up-and-down marching, they reached the small village of Kiora in the Mkondoa River valley, only to discover Farquhar's caravan stalled because of its leader's deteriorating health. Badly swollen legs suggested elephantiasis, to go along with a face, Stanley said, exhibiting "a deathly pallor."[19] In addition, nine of the caravan's donkeys had died, and the inventory of supplies showed that Farquhar had been overly generous in doling out *honga*. Stanley merged the caravans, and on May 11 the enlarged party took to the road again. After about eight hours, they crossed to the other side of the Mkondoa, thus veering away again from the route traveled by Burton and Speke. A west-by-northwest tracking led to Lake Gombo, yet to be seen by a European. A small and not very impressive body of water, Stanley wouldn't have stopped except for the need to search for a missing cooper. With nothing better to do during the search to find the man, he decided to reconnoiter the lake's northern and southern slopes. The resulting brief and not terribly detailed description constituted his first true contribution to the annals of geographic discovery.[20]

An incident occurred at Lake Gombo that nearly cost Stanley his life. As he explained it, Shaw and Farquhar showed up for breakfast one morning surly and uncommunicative. When pressed as to why, they began complaining about Stanley's ill treatment of them. In the heated exchange that followed, Stanley ordered Shaw to pack up and leave without further delay. Shaw later apologized and the matter seemed settled. But shortly after he retired that night, a bullet tore through Stanley's tent, barely missing him. Shaw at first denied firing his pistol, but upon further questioning claimed he'd had a dream about seeing a thief. Stanley said he warned Shaw to be careful firing guns in his direction and bade him good night. A possible murder attempt? A pathetic effort if indeed the case, which caused Stanley to think that Shaw might have become "momentarily insane."[21]

By now Stanley had given up on Farquhar, whom he disliked almost from the beginning anyway. He characterized his behavior while aboard ship as "lazy and insolent"; in Mauritius, the Seychelles, and Zanzibar, he described him as "normally inebriated" except during the morning; and in Africa he found him "useless," being "neither tailor, sail maker, carpenter, or anything else." All told, he was a "bad investment."[22] After the deaths of several of the donkeys used to transport Farquhar, Stanley's patience ran out. He ordered Farquhar carried by litter to Mpwapwa, the next village up ahead.

After two long, difficult marches the weary band of travelers reached Mpwapwa on May 17, relishing the prospect of a much needed opportunity to rest, resupply, and take on new porters. During the stop, an Arab ivory trader related another rumor about Livingstone: that he'd supposedly shot himself in the thigh while on the way to Umanyema.[23] So far no one knew anything about him firsthand.

In Mpwapwa, Stanley met two caravan leaders, Sheikhs Thani and

Hamed. Their paths had crossed several days earlier, and like Stanley they were on the way to Tabora. A proposal to join forces for the difficult march ahead appealed to Stanley, and he consented to meet them at Chunyu, a little more than five miles away at the base of the Usagara Mountains. Before leaving Mpwapwa, Stanley also made arrangements for Farquhar to be looked after, hoping he might recover in due course. Farquhar wished to go no farther and so didn't object. A servant remained with him.

The combined caravans left Chunyu on May 22 and traveled more than twelve hours in order to get across the thirty-two-mile wide Marenga Mkali as quickly as possible. *Mkali* means bitter, sharp, or fierce in Kiswahili, and by common usage a *marenga mkali* denoted especially severe stretches of wilderness or unoccupied country. On the first day Stanley fell ill and had to be carried by litter. Nevertheless, he managed to be back at the helm when the journey resumed at 3:00 A.M., and later that morning they reached Mvumi on the eastern border of Ugogo, an expanse of country that caravans dreaded entering. Although free of tsetse and sleeping sickness, its semiarid climate made water difficult to find even in good years, and there were few trees other than scattered baobabs to provide shade from the overhead sun. The heavy *honga* levied by many different chiefs intensified apprehension of what the days ahead held in store. Thoughts of trying to avoid payment were put to rest by large contingents of Wagogo warriors standing ready to back up the chiefs' demands. Stanley called them the "Irish of Africa—clanish and full of fight." Earlier, Richard Burton had labeled Ugogo "stern and wild,—the rough nurse of rugged men."[24]

During the crossing, Stanley suffered another attack of malaria and lost nine donkeys from drinking the brackish water of the Marenga Mkali. The tendency of people to stare at him hardly helped his disposition. They made him feel "not much better than a monkey in the zoological collection at Central Park, whose funny antics elicit such bursts of laughter from young New Yorkers."[25] In the midst of one such incident Stanley pulled out a whip, "whose long lash cracked like a pistol shot," in order to clear the way.[26] By now he had also adopted the standard caravan practice of using lashes to maintain discipline among the ranks of porters. Strategically, he also learned the tactics of convening a council to render judgment and leaving the task of administering the punishment to one of the headmen, rather than doing it himself. All told, Stanley came to loathe Ugogo, describing it as "a land of gall and bitterness, full of trouble and vexation of spirit, where danger was imminent at every step—where we were exposed to the caprice of inebriated sultans."[27]

Weakened by nearly two weeks of fever, Stanley wanted to stop for a while

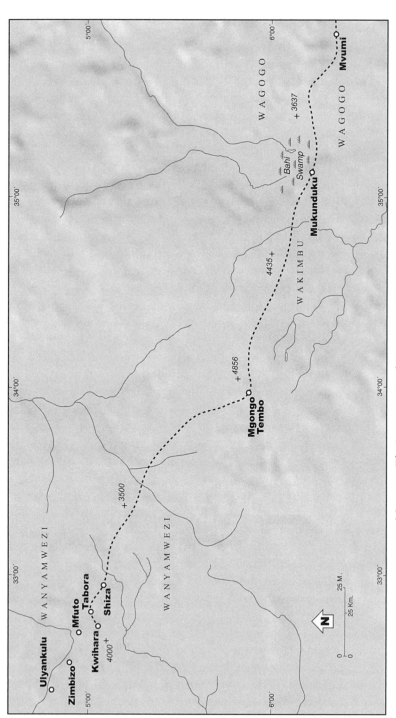

Map 3.2   The Journey to Find Livingstone, May–June 1871

in order to begin a quinine treatment. Sheikh Hamed said he couldn't afford another delay and would push on. Stanley told him to do as he pleased, feeling his caravan had enough firearms to see them safely through. After further consideration, Hamed decided to stay with the others, and two days later they broke camp and continued west, staying south of the large Bahi Swamp.

At Mukunduku, some indecision existed as to which route to follow in order to leave Ugogo for Uyanzi, with its promise of better times. The more usual southern route had a reputation for its costly *honga,* while an alternative northern one cost less but took longer. After spirited debate, they decided to take a poorly known third route because it looked to be the shortest of all and might avoid *honga* payments altogether. On June 8 they at last left Ugogo by climbing up a rugged escarpment covered by thorny acacia bushes to reach a woodland-covered plateau about 4,500 feet above sea level. Cooler days and numerous pools of clear water eased travel, as did the presence of some recently arrived Wakimbu settlers who eagerly sold food and, thankfully, didn't demand *honga.* During the journey, Sheikh Thani's caravan had to be left behind when some of the men came down with smallpox.

New and disturbing scenes suddenly started to appear with regularity. The village of Mgongo Tembo, a productive settlement when visited by Speke and James Grant in January 1861, now consisted of nothing "but blackened wrecks of houses," with the fields "a sprouting jungle" due to an Arab-led attack two years earlier.[28] Beyond Mgongo Tembo the road veered sharply northwest through country still showing no signs of people. What it offered instead was heat, thirst, and stinging bites of tsetse. One of the porters afflicted with smallpox fell by the wayside and the caravan pushed on without him, for, according to Stanley, it must proceed ahead like a ship in a hurricane, which can't wait for one who falls overboard. He had his eyes set on making Tabora in record time. A bit farther on, another example of the violence brought to this part of Africa by the slave and ivory trades caught their attention. Stanley reported that little remained except abandoned fields to tell of a once

> well-cultivated and populous district, rich in herds of cattle and stores of grain. All the villages are burnt down, the people have been driven north three or four days . . . the cattle were taken by force, the grain fields left standing, to be overgrown with jungle and rank weeds. We passed village after village that had been burnt, and were mere blackened heaps of charred timber and smoked clay; field after field of ripe grain years ago was left standing in the midst of a crop of gums and thorns, mimosa and kolquall.[29]

As they got closer to Tabora the countryside started to show signs of life, and visitors came with so-called news about Livingstone. One source described him as "a very old man, beard nearly white" who was on his way back to Ujiji after having gone to Umanyema, whereas another reported that he had died during the return. Yet a third proclaimed him to be a fat old man who had no men left except three slaves, while a fourth said he'd injured his shoulder in a fight with a lion.[30] Livingstone did have a run-in with a lion, but it had happened long before Stanley arrived on the scene, probably in the first or second week of February 1844 in what is now Botswana, during a hunt. He suffered deep gashes and a badly damaged humerus that impaired use of his left arm for the rest of his life. Given all the stories, Stanley considered anything he heard about Livingstone to be rumor and stuck with his plan to find him, even if this amounted to nothing more than finding his bones.

On June 22 the caravan reached Shiza, only a few hours from Tabora, which they set out for in the morning "with banners flying and trumpets and horns blaring."[31] In all, ninety-four days had passed since Bagamoyo. Stanley glowed with pride, as Burton and Speke needed 134 days, and Speke and Grant 115, to make the same journey. Tabora's governor offered greetings and, following pleasantries, led the caravan to nearby Kwihara, where a large *tembe* (a rectangular flat-roofed house characteristic of much of this part of Africa) served as a temporary abode for important visitors. The members of the other caravans were on hand to greet them. All told, the six caravans had lost ten men to dysentery and smallpox, but none to any kind of hostilities. Desertions proved more costly, reducing the original 192 to fewer than one hundred. Only twenty-five men were contracted to continue the journey to Ujiji.

Four days later Stanley went to town to thank the Arabs for the lavish amount of food they had sent to Kwihara. Their lifestyle struck him as extremely comfortable. They dressed immaculately and lived in large, solid houses. Local produce, including livestock, abounded, and gardens of citrus, mangoes, papaya, onions, and garlic provided variety to the diet. Wherever Arabs settled in the interior, agricultural innovations in the form of new crops and techniques leading to greater productivity almost inevitably followed.[32] Other items, including condiments, china, silver, jewelry, and Persian carpets, came via caravans from the coast. Conversations produced disquieting words about the chance of reaching Ujiji anytime soon. The direct road to the town passed through country under a young chief named Mirambo, and as part of a larger strategy to gain control of the region's trade, he wouldn't allow caravans from Tabora to pass. Mirambo means "corpses," testimony to how he'd achieved power.[33] Stanley accepted the Arab view that Mirambo was nothing more than a leader of bandits and agreed to join the military campaign then being planned. Following the promised quick victory, he intended to leave immediately for Ujiji. That Stanley sided with the Arabs is hardly surprising. He knew something of them from previous experience, and their help seemed crucial in the quest to find Livingstone. Africans, on the other hand, had yet to penetrate his consciousness much beyond dealing with porters and haggling over *honga*. And he certainly possessed little knowledge of the complexities surrounding competition for control of the slave and ivory trades that raged in this part of the continent. The stakes were immense, many factions competed, and warfare had become a way of life.

Stanley penned his first story for the *Herald* on July 4. It outlined the journey to date, and per instruction from Bennett, who only let a few higher-ups at the paper in on the mission, it carried no signature. Only when the story was published on December 22 did the public learn the name of the author and the intent of his mission.[34] Three days later a violent attack of malaria sent Stanley to bed for two weeks. The fever produced bouts of delirium and a total loss of time reckoning. Both Shaw and Selim also became ill, and it wasn't until July 29 that everyone felt well enough to join the Arab-led force assembled at Mfuto. With more than two thousand fighters at their disposal, they easily overran the village of Zimbizo on August 4. The next day, with Stanley still incapacitated by fever, some five hundred men led by twenty Arabs moved on Ulyankulu, reputed to be Mirambo's current place of residence. It, too, fell quickly, yielding ivory and slaves to the confident conquerors, who then split their forces. This played right into Mirambo's hands. He left the village upon learning of the intended attack to set an ambush along the road back to Zimbizo. Caught completely by surprise, all of the twenty Arabs and half of the troops in the contingent were killed. Stanley called the effects of the defeat "indescribable," noting,

> It was impossible to sleep, from the shrieks of the women whose husbands had fallen. All night they howled their lamentations, and sometimes might be heard the groans of the wounded who had contrived to crawl through the grass unperceived by the enemy. Fugitives were continually coming in throughout the night, but none of my men who were reported to be dead, were ever heard of again.[35]

In total disarray, the rest of the force fled in panic, fearing that Mirambo intended to finish them off. Contrary to the usual Wanyamwezi practice of forming fighting units only as needed, Mirambo had created a disciplined standing army composed of many mercenaries called *ruga-ruga* (literally, a king's levy) who owed allegiance only to him. Most carried muzzle-loaders. The Arabs thus had no idea of what they'd be facing. With four of his own party dead and others, including Shaw, having, Stanley said, "lost their heads," the situation appeared desperate. It could very well have numbered him among the victims if Selim hadn't had the presence of mind to round up a donkey and get Stanley aboard for the trip back to Mfuto and thence Kwihara.[36]

The debacle caused Stanley to abandon his plans to take the usual route to Ujiji. He decided, instead, to start in a southerly direction and thus away from country controlled by Mirambo. Only when it looked safe to do so would he turn toward Lake Tanganyika. First, though, the caravan, which had dropped to thirteen men, required attention. As he set about getting more porters, Stanley fretted that it might be necessary to abandon the goal of reaching Livingstone. Indeed, even if the doctor were still alive, he might not be for much longer because the caravan sent to resupply him was, like Stanley's, sitting idle in Tabora. Stanley's offer to take the doctor's goods along via the alternate route was turned down by the agent in charge on the grounds that a caravan couldn't possibly make it to Ujiji this way.[37]

On August 13 word arrived of Farquhar's death at Mpwapwa on or about May 27, and from his looks Shaw seemed on the verge of following him to the grave. Stanley attributed Shaw's condition to "the fatigue one endures from the constant marches" and to "his intercourse with the females of Unyanyembe," which "put the final touches to his enfeebled frame."[38]

More days of relative inactivity went by until sounds of gunfire echoed from the direction of Tabora on August 22. Mirambo's army, supported by large numbers of Wangoni, had the town under siege. Offshoots of the Zulu in South Africa, groups of Wangoni had been moving progressively northward in search of booty, and wherever they showed up periods of violence and instability inevitably followed. When the small Arab force sent to confront the attackers quickly met its end, throngs of people rushed to Kwihara. By nightfall Stanley counted one hundred and fifty men with firearms at his disposal should Mirambo decide to attack. Apparently satisfied with what they had taken from about a quarter of Tabora's houses, he and his allies broke off the engagement and headed their separate ways.

With the crisis over, Stanley resumed making travel plans for Ujiji. To compensate for having to cover a much greater distance by first going south, he wanted the caravan to move as fast as possible. Therefore, each porter would carry only fifty pounds of absolute essentials rather than the usual seventy-pound load. The Arabs once again cautioned Stanley about the like-lihood of ever reaching Ujiji, particularly since bands of *ruga-ruga* would almost certainly be encountered along the way. He ignored what they said, calling the words "false-hearted," suspecting that other motives, such as wanting him to stay and aid in future battles with Mirambo, prompted their entreaties.[39] Furthermore, Stanley had come to view finding Livingstone as something more than just an assignment. This is vividly revealed in a September 13 journal entry that reads, "The 'Apostle of Africa' Livingstone is always on my mind and as day after day passes without starting to find him I find myself subject to fits of depression."[40] Whether the statement reflected concern about the doctor's fate or his own possible failure can't be told.

Work on reconstituting the caravan, therefore, continued apace. The new additions included three boys Stanley purchased from a slave dealer for sixty dollars in gold.[41] One he renamed Kalulu (Swahili for "young antelope"), who became Stanley's most trusted companion. A complication involved Shaw's continuing downhill slide. Stanley described him as "so weak that that he can absolutely do nothing," and considered postponing the departure "until all damage is past, and he is sufficiently strong to travel."[42] Concerned about how long this could take, especially with rumors flying about that Mirambo might be launching another attack on the town sometime soon, Stanley set departure for September 20. Then, just before the appointed day, he suffered another attack of fever. Despite urgings from the Arabs, Stanley wouldn't change his mind about leaving because of having boasted to one of them "that a white man never breaks his word."[43] The statement reflects two things Stanley would demonstrate time and again in Africa: his sense of representing Europeans in general and his need to demonstrate moral superiority on their behalf. Furthermore, he ached to get away from Tabora, as the many weeks spent there had made the town a tedious and boring place to be. As for the mission, it could well turn out to be fruitless, especially since he had only fifty-four men and boys available to accomplish it.

The journey began ominously, as a succession of desertions and illnesses allowed for less than ten hours of travel over the first four days. Given that the threat of lashes didn't seem a sufficient deterrent, Stanley sent a man to Tabora to pick up the kind of neck chain caravan leaders used for harnessing slaves. Anyone caught sneaking off in the future would be harnessed by it just long enough to make the point.[44] Desertions continued anyway, prompting him to remark that soon the caravan "will be reduced to nothing."[45] Shaw also slowed them down. He couldn't walk and kept falling off his donkey. Finally, after a week of this and Shaw's continuous pleadings,

Stanley agreed to allow him to return to Kwihara. His chances of surviving looked bleak. Stanley, in fact, told him that with no one there to provide needed care, he might die.

Their pace quickened upon entering an "immense forest" that looked to be endless—"the new land which no European knew, the unknown, mystic land," Stanley mused.[46] A growing self-confidence based on having made it this far seems to have made exploring a more intriguing thought. Seven hours of marching led to the large fortified village of Ugunda, where caravans going south toward ivory country counted on hiring more porters. This time none could be found because the many wars raging thereabouts kept men away and otherwise occupied. Beyond Ugunda, the forest thinned, and intense heat, plus the stinging bites of tsetse and sword flies, tempered enthusiasm. The sight of a dead man by the trail also provided a vivid reminder of the dangers of smallpox, and several human skeletons gave testimony to war's grim results. While passing near a village called Manyara, Stanley said they were forced to stop because the chief "had never seen a white man before" and wanted to "know all about this wonderful specimen of humanity."[47] It actually turned out to be an agreeable, even amusing, visit, with Stanley claiming to have regaled the chief by exhibiting the wonders of European weapons and giving him a whiff of ammonia.

They next camped beside what Stanley identified as the Southern Gombe River, then dry. There is no such river, and given the direction they were traveling, the locale must have been near the juncture of the Ugalla and Katambuki Rivers. Much of the caravan's route from Kwihara to Ujiji is impossible to trace with certainty—most of the place names mentioned by Stanley cannot be found on later maps and he left few compass readings as guides. The best one can do in many instances is to use the landmarks he described as guideposts. Whatever the exact spot, the surrounding area proved to be a hunter's paradise, and for several days they stuffed themselves with game meat. No one really wanted to leave when Stanley gave the order to break camp on October 7. A few hours after getting under way the men suddenly stopped and a mutiny appeared imminent. According to Stanley, one of the leaders even leveled a rifle at him, and in response he brought his gun to the ready. But before any shots could be fired, Mabruki Speke, one of the "faithfuls" from Zanzibar, stepped in to calm things down. Sensing the need to maintain peace, Stanley said he pardoned everyone, including the leaders after they apologized. For not having performed his duties as captain properly by warding off the mutiny, Bombay received a lashing.

Two days later the caravan reached Ukonogo, a land short of water and full of tsetse and sleeping sickness. It also presented prospects of running

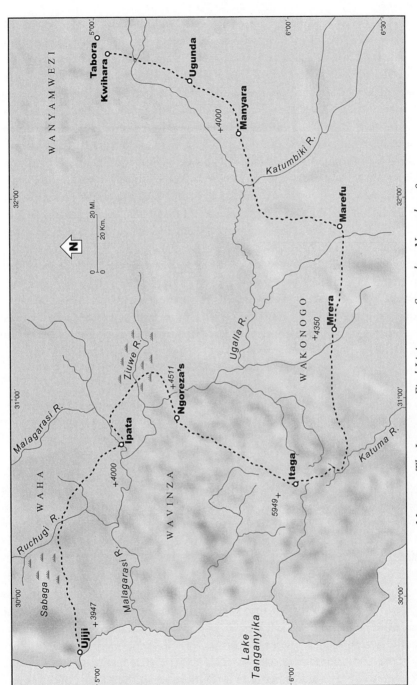

Map 3.3   *The Journey to Find Livingstone, September–November 1871*

into *ruga-ruga*, and any serious encounter would likely be their doom. At Marefu on October 10, Stanley changed travel plans. He wanted to continue south for a while longer, but word of fighting in that direction convinced him the time had come to turn west toward Lake Tanganyika. The country-side beyond Marefu also showed the effects of recent hostilities, including bleached skulls. Near the village of Mrera, Stanley saw his first herd of wild elephants. That it took him so long indicates how thoroughly the herds had been hunted between there and the coast. Stanley called a halt at Mrera to allow Selim time to recover from a bad case of dysentery. It also provided an opportunity to purchase grain for the difficult journey ahead. With ample food, including fruit, birds, and small game from the forest, and prospects of being only about ten days from Lake Tanganyika, spirits soared. Stanley said all had become friends again, the mutiny attempt having been forgotten.[48]

This particular march followed the rugged terrain marking the watershed of rivers flowing northward and those flowing to the south. And although Stanley said the area possessed "fair, lovely valleys and pellucide streams" that "the fairest scenery in California cannot excel," it appeared "almost uninhabited."[49] Once again, war had left its mark in charred villages and fields. A settlement along what Stanley called the Mpokwa River (probably the Katuma) looked to have been abandoned without a fight because

> The huts were almost all intact as they were left by their former inhabitants. In the gardens were yet found vegetables, which, after living so long on meat, were most grateful to us. On the branches of the trees still rested . . . exceedingly well-made earthen pots.[50]

The river provided an avenue through a dense forest, home to lions, leopards, and other wildlife, on the way to Rusawa. Although it was a populous district, the wide scattering of settlements meant few traders ever bothered to visit it. At Itaga, more than halfway between Unyanyembe and Ujiji, another decision had to be made about what route to follow. Still concerned that Livingstone would hear of his plans and flee, Stanley favored striking directly west to Lake Tanganyika, road or no road. But on being told that the Malagarasi River, which flowed into the lake, could be reached in two days, he opted to go there instead. It was October 25, a day Stanley would remember as the beginning of a "series of troubles."

First came differences over whether to remain longer at the next camp. The men felt it would be better to learn more about the country ahead before setting off, while Stanley, as usual, wished to push ahead immediately. Also as usual, he got his way and off they went, packing only enough food for the presumed short journey. After two tough days of mostly uphill traveling, the sight of a camp recently built by Arabs from Ujiji lifted the men's spirits. They couldn't be too far from their goal. But the Malagarasi was nowhere in sight. Based on the information provided, they should have reached it by now. Making matters worse, the area contained little potable water and no signs existed of humans in the vicinity. October 29 turned out to be especially grueling. As described by Stanley: "The country was cut up in all directions by deep, wild, and narrow ravines trending in all directions" and required a "long series of descents down rocky gullies, wherein we were environed by threatening masses of disintegrated rock."[51] With rations down to sweetened tea and a few fruits gathered from the forest, things took on a desperate look, so desperate that during the night Stanley heard the men imploring Allah for food. Clearly staying put would mean starvation, and so the next morning they broke camp determined, according to Stanley, "to travel on until food could be procured, or we dropped down from sheer fatigue and weakness."[52] About two hours later, one of the men spied a village in the distance, and they hurried toward it, firing guns to announce their arrival. It turned out to be unnecessary, for upon noticing people approaching, the villagers rushed forth to confront what they thought to be an enemy force. Satisfied that the strangers meant no harm, they freely supplied food, including meat, to quell everyone's hunger. The caravan had reached a place called Uvinza, under the jurisdiction of Chief Ngoreza.

From this point the easiest route trended north by east. It led to a formidable-looking marsh along the Ziuwe River, said to have swallowed all members of a thirty-five-man slave caravan not too long before. A natural bridge created by densely interlaced vegetation allowed them to cross it without mishap, and for the first time since Rusawa, they entered populous country. This would mean having to pay *honga* again on a regular basis. Stanley felt that "forty good rifles . . . could have made the vain fellows desert their country *en masse*" but concluded that those wishing to "come out of Africa alive" should act more prudently.[53]

The Malgarasi finally came into view on November 1. A crossing would be needed at some point, and the negotiations and final price tag for being ferried by canoes at Ipata led Stanley to describe the Wavinza as "worse than the Wagogo" for their greed.[54] The donkeys had to swim, and Stanley lost his best one to a crocodile. On the other side of the river, members of a passing caravan told of seeing a white man in Ujiji just eight days earlier. It must be Livingstone, Stanley thought, or at least hoped. He thus abandoned the river route for a more direct one across the broad, densely populated plains of Uha, one of eastern Africa's most productive agricultural regions. Thinking the *honga* paid at the first village sufficed for right of passage through the country, the caravan received an unpleasant surprise when the leader of a large force of warriors asked why customary dues had not been sent to the king. Stanley offered ten *doti,* but they demanded one hundred. For a brief moment he considered fighting; however, the prospect of a victory in such open country seemed slim, and after protracted discussions with some of his senior men, he handed over seventy-five *doti.* The next day produced another payment demand by the king's brother, one that Stanley said made him feel "savage" and "Able, ready, and willing to fight and die, but not to be halted by a set of miserable naked robbers!"[55] He knew, however, the only sensible thing to do was pay up. When informed that five more *honga* would have to be settled before leaving Uha, Stanley decided on another course of action—to move through an unoccupied stretch of thickly vegetated country marking the frontier with Uvinza.

Under cover of darkness they entered it early in the morning of November 7. A quick stop for breakfast at the Ruchugi River was followed by a march to what Stanley called Lake Musunya, probably a flooded portion of what today is known as Sabaga Swamp.[56] At one point, a woman burst into hysterics and Stanley used a whip to silence her. The next day brought them to a resting place in the forest less than a mile from a large Waha settlement. To avoid detection, Stanley ordered no fires lit and complete silence maintained. To be on the safe side, all the goats and chickens were killed. Using darkness again as protection, they left Uha just as morning broke. The new day revealed openly friendly people who surprisingly didn't demand *honga.*

As Friday, November 10, dawned, Ujiji lay only six hours distant. Anticipation resulted in a speedy and lighthearted march, and nearing the town's outskirts, the men, robed in their finest, unleashed the usual rifle fire salute. The sound produced a throng coming to greet them. It included Livingstone's servants, Susi and Chumah, who ended all doubts about the doctor being there. A few minutes later, Stanley said he noticed "a pale-looking and grey-bearded white man in a navy cap, with a faded gold band about it, and a red woolen jacket" standing amidst a group of Arabs.[57] Advancing cautiously, he uttered those four words that would follow him to the grave and beyond: "Dr. Livingstone, I presume?" While really wanting to run "to shake hands with the venerable traveller," Stanley claimed he exercised restraint in order to appear as a dignified Englishman would in such circumstances, a behavior more designed to make an impression on the Africans and Arabs than the doctor. Livingstone, too, exercised restraint by simply answering, "Yes," despite not having seen a European since March 1866. Interestingly, he first called his "finder" Henry Moreland, which means Stanley must have introduced himself in this manner.[58] Whether he later used Morton in Livingstone's presence can't be determined, because the doctor's journal notes always refer to Mr. Stanley and his later letters were always addressed to H. M. Stanley. Many years later, the Tanganyika government put up an obelisk with the words

Under the Mango tree
which stood here
Henry M. Stanley met
David Livingstone
10 November 1871

The doctor had returned to Ujiji on October 23, reduced to a living "skeleton" by illness and frequent lack of food during the more than two years it took to complete the round-trip to Umanyema. Instead of his lot improving,

The recreation of Stanley's meeting with Livingstone. Selim and Kalulu are just behind Stanley. *Henry M. Stanley,* How I Found Livingstone *(New York: Scribner, Armstrong & Co, 1872).*

it worsened because the man left in charge of his stores had sold them all. Nearly destitute, Livingstone could only afford to buy food for two slim meals per day, and the future looked even bleaker, since his resources would soon be completely exhausted. Little could be expected from the Arabs, as Mirambo's blockade had put them in difficult straits as well. Stanley's arrival, therefore, appeared to be a godsend. Indeed, Livingstone felt overwhelmed by the "generosity" offered and expressed being "extremely grateful" for it.[59] Later, in a letter to his daughter Agnes, he said of Stanley:

> He laid all he had at my service, divided his clothes into two heaps, and pressed one heap upon me; then his medicine-chest; then his goods and everything he had, and to coax my appetite often cooked dainty dishes with his own hand.[60]

The two men hit it off almost immediately and spent the day in easy conversation. Stanley did his best to update world events for Livingstone, who, in turn, told of his recent journeys, including seeing a horrific massacre of mostly women at a market in Nyangwe the previous July.[61] Its barbarity convinced him to return to Ujiji without further delay. As per usual for special occasions, Stanley popped the cork on a bottle of champagne. He described awaking in the morning "with a delightful sense of pleasure and fatigue of limbs" and "in a state of total confusion." Suddenly it dawned "that Livingstone had been found."[62]

Stanley's initial plan called for finding the doctor, getting a receipt for any goods delivered, and then returning with evidence of his accomplishment as quickly as possible. But Livingstone's demeanor and behavior were not at all like Kirk and others had described. Rather, to Stanley, he seemed "unaffected," a man who doesn't "mince words," and who "converses with me as if I were of his own age, or of equal experience." It added to his growing self-confidence and generated the feeling that he might yet become "somebody."[63] Thought of a return could be put off for a while longer.

On November 14 Livingstone proposed that the two of them go to Umanyema so that together they could "finish his discoveries" regarding the sources of the Nile. This caught Stanley completely by surprise, and after a few moments of not knowing how to respond, he replied, "I don't think I was made for an African Explorer; for I detest the land most heartily." The cause of such negative feelings, Livingstone suggested, was the "bile of fever" currently afflicting Stanley. Once over that he would "be able to see things differently."[64] Although the change didn't take place immediately, these conversations began Stanley's true African education, and he slowly started "to

Stanley dressed as he was for the meeting with Livingstone on November 10, 1871. *Courtesy of the Royal Museum of Central Africa*

see things differently." Soon, he would view much of Africa through a Livingstone-tinted filter.

Further discussion led to something far less time-consuming than going to Umanyema—an exploration of the northern end of Lake Tanganyika to determine the course of the Rusizi River and thereby add another piece to the Nile puzzle. Burton and Speke had tried, but turned back in the face of heavy rain, unaware that the Rusizi was only ten miles away. Just in case Shaw might still be in Kwihara alive, Stanley wrote him saying he'd be back around New Year's Day. In the meantime, Shaw should

> 1st Let no one take anything of Dr. Livingstone's goods out of my tembe, for any reason whatever. See that the men of Livingstone waste nothing.
> 2nd Finish the small boat as quickly & as efficiently as you can.
> 3rd Keep . . . all letters, newspapers & medicines with you until you hear from me again. Do not let them leave Unyanyembe.[65]

The northward journey along the eastern side of the lake began two days later in a large canoe provided by one of the Arabs. Stanley described the sights as resembling a world of "quiet scenic beauty," quite unlike anything he had witnessed before. The third day brought them to a village at the mouth of a small river, where Stanley

> imagined the scenery getting more picturesque and animated at every step, and thought it by far lovelier than anything seen near Lake George or on the Hudson. The cozy nooks at the head of the many small bays constitute most admirable pictures, filled in as they are with the ever-beautiful feathery palms and broad green plantain fronds. These nooks have all been taken possession of by fishermen, and their conically beehived-shaped huts always peep from under the frondage. The shores are thus extremely populous; every terrace, small plateau, and bit of level ground is occupied.[66]

This sense of serenity, much of it undoubtedly related to his growing respect and affection for Livingstone, lasted throughout the journey, one that presented only a few relatively minor crises, such as Stanley becoming feverish again and Livingstone suffering bouts of diarrhea. Contrary to reports heard in Ujiji, the inhabitants, the Barundi, proved to be friendly and even welcoming. When they reached the north end of the lake, the riddle of the Rusizi was solved: A brief reconnaissance proved it flowed into the lake and rose, the local chief said, near another, later shown to be Lake Kivu. As such, it could not be part of the Nile drainage system. The question of an outlet from Lake Tanganyika thus remained unsettled. Livingstone continued to

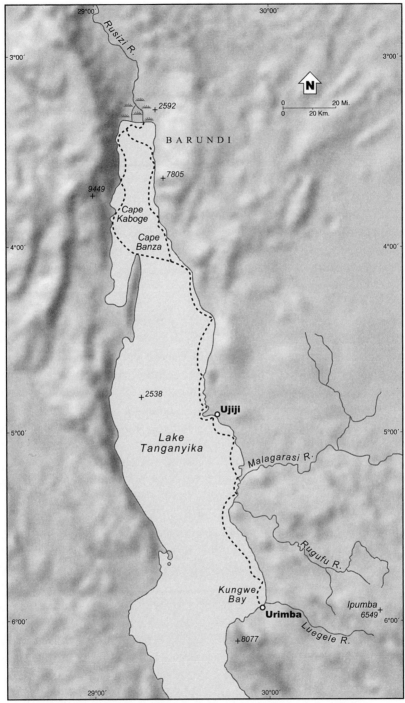

Map 3.4 Lake Tanganyika Explorations and the Start for Tabora,
November 1871–January 1872

believe there must be one. As the first Europeans to round the north shore, they corrected the conventional map, which showed it ending in a sharp point, instead of its more nearly straight-line shape.

In order to continue with mapmaking, the return to Ujiji started along the lake's western shore. Since it was considered more hostile territory, they made every effort to proceed quickly and cautiously. Only on one occasion did trouble seem possible. It occurred at Cape Kaboge, when a group of somewhat inebriated armed men mistook the party for Arab and Waswahili slave traders. But nothing untoward happened, thanks largely, Stanley said, to Livingstone's patient negotiations that removed any fears the men might have had concerning their intentions. From there they skirted past Cape Banza at the north end of the large peninsula that Stanley mistook for an island and paddled across the lake, pulling in to Ujiji on December 13 with all hands safely on board.

The question now became what to do next, and after considering several options, Livingstone decided to accompany Stanley to Kwihara in order to collect his still undelivered supplies. So as to avoid war-torn areas and paying *honga*, they went south to the village of Urimba on Kungwe Bay, and from that point headed directly east in order to connect with the trail Stanley had followed on the way to Ujiji. This was not a time for exploring, so far better to deal with the familiar rather than the unfamiliar.

During the coming days, Stanley suffered an annoying rash and bout of malaria, confirming his sense that in Africa "fever is never far off."[67] He used what energy he had to put the trip's logistical arrangements in order. Livingstone mostly copied field notes and wrote letters, including two for the *Herald*. They had discussed this from time to time, with the doctor wanting to know if correspondence from him might help enlist American support in suppressing the slave trade. Stanley gave an enthusiastic endorsement, saying the letters "would be . . . read by the thousands of the Herald's readers & from thence would be copied & quoted into other journals, so that it must bear fruit one way or the other."[68]

The journey got under way December 27, with one group, including Livingstone and Stanley, aboard two large canoes flying the flags of Britain and the United States. As they fluttered in the breeze, Stanley said he felt "a certain pride that the two Anglo-Saxon nations are represented this day on this great inland sea, in the face of wild nature and barbarism."[69] The others followed an overland route that required traversing a long stretch of unknown country south of the Rugufu River. When the canoes reached Urimba on January 3, the villagers claimed to have heard nothing at all about anyone approaching via land. But three days later the party showed up, its members exhausted but not much worse for the wear.

They had only a night's rest before beginning the march inland along the narrow valley of the Luegele River. The going proved tougher than expected, and no one, including the guide, knew the way through this stretch of country. Eschewing what appeared to be a northeasterly trending road headed toward three mountain ranges, Stanley decided to navigate by compass and proceed due east. During the fifth day of travel, he described entering a "beautiful parkland," in which

> the grass was very tall, and the rainy season, which had commenced in earnest, made my work excessively disagreeable. Through this tall grass, which was as high as my throat, I had to force my way, compass in hand, to lead the Expedition, as there was not the least sign of a road, and we were now in untravelled country.[70]

Then came several days of trekking up and down heavily forested ridges on mostly empty stomachs. By now all the meat had been consumed, and though signs of game abounded, the animals were widely dispersed due to the rains and, therefore, difficult to find.

A little farther on Stanley caught a brief glimpse of the first familiar landmark: what he had called Magdala Mount, after the mountain fortress in Ethiopia, on the way to Ujiji. The best bet is that he saw Ipomba, which at more than 6,500 feet is the highest point in the area. They got a closer look at it on January 14, and Stanley knew that familiar territory must be nearby. After a tough go through a dense, wet forest with only mushrooms and wild fruits to assuage their gnawing hunger, some of the men urged Stanley to change course to the southwest. He demurred, preferring to trust the compass to lead them in the right direction. And it did, for within two days they found his former camp at Mrera, where everyone ate their fill of maize, sweet potatoes, and beans. Stanley also shot two zebra and a giraffe to provide some highly welcomed meat. Another problem replaced food as the main concern—wetness and rocky terrain had virtually destroyed Livingstone's and Stanley's boots. This proved especially burdensome for the doctor, because of a recurrence of the foot ulcers that had plagued him so badly in 1870. The need for a rest was made doubly urgent with the return of Stanley's fever, and, thus, travel didn't resume until January 26. Livingstone, as always, wanted to walk, but to ease the pain he rode a donkey instead. This convenience didn't last long, as shortly after they had got under way, a large swarm of bees attacked and stung the donkey so badly that it died two days afterward.

Trudging on, they passed an Arab-led caravan headed in the opposite direction and learned about Shaw's death in Tabora. Stanley's surmise proved correct, which didn't surprise Livingstone, who supposedly said:

> I told you so for when you described him to me as a drunkard I knew he could not live. Men who have been habitual drunkards cannot live in this country any more than those who are slaves to other vices. I attribute most of the deaths on the Zambezi to much the same cause.[71]

Slowly the exhausted members of the caravan pressed forward, revisiting familiar stops. At one point Stanley's recurrent fever became so bad that he had to be carried in a litter for several days. And rain continued to soak everyone to the bone. At Ugunda on February 14 a surprise awaited their arrival, mail from Zanzibar. The first letter Stanley read contained depressing news. Bennett had balked at sending money to cover expenses. Relief came with the second one: He'd relented and expenses would be covered. Finally, on February 18, fifty-four days from Ujiji, Kwihara and "Home!" came into view and they advanced toward it with flags flying and rifle fire to announce their arrival. "It is the custom, for as they say, 'a great man does not enter a town like a snake'," noted Stanley.[72] The "great man" in this instance clearly meant Livingstone. Stanley never described himself in such terms.

As in Ujiji, Livingstone discovered his goods in complete disarray. The elements and theft had taken their tolls, so Stanley set about restocking them. The doctor wanted to continue looking for the sources of the Nile. Ever since Herodotus speculated that they issued from four springs, people had been trying to find them. Livingstone thought they existed somewhere in the Katanga region and figured the journey there could be completed in a year and a half.[73] Stanley, on the other hand, calculated it would take at least two years, and consequently he put enough goods together to last twice as long. But with the Mirambo wars still raging, no porters could be hired. The only way to get them would be to return to Bagamoyo, and do it as quickly as possible. He promised Livingstone to take his journals and more than thirty letters, including the two for the *Herald*, and put them in the right hands. Stanley wanted the doctor to leave with him. According to Livingstone, he

> Used some very strong arguments in favor of my going home, recruiting my strength, getting artificial teeth, and then returning to finish my task; but my judgment said, "All your friends will wish you to make a complete work of the exploration of the sources of the Nile before you retire." My daughter

Agnes says, "Much as I wish you to come home, I would rather that you finished your work to your own satisfaction, then return merely to gratify me."[74]

During his sojourn across Africa from 1853 to 1856, Livingstone came to believe himself an instrument of god and, as such, felt protected from mortal danger. And he needed to succeed in this quest. Going home having failed wouldn't do.[75]

The day Stanley feared, when he must depart from the company of the man who had, in many ways, become a surrogate father, was fast approaching. A March 2 journal entry records him thinking:

I shall have to leave some day and the sooner the better for him, for me, for all of us. I should like to stay with him longer—if the march of time could be arrested—and the hours could be so prolonged that they would not multiply into days. I have done my duty strictly by him, and now another duty seizes upon me to sever us.[76]

Besides, a longer stay would mean traveling during the *masika,* and so he chose March 14 as the dreaded day. The night before found Stanley in deep despair: "I bitterly regret," he noted, "the approach of the parting hour. I now forget the succession of fevers, and their agonies, and the semi-madness to which they often plunged me. The regret I feel now is greater than any pains I have endured."[77] Livingstone clearly had deep affection for Stanley, and in later correspondence referred to him as like a son. In a rather strange twist of fate, he'd lost his eldest son, Robert, in the American Civil War, and Stanley may just have helped fill that void.

The following morning the two men walked together for a short distance, and after bidding one another fond farewells, each turned in a different direction. The next night Stanley tried to compose a letter to Livingstone but never finished it. The numerous crossing-outs in the copy that survives illustrate an inability to come up with the right words. Two statements from what is readable, however, are useful in capturing the moment for Stanley. They confirm both his sense of personal loss and the call of duty. One reads, "The time then passed with you has been too short. I have not had enough of you. This will be a cause of keen regret to me in future, as it is now." The other notes,

It is a consolation, however, after tearing myself away, that I am about to do you a service—then I have not quite yet parted from you, you and I are not quite separate—though I am not present to you bodily. You must think of me daily until your caravan arrives. Though you are not before me visibly—I must think of you constantly until your last wish has been attended to.[78]

The way back to Bagamoyo mostly followed the way taken in. At first, the small party moved fast, crossing Ugogo without major incident and paying only the occasional *honga.* The *masika,* however, broke on March 18, much earlier than usual. Upon reaching Mpwapwa on April 7, Stanley tried to locate Farquhar's grave. Finding no evidence, he put a pile of stones on the presumed spot.[79]

Beyond Mpwapwa, rain poured down day after day, making the conditions of the previous year look mild by comparison. At Mkondowa Pass they waded through shoulder-deep water and then pushed on "over marshy bottoms, up to the knees in mire, under jungly tunnels dripping with wet, then into sloughs arm-pit deep."[80] Once across the swollen main channel of the Mkondowa, Stanley gave in to reality and ordered a halt at Rehenneko until conditions improved. Ten days later, the rain finally stopped, but that wasn't much consolation, for ahead lay the Mkata River, then in full flood, which left only a few higher spots above water. Two eight-hour marches were needed to make the crossing, and on the other side a six-mile-wide lake created by the juncture of four streams greeted their eyes. Once again, the men went into the water, sometimes having to swim.

A little farther on they came upon a devastated Simbawenni; the town's front walls had been washed away and about fifty houses destroyed by a rampaging tributary of the Ngerengere River, the Morogoro. Debris littered the valley, transforming a former "Paradise . . . into a howling waste."[81] The other side of the Ngerengere presented even worse horrors. From a report given him, Stanley estimated "nearly ONE HUNDRED VILLAGES . . . were swept away" in a flood six days earlier caused by a rare hurricane on April 15. The scene he described as being

> simply awful. Wherever we look, we find something very suggestive of the devastation that has visited the country; fields of corn are covered with many feet of sand and debris; the sandy bed the river has deserted is about a mile wide; and there are but three villages standing of all that I noticed when *en route* to Unyanyembe.[82]

Only minor ordeals marked the last days of the journey, and on the evening of May 6 the weary men trooped into Bagamoyo, having covered the distance from Kwihara in fifty-three days, despite the conditions. Stanley's objective of finding Livingstone and getting back to tell the world about it had been accomplished. As proof he carried a journal signed by Livingstone with the words 'positively not to be opened.'[83] Remarkable serendipity had allowed all this to be accomplished—the long trip to India, the wait for porters in Bagamoyo, the time spent in Tabora and the subsequent detour, and Livingstone's leaving Nyangwe. Take even one element from the equation and Stanley would have arrived too soon, presenting prospects for either waiting there or tracking the doctor down. Neither seems plausible, and without finding Dr. Livingstone, the coupling of Stanley and Africa is unlikely ever to have happened. For one thing, it provided the necessary fame. He'd linked himself to a cultural icon. Furthermore, the seeds of interest had been planted. A lengthy list of farewells Stanley bade Africa in his final dispatch to the *Herald* shows that the seeds remained ungerminated.[84]

CHAPTER 4

Out from Africa and Back Again

TRIUMPH, DISASTER, AND A NEW BEGINNING

Awaiting Stanley's arrival in Bagamoyo were Royal Navy Lt. William Henn and Livingstone's youngest son, Oswell, both members of the Livingstone Search and Relief Expedition (LSRE), which had arrived a week earlier. Stanley learned of its existence two days beforehand, but that's all he knew. An undertaking of the Royal Geographical Society, the expedition was hastily assembled following the *Herald*'s publication in the December 22, 1871, edition of Stanley's letter from Unyanyembe revealing the purpose of his mission and the unsettled conditions brought on by Mirambo's rise to power that appeared to threaten it. Prior to this time, official sources steadfastly maintained that Livingstone was safe and well provisioned, and some, including Richard Burton, continued to claim the doctor could readily take care of himself, no matter the circumstances. He'd been doing just that for three decades in Africa. Furthermore, meddling in his affairs would probably just lead to grief. Better, as Francis Galton put it, "to defer action till some intelligence of his wishes and whereabouts had been received."[1]

Stanley's words proved to be enough "intelligence" for the public, and opinion began clamoring for something to be done. With Foreign Office approval as an impetus, the Royal Geographical Society swung into action by contributing five hundred pounds and launching a subscription campaign that quickly raised more than four thousand pounds from an array of sources, the Treasury not included, to finance an expedition. Lt. Llewellyn Dawson agreed to head it, and Henn was given the post of second in command. The ship carrying them left England on February 9, and at Zanzibar, Charles New, a Methodist missionary with six years' experience in East Africa, signed on as well. The job of hiring porters fell to consul Kirk.

When Dawson learned of Stanley's success and imminent arrival, he resigned command, feeling the charge to resupply Livingstone no longer applied. After conversing with Stanley, Henn, too, thought it not worthwhile to go ahead, although he wanted to consult with Kirk before making a final decision. Oswell agreed to go with the caravan Stanley was forming should the LSRE be officially dissolved.

Zanzibar put on a great display for Stanley's May 7 arrival. A visiting American described it as a "great sight," the beach "lined with people, native and white, who testified their delight by an unceasing discharge of small arms."[2] During a meeting with Dawson, Stanley confirmed the rightness of the lieutenant's decision, remarking that "Most certainly it would be useless for you to go to search for Livingstone now."[3] He also spoke with New, who'd lost interest in the expedition following a dispute about whether he or Henn would assume command. Henn's letter of resignation to Kirk sealed the matter—there would be no LSRE, at least for the time being.

The large cache of goods collected in anticipation of the relief effort greatly simplified Stanley's task of provisioning his own Livingstone-bound caravan. Oswell provided money for additional purchases but then suddenly did an about-face. Suffering from malaria and dysentery and facing the prospect of crossing a flooded countryside, he bowed to advice and decided to go home. Kirk helped Stanley find a young Arab named Mohammed bin Galfin to replace him, and on May 27 a contingent of fifty-seven men, none slaves, according to Livingstone's wishes, departed Zanzibar for Tabora. In a letter, Stanley wrote to Livingstone, "And now, my dear and good friend, I have done to the utmost of my ability what I have promised. . . . All I can do now, is to wish you the blessing of God, and the Providence who has watched over you so long."[4] The caravan reached Tabora on August 14, thus bettering Stanley's time the previous year. Fully resupplied, Livingstone resumed his quest to find the sources of the Nile two weeks later.

Homeward bound, Stanley boarded the steamer *Africa* on May 29, accompanied by Oswell, New, Henn, Selim, and Kalulu. Dawson had gone ahead separately a few days earlier. The schedule called for them to make a connection to Aden in the Seychelles, but due to the *Africa*'s slow pace they missed it by less than a day. Hating even short delays, Stanley didn't relish the thought of sitting idle until the next ship came along in a month's time. The wait turned out to be a blessing in disguise, as it provided an opportunity for him to recoup his health in a restful setting.

At Aden on July 10, Stanley found a cable from George Hosmer, the *Herald* bureau chief in London, waiting for him. It read:

> Mr. Bennett sends the following
>
> You are now famous as Livingstone having discovered the discoverer. Accept my thanks, and the whole world. Recruit your Health at Aden or Elsewhere. Forward by Special Messenger Livingstone's letters and anything further you may have. accept in addition assurance fellow correspondent that more splendid achievement energetic devotion and generous gallantry not in History of Human Endeavor.[5]

Before leaving Zanzibar, Stanley had written to Bennett, saying, "Congratulations to you on the successful termination of this arduous enterprise, because the glory is due to the *Herald*."[6] Each could share in the moment, perhaps the last truly felt mutual one between the two.

Unsure of what to do next, Stanley cabled back asking if he should proceed to China as discussed in Paris or return directly.[7] With no immediate reply forthcoming, he decided to continue on to Suez, where a second telegram from Hosmer said that while he was "quite free to come to England," it would be better to do this "slowly" after mailing Livingstone's letters and his own stories from Alexandria. Bennett wanted to synchronize their publication with Stanley's arrival in London in order to create the biggest possible news splash and feared telegraphing the stories might lead to leaks. If Stanley found this course of action "impracticable," Hosmer suggested they meet at some convenient place along the way. For Stanley such a delay seemed more than "impracticable," because he had promised Livingstone that all his letters—those to family members as well as the ones for the *Herald*—would be delivered promptly. Letting him down this way seemed unthinkable.[8] Thus, after dismissing Selim from his employ at Port Said, he set out with Kalulu for Marseilles to rendezvous with Hosmer.

During their get-together early in the morning of July 24, Stanley heard some good news. Bennett had changed his mind and the letters could be cabled ahead for immediate publication. After a couple of days in Marseilles, mostly spent buying clothes, Stanley and Kalulu took the train for Paris, arriving to accolades and a round of celebrations organized mostly by the city's contingent of Americans, who would soon form the Stanley Club. At a July 31 banquet, they toasted him as

> Henry Stanley, the discoverer of the discoverer. We honor him for his courage, energy, and fidelity. We rejoice in the triumphant success of his mission,

which has gained him imperishable renown and conferred additional credit on the American name.[9]

As further tribute, the chef created a special dish called *poularde à la Stanley aux truffes.*[10]

Other, less complimentary forces were by now blowing in the wind. Stanley got a hint that he might face some unpleasantness from U.S. and Canadian press clippings he read while still a few days out from Bagamoyo. Although most praised his accomplishments and took great pride in an American having found Livingstone, some expressed doubts about the veracity of his first letter from Kwihara. One skeptic went so far as to suggest that "the explorer had never wandered farther than the wilds of Central Park in his search for the lost traveller."[11] Such comments proved mild, though, compared to the firestorm brewing in Britain. The first salvos came from the halls of the RGS, and most particularly from Henry Rawlinson, who, in his May 13, 1872, presidential address, made light of Stanley by remarking,

> There is one point on which a little *éclairissement* is desireable, because a belief seems to prevail that Mr. Stanley has discovered and relieved Dr. Livingstone; whereas, without any disparagement to Mr. Stanley's energy, activity and loyalty, if there has been any discovery and relief it is Dr. Livingstone who has discovered and relieved Mr. Stanley. Dr. Livingstone, indeed, is in clover while Mr. Stanley is nearly destitute. . . . It is only proper that the relative positions of the parties should be correctly stated.[12]

And although the majority of the British press initially praised Stanley's achievement, the compliments sometimes contained not-so-subtle reservations. The *Echo*, for instance, called it "a great exploit on the part of the New York Herald to have sent out the expedition which has discovered Dr. Livingstone," but then added, "We could, of course, have wished the honour of the discovery had fallen to countrymen of our own."[13] An editorial in the *Spectator*, while admitting that "a great deed has been accomplished," also used language such as the "utter *bizarrerie* of the whole story," "cold calculation," and "its pathetic incidents related with careful eye to stage effect" to describe what Stanley told *Herald* readers. It then questioned the worth of Livingstone's and Stanley's activities, noting that,

> Dr. Livingstone's discoveries do not "open" Africa. Mr. Stanley's enterprise does not bring those great lake regions, those numerous tribes, all that wealth of land and men, one whit nearer to the world which alone could use them.

No tribe will be civilized by that kind of contact. No nation will be enriched by that kind of knowledge. No living man, unless it be Dr. Livingstone and Mr. Stanley themselves, will be the nobler, or the better, or the more competent for all that profuse pouring-out of some of the noblest qualities of men, for all that patience and courage and sagacity in the investigation of natural facts.[14]

Stanley's references to Kirk's supposed negligence in forwarding supplies to Livingstone created a particular bone of contention. He first broached the subject in a long letter to the *Herald* written at Kwihara on September 21, 1871. Among other things, he chastised Kirk for letting a resupply caravan sit idle in Bagamoyo for three and a half months, claiming this "showed great unkindness towards the old traveller." Furthermore, in his view, a prompt departure would have allowed the caravan to get through before Mirambo set up the blockade.[15] Stanley came back to the issue during an interview in Marseilles with a reporter from the *Daily Telegraph*, who concluded,

The substance of these statements is that Dr. Kirk failed in rendering to Livingstone that proper support which might have given England the honour of finding him. Mr. Stanley complains of the long time that Dr. Kirk took in sending on goods, which were moreover given in charge of men who showed themselves unworthy of the trust.[16]

He pressed the issue again during the July 31 banquet in Paris. An attempt to soften his remarks by saying he was "simply fulfilling a solemn promise" to air Livingstone's concern about ill treatment and have it "thoroughly investigated," didn't help matters much.[17] A journal entry made later that night shows Stanley knew he'd blundered:

I was led by the warmth & glow of the occasion to speak more hot-headedly about Kirk than I intended, but there is something in the atmosphere, or the wine, or something which carried me on. I must endeavor to restrain myself for though I do think that Kirk has behaved abominably to his old friend . . . it does not do, to run a tilt at any body in a mixed assemblage of this kind."[18]

It's true that Livingstone had become upset with Kirk, but mainly because he hired firms in Zanzibar that used slaves as carriers and not for delays or being "ill treated."[19] As he put it in a letter, "It is simply infamous to employ slaves when any number of freemen may be hired!" But the doctor didn't intend this as a criticism per se of Kirk. As he told him, "I am sorry to hear by note from Oswell that you had taken my formal complaint against certain banyans and Arabs as a covert attack upon yourself: this grieves me deeply, for it is a result I never intended to produce."[20] Others quickly jumped in to defend Kirk, which by extension meant attacking Stanley, in this instance for having unduly influenced Livingstone. In a July 29 letter to the *Daily Telegraph*, Oswell proclaimed, "Let me state at once that Dr. Kirk is totally unworthy of the accusations which are daily reaching the public, and can have but one source."[21] It's doubtful that Stanley could have influenced the doctor in his opinions of Kirk, or anyone, for that matter. They'd already been formed. Perhaps, all he did was bring them to the surface again.

Another sore point involved Livingstone's letters. The RGS refused to acknowledge Stanley's accomplishment until he produced them. As of the beginning of August, only those written for the *Herald*, ones Rawlinson described as "too vague in their present shape to admit of useful geographical discussion," had been made public.[22] The delay resulted from Stanley's wanting to be sure the letters reached secure hands, and thus he waited until meeting Lord Lyons in Paris before parting with them. Then attention suddenly shifted to the legitimacy of the letters, the implication being that Stanley had done the writing. The *Saturday Review* editorialized, "It would seem that Livingstone has profited by his residence in the heart of Africa to acquire considerable familiarity with American literature and slang, and to hit off the racy, sub-erotic flavour of the *New York Herald* with some success." It went on to express concerns about the content of the published letters because they "tell us so little about Livingstone himself, or about the tribes among whom he has lately been sojourning, and are made up of stale talk about the familiar atrocities of slavery." There also appeared to be a mistake regarding drainage patterns that the editorial claimed "so cautious and careful a geographer as the Doctor" would hardly make.[23] Comments such as these suggest that Bennett and the *Herald* were as much targets as Stanley. The fact that the paper was so profitable probably added to the venom. Furthermore, Bennett disliked the English and said so on many occasions. His Scottish ancestry no doubt played some role in this. Livingstone's other son, Tom, had no problem with the authenticity of the letters and other writings he saw and made this be known in a letter to the London *Times* on August 2. The next day a representative of the Foreign Office, replying to Stanley's complaints about his treatment, expressed the view that members there "have not the slightest doubt as to the genuineness of the papers which have been received . . . and which are being printed."[24] Nonetheless, questions lingered, as evidenced by a strange piece printed in the August 10 edition of the *Echo* and signed by someone calling himself the Author of the "Rosicrucians." It had this to say:

SIR—I would beg to put the following questions:—

First.—Is Mr. Stanley a Spiritualist?

Second.—Has Mr. Stanley been among the Mediums?

Third.—Are the letters of Dr. Livingstone to be supposed to be written by him through a mediumistic means; and, are they to be accounted as truly [thus] by Dr. Livingstone, but by Livingstone secondarily?

Fourth.—In rescuing Dr. Livingstone, why did not Mr. Stanley bring Dr. Livingstone with him?

Fifth.—*Is Livingstone dead?*

I am no Spiritualist. I have no sympathy with the extraordinary opinions attributed to Spiritualists. But I should like the above questions answered. Your insertion of this letter would oblige. I speak for very many worthy people, sincerely interested in Dr. Livingstone.[25]

Hurt to the point of anger, Stanley considered this the paper's view, and it deepened his suspicion of English reporters, whom he accused of having "a singular tone for insinuation" instead of saying outright what they mean. He thought the RGS to be behind most of the insults, pointing to Rawlinson's comments and a statement made by Horace Waller claiming that only "the steel head of an Englishman could penetrate Africa."[26] A lay Anglican missionary who joined the Zambezi expedition in 1860, Waller had become one of the staunchest antislavery activists in the circle of Britain's aristocrats and a man of considerable influence within the RGS.

Much of the society's reluctance to recognize Stanley publicly—no one from it showed up to greet him when he reached England on August 1—centered on his supposed failure to do "real" exploring. Explorers were supposed to be motivated by science and a desire to bring change, and since Stanley didn't fit that model, it was hard for the establishment to give him credit.[27] Kirk, for example, said Stanley had taken the "dull and well-known route to Ujiji, in which there can be little of interest left for an unscientific traveller." Rawlinson concurred by characterizing the journey as one of a "practical and utilitarian character, instead of being conducted for scientific objects."[28] Behind such statements lurked a wounded national pride. As later stated in a summary of the society's first one hundred years,

> The Council of the Society thought it incongruous and almost an impertinence that a newspaper reporter should have succeeded where a British Officer, backed by authority of the Royal Geographical Society had failed. No enthusiasm was shown when Stanley reached England in the late summer.[29]

Tired of waiting for due recognition, Stanley called at the society's new Saville Row headquarters on August 5 and arranged to speak with several of its more prominent members the next day. During the meeting, Galton, then president of the Geographical Section of the British Association, invited Stanley to read a paper about his journey with Livingstone at the association's annual meetings in Brighton on August 16. As a goodwill gesture, Rawlinson sent Stanley a citation, thanking him for "the transmission of direct intelligence from Dr. Livingstone" and praising the expedition's "energy, perseverance, and courage."[30]

Despite these overtures and many invitations from prominent figures, the damage in many ways had already been done, and each slight caused Stanley to grow more bitter. He fumed over "anonymous and hostile" letters that contained comments such as "look out for tomorrow's papers!" and "you detestable Welsh-Yankee what right have you to put your finger in our English pie?" No day passed, he said, without the mail bringing "numerous proofs of English hate." In his mind the RGS continued to be the prime suspect. Even though members wrote him "nice personal letters," he thought they probably continued to inspire "many of the nasty articles in the leading papers." Fear that the geographers intended to "pulverise" him in Brighton further raised his suspicions.[31] Stanley's growing self confidence was thrown into reverse, and the Brighton experience would diminish it further.

Stanley started his speech to the association with an extemporaneous and highly dramatized version of how he'd come to search for and find Livingstone, before getting to his prepared text titled "Discoveries at the Northern Head of Tanganyika." Save some of the geographers, the nearly three thousand people in the audience, including Napoleon III and Empress Eugenie, enjoyed the presentation. According to the *Scotsman*, Stanley's "opening remarks were . . . characterized by a rollicking good nature, mixed with a strain of sententious talk that won the sympathies of his hearer."[32] Although critical of "occasional passages of somewhat highflown and inflated diction," the review in the *Standard* concluded that "In its way, it is as admirably effective a piece of narrative as we could have had" and that any excesses could "be excused and accounted for."[33] A brief question-and-answer period followed that included several sharp exchanges with RGS members over Livingstone's theory of the Lualaba River being connected to the Nile. Stanley reacted by saying,

> I am not a man of science. I simply went to find Livingstone. . . . As for the sources of the Nile, you can make what you like for the present . . . but for an ultimate decision upon the value of his discoveries you must wait until Livingstone can come home, and prove for himself his own opinions.[34]

At the event's conclusion, the chair proposed that Stanley be accorded "a formal vote of thanks," as one reporter noted, "ere any one could second it the hall was ringing with applause."[35]

Stanley was more annoyed than pleased. He interpreted laughter at several points during the talk as directed at him and resented some of the questions and comments, which he didn't anticipate being part of the program. Galton's accusation of having done "sensational geography" particularly rankled. It all boiled over the next day during informal remarks to the Brighton and Sussex Medico-Chirugical Society. A reporter said that during Stanley's description of Livingstone's medical knowledge, a noise came from the audience which he

> apparently regarded as a derisive laugh, either at something he said or his manner of saying it. This appeared to annoy Mr. Stanley exceedingly; and at once quitting the humorous and cheerful style in which he had been speaking, he adopted a stern, emphatic, and impassioned tone; protesting that he had not come to be laughed at, and that he had had quite enough gratuitous sneering of late without their adding to it.

After making reference to accusations of "sensationalism" and asking why people still questioned his statements, he bowed quickly and strode from the room.[36]

Some of the follow-up in the press took Stanley's side, whereas other editorials used the event to heap further criticism on him. But overall the tide had already begun to turn in Stanley's favor. A major boost came from Edward Arnold, the highly respected editor of the *Daily Telegraph* and an RGS fellow, who in a letter to Arthur Helps, Clerk of the Privy Council, said,

> How shameful is this jealousy against Stanley and the newspapers—for having saved Livingstone and his priceless discoveries unofficially! As an old traveller—and having closely questioned the American—I do not fear to say that a cooler, finer piece of quiet derring-do was never told. But after hinting that he was a swindler—and then saying that 'Livingstone had rescued Stanley'— the Royal Geographicals have handed the great business over to a sub-section of the B.A. at Brighton; Stanley does not care—but think how mean and petty it all appears to the Americans! Can you not whisper in the right ears that the hour is passing when this pitiful behavior might be neutralized? A gracious note from the Court—a kindly compliment from the good Queen's lips— would sweep the gathering evil of this stupid officialism away, and be re-echoed in proud pleasure from American hearts. I write this to you as at once

sympathetic and influential, and "write it out of my own head"—but indeed some such thing ought to be done.[37]

An experienced Africa hand named Winwood Reade went public on Stanley's behalf in a long letter to the *Pall Mall Gazette*. He stressed five points: 1) the meeting with Livingstone clearly took place; 2) Livingstone wrote the letters in a style suitable to the *New York Herald*; 3) Stanley couldn't possibly profit from forgeries; 4) nothing seemed "exaggerated or unnatural" in the description of the meeting between Stanley and Livingstone; and 5) even if Stanley hadn't found the doctor the journey to Ujiji "would have been a remarkable exploit." He closed the letter with

> People in general know little about Africa, and our geographers are incompetent to lead public opinion upon such matters, or even to find out the truth themselves. There is no country where African travellers excite so much attention as in England, and it perhaps follows as a matter of necessity that there should be no country where so many silly things are said against them.[38]

The first official signal of approval to Stanley came in a letter from Queen Victoria through Lord Granville. It read,

> Sir—I have the great satisfaction in conveying to you, by command of the Queen, Her Majesty's high appreciation of the prudence and zeal which you have displayed in opening communication with Dr. Livingstone and relieving Her Majesty from the anxiety which, in common with her subjects, she has felt in regard to the facts of the distinguished traveller.
>
> The Queen desires me to express her thanks for the service you have rendered, together with Her Majesty's congratulations on your having so successfully carried out the mission which you fearlessly undertook.[39]

A jewel-bedecked gold snuffbox accompanied it, and to top matters off, the queen received Stanley at Dunrobin Castle in Scotland on September 10, with Rawlinson, rather ironically, making the introductions. Their ten-minute conversation was mostly about Livingstone and Africa, and Stanley came away impressed with Her Majesty. After another brief meeting the next day, he remarked, "she was kind as I could wish." Victoria was less complimentary, calling Stanley "a determined, ugly little Man—with a strong American twang."[40]

Her comment points to another controversy surrounding Stanley, his nationality. Many, like the queen, thought him to be American. Birthplaces speculated upon included Missouri, Louisiana, Connecticut, and New York

City. Samuel L. Clemens (Mark Twain) signed a congratulatory letter "your fellow Missourian."[41] Wales also came up, and Stanley began to get letters, often with requests for money attached, from purported Welsh relatives. He kept quiet during the ruckus despite being highly annoyed. Why should anyone care about his ancestry when he didn't? Later he would say,

> Few men have less cause to boast of their ancestry than I have. Though British-born—& though secretly found of even that small fact—I dare not boast of it. If birth as Lord Thurlow says is an accident of an accident, it was assuredly so in my case. A cloud hangs over my ancestry which causes me to be incurious about my origin and as I left my native soil from necessity, was reproached for revisiting it, and did disclaim my relatives, there is no excuse for me to feel pride in my blood, or my country & therefore am as free from passion or pride on the point of birth as any man.[42]

Ancestry, however, did matter to some, especially within the RGS hierarchy. Letters went back and forth among them concerning a need to make the public and the queen aware of Stanley's humble origins, assuming this would delegitimize him.[43] Her gift and reception put an end to this strategy. On the other hand, resentment continued to be expressed about Britain having been upstaged by a mere reporter for a second-rate American newspaper. It surfaced with another RGS proposal to relieve Livingstone, this time by sending an expedition up the Congo River. Stanley thought success unlikely and told Clement Markham, now the society's secretary and a strong supporter of the idea, that "The doctor knows when he wishes to be relieved, and will notify his friends of the fact. Why then not wait for his request?"[44]

The society opted to go ahead anyway, putting Royal Navy Lt. W. J. Grandy in charge. It also revived the original search and rescue plan, this one commanded by Verney Lovett Cameron, another Royal Navy lieutenant. Both men left Liverpool on November 30, 1872, and both experienced long delays in organizing their caravans. Grandy got as far as Lukangu on the Congo, and Cameron managed to reach Tabora. Upon learning that Livingstone had died on May 1 at a village called Chitambo, south of Lake Bangweulu in present-day Zambia, Grandy turned back. Three other Europeans had left with Cameron. One died from malaria, and another shot and killed himself while delirious from fever. The third accompanied the procession taking Livingstone's preserved body to Bagamoyo, despite Cameron's advice to bury it in Unyanyembe. He then forged ahead to explore Lake Tanganyika and eventually cross the continent.[45] Interestingly, Cameron had hoped Stanley might be able to join his expedition and, when this proved impossible, expressed hope that they might be able to work together at some future date.[46] It never came to pass.

Stanley's adversarial relationship with the RGS continued, sparked, from his perspective, by his not having been awarded one of its coveted gold medals. In spite of Queen Victoria's recognition, a few higher-ups still saw him as undeserving. Markham thought he merited only "a jolly good dinner" and repeated the charge that Stanley hadn't done any real geography.[47] The well-known explorer James Grant considered one hundred guineas and a lifetime membership in the society to be reward enough, claiming that Stanley's accomplishment didn't measure up to those of past medal recipients. Grant called him a "snob" and a man "wanting in moral character."[48] But the longer the RGS delayed, the more face it lost in the eyes of the public. One publication called it "more crackbrained than any other body of men professing wisdom on the face of the earth."[49] As a result, the powers that be finally gave in and presented Stanley with the Victoria Medal for 1873 at a testimonial dinner on October 21. To do so required suspending the rules governing the time of year for the award and taking an informal, rather than the usual formal, vote. A letter Stanley sent to Markham may well have played a role in this unusual action. After threatening retaliation unless Galton apologized for the "sensational geography" accusation and questioning his nationality in public, he went on to say that

> There is only one other way of silencing all these accusations against the Society, to show that they are all groundless—which I hope you have sufficient discernment to perceive. It is by far the most effectual, and requires no public retraction of any word or deed. If you did that there could be no more said, the very deed would show the confidence you had in me. But I leave to you to suggest and to proffer.[50]

A whirlwind lecture tour focusing on Scotland followed. Large, enthusiastic crowds greeted Stanley just about everywhere, and many communities presented him with their freedom awards, the equivalent of keys to the city. A series of talks in England was no less successful, and upon its completion, Stanley spent time with Livingstone's good friends Emilia and William Webb at Newstead Abbey near Nottingham before boarding the steamer *Cuba* in Liverpool on November 9, 1872, for a "homecoming" in New York City.

How I Found Livingstone came out just days before the crossing. Once again Stanley felt the sting of criticism. Some reviewers found the book's seven hundred–plus pages far too many, and others raised objections about the dramatic style of writing. The reviewer for the *Spectator* called it "distasteful as a literary production," while his counterpart in the *Manchester Guardian* editorialized,

> The race of special correspondents have developed a language of their own, which is not English, and Mr. Stanley exhibits strongly all the peculiarities of the New York variety of the species. His energy in the coinage of language is equally surprising and misplaced, and in addition to the general unpleasing effect which a style of this description has on one accustomed to retain some respect for the "pure wells of English undefiled," our author is frequently guilty of bad taste and positive vulgarity.[51]

It didn't help that in a "Valedictory" section Stanley continued to harp about the Livingstone Search and Rescue Expedition, Kirk, and the behavior of geographers. Still, the book was such a huge success with the public that it required a third printing before Christmas. This and later editions contained only a few brief references to Kirk. Stanley finally realized the war with him brought more grief than gain.

The story Stanley told was interlaced with recommendations that Europe, and particularly Britain, involve itself more in Africa's affairs. It's not clear when he began to think seriously about this, but it likely occurred sometime during the stay with Livingstone. Mirroring many others with a similar imperial bent, Stanley stressed two things to readers: the need to bring "civilization" to the continent and the riches awaiting those willing to take on the task. He considered the area between Morogoro and Simbawenni as having great promise for "some civilized nation, which in some future time will come and take possession of it." And if that nation built a railway, drained the marshes and swamps, and cleared forests, he felt settlers could be lured into coming. Their presence would serve to speed the pace of development and help relieve pressure on the more populous portions of Europe, a growing concern at the time.

The Wami River appeared to him as an ideal artery to carry the civilizing process from the coast inland, for it would "open direct trade to Usagara, Useguhha, Ukutu, Uhehe; to get ivory, the sugar, the cotton, the orchilla weed, the indigo, and the grain of these countries." Exploiting the potential of the rich soil of Ukawendi required the presence of "civilized people" (i.e., Europeans) to overcome the region's general unhealthy status. The same held for the Wanyamwezi's future. They would need a "philanthropic government" and the "charity of civilization" for their potential to be realized.

In keeping with the times, Stanley considered missionaries central to the civilizing process, and so he identified places where their efforts might be concentrated to greatest effect. Usagara ranked high on the list, for here, Stanley claimed, a missionary could live "amid the most beautiful and picturesque scenes a poetic fancy could imagine" and find "gentle people are at his feet ready to welcome him!" By following the Malagarasi River, missionaries could engage in "conversion-tours to Uvinza, Uhha, and Ugala," and he said a "beautiful spot" for a mission station existed on the eastern side of Lake Tanganyika. The site could accommodate a large congregation, be defensible, and have access to needed supplies in a setting where "the docile and civil people of Ukaranga but waited religious shepards." To be successful, he emphasized that the missionary

> must know his duties as well as a thorough sailor must know how to reef, land, and steer. He must be no kid-glove effeminate man, no journal writer, do disputatious polemic, no silken stole and chausable-loving priest—but a thorough earnest laborer in the garden of the lord—a man of the David Livingstone, or of the Robert Moffat stamp.

As a further indication of Livingstone's profound influence on his thinking, Stanley now saw ending the slave trade as this part of Africa's most urgent need. It was an "abomination" and he worried in particular about the trade's effects on the Wanyamwezi, who seemed to be on the verge of "extermination." He recommended first seizing control of the Indian Ocean ports, for once this was accomplished, an antislave squadron would be able to follow the Wami River to within twenty miles of Simbawenni. After an overnight march, they could burn the town and thereby "break up this nucleus of the slave trade in East Africa at once and forever."

Stanley's views about Africans aren't easily pigeonholed. On occasion he reflected current thinking by describing them as "savages," "barbarians," or "children." In addition, he fell into the race trap, where *Negro* meant *inferior,* an idea he seems to have developed while living in the American South.[52] For example, Stanley said that when a Mswahili man leaves a coastal town for inland village, "he sheds his shirt that had half civilized him, and appears in all his blackness of skin, prognathus jaws, thick lips—the pure negro and barbarian." By way of contrast, he called the Wahumba, actually Maasai,

> a fine and well formed race. The men are positively handsome, tall with small heads. . . . One will look in vain for a thick lip or flat nose amongst them; on the contrary, the mouth is exceedingly well cut, delicately small; the nose that of the Greeks, and so universal was the peculiar feature, that I at once named them the Greeks of Africa. Their lower limbs have not the heaviness of the

Wagogo and other tribes, but are long and shapely, clean as those of an ante-lope. Their necks are long and slender, on which their heads are poised most gracefully. Athletes from their youth, sheperd bred and intermarrying among themselves, thus keeping the race pure, any of them would form a fit subject for the sculptor who would wish to immortalize in marble an Antonius, a Hylas, a Daphnis, or an Apollo. The women are as beautiful as the men are handsome. They have clear ebon skins, not coal-black, but of an inky hue.

He was not the first, nor would he be the last, to portray the Maasai as the "noble savage" ideal.

Stanley bought into prevailing notions of racial purity and found people of "mixed" backgrounds the worst of the lot. They are, he said,

neither black nor white, neither good nor bad, neither to be admired nor hated. They are all things, at all times, they are always fawning on the great Arabs, and always cruel to those unfortunates under their yoke. . . . Cringing and hypocritical, cowardly and debased, treacherous and mean. . . . He seems forever ready to fall down and worship a rich Arab, but is relentless to the poor black slave. When he swears most, you may be sure he lies most, yet this is the breed which is multiplied most at Zanzibar—this syphlitic, blear-eyed, pallid-skinned abortion of an Africanized Arab.

Yet the same man could say that if a "white stranger" walked through the native quarters of Zanzibar, he would begin "to learn the necessity of admit-ting that negroes are men, like himself, though of a different colour; that they have passions and prejudices, likes and dislikes, sympathies, and antipa-thies, tastes and feelings, in common with all human nature." Despite his own keenest observations, Stanley claimed he could not "detect any great difference between their nature" and his own. He'd expressed similar thoughts in 1869 by concluding that the "scale of their education" was the only thing separating people when it came to intelligence.[53] Europeans held the advantage, and repeating the paternalism fashioned during his American West days, he believed it was thus incumbent on them to help lift Africans to the same material and spiritual level.

When the *Cuba* dropped anchor on November 20, everything looked to be in place for a triumphal return. Crowds lined the dockside and a large banner carried the greeting WELCOME HOME HENRY M. STANLEY![54] Nonethe-less, apprehension gripped Stanley. He chafed at commentary that seemed to brand him a "liar-forgerer, imposter, and murderer."[55] Such accusations were given a boost by a letter from Lewis Noe published in the *New York Sun*, a bitter rival of the *Herald*, on August 24. Noe painted a very dark picture of Stanley, with claims about having been lied to, bullied, beaten, and even threatened with death by Stanley during their Turkey adventure. Noe went on to portray Stanley as having a "cruel and revengeful nature" that made him "capable, if a sufficient inducement existed, of any crime."[56] A follow-up interview appeared in the August 29 edition of the *Sun,* in which, among other things, Noe claimed that Stanley's skill at copying would have allowed him to forge the Livingstone letters.[57] By this time, numerous people on both sides of the Atlantic passing themselves off as experts had claimed that handwriting, spelling, style, and facts all pointed to Stanley as the writer. Although penmanship was something he clearly excelled at, the charges proved baseless.

Cook wrote Stanley about the comments, saying that they "ought not to go uncorrected," and told a *Chicago Times* reporter that Stanley had been "Basely slandered" by Noe.[58] Stanley responded by labeling the charges "most atrocious falsehoods" and claimed that "a detailed refutation" would be undignified and unworthy.[59] Edward Morris also jumped in to defend Stanley. When asked by a *Herald* reporter at the end of a lengthy interview if he believed Stanley's version of the incident, Morris replied, "Most undoubtedly, and I again say that Mr. Stanley is my friend, and any testimony I can offer in his favor will be gladly given."[60] As it turned out, very few people paid attention to Noe, and the incident vanished from public view. In early October Cook told Stanley that the "excitement in regard to Noe's statement about us has entirely subsided in this country."[61] During the hubbub on both sides of the Atlantic, the public did learn one thing for certain: Stanley had been born in Wales, not the United States.

Stanley's first days in New York City indeed proved welcoming, with newspapers praising his bold actions. The *New York Evening Mail* editorialized that "Certainly the young journalist deserves all the recognition of his daring, persistence, and good sense. Wherever he goes he will find such welcome as is rarely extended."[62] The *Tribune* remarked that Stanley "has honored the country that nourishes such men and develops such spirit and daring."[63] And following the trend set on the other side of the Atlantic, the American edition of *How I Found Livingstone* sold out within a week. Even the *Herald*'s New York rivals found mostly positive things to say about the book. The reviewer for the *Tribune* found the narrative of "extraordinary interest," while the one for the *Times* said,

It moves steadily forward, with an animation and certain vigor, freshness, and breeziness unusual in works of its class, while the sensationalism that marked the letters in which Mr. Stanley first communicated his experiences to the public, is toned down so thoroughly as to show that he fully understands the difference between making a book and writing for the New-York *Herald*.[64]

Numerous festivities filled Stanley's calendar. According to the *Herald*, the one at the Lotos Club consisted of "a very brilliant assemblage, and was marked throughout by great enthusiasm and heartfelt pleasure."[65] A dinner at Delmonico's hosted by the American Geographical Society followed. Unlike in England, Stanley had no problems with the American geographical establishment. But he had to miss the AGS's official welcoming ceremony because of illness brought on by fatigue.

Each day crowds gathered outside the hotel hoping Stanley would grace them with an appearance. The glow, however, began to fade when an eagerly awaited four-part lecture series at Steinway Hall bombed. Scarred by the Brighton experience and wanting to prove his knowledge of Africa, Stanley gave the audience a factual report, not the tales of adventure they'd come to hear. Even the *Herald*'s reviewer criticized him, calling the part of the lecture about Livingstone "intolerably dull," because "In everything he overlooks the personal and peculiar and treats only the geographical and common place."[66] As a result, not enough customers showed up at the third performance to make it worthwhile going on. A quick apology from the *Herald* for the harsh tone of the review and wishes that a lecture scheduled for Brooklyn would "be able to cure the terrible wound of this day" didn't go far toward alleviating the sting.[67] Compounding matters, the "Dr. Livingstone, I presume?" greeting had by now become a commonplace joke, and Stanley saw his whole journey spoofed in a vaudeville farce titled *Africa*. A broadside hit the streets of New York with a parody of the Stanley-Bennett exchange:

Mr. Bennett (in bed, 4 A.M.): Mr. Stanley have the Ten Tribes ever been found?
Mr. Stanley (in room adjoining, also in bed): No, sir; not to my knowledge.
Mr. Bennett: Can they be found?
Mr. Stanley: I should judge so.
Mr. Bennett: Will you find them?
Mr. Stanley: I will sir.
Mr. Bennett: Start immediately; draw on me as large a sum as you like, and don't come back until you have found all the Ten Tribes, whom you must send to America as speedily as possible.
And Mr. Stanley takes the first boat—anywhere; and depend on it, the news will soon be flashing along the line: "Glory! I have just found Tribe Number One. The Reubenites are well, and send congratulations!"[68]

The New Year didn't bring immediate cheer. An anticipated multicity lecture tour fell through, and a proposal by Stanley for another African expedition prompted the editor of the *New York Times* to write that it "would be like threshing out the beaten straw."[69] While money posed no problem—he was still drawing a full salary from the *Herald,* and book royalties poured in—uncertainty about when Bennett would come up with another reporting assignment produced almost overwhelming anxiety. To keep busy, Stanley set about putting the final touches on a novel called *My Kalulu, Prince, King, and Slave: A Story of Central Africa.* He claimed to have written it "for those clever, bright-eyed, intelligent boys, of all classes, who have begun to be interested in romantic literature, with whom educated fathers may talk without fear of misapprehension, and of whom friends are already talking as boys who have a promising future before them."[70] The story portrays Kalulu as a young African prince who falls into the hands of slavers. He later escapes and meets up with an Arab boy named Selim, also taken as a slave. Eventually, both of them escape, become blood brothers, and dedicate their lives to ending slavery in central Africa. By writing such a book, Stanley felt he might "be able to describe more vividly . . . the evils of the slave-trade in Africa—how it begins, how it is conducted, and how it sometimes ends."[71] Although the novel achieved neither commercial nor artistic success—it turned out to be Stanley's only attempt at writing one—Livingstone's influences on his thinking about slavery and the slave trade are clearly evident. Both must be abolished. Contrary to most thinking at the time, he had Africans and Arabs leading the way. Indeed, the novel is bereft of European characters. For this reason alone, *My Kalulu* ought to receive more attention than it has from those interested in European writings about Africa. That the book has been accorded so little notice may again reflect prevailing views of Stanley. It doesn't fit the current stereotype of the explorer as an oppressor by default.

In April Bennett finally summoned Stanley to Paris, the magnate's adopted home. The meeting took place at the Hôtel des Deux Mondes on May 3, with Bennett issuing an assignment to cover Spain's ongoing civil war. Stanley wasn't pleased. It meant going back to old ground, the salary of one thousand per year was half what he wanted, and this time he wouldn't be the only *Herald* correspondent on the scene. As usual, though, Stanley did as instructed, and for four months between mid-May to mid-September he reported from Madrid and other places in the country. Several times he found himself caught up in skirmishes with Carlist forces. One near Pamplona caused him to note that "Their followers shoot fairly well at long ranges with their Remingtons and why I have not been hit as several poor fellows near me I do not know."[72] Fate, luck, whatever, Stanley continued to escape when others fell. Shortly thereafter Bennett once again requested his presence in Paris. The venue would change—he would be going to the

Gold Coast (now Ghana) to follow the British campaign against the Ashanti, or, more properly, Asante, Kingdom.[73]

The crisis was just the most recent one in a conflict between two imperial powers over control of the region's coastal trade going back to 1803. A British victory in 1826 stabilized the situation for a while, but one of the conditions imposed on the Asante—that they free a string of recently conquered territories along the coast—sat poorly with them. In 1867 an opportunity arose for the Asante to retrieve what they felt rightly theirs. Kofi Kakari had just been installed as the new king, or *asantehene*, and technically a state of war existed with Britain because the Asante had refused to hand over a presumed gold thief five years earlier. Under pressure from his councilors, Kakari vowed to reclaim the lost lands, and during 1868 and 1869, his armies probed southward into a British-created protectorate surrounding a string of coastal forts and castles. Only a thin line of West Indian troops, a few Royal Marines, and local militia, most of whose members came from the Fante Confederation, an Asante foe, guarded the protectorate. Sensing that they had an overwhelming military advantage, the Asante launched an all-out attack in December 1872, employing a force estimated at around eighty thousand men. By June 1873 it looked as though success would be theirs; however, stiff resistance from the better-armed West Indians and Royal Marines produced a stalemate. Then diseases began to take their toll, with malaria, yellow fever, elephantiasis, Guinea worm, and smallpox inflicting more casualties on the Asante than the fighting. Suffering from hunger as well, the army withdrew.

Britain reacted to the situation by sending one of its most respected military commanders, Maj. Gen. Garnet Wolseley, to the Gold Coast with orders that the Asante "pay compensation and give assurances of good behaviour for the maintenance of future peace."[74] Commitments to the abolitionist lobby also played a role in prompting a response. Wolseley discovered a near-panic situation when he reached Cape Coast Castle on October 2, 1873. A reconstituted Asante army seemed on the verge of overrunning the nearby the fort of Elmina, and if it fell, then surely Cape Coast would be next. Elmina's defenses held, and the Asante retreated with little to show for their efforts other than dead and wounded men.

By this time, Stanley and others intending to join the expected British march on the Asante capital of Kumasi were already en route aboard the African Steamship Company's *Benin*, which departed Liverpool on September 30. The voyage turned out to be a trying one, for when the ship dropped anchor at Funchal, Madeira, a quarantine notice resulting from a case of cholera on a French brig harbored in Liverpool at the same time as the *Benin* prohibited the passengers and crew from going ashore. The same thing happened two days later at Tenerife in the Canary Islands. Consequently, everyone had to wait until an October 16 docking at Freetown, Sierra Leone, to stretch his legs on land. Stanley developed an immediate loathing for the place. Its lack of fresh air, he felt, had "caused the fragile European to sicken, and fade, and die." Furthermore, it looked to him as though the British had accomplished virtually nothing after nearly a century of occupation, and he called the Africans a bunch of "insolent, lying, thieving negroes."[75] Much to his relief, the stopover lasted only twelve hours, and on the morning of October 22 the *Benin* dropped anchor in the surf outside Cape Coast Castle.

A meeting with Wolseley took place that same evening. He had a reputation for being hostile to correspondents, referring to them as "those newly invented curses to armies, who eat the rations of fighting men and do no work at all."[76] Stanley, however, came away impressed. Except for his soldierly appearance, he said, he might have mistaken the general for "a first-class special correspondent, just the man to have seized an item and dared a general-in-chief to lay hands on him, just the man to be sent to any part of the world to collect news." With "eager eyes [that] betray the inquisitive and indomitable energy," Stanley felt that the "British Government could have found no worthier man to entrust the castigation of the Ashantees to."

On the other hand, Cape Coast Castle provided Stanley with another opportunity to criticize the British over their presumed failures in Africa. After more than two hundred years of British rule, the only accomplishments Stanley could detect consisted of "a Government house, post-office, and two or three other offices, and a church." And he puzzled over why they chose it over Elmina, which possessed a superior fort and harbor and seemed healthier, as the place from which to launch the invasion. In addition, Stanley considered the people at Cape Coast more "advanced" because of an earlier Dutch presence that had "inculcated in them industrious habits."

As one day succeeded another without any sign of a military campaign being imminent, Stanley and the other correspondents began to worry that the affair would end in a negotiated settlement, an event hardly worthy of the time and money spent getting there. Much of the delay stemmed from Wolseley's ultracareful planning. One to leave as little to chance as possible, he first sent a contingent of reorganized Fante troops ahead to clear out any Asante they might find between Cape Coast Castle and the Pra River. They also had instructions to secure the cooperation of all local chiefs, in order to remove the possibility of unexpected troubles hindering the army's advance. As a further precaution, Wolseley ordered a string of well-equipped stations built along the projected line of march. He specified that each one have pit latrines, a hospital to care for the sick and wounded, and fires constantly

burning to warm the men at night.[77] Finally, Wolseley wanted British reinforcements before going into battle. While the government said no to the
request, he waited in hopes of its eventually being honored.

To relieve boredom, Stanley tried to convince several other reporters to
sail with him to Accra on the *Dauntless*, a small steam-powered craft provided courtesy of the *Herald*. Only one agreed, and as they coasted eastward,
Stanley felt refreshed "to see real nature once more after all the dreary waiting for active life at Cape Coast Castle." Along the way, they passed Cor-
mantine, the first British settlement on the Gold Coast and once a great slave
mart, Apam, a former Dutch fort destroyed by the Asante in 1811 and the
still active trade center of Winneba, before reaching Accra. Here the two
men spent a day exploring the old fort and speaking with several British
traders, who told them about Capt. John H. Glover's planned assault on the
Asante via the Volta River. They also visited the Basle Mission House and
its educational facility at Christianbourg, several miles outside Accra.

All of this together hardly made for much of a story, and the only thing
of note Stanley learned upon returning to Cape Coast was that the British
government had finally agreed to send additional troops. But when they
might show up remained unclear, and desperate to find something worthwhile to write about, he decided to see what could be learned about Glover's
intentions along the Volta. Stanley invited George A. Henty, a reporter for
the *Standard* he met during the Abyssinian campaign and later dubbed "the
Prince of Storytellers" for his many heroic tales for boys, to join him on the
Dauntless for a journey to find Glover. Upon reaching Ada at the river's
mouth, they learned that his camp was close by. Stanley had heard nothing
but glowing praise for the captain, particularly regarding his efforts while
governor of Lagos Colony, and he came away from their conversation even
more impressed. Glover struck him as "a great man," and he doubted that
he would "soon see his equal on the West Coast of Africa in the purely
administrative and the organizing line."

All told, Glover had some twenty thousand Africans under him, and Stanley thought that with the addition of one hundred British officers, Wolseley's
army would be unnecessary. But the Volta operation had been designed as a
diversionary tactic, and when Glover finally moved out on January 15, 1874,
only eight hundred well-trained Hausa troops marched with him.[78] Two
other flanking operations were also part of the battle plan.

Their conversation with Glover over, Stanley and Henty boarded a
steamer to discover what they could about the little-known Volta. They
didn't have much time and traveled only as far as the force's second staging
point at Bakpa. The river struck Stanley as typically tropical, fringed by man-

groves and having a "wayward course" with numerous channels. No signs of human habitation were visible, which he attributed to the "fatal air" emanating from the marches. To live there and breathe it "would be like eating from the forbidden fruit." Hurrying back to Cape Coast, they arrived just after the disembarkation of the new troops. Numbered among them were the famous 42nd Highlanders, or Black Watch, and Stanley looked forward to seeing "a splendid body of kilted men." To his dismay, however,

> they had left their kilts behind them, and . . . were breeched, like ordinary British soldiers, in the unpicturesque Norfolk grey. The cause was, I am told, the kilts were not fit for bush-work; that the authorities feared that thorns and cacti would have so wounded the epidermis of soldiers, that they would in a short time be disabled from active service.

On a more positive note for Stanley and the other reporters, active preparations had begun for the advance against the Asante, and on December 27 the army moved out. The first segment of the journey went through the infamous "bush," or what, Stanley said,

> should be more appropriately called jungle. It is so dense in some places that one wonders at first sight how naked peoples can have the temerity to risk their bodies in what must necessarily punish their unprotected cuticles most painfully. The jungle probably covers many thousands of acres, literally choking the earth with its density and luxuriance. It admits every kind of shrub, plant, and flower into close companionship, where they intermingle each other's luxuriant stalks, where they twist and twine each other's long slender arms about one another, and defy the utmost power of the sun to penetrate the leafy tangle they have reared ten and fifteen feet above the dank earth.

After a short stretch of more open country, they entered a forest where, according to Stanley, "powers of description fail. In density and wild luxuriance it eclipsed everything I have ever seen in Africa. I do not suppose that anything in Brazil can give one a more thorough realization of tropical luxuriance." A well-constructed road eased travel, however. Stanley complimented the engineers, saying they "have done their work so well that it becomes a pleasure to walk the smooth, broad road." He, like many others at the time, viewed roads as tangible evidence of progress and symbols of the ability of humans to dominate nature. Before the decade was out, an opportunity to oversee their construction in Africa would be his.

Wolseley had chosen Prasu on the Pra River as the staging point for the invasion and waited there while straggling supply lines caught up. Never one

Map 4.1   The March to Kumasi, December 1873–February 1874

to let an opportunity to criticize military tactics go without comment, Stanley told readers,

> You must remember, as you pass your judgment on the glaring mistake of the authorities here, that the detention of the white regiments at the unhealthy stations on the road means much more than delay—it means sickness and mortality—and also remember that to make carriers of West Indian negroes, who are as little capable of standing this climate as white troops are, is to make them nearly all unfit for the active prosecution of the war.

During the wait, a Reverend Kuhne, one of several Basel missionaries captured by the Asante more than four years earlier, walked into camp. Released because of his deteriorating health, he reported that Kakari would not fight because the army had been severely weakened by losses from battle and disease. This seemed to be confirmed by communications coming directly from

Kumasi, and from the fact that an advance force of African troops made it to within twelve hours of the capital without difficulty. To Stanley it appeared

> that there is no fighting spirit left in the king of Ashantee, and that the British campaign of 1873–74 is destined to end in a peaceful parade at Coomassie. . . . It is rather disheartening to officers who have dared the fatigues and the climatic dangers of Africa to be told that peace will be made. It is more disheartening for an expedition which numbers so many Europeans to have to go through the form of marching to Coomassie only to sign a peace—such a peace as has already been made too frequently. It must be annoying to Great Britain, after such an expense—after cherishing the delusion that now she had the opportunity to crush the insolent Power which has insulted her representatives during the past century—to be told she shall not have the power to punish or avenge wrongs; but she shall have her expedition, the losses of life she has incurred, the sickness and the fever her sons have endured, all for nothing.

Continuing on, he thought,

> There is only one hope remaining, after this probably tame ending of the expedition, that, as the troops enter Coomassie, this event may not be accepted by the Ashantees as a sign of amity. The king may be willing to declare his readiness to sign a treaty, to send any number of hostages to Cape Coast Castle, to pay any reasonable sum as an indemnity to the Assins and Fantees for the losses they have sustained; but will he be willing to allow an invading army to occupy his capital and dictate terms of peace to him from an apartment in his own palace? That he will fear some treachery on the part of the white men, some deep scheme of revenge, some bloody massacre, some wholesale spoilation, is the only hope left to the English that they will not be permitted to enter Coomassie bloodlessly or without some opportunity of inflicting a punishment on the savages, that it may become a tradition among them of what may be expected should they venture to attack any territory under the protection of white men again.

On January 19 Wolseley moved his force of over 3,500 combat troops and more than three thousand supply carriers to the other side of the Pra, where burned villages and occasional skeletons provided vivid reminders of recent Asante raids. Thick forest stands once again lined the road until they entered the 2,000-foot-high Moinsi Hills, which Stanley said provided relief because of the "pure, healthy air" at this altitude. On the other side stood Fomena, the recently abandoned capital of the Moinsi Kingdom. It impressed Stanley by having a broad central avenue, enough good houses for the white troops, and an array of fine crafts left behind by the people. These included wooden stools displaying a "perfection of workmanship," ladles that a "European turner would be proud of," and "excellently done" sandals. He had a sharp eye for items of utilitarian value and never hesitated to pay the makers, no matter their origins, compliments. The comments also show a developing appreciation for African skills, a none-too-common sensibility among late-nineteenth-century travelers.

They spent four days at Fomena to make sure everything was in place for the final leg of the march. Kakari wanted to negotiate a settlement, but he could not acquiesce to Wolseley's demands of fifty thousand ounces of gold and six royal hostages, including the Queen Mother, without losing face and maybe even the throne.[79] Meanwhile, several other newly released prisoners came into camp claiming that

> The king emphatically declares 'he has no palaver with white men,' and that his sole object in sending his army of invasion, February 1873, was to recover his provinces of Akim, Assin, and Denkerah—his right by conquest long ago—tributary to him until they rebelled. He wishes to be a friend to the white people, and to establish commerce with them.

Wishing to avoid war, Kakari told them he might be able to find enough gold to pay the indemnity if the advance were halted.

Wolseley had no intention of doing any such thing and set the army and its followers on course for Kumasi. About ten miles from Fomena, the reporters got their wish—a large Asante army positioned dead ahead. Fighting broke out on the 31st, with the main battle occurring around the town of Amoafu. By midday, the superior firepower from cannons and Snider rifles won this round of the battle for the British. During the engagement, Wolseley later remembered Stanley acting gallantly:

> Not twenty yards off were several newspaper correspondents. One, Mr. Winwood Reid, a very cool and daring man, had gone forward with the fighting line. Of the others one soon attracted my attention by his remarkable coolness. It was Sir Henry Stanley, the famous traveller. A thoroughly good man, no noise, no danger ruffled his nerve, and he looked as cool and self-possessed as if he had been at 'target practise.' Time after time as I turned in his direction I saw him go down to a kneeling position to steady his rifle as he plied the most daring of the enemy with a never-failing aim. It is nearly thirty years ago, and I can still see before me the close-shut lips and determined expression of his manly face which—when he looked in my direction—told plainly I had near me an Englishman in plain clothing whom no danger could appal. Had

I felt inclined to run away, the cool, firm, unflinching manliness of that face
would have given me fresh courage. I had been previously somewhat preju-
diced by others against him, but all such feelings were slain and buried at
Amoaful. Ever since I have been proud to reckon him amongst the bravest of
my comrades, and I hope he may not be offended if I add amongst my best
friends also.[80]

Stanley never mentioned the event, nor did he refer to Wolseley, either at
the time or later, as a best friend, and there is no other source to confirm or
deny what happened.

The war, however, had not yet been won, for on the other side of the Oda
River stood another ten to twelve thousand Asante troops poised for battle.
The fighting began February 4 at 7:40 A.M., with British progress slow at
first. Indeed, for a time the outcome seemed in doubt. But after securing the
village of Odaso, Wolseley changed tactics and ordered the Black Watch to
advance quickly. "Then began," wrote Stanley, "the sublime march to Coomassie, the most gallant conduct and most impressive action of the Ashantee
campaign. It was on the 'fire fast' and 'advance fast' principle" that quickly
overwhelmed the opposition. At 6:00 P.M. the first troops entered Kumasi,
only to find it abandoned. Wolseley secured the city and ordered the execution of anyone caught looting. Cover of darkness allowed much to be taken
in spite of the threat.

During the march, Asante sacrifices and other killings became a favorite
topic of reporters' stories, and in a grove adjacent to the city, they got an
opportunity to provide another justification for the march on Kumasi. As
Stanley described it, he first detected smells "so suffocating that we were glad
to produce our handkerchiefs to prevent the intolerable and almost palpable
odour from mounting into the brain and overpowering us." They came from
a place labeled Golgotha, the reputed royal execution ground, where he
reported seeing "forty decapitated bodies in the last stages of corruption, and
countless skulls which lay piled in heaps and scattered over a wide extent."
Previous visitors had commented on the site, and using their estimates of
numbers killed per year, Stanley calculated that more than 120,000 people
"must have been slain for 'custom'" since the middle of the eighteenth century. The figure was pure fantasy designed to rouse readers and justify the
destruction wrought by the army.

As at Magdala, everything of value that could be carried away was, and in
similar fashion, Wolseley ordered Kumasi put to the torch. The General later
recorded that "In my heart of hearts I believed that the absolute destruction
of Koomassee with its great palace, the wonder of Western Africa, would be

a much more striking and effective end to the war than any paper treaty."[81] With the possibility of total destruction staring him in the face, Kakari sued for peace and signed the Treaty of Fomena containing ten articles, including one demanding an indemnity of fifty thousand ounces of gold that effectively ended the Asante's imperial ambitions.[82] The humiliation also ended Kakari's tenure as *asantehene*, and a decline of power at the center further weakened the state. Its independence came to a formal end with the establishment of a British Protectorate in 1896.

Given the onset of the rains and the risk of disease outbreaks, Wolseley decided to get his men back to Cape Coast and not wait for the other armies to reach Kumasi as originally planned. Glover's advance, in fact, had become bogged down. The weeklong return to Cape Coast lacked the drama of the return from Magdala—animals not dying by the hundreds and no torrents of water to cross—and overall the campaign hardly measured up to Abyssinia. Still, in a similar fashion, Stanley had been able to fill the *Herald* with thrilling stories of another British victory over an African imperial contender. Richard Burton had a different view of the campaign. He called it "ignoble. . . . A poor scuffle between the breechloader and the Birmingham trade musket."[83]

Despite railings at perceived failures in Sierra Leone and the Gold Coast, Stanley continued to push for Britain to increase its activity in Africa. The problem all these years, he thought, centered on the country's inaction. The Gold Coast seemed an almost ideal place to begin a change in direction, for he considered the Asante "born traders" who could help make it as "rich an acquisition to the British Crown as the Island of Cuba to the United States." In turn, Stanley argued that by freeing them from despotism of the past "a change of masters would be a glorious thing for the Ashantee." Furthermore, with Hausa troops manning garrisons, he saw the Gold Coast having the potential to be the "nucleus of a great empire . . . that in the process of time will rival that of India." Rhetorically, at least, Stanley had joined the ranks of ardent imperialists, and at the end of the decade, he would get a chance to put his words into practice.

The ship taking Stanley and most of the other correspondents home sailed from Cape Coast on February 19. During a call at São Vincente in the Cape Verde Islands on February 25, word of Livingstone's death finally reached him. As displayed in a journal entry, a distraught Stanley suddenly claimed finding a new purpose in life:

> Poor Dear old man! Another sacrifice to Africa! His mission, however, must not be allowed to cease; others must go forward & fill the gap. . . . May I be

selected to succeed him in opening up Africa to the shining light of Christianity, but not after his method! Each man has his own way. His I think has its defects, though the old man personally has been nearly Christ like for goodness, patience & self sacrifice. The selfish and wooden headed world requires other promptings other than the Gospel, for man is a composite of spiritual and the mundane. But may Livingstone's God be with me as He was with Livingstone in all his loneliness, and direct me as He wills. I can only vow to be obedient, & not slacken.[84]

When exactly he wrote these words, however, can't be determined, as the journal was compiled at least a decade later.

Stanley went to Southampton to meet the ship carrying Livingstone's remains and served as one of the pallbearers at his state-sponsored April 18 burial in Westminster Abbey. Afterward, he stayed in London to put the finishing touches on *Coomassie and Magdala,* a task that consumed him for three weeks. An attempt to publish the Abyssinian part in 1869 met with no success, and his publisher dissuaded him from trying again in August 1872 because of concerns that it might hurt the sales of the Livingstone book. With this task out of the way, Stanley's thoughts turned to completing what the doctor had left unfinished. He claimed he bought more than 130 books on Africa and spent hour after hour "inventing and planning, sketching out routes, laying out lengthy lines of possible exploration, noting many suggestions which the continued study of my project created."[85] An opportunity to put all this preparation into practice materialized during a chance meeting with Edwin Arnold, his former defender. They talked about Livingstone and "the unfinished task remaining behind him," and when asked by Arnold, " 'And what is there to do?' " Stanley said he answered,

The outlet of the Lake Tanganyika is undiscovered. We know nothing scarcely—except what Speke has sketched out—of Lake Victoria; we do not even know whether it consists of one or many lakes, and therefore the sources of the Nile are still unknown. Moreover, the western half of the African continent is still a white blank.[86]

Convinced of Stanley's skills and resolve, Arnold said his paper, the *Daily Telegraph*, would put up six thousand pounds for a new expedition if the *Herald* matched it. Seemingly caught off guard when Stanley contacted him about the idea, Bennett said yes but committed himself to nothing more specific at the time. In fact, Bennett seems to have had little enthusiasm for such a venture: He'd grown tired of Stanley being the center of attention and reportedly "would break out into fury when Stanley came unto the news."[87] And Bennett didn't like sharing stories, especially with other newspapers. When Stanley called at his office in New York on July 8, Bennett brusquely responded that he was busy. Stanley would have to come back another time. When they did get together three days later, Bennett refused to sign a contract, saying, according to Stanley, that it "was against all custom with him." But he did agree to make a bank deposit, which the *Telegraph* "might draw upon, as the necessity of the case demanded it."[88] Whatever the cause, Bennett changed his tune, for on July 26 a *Herald* editorial proclaimed that Stanley would be "the ambassador of two great powers, representing the journalism of England and America, and in command of an expedition more numerous and better appointed than any that has ever entered Africa."[89] To Stanley's great delight, the Anglo-American Expedition (AAE) could now go forth with him at the head. A journal entry shows the victory was a personal one. The expedition, he noted, "would compel those who doubted that I had discovered Livingstone at Ujiji to confess themselves in error; and the member of the Royal Geographical Society who called me a 'charlatan' to retract the libel."[90]

Donations poured in, and hundreds volunteered to go along. Some of the military men impressed Stanley, but he found most of the civilians to be either "madmen" or "fools" who furnished "unblushing falsehoods" about their qualifications.[91] That he'd done the very same thing on past occasions makes the statement appear hypocritical. On the other hand, it could represent a rejection of former behavior. In the end, Stanley selected only three men: Frederick Barker, a persistent clerk at the Langham Hotel in London, who had to get his mother's permission, and Frank and Edward Pocock, two young fishermen from Kent recommended by Arnold. Stanley felt the brothers would be valuable for piloting a wooden boat he planned to use on rivers and lakes. The specifications called for it to be forty feet long and in five sections, each weighing sixty pounds, a load for one man. Stanley named the boat the *Lady Alice,* after Alice Pike, the beautiful and vivacious seventeen-year-old daughter of a wealthy Cincinnati whiskey magnate he met at a dinner party in London on May 13. She intrigued him, appearing "constrained even to being frigid," yet dressing in a "fast" style, with a bearing of "inordinate vanity." That his feelings toward her quickly progressed beyond intriguing is evidenced by a musing three days later. It reads, "I fear if Miss Alice gives me as much encouragement long as she has been giving me lately I shall fall in love with her, which may not perhaps be very condusive to happiness, for she is the very opposite of my ideal type."[92] He did indeed fall in love, and an engagement quickly followed. During July, when both were back in the United States, they signed a marriage promise stating, "We solemnly pledge ourselves to be faithful to each other, and to be married one to another, on the return of Henry Morton Stanley from Africa. We call God to witness this our pledge in writing." She went on to tell him "Take good care of yourself and come back as quickly as possible & I will marry you." A date was even specified—January 14, 1877.[93] They dined together the evening before Stanley's departure. After kissing her good night, he recorded,

> At this moment there's no doubt in my mind that she is faithful, and loyally determined to marry me, and she evidently believes that she will. But two years is such a long time to wait, & I have much to do, such a weary journey to make before I can ever return. No man had ever to work harder than I have for a wife.[94]

Bidding Alice a fond farewell the next morning, he left for London to take care of last minute details and await completion of the *Lady Alice*. Two other boats had been ordered as well, a Yarmouth yawl called the *Wave* and a specially constructed rubber pontoon he named the *Livingstone*. When all that could be done had been done, Stanley boarded the steamer *Euphrates* on August 15, bound once again for Zanzibar.

CHAPTER 5

The Longest Journey

ACROSS AFRICA 1874–1877

A mostly familiar Zanzibar greeted Stanley when he strolled ashore on September 21, 1874. One important change, however, had occurred—it no longer trafficked in slaves. With Livingstone's writings from the continent and Kirk's from Zanzibar providing extra ammunition, the Gladstone government gave in to the demands of the antislavery lobby and sent a "special mission" to the island in January 1873. Headed by the highly respected former governor (1862–1867) of Bombay Henry E. Bartle Frere, the mission sought to convince Barghash of the need to abolish the trade once and for all. After two months of negotiations, Bartle Frere left with nothing concrete in hand. The job of winning over the sultan fell to Kirk, who made it clear that failure to comply with Britain's wishes would almost certainly result in a blockade. Strapped for cash—the devastating storm of April 1872 had leveled the island's valuable clove and coconut plantations, and Mirambo still held the ivory trade hostage—Barghash caved in and signed a treaty on June 5, 1873. It affirmed the closure of Zanzibar's slave market, made the trade illegal at all ports under the sultan's jurisdiction, and required that freed slaves be accorded protection.[1] Barghash cleared the market that very day and followed with a proclamation ending with "Whosoever, therefore, shall ship a slave after this date will render himself liable to punishment."[2] The treaty said nothing, however, about inland trade. Bringing it to a close would take considerably longer, and even on Zanzibar and Pemba slavery as an institution persisted until 1897.

Stanley stayed with American Augustus Sparhawk, another John Ber-

tram & Co. employee, who'd befriended him in 1871. Sparhawk also provided space for storing the many goods being assembled by the expedition.
The focus on exploration required taking along chronometers, sextants,
compasses, barometers, thermometers, almanacs, a sounding line, a plani-
sphere, photographic equipment, pedometers, timepieces, and charts.[3]
These, and a good number of Snider rifles and ammunition, were brought
from England. Zanzibar could be relied on for providing everyday items and,
of course, goods for paying *honga*.

Stanley figured that in excess of three hundred men would be needed to
carry all the loads, but to his chagrin, prospective candidates demanded
much more pay than they had before. He placed the blame on Cameron for
doling out profligate salaries in 1872. Stanley called him a "foolish fellow,"
who doubled the usual amount.[4]

Enough time was available during preparations to do some exploring
along the Rufiji River. Despite skepticism derived from two prior expeditions about the river's potential as a route to the interior, Stanley remained
optimistic that Richard Burton's assessment of it as "the counterpart of the
Zambezi," would be correct.[5] At least he'd go see for himself.

Accompanied by the Pococks, twenty-four Wangwana, two cabin boys,
and an English bull terrier named Jack, Stanley set sail for the Rufiji on September 30 in the *Wave*. They first stopped at Dar es Salaam. Its secure natural
harbor had caught the eye of Barghash's predecessor, Seyyid Majid, who
started building a city he hoped would eventually rival or even surpass Zanzibar. After Seyyid Said died in 1856, his eldest son Thueni took control in
Oman, with Zanzibar left to Majid. But interest languished after Majid's
death in 1870, and Stanley found the port "silent and comparatively
deserted." Still, like the sultan, he valued its potential, and thought a plan
being discussed in England about using Dar es Salaam as a place for settling
freed slaves a capital idea. Many good houses stood uninhabited, the prospects for commercial developments seemed considerable, and no European
flag currently waved above it.

After a brief visit to Kwale Island, the party steered back toward the mainland and entered the northernmost channel, cutting through the mangrove
forests of the Rufiji delta on October 6. Not too long thereafter, the *Wave*
ran aground, but with little damage done, the crew quickly had it moving
again. Upon passing the twenty-mile mark Stanley concluded that steamers
as large as those plying the Mississippi could easily be accommodated. By
forty miles the *Wave* was into uncharted waters and still running smoothly.
Even the many hippos and crocodiles cooperated by not getting in the way.

As for the inhabitants, they seemed more amused than anything else, wondering why anyone would come so far just to have a look at water.[6]

At a bank of sand bars a few miles farther on, Stanley turned the *Wave* around, even though he thought a sturdy boat like the *Lady Alice* might be able to sail past the bars and go a couple of hundred miles farther upstream. All in all, prospects appeared bright. The valley seemed rich and populous, and the river looked to be an ideal artery for launching attacks to crush the slave trade. On the way back through the delta they reconnoitered its two other major channels and then visited Mafia Island. A mere ten miles from the mainland, it struck him as another highly promising place to locate a colony of freed slaves. Once securely established, he felt they could use the Rufiji to open trade with people upcountry.[7] After spending a night in Bagamoyo, the *Wave* brought the party back to Zanzibar on October 16 without mishap. Its purpose fulfilled, Stanley sold the boat to the Universities Mission to Central Africa for one hundred pounds. The Pococks performed their tasks admirably and enjoyed this stint of exploring with Stanley. Frank described him as "a good man to be away with."[8]

The Rufiji visited, their full attention could be focused on preparations for the long and uncertain journey ahead, although the onset of Ramadan slowed the pace of activity. The monthlong fast meant that little heavy work could be accomplished. Stanley filled part of the time by mapping out a more direct route from Bagamoyo to Mpwapwa that cut across Maasailand. Then would come the long march to Lake Victoria to determine whether it was one body of water or possibly as many as five smaller lakes. During this phase of exploration, Stanley hoped to meet with Mutesa, the *kabaka,* or king, of Buganda, the richest and most powerful state in this part of the continent. He also wanted to make contact with Rumanika, the ruler of Karagwe, a Bahaya kingdom south of Buganda. These would be preludes to a trip to Lake Albert. Stanley had two reasons for going there: to check on earlier speculations about the lake's length and breadth and to have his letters and newspaper dispatches sent down the Nile via Equatoria, an Egyptian-held province in the southern Sudan.[9] Col. Charles "Chinese" Gordon of Taiping Rebellion fame was its current governor. His next destination would depend on time and circumstances. It might be all the way to the west coast or south to find the headwaters of the Nile.

More immediately, additional porters had to be hired, and to his great consternation, Stanley found that the sections of the *Lady Alice* weighed more than twice the specified sixty pounds. With funds running low, he considered selling the boat, although this would undoubtedly doom the expedition, as finding enough canoes to replace it seemed an impossible task.[10]

Inquiries turned up a shipwright named Ferris who said he could make the necessary modifications. When the work was completed, Stanley congratulated himself on having a boat that could be carried "any distance without distressing the porters, with twelve men, rowing ten oars and two short paddles, and able to sail over any lake in Central Africa."[11]

At the end of Ramadan, the largest, best-equipped, and most heavily armed European-led exploration of Africa's interior ever put together was ready to go. Joining Stanley aboard the dhows headed for Bagamoyo on November 12 were the Pococks, Barker, 237 Africans (including many "faithfuls" who had been with him in 1871–1872), five dogs, six asses, more than eighteen thousand pounds of supplies, and the two boats.[12] The rubber pontoon would never see service. Just as in 1871, Bagamoyo got under Stanley's skin, this time by tempting the men with all kinds of opportunities to drink and carouse. When that happened, arguments and fights almost inevitably broke out. This time, though, the stay turned out to be a short one, and at 9:00 A.M. on November 17 the Anglo-American Expedition, some 356 strong after adding additional porters, began its westward journey, flying both the Union Jack and the Stars and Stripes. Stanley now stood in command of his own army, "faithful" Manwa Sera served as captain of the troops, and a drummer boy marched at the head of the procession. Unfortunately, the day turned out to be brutally hot, and men and animals started to wilt. Two porters failed to make it to the first camp, and one of the mastiffs, Castor, succumbed to heat prostration. A second survived only a few days longer. During the halt, Stanley had to settle a sticky situation when a contingent of the sultan's soldiers came to collect some women who decided to leave their masters in Bagamoyo for the company of expedition men. To maintain Arab goodwill he ordered them sent back over loud protestations, both by the women and their newfound companions. On a brighter note, the *Lady Alice* did an "admirable job" ferrying the Kingani River.

Stanley liked what the new route presented, noting the landscape across the river was like "a stretch of beautiful park land, green as an English lawn, dipping into lovely vales, and rising into gentle ridges."[13] But looks could be deceiving, and thus during a stopover at Rosako, he arranged for all the men who had not previously been infected by smallpox to receive vaccinations. From here the expedition headed for the Wami River. Noting its many boulders, Stanley concluded that navigation wouldn't be possible during the dry season, thus making it far less valuable than he'd originally thought. The route from the Wami led upward into the Nguru Mountains, nearly seven thousand feet at their highest. Once again Stanley waxed enthusiastically about the scenery, describing one section as "grand and impressive" and another as reminding him of scenes from the Alleghenies, with water "flow-ing clear as crystal from numerous sources."[14] His use of English and Ameri-can scenic comparisons served two purposes: providing readers with something familiar, if even just a name, with which to identify and creating more favorable impressions of Africa's livability, a theme he would repeat in different contexts many times in years to come.

Nothing barred the way, not even the Maasai, known to prey upon pass-ing caravans. The size and armaments of Stanley's entourage discouraged the *el moran,* as the young warriors are known, from trying anything. Conse-quently, the expedition reached Mpwapwa on December 12, after only twenty-five days on the road, less than half the time it took Stanley to get there in 1871. From previous experience, Stanley anticipated losing men to desertions and illnesses, for while still in Zanzibar he wrote that after about three weeks travel, "Scores will have deserted, the strong will have become weak, the robust sick."[15] The number turned out to be fifty. To complicate matters, the previous growing season around Mpwapwa had been a poor one and therefore food sold "at famine prices."[16]

A surprise awaited Stanley—Phillippe Broyon, a Swiss adventurer-trader who'd just recently met Mirambo, becoming the first European to do so. Stanley didn't mention the meeting in either *Through the Dark Continent* or newspaper dispatches, but he does refer to Broyon's existence in a diary entry on a later date.[17] What conversations and relationship the two men might have had seem lost to history.

In a letter to Edward Levy, Stanley fretted about the greater-than-expected costs of the expedition and, in particular, how this might interfere with doing right by the Zanzibaris. As he explained, should he decide to cross the continent,

> probably £200 will have to be paid toward getting the poor fellows back to Zanzibar, though I have not bound myself by any agreement to take them, or send them back to Zanzibar, but you will agree with me that it would be a sin to desert them 4000 miles from their homes after such faithful service, always supposing that we reach the west coast of Africa.[18]

While not yet having made a final decision, it's clear he was seriously think-ing about making such a journey if possible.

A rather depleted and dispirited caravan thus faced the waterless Marenga Mkali. Stanley described the day and a half it took to get through it as excru-ciating, for "the heat was intense, the earth fervid, the thorny jungle a con-stant impediment & a sore trouble, & its exhalations nauseating."[19] So as not to have a repeat of 1871, they carried fifty gallons of drinking water for the crossing. Entering Ugogo on December 16 hardly served to raise Stanley's spirits. To him it represented "the most unloveable country in Africa," a place "hateful to the eye and bitter to the mind."[20] His mood wasn't helped by a strength-sapping fever.

Illness, lack of food, numerous tribute negotiations, intense heat, and the downpours that began December 23 at Dodoma intensified Stanley's feelings. In a letter to an unidentified friend written on Christmas Day, he lamented,

> It has been raining heavily the last two or three days, and an impetuous downpour of sheet rain has just ceased. On the march, rain is very disagreeable; it makes the clayey path slippery, and the loads heavier by being saturated, while it half ruins the cloths. It makes us dispirited, wet, and cold, added to which we are hungry—for there is a famine or scarcity of food at this season, and therefore we can only procure half-rations. . . . I myself have not had a piece of meat for ten days. My food is boiled rice, tea, and coffee, and soon I shall be reduced to eating native porridge, like my own people. I weighed 180 lbs. when I left Zanzibar, but under this diet I have been reduced to 134 lbs. within thirty-eight days. The young Englishmen are in the same impoverished condition of body, and unless we reach some more flourishing country than famine-stricken Ugogo, we must soon become mere skeletons.[21]

It would be quite some time before anything resembling "flourishing country" was seen. In fact, conditions only worsened, causing more of the men to desert, and Stanley at one point thought the whole project to be "doomed."[22] A march across a broad waterless plain on December 29 proved to be especially taxing. Five men with two guns disappeared, and Stanley learned that as many as fifty others planned on slipping away as soon as they could. To head them off, he had the leaders "clapped in chains and flogged." A large group Wagogo warriors brandishing spears added further tension to the day, but they caused no trouble, being content with the display.[23] The sick list continued to grow and included those with "fever, sore feet, opthalmia, and rheumatism."[24] Although ill himself, Stanley said, he often had to intervene to keep quarrels from turning into fights.

When the march resumed on December 31, Stanley decided the state of affairs called for the quickest possible trip to Lake Victoria, and thus he plotted a route going straight north rather than connecting with the usual one that Speke had followed in 1858. A cordial reception by villagers at Mwenna made it look like a good decision, but then during the night of January 3, 1875, heavy rains produced a six-inch stream of water running through the camp. According to Stanley,

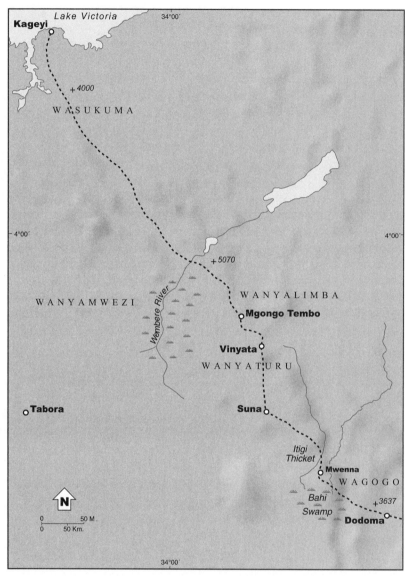

Map 5.1   Journey to Lake Victoria, December 1874–February 1875

Every member of the expedition was distressed, and even the Europeans, lodged in tents, were not exempted from the evils of the night. My tent walls enclosed a little pool, banked by boxes of stores and ammunition. Hearing cries outside, I lit a candle, and my astonishment was great to find that my bed was an island in a shallow river, which, if it increased in depth and current, would assuredly carry me off south towards the Rufiji.[25]

The next day, they climbed nearly a thousand feet to the plateau making the western boundary of Ugogo. Looking back, Stanley again registered his feelings about the land and its people:

A farewell to it [Ugogo], a lasting farewell to it, until some generous philanthropist shall permit me or some other to lead a force for the suppression of this stumbling block to commerce with Central Africa. This pleasant task and none other could ever induce me to return to Ugogo.[26]

He would return more than a decade later, but not in this capacity.

Because of being off the caravan trail, no one was sure what lay ahead. Before long, they found themselves ensnarled in a dense thicket virtually impenetrable to all but elephants. A group guarding the rear got separated, and five of its members and a donkey never reappeared. Few settlements existed on the other side, and food couldn't be found to replenish the rapidly dwindling stores. Worried about impending starvation, Stanley sent volunteers ahead to try to find a place to purchase grain. Meanwhile, those remaining behind managed to get by on a small amount of oatmeal and a few bush fruits until the volunteers returned from a village called Suna with just enough millet to provide everyone with one small serving. Necessity required a blistering pace to get more food, and they covered the twenty-seven miles to the village in two days.

Additional men disappeared along the way, and the "deplorable" state of many others forced Stanley to call a halt at Suna. As he noted in his journal,

Having arrived here I must now wait until my people are . . . refreshed and perfectly rested. I propose to deal very liberally with all to repay them for their sufferings. God knows how much I feel for my poor people & under the circumstances I have done what prudence & wisdom would have suggested ought to be done. Had I delayed our arrival here I might have lost 50 instead of ten.[27]

Three days of rest and eating their fill did wonders for almost everyone. The major exception was Edward Pocock, who started running a high fever.

Other symptoms included a black tongue, pains in his back and knees, giddiness, a "great thirst," and small pimples that indicated a mild case of smallpox.[28] Sensing growing restiveness among the villagers, Stanley decided to leave before anything unpleasant happened. Edward's strength continued to wane, and the next night he passed away, with typhus rather than smallpox the likely cause. They buried him beneath a large acacia tree, marked by a cross Frank carved into the trunk. After a prayer service, Stanley said everyone retreated "to brood in sorrow and silence" over their fallen comrade.[29] Just a few days earlier, however, Stanley had described him as "one of the most useless of men" who needed constant reminders to do his two simple jobs of blowing bugle and looking after the men in charge of the donkeys.[30]

A little ways farther on, the landscape changed to an open boulder-strewn plateau marked by numerous Wanyaturu or Warimi homesteads and large herds of cattle. Porters continued to "drop off most mysteriously," and a "faithful," Kaif Halleck, decided to stay behind for a short rest because of a bad attack of asthma. It proved an unwise decision, as Halleck was killed while waiting for escorts to bring him forward to the next camp at Vinyata. Stanley quickly put everyone on full alert and vowed to never again leave a sick man behind without adequate protection. He'd break the vow more than once. However, the arrival in camp of a *mganga*—a healer—with an offering of an ox struck him as a "propitious omen." They exchanged greetings and gifts, and the *mganga* returned the next day for another round of pleasantries. Then, shortly after he departed, war cries rang out, followed by the approach of a large body of men armed with spears, shields, and bows and arrows. Their leader blamed members of the expedition for stealing milk and butter and insisted on being compensated for the loss. If payment was not immediately forthcoming, he said they would attack. Stanley gave him some cloth and thought the crisis over. It wasn't, for shortly thereafter, a Zanzibari stumbled into camp, reporting an ambush that had wounded him and taken his brother's life. The Wanyaturu then followed through on their threat. Stanley said he made the first kill and that after suffering fifteen fatalities within seconds, the attackers broke off the engagement.[31] Puzzled by the hostility, he surmised that the only reason must have been "a desire for plunder & a savage thirst for blood."[32] A more plausible explanation is that the Wanyaturu were simply trying to defend themselves from presumed foreign invaders. They'd suffered attacks before and nothing indicated differently this time.

Emboldened by driving off an even larger force of warriors the next morning, Stanley decided to launch a counterattack. His mind-set is captured in a letter to Alice, in which he wrote that the time had come "to teach these savages a lesson of the severest kind, that large Expeditions like mine, though strongly disposed to be peaceful were not to be attacked with impunity."[33] A fierce battle erupted, and when the initial detachment sent into combat somehow strayed too far afield, it lost everyone except the messenger who brought back the bad news. But the Wanyaturu took even greater casualties, and when they failed to show up again at daybreak, Stanley said he decided "to seal our victory with a fresh display of force." Accordingly, he instructed the *askari* to proceed "to the extremest limits of the valley and burn all the villages that were left standing and bring in enough grain and other food to last a week."[34] By noon, Stanley could report being in a "now silent and blackened valley" and feeling satisfied that the Wanyaturu had been left "to ponder on the harsh fate they had drawn upon themselves by their greed, treachery and murder, and attack on peaceful strangers."[35] Their dead totaled thirty-five, although Stanley admitted the number killed must have been much higher.[36] The expedition lost twenty-two men.

Pillagers located a bounty of badly needed food, including sorghum, millet, peas, beans, chickens, eggs, sheep, goats, honey, and the local beer, *pombe*.[37] A few miles beyond Vinyata, good fortune produced a regularly traveled road, although to where no one knew. It eventually led to a place called Mgongo Tembo, or elephant's back after the shape of a prominent rock, ruled by a friendly chief named Marema, who'd hosted Burton and Speke at a village farther south. With the onset of increasingly unsettled conditions there, Marema moved on, seeking safer conditions for his people. He found them among the peaceable Wanyilamba. During one of their conversations, the chief informed Stanley of Mirambo's presence in Usukuma, through which the expedition would have to pass on the way to Lake Victoria. Convinced that he couldn't afford a detour this time, Stanley opted to take his chances with Mirambo and set off for Usukuma on February 1.

The first leg of the journey produced more deaths from disease and more desertions, before a welcoming sight came into view at the Wembere River valley—a large plain teeming with wildlife. Given the unexpected opportunity, Stanley decided to spend a few days there to replenish the meat supply, while parties fanned out to see if they could find more to eat and locate deserters. Concerns about food finally ended when they encountered the Wasukuma. Closely related to the Wanyamwezi, they'd been blessed with a more bountiful country. At the first stop, on February 9, Stanley said,

> The products of the rich upland were . . . laid before our feet, and it must be conceded that the plenteous stores of grain, beans, potatoes, vetches, sesamum, millet, vegetables, such as melons and various garden herbs, honey, and

tobacco, which we were enabled to purchase . . . were merited by the members of the long-suffering expedition. The number of chickens goats that were slaughtered by the people was enormous. . . .

With the rewards they received, the Wangwana, and Wanyamwezi men, women, and children, revelled in the delights of repleted stomachs, and the voice of the gaunt monster, Hunger, was finally hushed.[38]

Joined by some fresh porters, a restored expedition set off again on February 13, with Stanley increasingly worried about the prospects of running into Mirambo. As a result, he decided to avoid heavily populated country and take a "jungle" road. Nothing of Mirambo or of his men was ever seen, and, indeed, on a couple of occasions, villagers mistook the expedition for Mirambo's army.

Among hospitable people who freely provided food, the pace of the march quickened. For the first time in quite a while, Stanley felt "free," adding that they "enjoyed something of the lordly feeling to which it is said man is born, but to which we had certainly been strangers between the ocean and the grassy plains of Usukuma."[39] At last, on February 27, after traveling more than 720 miles from Bagamoyo in 103 days, their destination came into view, and that night the expedition's members, now numbering 166, bedded down next to a small village called Kageyi on the south shore of Lake Victoria. While not a churchgoer, Stanley did believe in the Christian God, as is revealed by a journal entry expressing thanks for having made it to this point:

This day we dedicated to rest and a feeling of gratitude to Almighty God who has wonderfully preserved us through manifold dangers, from ferocious savages whose fierce hearts thirsted for our blood, from the sickness which has overtaken so many of our fellows, from hunger which has killed numbers of our people. 'Tis true we are much reduced in pride of numbers but thanks to Providence who has watched over us night and day we are still strong to cope with robbers and fractious people, though my prayer is that we meet no more, for to conquer costs many a valuable life. We can barely believe that our long march to this place has terminated, or that we have not tomorrow to brace ourselves for another day's long march. How my weak and sick and wearied men rejoice at the sweet repose before them. They celebrate it with songs and shouts, while I deep in my inmost heart feel nothing but devoutest thanks to my God.[40]

The local chief Kaduma welcomed them, and while the men recuperated, Stanley set about readying the *Lady Alice* for sailing the lake. The rigors of the journey had caused some damage to the boat, but nothing that couldn't be easily repaired. However, useful information and guides eluded Stanley. The villagers knew nothing about the extent of the lake, and they expressed fears of people living along its shores. Some were described as "gifted with tails," another group supposedly "trained enormous and fierce dogs for war," and a third was said to be "a tribe of cannibals, who preferred human flesh to all other kinds of meat."[41] Undeterred as usual, Stanley selected ten of his own men to make up the crew, and on March 8, 1875, they headed the *Lady Alice* eastward along the southern shore of an arm of the lake Stanley named Speke Gulf. In this he followed the usual practice of using European names to designate newly described features of the landscape. It didn't end until 1901, when the Royal Geographical Society issued a publication titled "On the Giving of Names to Newly Discovered Places" that encouraged the use of local names instead. In the meantime, Stanley-given names became more common on late-nineteenth-century maps of eastern and central Africa. The earlier run-in with the RGS may have induced him to go overboard just to show that he'd been where he said he had.

Save a brief storm, the several days required to reach the eastern end of the gulf passed without mishap. By following the northern shore on the return trip, Stanley confirmed that Ukerewe was an island, not an extension of the mainland as some suspected, and once they reached waters, it became apparent that Speke Gulf was part of Lake Victoria. Some fishermen demonstrated that people thereabouts didn't stray far from home by saying eight years would be needed to round the lake. A new hazard presented itself: colonies of hippopotami lolling in the water. While sometimes they paid no attention to the approach of the boat, at other times it sent them into an attack mode that required deft maneuvering to avoid being overturned. The human situation changed along the densely populated coast surrounding Kavirondo Gulf. Stanley wanted to go ashore to learn the names of some of the villages, but a large gathering of men carrying spears caused him to think better of it. The security of a small, unpopulated island a safe distance away seemed a wiser choice.

On March 24 the boat reached the northeastern end of the lake, requiring a turn to the west. Patient negotiations at the village of Muwanda produced vegetables and meat; however, the next day a storm blew up, forcing the crew to take cover on a small nearby island. Shortly after they landed, several canoes came calling, and upon accepting a bead necklace, the paddlers provided information about the surrounding countryside. Then a third canoe appeared with a request from their chief to move the *Lady Alice* closer to shore. Suspicious of the reason, Stanley opted to stay put. In the morning a larger party of paddlers repeated the request, and not liking their looks, Stanley weighed anchor, pretending to comply. The canoes followed, but the *Lady Alice* in full sail quickly outdistanced them.

A tricky situation at Mombiti didn't end as peacefully. The resident Bavuma islanders first hurled stones at the boat, and then on March 28 an attempt to trade turned ugly. According to Stanley, during a bargaining session for potatoes with members of one canoe party,

> other canoes came up and blocked the boat, while the people began to lay hands on everything; but we found their purpose out, and I warned the canoes away with my gun. They jeered at this and immediately seized their spears and shields, while one canoe hastened away with some beads they had stolen, and which a man insolently held up to my view, and invited us to catch him. At the sight of this I fired, and the man fell dead in his canoe. The others prepared to launch their spears, but the repeating rifle was too much for the crowd of warriors who had hastened like pirates to rob us. Three were shot dead, and as they retreated my elephant rifle smashed their canoes, the result of which we saw in the confusion attending each shot. After a few shots from the big gun we continued on our way.[42]

The Bavuma had had enough, and the next day, after passing the outlet of the Victoria Nile, the *Lady Alice* entered Buganda waters. A warm reception and an offer to take them to Mutesa greeted their arrival.

On April 2, Stanley reported seeing six canoes, crowded with men, coming round a point. They wore white garments like the Zanzibaris and turned out to be subjects of Mutesa who brought his greetings and a request for Stanley to come for a visit as soon as possible. Pausing only long enough to partake of a much appreciated feast, the voyage resumed, with nearly two hundred escorts accompanying the *Lady Alice* as she sailed toward the man reputed to be the most powerful ruler in all of Central Africa.

At Usavara, Stanley met the *katikiro,* Buganda's equivalent of a prime minister, who, amid much ceremony, led him to a newly constructed hut. After being questioned and fed, Stanley and his men received instructions to clean up for an audience with Mutesa. Speke had had many meetings with him during his four month stay in 1862, and the picture he painted was of a tyrant, capable of about any kind of brutality on a whim. The now fully mature thirteenth ruler of Buganda made a different impression on Stanley. He described Mutesa as "an intelligent and distinguished prince" who garnered honor and respect rather than fear and came away convinced that "if aided in time by virtuous philanthropists, [Mutesa] will do more for Central Africa than fifty years of Gospel teaching, unaided by such authority, can

Mutesa's royal reception at Usavara as remembered by Stanley. *Henry M. Stanley, Through the Dark Continent (New York: Harper & Brothers Publishers, 1878).*

do." As ruler of an estimated nearly three million people occupying seventy thousand square miles of territory, he could become "the possible fruition of Livingstone's hopes" for civilizing equatorial Africa.[43]

Leisure and further conversations with Mutesa occupied the next several days. Stanley's ability to speak some Kiswahili helped the two men understand one another and build rapport. When the royal party set off for the return to the palace atop Rubaga Hill, near present-day Kampala, Stanley followed. Three hours of travel revealed a very different country than any they had seen so far, one of green hills and clear streams in which round huts "were buried deep in dense bowers of plantains which filled the air with the odour of their mellow rich fruit."[44] Stanley's appreciation of the country's beauty and wealth and his respect for the people grew with each passing day. He saw a future "dressed in the robe of civilization"; a land with church spires on each hill, of "waving fields of grain," of "smiling affluence and plenty," the bays lined by sailing vessels; and "full of sounds of craftsmen at their work, the roar manufactories and foundries and the ever buzzing noise of enterprising industry."[45]

At a meeting with Mutesa on April 10, in which he attempted to show him Christianity's merits over those of Islam, Stanley heard about the presence of another European in the capital. He thought the man must be Cameron, but he discovered instead Col. M. Linant de Bellefonds, who'd come with forty soldiers from Gordon's headquarters in Equatoria to establish commercial relationships between Egypt and Buganda. The two struck up a friendship, and Stanley gave de Bellefonds his dispatches for the *Daily Telegraph* and the *Herald*, anticipating that they would get to the papers quicker via the Nile route. A fanciful story was invented about how the dispatches reached their destination. It had de Bellefonds and all but four of his party being killed by the Bari as they attempted to return to headquarters in Equatoria. Miraculously, some of Gordon's troops were said to have found the letters, in one version in de Bellefonds's boots. While de Bellefonds died at the hands of the Bari, this came after the dispatches had already been sent.[46]

One of the dispatches proved to be especially crucial. It included an appeal for missionaries to continue the work of conversion just begun. Stanley wanted those of the "practical" type who can "cure . . . diseases, construct dwellings, understands agriculture and can turn his hand to anything, like a sailor." Because of all the export possibilities, including ivory and coffee, he felt the costs of building a mission station would be repaid "tenfold."[47] Publication of the dispatch on November 25, 1875, created enormous excitement. Donations flowed in, and a year and a half later the first Church Missionary Society representative entered Buganda. Others soon followed, including the Catholic White Fathers. Mutesa welcomed them and invited Europeans to visit as suggested by Stanley. A shrewd man with great ambition, he felt they could be useful in widening Buganda's sphere of influence and consolidating his own position. As for the missionaries, they found a fertile field for converts. Due to scandals and intrigues, many Baganda no longer trusted or believed their traditional priests and thus responded positively when a new religion became available.[48] The new religion, whether Catholic or Protestant, also promised them education, a lure that to this day wins converts all over Africa.

Stanley next wanted to explore Lake Albert, which necessitated collecting the rest of the expedition from Kageyi. De Bellefonds went along as far as Usavara. He'd grown fond of Stanley, calling him a "fine-hearted fellow, a frank, excellent comrade, and a first-rate traveler," who'd be missed like a brother.[49] The return trip went from bad to worse. First, only ten of the thirty canoes promised as an escort showed up for the scheduled departure from Usavara on April 17. Magassa, in effect the admiral of the Bugandan fleet, said not to worry because the rest could be secured at the nearby Sese Islands. After he left to get them, the *Lady Alice* and two canoes coasted slowly southward. Magassa caught up with them on the evening of the 21st, without bringing a single new canoe. In fact, he now had only five, the others having been abandoned as unfit. Magassa departed, saying he would soon bring the full compliment of canoes.

With food about to run out, the *Lady Alice* put into shore near the village of Makongo a few days later. Dawn found the camp surrounded "by a large number of natives who came armed to the teeth with bow, spear & shield."[50] Stanley had entered a disturbed border zone between Buganda and Buhaya only nominally under Mutesa's control. As in Ituru, more often than not, strangers meant trouble, and the island's chief stated that in order to avoid problems, the party should leave immediately for nearby Busira Island. He promised to send food when they got there. Stanley complied with the request and from Busira spied Magassa in the distance, leading fourteen canoes. A messenger hurried to tell him to come the next morning, as Makongo had provided only enough bananas for one day and they urgently needed more food. By 10:00 A.M., with Magassa still nowhere in sight, Stanley proceeded to what he called Alice Island (probably Kerebe).[51] Although the people acted friendly, he thought the asking price for food exorbitant, and thus decided to see if it might be more reasonable on Bumbire Island.

During the approach to the island, Stanley noticed a small cove, and by now desperate for food, he decided to risk going ashore, even though shouts could be heard coming from a large group of Bahaya assembled on a ridge overlooking the cove. They must have been forewarned of the party's coming. As the crew brought the *Lady Alice* onto the beach, the men from the hill rushed toward them. Stanley prepared his guns and ordered the boat back into the water. The crew didn't move, he said, either because they thought him "too suspicious" or because of "their dread of starvation." Just when it looked as though entreaties had diffused the situation, several Bahaya pulled the boat farther up the beach. An attack seemed likely, and Stanley said he readied his pistols but was told by his men to be "patient." He listened and things calmed down, with Shekka the leader of Bumbire saying the party should remain until the local chief, Antari, was informed of its presence. As an act of good faith, Stanley gave Shekka several pieces of cloth and some beads. Suddenly, without warning, the *Lady Alice*'s oars were seized, apparently to make sure the newcomers stayed put. After this, the Bahaya departed, only to return a short while later in even greater force to demand more cloth and some pieces of iron. Lacking the latter, Stanley offered twenty cloth pieces for the oars. According to him, they replied, "prepare for war," and to make the threat real, the warriors advanced "with drawn bows." Stanley again instructed his men to get the *Lady Alice* into the water, despite having no oars. This time they did so immediately, and when free of the shore, he began using the elephant gun to keep canoes from pursuing them. All told, the volleys may have killed as many as eight Bahaya, including, he later learned, a woman and an infant. Then, rounding the cove, two canoes closed in, shutting off their escape route. Stanley fired at them and claimed both canoes sank, with five or six of the occupants dead from bullets or drowning. After that the *Lady Alice* sailed to safety.[52]

Torn-up seats and footrests served as paddles. Nature made progress even more difficult by alternating between periods of dead calm and severe storms, and on several occasions the *Lady Alice* almost capsized. Finally, during the afternoon of April 30, exhausted and nearly starved, they stumbled ashore on an uninhabited island near the entrance to Bangwe Bay Stanley

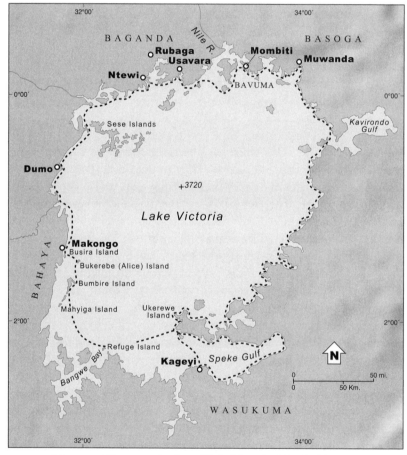

Map 5.2   Circumnavigation of Lake Victoria, March–May 1875

named Refuge. It yielded four ducks and some green bananas and berries to dampen gnawing hunger pangs. A second day of rest and more bananas restored enough strength to allow the journey to resume. Stone throwing kept the boat away from the shore the next day, but a storm forced a landing on Ukerewe Island. Fortunately, one of the crew hailed from nearby, and the inhabitants provided more than enough food to satisfy everyone's needs. A hard nine hours of rowing brought the *Lady Alice* to Kageyi on May 5. During the circumnavigation's nearly two months and one thousand miles, Stanley's two primary goals had been accomplished. In terms of exploration, Lake Victoria was shown to be only one body of water. For this alone, Rawlinson said Stanley deserved "a very high place among African discoverers."[53] More important in the long run, contact with Mutesa had been established.

Stanley noticed several of the shore party's members missing. According to Frank Pocock, Fred Barker had died quite suddenly twelve days earlier from a mysterious disease marked by an excessive drop in temperature. A cairn with a stone simply inscribed F. B. 1875 STANLEY marked the grave.[54] Dysentery claimed the lives of five others, including the intrepid Mabruki Speke, who'd worked for Stanley in 1871–1872 and, before him, Burton, Speke, Grant, and Livingstone. On a more positive note, everyone else looked reasonably healthy. They'd eaten well, thanks in large measure to continued cordial relations with Kaduma. Stanley certainly needed his fair share of food, having become a virtual skeleton at 115 pounds. Yet he managed to lose seven more during a five-day bout with fever.

With Magassa still missing, and harboring suspicions that he would likely never show up, Stanley considered taking an overland route to Buganda. Reports of warfare and generally unsettled conditions along the way scuttled the option, and so while he convalesced from yet another attack of fever, Kaduma and Frank went to Ukerewe to find out if its ruler, Rukonge, might be able to furnish the needed canoes. They returned with fifty to bring the full expedition to Ukerewe. Fearful that a side trip like this might delay progress indefinitely, Stanley decided to send the canoes back and go see Rukonge himself. A series of negotiations during the first week of June produced an agreement for twenty-three canoes.

As per Rukonge's instructions, Stanley ordered the paddles taken away and secured when all the canoes reached Kagevi. The chief knew his people feared crossing the lake, and so he told the crews that their mission was to bring the expedition's members to Ukerewe. He also knew that once they learned the truth, at least some of them would refuse to go with Stanley, and thus the deal included a proviso that anyone wishing to return home could do so freely. All opted for home, and ten canoes had to be given over to the job of taking them back. Stanley hoped some of the men would change their minds, but after a week of no news, much less volunteers, from Ukerewe, he decided the time had come to start for Buganda. The first contingent left on June 21. The others would follow when a secure camp had been built on Refuge Island.

Within hours, the canoes, most of which proved to be rotten, began sinking. Frantic efforts saved their occupants, and they, along with salvaged cargo, found safety on a nearby island. All told, five canoes were lost, and it required several days to replace them, repair the others, and purchase additional food. This delayed getting to Refuge Island until June 24. Stanley left a small contingent to construct the camp while he and the others returned to Kageyi. Along the way, three canoes got separated from the others, and although two eventually showed up with all aboard, nothing could be learned of the third. After waiting more than a week for it, Stanley bade farewell to Kaduma and Kageyi for the last time. Only a year later did he learn that the men in the third canoe had ditched it and returned to Unyanyembe.

Illness overtook Stanley, and he spent the first five days on Refuge Island confined to his hut. As a result, the next leg of the journey to Mahyiga Island didn't start until July 18. Three days distant and only five miles south of Bumbire, Stanley decided to build a particularly strong camp, thinking that unless the Bumbire islanders "made amends of their cruelty and treachery," he would "make war on them."[55] For amends he demanded that Shekka and two subchiefs be handed over to his custody. To make sure this happened, Stanley took the ruler of an adjacent island and several others hostage. The price for their release would be the three men. Only Shekka could be located, and when he was delivered, Stanley ordered him put in chains.

Meanwhile, between July 27 and 29, sixteen large Baganda canoes carrying nearly five hundred men pulled into Mahyiga. Mutesa had heard rumors about Stanley and his men having perished on Lake Victoria, but doubting their veracity, he sent out search parties to find the truth. News of the situation brewing at Bumbire prompted those nearby to go to Mahyiga immediately. Buoyed by this imposing addition to his force, Stanley sent a message to Antari stating that he would release Shekka upon payment of "5 bullocks, 30 bill-hooks and 40 spears." If they failed to comply, he vowed to "punish the natives of Bumbireh" and take Shekka to Mutesa for whatever the kabaka might wish to do with him.[56]

Antari's rejection came August 3, along with a promise to attack if Stanley failed to release Shekka and the other hostages. The threat became real when a group of Baganda sent to collect provisions on the mainland opposite Bumbire walked into an ambush that killed one and seriously wounded eight others. A discussion took place that night concerning what course of action to follow, and with the full Anglo-American Expedition now at Mahyiga to join the Baganda, Stanley decided the time was ripe for revenge. Consequently, the next day he loaded 280 men, fifty carrying rifles, into eighteen canoes for the showdown at Bumbire. Seeing an opponent well prepared for battle, Stanley first ordered the canoes to turn broadside out of spear and arrow range and have the riflemen fire at will. After about an hour of taking heavy casualties, the Bahaya retreated from the shore to a nearby hill slope that remained within range. The barrage continued for approximately another hour. Sensing an opportunity for a decisive victory, Stanley instructed his men to move toward shore and feign a landing. This drew the remaining Bahaya back down the slope and into a full fusillade that shattered their resistance. At least forty-two of them were killed and more than one hundred wounded, while the combined AAE-Baganda forces suffered only two minor injuries.[57]

The following morning a party swollen to 685 people carried by thirty-seven canoes and the *Lady Alice* departed Mahyiga for Buganda. Those on Bumbire quietly watched as they passed by, and on August 12, having met with many jubilant receptions along the way—news of the victory had spread almost instantly—Stanley disembarked the expedition at Dumo, the village chosen as the base camp for an exploration of Lake Albert. In addition to the lake's size, the issue of its relationship to the Nile remained unsettled. In particular, did the river, as some surmised, flow both into and out of the lake?

Dumo swirled with talk of an impending war between Buganda and Buvuma, where Stanley had earlier run into difficulty. In need of guides for the journey to Lake Albert, he set off for Rubaga to see about securing them before hostilities began, taking along only those needed for manning the *Lady Alice*. Frank and Manwa Sera could be trusted to keep order in Dumo. A key part of his strategy involved convincing Mutesa to establish a trade route to the lake, so that the Nile could be used for exports and imports, thus reducing reliance on caravans to the coast.[58] Upon hearing that the *kabaka* had already left for the front, Stanley altered his course to meet him there. With several hundred Bavuma canoes said to be patrolling the lake, he didn't want to risk losing the *Lady Alice* and left it at Ntewi before going to Jinja, the army's gathering place. Mutesa greeted him warmly noting that he couldn't supply guides with a war about to start. At its conclusion, though, he promised to provide not just guides but a whole army as an escort to Lake Albert. A powerful show of force would be needed for safe passage through the rival kingdoms of Unyoro and Ankole.[59]

Stanley estimated the Baganda army at 150,000 men, and as it and a cortege of fifty thousand women, plus large numbers of children and slaves, moved out on August 27, he followed. The Bavuma chose to assemble in force on Ingira Island, and Mutesa planned to capture it from a mainland point, just seven hundred yards away, before invading their Bavuma Island homeland. Despite his overwhelming numerical superiority, the *kabaka* worried about having fewer war canoes and men far less skilled at fighting on water than the opponent. To overcome this deficiency and hasten the war's end, Stanley suggested building a rock causeway to the island. He estimated it wouldn't take more than five days to complete. Vigorous work began almost immediately. After five days the causeway extended only 130 yards, mainly because it measured close to one hundred feet wide instead of the recommended ten feet. Stanley's role changed from adviser to active participant when he reportedly killed five Bavuma with cannon fire and two with rifle shots on September 6.[60] Mutesa's decision to pursue a negotiated settlement was scuttled when the Bavuma massacred all fifteen delegates as soon as they reached Ingira. A long, difficult war now seemed inevitable.

Stanley wrote a letter at this time that shows how much the post-Livingstone experience still rankled and how desirous he was to prove himself to others. Following a few brief comments on the local scenery, he went on to say,

> On Lake Albert I hope to meet other whites, so that there may be many witnesses of my being in Africa. I wish I could meet with some of those doubting Thomases here, in some wilderness. Had Cameron emerged from Africa yet? If so what success has he had? If I come through, his journey will be a mere tour compared with mine; though if he arrives in England safe he will deserve all the applause he can get. I am, however, not labouring for applause. I am labouring to establish a confidence in the minds of right-minded people, which my vicious foes robbed me of.[61]

During lulls in the action, Mutesa and Stanley spent much time conversing, and one of the things they talked about involved the relative merits of Christianity and Islam. Stanley thought the *kabaka* had earlier become a Muslim, but while he was interested in Islamic theology to the point of learning Arabic in order to read the *Qur'an,* Mutesa never converted. Stanley presented him with an abridged version of the Bible translated into Kiswahili and felt increasingly confident about having convinced the ruler of Buganda to adopt Christianity. Dallington Muftaa, a teenager who'd joined the expedition from the Universities Mission in Zanzibar, did the translation, which was copied by one of Mutesa's scribes. Dallington also acted as an interpreter when necessary. According to Stanley, the *kabaka* "announced his determination to adhere to his new religion." As testimony he would have a church built, and "do all in his power to promote the propagation of Christian sentiments among his people, and to conform to the best of his ability to the holy precepts contained in the Bible."[62]

With no peace in sight, Mutesa sent some forty canoes against Ingira. Since the resulting battle left the situation unresolved, he followed with an all-out attack by 230 canoes. This, too, failed, as did two more battles. As feared, the Bavuma showed their superiority on the water. And now the Basoga seemed ready to attack on land. There was talk of retreat, and Stanley said he urged Mutesa to fight on until both the Bavuma and Basoga agreed to pay tribute. He'd even devised a "floating fort" armed with one hundred musket-shooters to strengthen the Baganda hand, hoping it might help end a war that looked like it could last at least another six months. Although the Bavuma mostly avoided the fort, they hadn't the manpower to sustain the war much longer. Word that the Baganda were planning to launch a major offensive convinced them to give up the fight, and on October 13 they agreed to pay tribute to Mutesa. Stanley said "glad shouts" rang out from both sides, and a grand celebration took up most of the next day. At its completion, the former adversaries camped together.[63]

As if there had not already been enough carnage, a fire raged through the camp during the early-morning hours, forcing its thousands, which included Stanley and his men, into panic-stricken flight. Convinced that Mutesa ordered the fire set to punish the Bavuma, many of whom were sick and wounded and could not escape, he refused an offer to join the royal party. The *kabaka* denied any involvement and sent a message "that he had arrested several persons suspected of having fired the camp and that he himself had suffered the loss of goods and women in the flames."[64] Satisfied by Mutesa's disclaimer, Stanley agreed to meet him on the other side of the Victoria Nile.

Stanley marveled at Buganda's agricultural productivity, based on soils that appeared to have "inexhaustible fertility." With Buganda's population of several million, the market potential for European goods seemed enormous, and he thought a railway connecting the lakes of the region would be a great catalyst to development, just as railroads had been in Britain and America. Henceforth, building railroads would be right at the top of his priorities for Africa.

Discussions with Mutesa continued. Religion again was a favorite subject, although his conversion to Christianity now seemed "nominal" to Stanley. Mutesa, in fact, hadn't converted. He recognized the value an alliance with Europeans might bring, both in securing Buganda's dominance over neighboring states and in fending off Egyptian advances from Equatoria, and thus manipulated Stanley, just as he had the Arabs. Nevertheless, the *kabaka* kept to his end of the bargain by starting work on the promised church by the time Stanley left on November 12 to collect the *Lady Alice* from Ntewi for the return to Dumo.

On November 26 the journey to rendezvous with the Baganda military escort under General Sambuzi began. When they reached the agreed-upon point at the Katonga River, no one was there, and more than a week passed before word came of Sambuzi having started on his way. To speed things up, Stanley took the expedition across the half-mile-wide, grass-and-papyrus-choked Katonga, only to wait until December 22 for Sambuzi and the majority of the Baganda to make an appearance. The rest of Sambuzi's force had gone directly to the frontier settlement of Kawanga, where final preparations for the journey to Lake Albert took place. As they departed for Bunyoro on New Year's Day 1876, Stanley estimated Baganda numbers at 2,800, including five hundred women and children, to add to his own force of 180. Of the roughly one thousand fighters on hand, one hundred carried rifles.[65]

Unyoro presented a striking visual contrast to Buganda. Instead of a landscape dominated by "soft pastoral scenes," it displayed mountain masses of great altitude—bare and serrated hilly ridges, isolated craggy hills, separated by a rolling country, whose surface often presented great sheets of ironstone rock, mixed with fragments of granite."[66] For food, sweet potatoes and greens replaced bananas and plantains. Along the way, Frank Pocock said they passed a summit "crowned with snow."[67] Stanley didn't mention the snow, but instead described a "blue mass" in the distance, which he named Gordon Bennett. Years later he would give it another name. The track along the north side of the Katonga River took them through a largely uninhabited section of Unyankole, characterized by cold nights and mornings foggy enough to restrict vision to fifty yards. Stanley found the scenery spectacular and labeled one section "the Switzerland of Africa" because "Peaks, cones, mountain humps, and dome-like hills shot up in every direction, while ice-cold streams rolled between riven and dismantled rocks, or escaped beneath natural bridges of rock, with furious roar."[68]

To this point no opposition had been encountered; indeed, the inhabitants often secreted themselves or fled at the approach of the large, well-armed force. The journey ended January 11 on a plateau overlooking what

Stanley thought to be Lake Albert, although it turned out to be the much smaller Lake George. He may have caused the confusion by asking to be taken to Luta Nzige, a Kiganda term for a body of water that eats locusts, as they often perished there by the thousands when swarming.[69] A treacherous-looking escarpment led to the shore, and while some of the men were scouting for a safe way to negotiate it, a large contingent of Banyoro warriors suddenly appeared on the crest of a nearby hill. Under their king, Kabarega, the Banyoro had become the dominant regional power and frequently sent forces on cattle raids of Banyankole villages. Sambuzi tried to convince them that they'd come only to explore the lake and would be leaving in three days. Suspecting more malevolent intentions, their leader replied that since the Banyoro were already "fighting with white men," war could be expected "on the morrow."[70] "White men" in this instance meant Samuel Baker, who led an Egyptian army into Bunyoro in 1872, and Baker's successor, Col. Gordon, whose forces periodically made sorties into the country's northern frontier.

Afraid a fight would be a costly one, many of the Baganda expressed a desire to go home immediately. Stanley responded by asking Sambuzi to allow two days for exploring the lake. When reports came back indicating that the descent to the lakeshore would be extremely difficult, perhaps even dangerous, entreaties to leave intensified. Stanley again argued for two more days, promising that afterward he would release the Baganda from all their obligations and give them half his trade goods to boot. Sambuzi refused the offer and said those under him would depart first thing in the morning This left Stanley with no option other than to join the retreat.

By marching from before dawn until sunset, they re-entered Buganda on January 17, having fended off only occasional forays at rear guards that did little damage. After the Baganda departed, Stanley sent a letter to Mutesa complaining about Sambuzi's failure to do as instructed and accusing him of stealing three loads of beads. The *kabaka* responded with an apology and an offer to provide sixty thousand, and, if needed, a hundred thousand, men for another try at Lake Albert. Dallington, who'd stayed behind as a kind of Christian emissary to the court, wrote a note urging the same thing.[71] Stanley, however, had already decided to head for Kafurro in Karagwe, where Arabs maintained a supply depot. From there the quest for the source of the Nile could continue. Furthermore, Stanley no longer trusted the Baganda. Their actions convinced him that "Henceforth the Expedition should be governed by one will, guided by one man, who was resolute not to subject himself, or time, to any man's caprice, power, or love."[72] That one man, of course, was Stanley.

After a series of relatively uneventful yet tedious marches, the expedition made it to Kafurro on February 25. Thanks to a trader named Hamed Ibrahim, Stanley met Rumanika two days later at his capital about three miles away. He seemed the exact opposite of Mutesa. Instead of having a "nervous and intense temperament," Stanley described him as displaying the "pleasing character of a gentle father" to go along with an imposing six-foot, six-inch stature. Known for his hospitality, he'd cared for an extremely ill Grant, while Speke went on to Buganda. Rumanika gave permission for an exploration of Karagwe, reportedly saying, "It was a land . . . white men ought to know."[73] Stanley started with a nearby lake that led via twisting channels to other lakes. It was clear that they all lay along a river, one he called the Alexandra Nile (after Princess Alexandra, the wife of Edward, Prince of Wales [later King Edward VII]) and that this river in all likelihood represented the "Mother of the River at Jinja," as the Baganda claimed. He'd found the Kagera River.

Next came a journey to the hot springs at Mtagata, some thirty-five miles north of Kafurro. Reputedly possessing healing properties, its waters drew many visitors. Stanley enjoyed several relaxing baths but had little good to say about drinking the water. Instead of acting, as claimed, like a laxative, he blamed it for triggering a bout of fever. Back in Kafurro, Stanley tried to elicit some useful geographical information from Rumanika and others. What they said sounded mostly like fable, and he decided the time had come to start moving again. The source of the Nile awaited discovery, and maybe another way to Lake Albert could be found.

When the expedition picked up stakes on March 26, it included three of Rumanika's sons to serve as guides through Karagwe. Stanley's opinion of Rumanika had grown even more positive, especially when compared with Mutesa. As he noted in his journal, "During my wanderings through his country, his name was all sufficient to provide protection & to ensure noble hospitality, and though he is so mild & gentle, readier obedience is paid to him by his subjects than to the stern implacable Mtesa by the Waganda."[74]

At the southern border of Karagwe, Stanley had to figure out where to go next. Exploring Rwanda was dismissed because of reputed Batutsi hostility toward strangers. Instead he decided to return to Ujiji to settle the question of whether Lake Tanganyika possessed an outlet. The most direct route passed through Uha, which presented the prospect of one *honga* demand after another. They couldn't afford this, as local food shortages had taken a large toll on trade goods. A longer journey through less populous country would be necessary.

Their route took them across the watershed separating the streams flowing toward Lake Victoria from those headed via the Malagarasi River to Lake

Tanganyika, and on April 13, they reached northern Unyamwezi. After a few days to rest and resupply, the journey resumed, with Bull, the last of the five dogs, the only casualty. The eulogy Stanley penned captures the special roles companion dogs played during his journeys and also displays the melodramatic style readers often loved and critics hated:

> Poor Dog! Good and faithful service he had done me! Who more rejoiced than he to hear the rifle-shot ringing through deep woods! Who more loudly applauded success than he with his deep, mellow bark! What long forest-tracks of tawny plains and series of mountain ranges had he not traversed! How he plunged through jungle and fen, morass and stream! In the sable blackness of the night his voice warned off marauders and prowling beasts from the sleeping camp. His growl responded to the hiddeous jabber of the greedy hyena, and the snarling leopard did not dismay him. He amazed the wonderous savages with his bold eyes and bearing, and by his courageous front caused them to retreat before him; and right bravely did he help to repel the Wanyaturu from our camp in Ituru. Farewell, thou glory of thy race! Rest from thy labours in the silent forest! Thy feet shall no more hurry up the hill or cross the mead and plain; thy form shall rustle no more through the grasses, or be plunging to explore the brake; thou shalt no longer dash after me across the savannahs, for thou art gone to the grave, like the rest of thy companions![75]

The ready availability of food and small tribute demands made for "capital marches" of ten to fifteen miles per day. Then on April 18, they encountered people busy making preparations for an expected attack by Mirambo. Determined to keep going forward, Stanley finally met the man he dubbed the "the African Bonaparte" four days later at Serombo, a substantial village of fifteen hundred houses.[76] Anticipating a tyrant, he instead found "A handsome, regular-featured, mild-voiced, soft-spoken man, with what one might call a 'meek' demeanor, very generous and open-handed." They became blood brothers, exchanged gifts, and parted the next day, in Stanley's view, "on the very best terms with each other."[77] Stanley respected strength and good manners no matter the source.

Beyond Serombo the possibility of being attacked by Wangoni became a concern. Even Mirambo paid them tribute. Many *ruga-ruga*—the term now used generally to refer to any kind of predatory band—also operated in the vicinity, with villages surrounded by stockades and recently abandoned farmlands giving ample testimony to the wars and raids afflicting this part of Unyamwezi. A watchful eye had to be kept, and while a few anxious moments did occur, the march continued without major incident. The five guides Mirambo provided undoubtedly helped smooth the way.

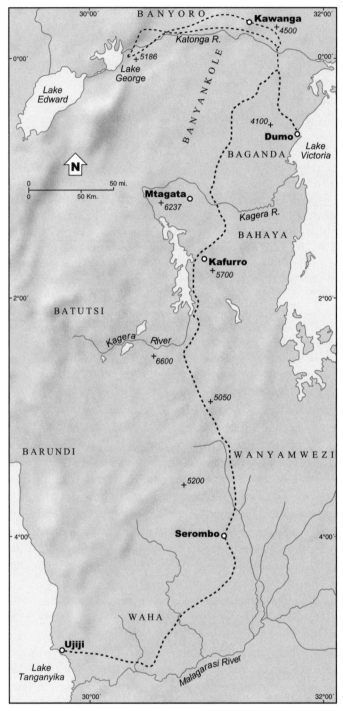

Map 5.3   To and From Lake George to Ujiji, November 1875–May 1876

On May 20 the expedition crossed the Malagarasi River north of where it bends westward, and a week later Stanley found himself in Ujiji. The place seemed pretty much the same to him except that Livingstone, "the grand old hero, whose presence once filled Ujiji with such absorbing interest . . . was gone!"[78] Something else vital was missing as well: mail. The lack of letters and newspapers in a year and a half made the task of figuring out an itinerary more difficult.

Stanley knew of Cameron's claim that the Lukuga River, on the other side of Lake Tanganyika, was a likely outlet. However, evidence obtained from two veteran travelers, including Cameron's guide, and from Arabs familiar with the area, suggested otherwise. Furthermore, the lake's water level clearly stood higher than it had in 1871, and longtime residents told him that the rise had been going on for quite a while. An outlet would preclude such a thing from happening, and reports indicated the Lukuga was too slow moving to be one. Stanley thought it might just be an arm of the lake. Still, he decided to withhold challenging Cameron until he'd had a look for himself.[79] The mission began on June 11, using the *Lady Alice* and a large teak canoe to carry Stanley, thirteen of his best men, and two guides from Ujiji. He could have cut diagonally across the lake but instead decided to go south to its end in order to do more exploring.

Some tense moments followed a couple of days of uneventful sailing. The first occurred when a band of *ruga-ruga* strolled into camp during a feast featuring two zebras shot by Stanley. After accepting some meat and having a smoke, they left without incident. Then the next night some sixty armed men decided to make themselves guests. Sensing that matters might turn ugly in the morning, Stanley arranged a quiet departure before they awoke. A third tense moment took place at the village of Kibwesa two days later. The guides from Ujiji said they'd been there to trade five weeks earlier, but the village now showed no signs of life. Stanley feared a trap and instructed the men to approach it cautiously. Six corpses lay along the path, and the village proved to be abandoned, the remaining occupants apparently having left in haste, "for all the articles that constitute the furniture of African families lay scattered in such numbers around us that an African museum might have been stocked."[80] No one could figure out what might have happened, especially since a ten-foot-deep ditch surrounded the village and the view allowed easy detection of an approaching enemy.

After that, uneventful days again became the norm, allowing Stanley time to take numerous measurements and draw detailed sketches of the shoreline. At the lake's southern end he saw more evidence of its rise, as well as the point from which Livingstone left on his last journey. Although a storm caused the canoe to be beached, the *Lady Alice* made it safely to the Lukuga on July 15. Reconnaissance found no current flowing through the narrow, papyrus-choked channel in either direction; however, Stanley concluded that if the lake kept rising, the Lukuga would breach the clogged channel and pour to the west. In other words, it would become an effluent if it wasn't one now. Less than three years later, Joseph Thomson proved Stanley's surmise correct, as he found the Lukuga flowing so swiftly toward the Lualaba River that "not for any reward would the canoe-men venture into it."[81]

The Watumbwe and Waholo-holo on the western side of the lake turned out to be friendly. By way of contrast, a party of Wabembe didn't welcome the strangers. Along with what Stanley called Burton Gulf, now Maganza Bay, a brief encounter took place in which he reportedly shot and killed four of them and wounded another. This ended the exploration, and the *Lady Alice* headed back across to Ujiji, which it reached on July 31. The success of the journey led Stanley to boast that

> Lake Tanganyika, despite its extreme length, is to be subject no more to doubts and fanciful hypotheses, for it has been circumnavigated and measured and its enormous coast line laid down and fixed as accurately as a pretty good chronometer and solar observations will admit. Captain Burton's discovery is now completed whole, with no corner indefinite, no indentation unknown.[82]

And he had shown that the lake could be taken out of the Nile picture, which nevertheless remained incomplete because of uncertainties regarding the Lualaba. Did the river join the Nile, or did it become the Congo? Had Cameron already figured this out? Without news from the outside, Stanley couldn't know for sure. A trip to Nyangwe in Umanyema would be required to resolve the issue. How to proceed after that, however, remained uncertain to him, as is revealed in a letter to Alice Pike dated August 14, in which he noted,

> I am in the centre of Africa, and want to strike from here to the western ocean, the Atlantic, to come to *you*. The eastern half is done, the western half must be traversed now and it is an entirely new country. With good fortune I could reach the ocean in 9 months from the day I leave Ujiji, but I doubt whether it is to be done under the circumstances in that time. I permit myself to hope I can do it in a year. I am not sure whether I shall attempt to reach the Western Ocean, or to reach some known point on the Congo, and return to Zanzibar. To reach some unknown point on the Congo would take five months or six from here. If I returned the same way I came I could travel quicker back than I could forward and this place might be reached again. That makes ten

months from here to Zanzibar . . . you see it takes time anyway. If I went westward & so to England, I might reach England in August or September 1877, if I returned to Zanzibar, by November or December 1877. If I adopted the first road I should have traversed 5,400 miles of Africa, and across by the latter I should have done 6,000 miles. The time engaged in doing it would be 3 years, just one year longer than I estimated. But estimates are invariably wrong, and it is not fair to tie a man down to mere estimates. We have all done our very best. No Expedition has done so much, or nearly so well as we have.[83]

A raging smallpox epidemic in Ujiji threatened to scuttle Stanley's plans. Among the victims were many of the town's Arabs and eleven of the Wangwana, ten of whom somehow managed to avoid being vaccinated at Rosako. And desertions continued apace. Stanley expected these during stops at Arab centers, where stories usually circulated about the dangers facing those who ventured into unknown lands. As for Umanyema, a persistent rumor claimed it to be full of cannibals. In an effort to avoid further losses, Stanley tried to get away from town as quickly as possible. A bout of fever foiled the attempt. When Stanley recovered sufficiently to call muster on August 25, he counted only 132 of the 170 who had walked into Ujiji with him. Fearing further desertions, he selected thirty-two of "Those who did not bear a good character for firmness and fidelity" and had them put into canoes for safe keeping, while the "firm and faithful" were allowed to go by land from Ujiji to the lake's crossing point at Kabogo.[84] In spite of these precautions, still others managed to steal away during the four-day journey, and more made the effort upon reaching the base camp at Mtowa on the other side of the lake. They included Kalulu, who disappeared on September 14. His freedom lasted only one day, as a search party found him hiding on an offshore island.

The expedition finally headed west on September 16, taking the usual Arab-Waswahili route to Nyangwe. Soon the difficulties of previous weeks began receding from view. Forests provided a bountiful supply of fruit, honey, and buffalo meat, while despite Arab warnings, the peoples they encountered showed no signs of hostility and traded willingly. The tranquillity caused Stanley to remark, "How thankful should men be, who fire for action, that there exists such a field as Africa for them!"[85] It was quite a change from when he told Livingstone about detesting the land "most heartily." Although ruined villages indicated the slave trade had come this way not too long ago, it seemed to have left the Uhombo basin untouched, for here Stanley found a "beautiful and productive place." He described it as literally overflowing with food: "There is palm butter for cooking—luscious

sugar cane to chew, fine goats & fat chickens for meat. Potatoes, beans, pea-
nuts, manioc, tender ears of corn for roasting, millet & matama grain for
flour, ripe beans, for dessert—banana & palm wine to drink and an abundance of soft-cool water to drink." As a bonus, the inhabitants were friendly
and willing to trade. They reportedly told him that if he should ever return,
he could expect the visit to be "much more pleasant."[86]

Beyond Uhombo the trail traversed more difficult country. Stanley
described nature here as "too robust and prolific":

> Her grasses are coarse, and wound like knives and needles; her reeds are tough
> and tall as bamboos; her creepers and convolvuli are of cable thickness and
> length; her thorns are hooks of steel; her trees shoot up to the height of a
> hundred feet. We find no pleasure in straying in search of wild flowers, and
> game is left undisturbed, because of the difficulty of moving about, for once
> the main path is left we find ourselves over head amongst thick, tough,
> unyielding, lacerating grass.[87]

At the border of Umanyema, the grasses gave way to a dense forest of a kind
Stanley had never seen before. He had trouble finding words to describe it.
Livingstone had passed this way, and at Kabambare Stanley engaged in several conversations with a chief who remembered well the eight long months
the doctor had spent here regaining his health. By now, however, the slave
and ivory trades had made the people more suspicious of strangers. Sometimes they simply fled, leaving food behind for the expedition to collect.
Smallpox had paid a recent visit, and intervillage wars raged. Stanley noted
that on three occasions he turned down requests to take sides in battles.[88]
The valley of the Luama River provided a convenient corridor for travel, and
by following it they reached the Lualaba on October 17. Stanley likened the
rivers' appearance to the Mississippi above where the Missouri enters and
claimed feeling "a secret rapture" while gazing at the "superb river" that
"Nature had kept hidden away from the world of science."[89]

Encouraged by having found the Lualaba so easily, the men picked up
their marching pace and covered eighteen miles the next day to find a group
of Arabs at the village of Tubanda, later called Kasongo. Among those present was Hamid bin Muhammed el Murjebi, better known as Tippu Tip
(sometimes seen as Tippu or Tippoo Tib), Umanyema's leading slave and
ivory trader. Born in 1837 on Zanzibar, he accompanied his father and uncles
on trading expeditions while still a youth and then around 1860 began independent operations. The origin of the nickname has never been determined.
He claimed to have gotten it from the "tip-tip" sound of his men's musket

fire during a battle. Another view attributed it to a persistent eye twitch. Stanley was impressed, describing Tippu Tip as

> the most remarkable man I had met among the Arabs, Wa-Swahili, and half-castes in Africa. He was neat in his person, his clothes were of spotless white, his fez-cap brand-new, his waist was encircled by a rich dowlé, his dagger was splendid with silver filigree, and his *tout ensemble* was that of an Arab gentle-man in very comfortable circumstances.[91]

And to Stanley's great relief, a rumor he'd heard in Ujiji proved to be true— Cameron had left the Lualaba because he had been unable to hire canoes to get him past the reputedly hostile peoples immediately downriver. Instead, he took Tippu Tip's advice and followed a more southerly route through Katanga toward Portuguese-held territory. Faced with the same predicament, Stanley concluded that he would need Tippu Tip's cooperation in order to proceed, whether along the river or overland. Accordingly, he proposed that the two join forces and travel together until reaching "the place where the river turns for good either to the west or east." Despite objections from family members about going with a European, Tippu Tip agreed to supply an escort for "a distance of sixty camps," in effect three months of travel, beyond Nyangwe for five thousand dollars according to Stanley or seven thousand as Tippu Tip said. Marching time would be four hours per day, and if Stanley decided not to continue, the money would still be owed. If Tippu Tip violated the agreement, he would get nothing.[92]

Their talks concluded, Stanley led the expedition to Nyangwe, a bustling market town divided into two sections. A modest one on the flatlands along the river housed the porters, whereas the larger and more copious section for the Arabs and Waswahili stood on two hills about forty feet above the river.

Stanley reported that his men were in great shape, in spite of having covered the 338 miles from Lake Tanganyika in forty-three days. No one had died or become seriously ill. The only injury of note occurred to Kalulu, who suffered an accidental, but non life-threatening, gunshot wound. The countryside around Nyangwe, however, didn't look so healthy. Ruined villages stood everywhere, their number suggesting to Stanley that a population once about 42,000 had been reduced to no more than 20,000 in the eight years since the Arabs arrived.[93] He attributed much of the devastation to Umanyema being a lawless frontier. Instead of the newcomers fighting among themselves as they did in the American West, the Arabs, he proclaimed

> invest all their spleen on the natives with most awful consequences. The spearing of the most worthless Arab slave causes all the Arabs to combine and rush

upon a large section equal to an English county in size and massacre, loot, & burn in revenge.[94]

Three such reprisals took place from October 15 to 27, and when asked why they acted so harshly, an Arab replied that the natives killed whenever they had the opportunity and that this was the way "to pay them." Stanley thought that the pay involved more than revenge:

> It meant a cut-throat grab at whatever is of value be it a woman, child, goat, chicken, corn, bananas, even a gourd or a knife, spear, or a stool. When natives run away half dead from fright with the racking noise of musketry & whistling gunshot in their ears it may be imagined that many articles of such kind are picked up to the enrichment after a sort of the victorious party.[95]

During the wait in Nyangwe for Tippu Tip, Stanley penned a long description about the evils of the slave trade. Having previously witnessed its conduct, he had now reached the source of supply, or, as he put it, the place where slaves were "grown, reaped, and harvested." He felt the only hope for ending the horror resided with Britain. It should "employ her real and vast influence at once, energetically and resolutely, to rescue inland Africa, and to check these wholesale murders of inoffensive tribes in the interior of the continent."[96] Stanley would repeat this plea for British engagement for many years hence, to little or no avail.

Tippu Tip brought a huge contingent of men, women, and children with him to Nyangwe. Rifles and muskets totaled two hundred. The AAE counted 154 members, after adding six new recruits. Weaponry included twenty-nine Sniders, thirty-two muskets, two Winchesters, two double-barrel shotguns, and ten revolvers. The combined force comforted Stanley because "Few tribes will care to dispute our passage now. I look forward in strong hopes of to do some valuable exploration."[97] On November 5, the journey began, headed toward a vast, unknown forest where reports claimed "one may travel days and days and weeks and months without ever seeing the sun." And "terribly vicious dwarfs, striped like zebras, who deal certain deaths with poisoned arrows" supposedly awaited those who dared venture this way. By now Stanley reckoned that the Lualaba could not be the Nile. It seemed "too mighty a river," and after flowing north, he figured, it must turn southwest to join the Congo. In any event, the river would be followed "come fair or come foul, fortune or misfortune."[98]

Thinking it easier, they followed a trail inland from the eastern side of the river. Within a few days, however, the ranks became "utterly demoralized." Dew and perspiration soaked clothing and

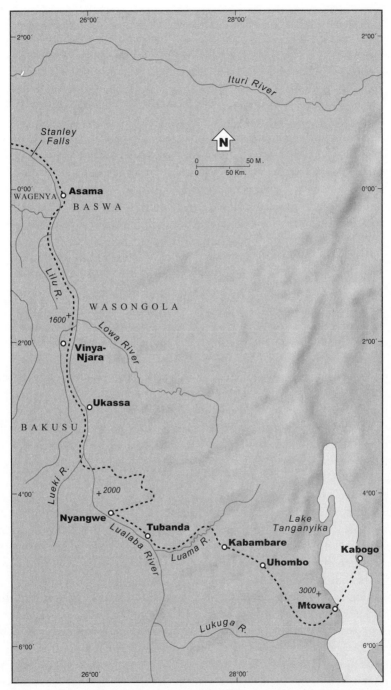

Map 5.4 From Lake Tanganyika to Stanley Falls, September 1876–January 1877

Every man scrambles as he best may through the woods; the path, being over a clayey soil is so slippery that every muscle is employed to assist our progress. The toes grasp the path, the heads bear the load, the hands clear the obstructing bush, the elbow puts aside the sapling.[99]

The twenty-four men carrying the sections of the *Lady Alice* had it even harder and each day straggled into camp well after the others. The ravages of the slave trade were everywhere to be seen. Tippu Tip claimed that slaves "only require to be gathered." After hearing this, Stanley lamented, "Today I sit me down to weep & sigh over fair Nyangwe's piteous state."[100]

Stanley again wondered about where to go after reaching the presumed joining of the Lualaba with the Congo. Should he continue to the Atlantic or head north to seek answers for the remaining questions about the source of the Nile? The latter option looked more promising, especially with regard to getting his men back to Zanzibar. He felt morally bound to do this, but the final decision could be put off for a while longer.

On November 10 Stanley ordered a badly needed rest. Once beyond the reach of the slave and ivory trades, the forests' inhabitants showed little evidence of having had much contact with the outside world. Four days later, three hundred of Tippu Tip's party departed, taking a northeasterly route to an area reputedly rich in ivory. The rest continued their trek "through the doleful, dreary forest" that reduced both Stanley and Frank Pocock to their last pairs of footwear.[101] So bad had things become that on November 16 Tippu-Tip asked to terminate their contract and return to Nyangwe, requesting half the expedition's men for escorts. Stanley thought it insane, although he did offer to turn back once they reached the confluence of the Lualaba with the Congo. Tippu Tip balked at first but eventually consented to go as far as the Lomami River.[102]

Upon reaching the Lualaba again on November 19, Stanley calculated the straight-line distance to be only forty-one miles due north of Nyangwe. As the other bank appeared to have fewer obstacles, he ordered the *Lady Alice* reassembled and floated for the first time since Lake Tanganyika. Some riverside villagers helped with the crossing by providing canoes; however, that night they all vanished into the forest. An attempt by two members of the expedition to buy some food the next day led to a shooting, and after that no villagers could be found anywhere in sight.

On November 22 Stanley and a crew of thirty-three headed downstream on the *Lady Alice,* while everybody else, including Frank Pocock and Tippu Tip, continued overland, the plan being to meet at the next village that had food for sale. But the same thing happened at each village they came to—the people ran away, often shouting *wasambye, wasambye,* a word Stanley recorded as having two meanings—those who wore cotton clothes and the uncircumcised.[103] At the point where the Lueki River (Stanley's Ruiki) enters the Lualaba, he considered the water too deep to cross on foot and so put ashore in order to ferry the land party across when it got there. After two days went by without any sign or even word of its approach, he sent five men back upriver to find out what had happened. Meanwhile, Stanley engaged in a little exploring along the Lueki in the *Lady Alice*. Finally, the next day, the land party made its appearance, unknowingly having taken a path leading away from the river and straight into an attack by Bakusu warriors.

The practice of villagers fleeing upon being approached repeated itself, which meant that provisions often could be had simply by taking what they left behind. Stanley would have preferred friendly contact, and thus after some expedition members shot two other locals, he ordered "that no native should be molested unless he was near camp at night" and that during the day "they could come & go as they pleased."[104] Disappearing villagers turned out to be the least of their worries, for at Ukassa, rapids barred the way and Stanley discovered an ambush waiting, which he claimed to have dispersed with gunfire, killing two of those lying in wait. Meanwhile, several canoes overturned attempting to shoot the rapids, and while no lives were lost, four irreplaceable Snider rifles disappeared beneath the water.

Although a string of marketplaces made it easier to buy supplies, other problems worsened. Health became a particular concern. According to Stanley, by December 4,

> The small-pox was raging, dysentery had many victims, over fifty were infected with the itch, some twenty suffered from ulcers, many complained of chest-diseases, pneumonic fever and pleurisis: there was a case or two of typhoid fever, and others suffered from prolapsus ani and umbilical pains; in short, there was work enough in the Expedition for a dozen physicians. Every day we tossed two or three bodies into the deep waters of the Livingstone.[105]

A large abandoned canoe was redesigned to carry the sick, and seeing how well it worked, Stanley surmised that a flotilla of similar-sized ones would allow everyone to travel by water after Tippu Tip and his party turned back.

Two days later, those traveling by river set up camp to wait for the land party to arrive. At about 4:00 P.M., war horns blared the approach of fourteen canoes filled with Wasongola ready for battle. Unmoved by pronouncements of the expedition's peaceful intent, they barraged the camp with arrows. Using fire from the shore as cover, Stanley said he took the *Lady Alice* to midstream to bait a trap by allowing the canoes to come within about fifty yards before ordering the crew to commence firing. The Wasongola responded with another fusillade of arrows that inflicted wounds on three expedition members. Within minutes, though, Wasongola casualties became so great that they broke off the attack and retreated downstream as fast as possible. Furthermore, the land party had once again run into problems with the Bakusu. The resulting skirmish produced three deaths and four with serious wounds among the ranks. In addition, cases of smallpox started showing up, and before the outbreak subsided, the Lualaba provided graves for eight more victims, including one of Tippu Tip's concubines.

At a place called Vinya-Njara the river party experienced another bow and arrow attack as it attempted to set up camp on December 18. It came as a complete surprise, since a blood brotherhood ceremony had been conducted earlier that day and people along the banks of the river had told them, "Go in Peace!" Stanley described a furious battle taking place, and when the assault continued during the night and into next morning, he decided "sufficient cause" existed "to make war." It was either that or "being heaved a headless corpse into the river."[106] During a reconnaissance along the river Stanley discovered the "nest" harboring the attackers. He shot the chief, which put the others to flight.[107] Two days later another confrontation occurred just after the land party arrived in camp. A nighttime lull allowed a party to find the attackers' canoes, which were either set adrift or confiscated. This helped bring about a peace settlement that yielded additional canoes. The expedition's casualties during the two battles numbered four killed and thirteen wounded.

The two leaders agreed that they could now part company. To make sure none of Stanley's people would choose to go with him, Tippu Tip said any that tried would be killed without hesitation. After a Christmas celebration, which included boat and foot races, the journey down river resumed. Per request, Tippu Tip waited at Vinya-Njara until the end of the year in case the expedition decided to turn back. Stanley's outlook suddenly brightened. At least for a while they'd all be traveling by water. Enough canoes had been found and confiscated to make this possible. And despite facing completely unknown country, he felt confident about reaching the Congo River sometime soon.

Unlike the area immediately above Vinya-Njara, the river below presented a succession of villages along its banks, although in most instances the inhabitants again kept their distance, sometimes brandishing spears and calling out, "meat, meat." More constant were the sounds of the forest. As Stanley colorfully described them,

The hum and murmur of hundreds of busy insect tribes make populous the twilight shadows that reign under primeval growth. I hear the grinding of millions of mandibles, the furious hiss of a tribe just alarmed or about to rush to battle, millions of tiny wings rustling through the nether air, the march of an insect tribe under the leaves, the startling leap of an awkward mantis, the chirp of some eager and garrulous cricket, the buzz of an ant-lion, the roar of a bull-frog. Add to these the cackle of twigs, the fall of leaves, the dropping of nut and berry, the occasional crash of a branch, or the constant creaking and swaying of the forest tops as the strong wind brushes them or the gentle breezes awake them to whispers. Though one were blind and alone in the midst of a real tropical forest, one's sense of hearing would be painfully alive to the fact that an incredible number of minute industries, whose number one could never hope to estimate, were active in the shades. Silence is impossible in a tropical forest.[108]

The first crisis occurred on December 30, when a storm caused several canoes to founder near where the Lowa River enters the Lualaba. Two members of the expedition drowned, and Stanley feared a rebellion might break out as a result. Instead, their loss was attributed to the workings of fate. Then came three days of hostile challenges and more exclamations of "meat" being in the vicinity. On New Year's Day 1877, Stanley said he nipped one attack in the bud by hitting two men with his first shot, and the next day he noted, "About 6 natives fell . . . in the passage down river."[109] January 3 brought a more serious engagement that cost the expedition two dead and ten wounded. Stanley had been warned the day before about a hostile reception, and when confronted he figured it was fight or die, either by having their throats cut or by drowning. Shortly thereafter, a brief encounter with the Baswa took place just above a potentially more dangerous enemy, the first in a series of rapids that would bear the name Stanley Falls (now Boyoma Falls). Convinced that the rapids could easily destroy the canoes, Stanley ordered a twenty-foot path cut along the river's left bank to have them carried around. An attempt by the Baswa to harass the workers failed in the face of rifle fire, and in retaliation Stanley ordered a raid on their home island to take food and other supplies. Rapids surrounding the island required clearing another path on the left bank, and this time Bakumu warriors tried to block the way. They, too, retreated after being fired upon.

A different kind of crisis ensued when the canoes returned to the water. While six of them managed to make it to an island, the seventh got smashed to pieces in the rapids. All aboard swam safely to shore except one of the Zanzibaris, who managed to climb onto a rock in the middle of the raging waters. A rescue attempt resulted in two others becoming stranded, and all efforts to get them off that day failed. Somehow they hung on through the night, and in the morning all three made it safely to shore by clinging to a cable fashioned from forest rattans. Meanwhile, a second canoe capsized, with an outcome less fortunate for the steersman, who drowned.

Getting beyond this point required cutting another path through the forest. At first the enemies consisted of biting red ants and burrs. Such irritants soon gave way to another confrontation, this time with the inhabitants of Asama Island, on January 18. While Stanley engaged them on the river, other armed members of the expedition succeeded in capturing two of their villages. A peace accord followed, producing an opportunity to trade for badly needed bananas.

Downstream from Asama, the river widens, and the following evening the expedition camped at what appeared to be a marketplace. Expecting traders to appear in the morning, they instead awoke to find the camp surrounded by a net. An attempt to cut it was met with a spear attack. Rifle fire caused the launchers to retreat. Eight didn't get away and told of having set the net so as to get "man-meat."[110] Four were taken along as guides to the sixth cataract, where a navigable channel allowed for an easy way around the swirling waters.

The next cataract, faced on January 25, promised a more difficult challenge. Stanley described the water falling "into a boiling and tumultuous gulf, wherein are lines of brown waves 6 feet high leaping with terrific bounds, and hurling themselves against each other in dreadful fury."[111] Matters were compounded by a series of Wagenya assaults on the camp, that required a staunch defense by perimeter forces to fend off. Once freed from this threat, Stanley divided the expedition, some members following the shore, others guiding the canoes through a narrow channel. By midmorning on January 28, the last barrier in the fifty-six-mile-long series of rapids had been passed. Compass readings showed them being north of the equator and on broad, placid waters flowing in a west-by-northwest direction. Although the sailing was smooth, the people along the river remained suspicious and sometimes hostile. In fact, three separate attacks occurred on January 29, bringing the total to twenty-four since November 23, 1876. Another occurred the next day at Yangambi, a village located across from where the Lomami River joins the Congo. Perhaps because of the unsettled conditions, Stanley missed it. His Lomami was the much smaller Lilu, which enters south of the Falls. Stanley described this attack as having been

met with instant punishment. In an instant we had landed spearmen and musketeers, and in their rear fire was set to the village. We then withdrew to a

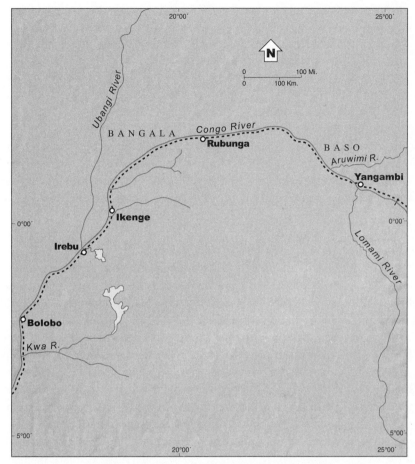

Map 5.5   The Journey along the Upper Congo, January–March 1877

grassy islet to observe the effect on the natives, lunched, and as they had drawn together on the banks, made a second attempt. But the fire and their losses in dead quelled their courage.[112]

Conditions only worsened, for during the afternoon of February 1, where the Aruwimi joins the Congo, huge war canoes closed in from two directions. Stanley ordered his canoes to drop anchor and form a line, with the *Lady Alice* positioned fifty yards in front. After five minutes of intense musket fire, the attackers, presumably Baso, moved upriver to re-form for another assault. Before they could, Stanley, clearly in a vengeful mood, decided to retaliate. "Our blood is up now," he said, because

It is a murderous world, and we feel for the first time that we hate the filthy, vulturous ghouls who inhabit it. We therefore lift our anchors, and pursue them upstream along the right bank, until rounding a point we see their villages. We make straight for the banks, and continue the fight in the village streets with those who have landed, hunt them out into the woods, and there only sound the retreat, having returned the daring cannibals the compliment of a visit.[113]

Pursuit led to a temple laden with ivory, and the men helped themselves to as much as they could carry. Stanley's assumption that the attackers were cannibals came from skulls and bones that looked human but may well have come from the pygmy or bonobo chimpanzees that inhabit this part of Africa, and the frequent taunts about becoming "meat." In any event, the likelihood of encountering further trouble led him to give up on the idea of exploring the Aruwimi.

Faced with declining numbers and seemingly still somewhere in the middle of the continent, Stanley became despondent, feeling that "To continue this fearful life was not possible. Some day we should lie down, and offer our throats like lambs to the cannibal butchers."[114] Nevertheless, on they went, with danger ever present, not only from human enemies but also from storms, rapids, and whirlpools. Then on February 8 the food ran out. Prepared to fight for it, Stanley maneuvered his canoe toward the village of Rubunga on the left bank. At first the people fled, but with coaxing they came back in a friendly, not hostile, mood. A blood brotherhood ceremony with the chief sealed a pact of friendship and enough food came along with it to end fears of starvation, at least for the moment. Upon asking the name of the river, the chief replied "*Ikuti ya Kongo*" (this is the Congo), confirming Stanley's view that since leaving the falls they'd been on it.[115]

The sight of four Portuguese muskets in Rubunga bolstered hopes that the river flowed to the sea, the destination Stanley had finally decided upon. Downstream from Rubunga all seemed well until spears rained down and war canoes closed in from the front and the rear just after they'd departed on the morning of February 11. According to Stanley, the Snider rifles "soon cleared the river with great loss to the savages." Yet that afternoon, another attack had to be fended off. After a couple days' reprieve, with only assaults from horseflies, mosquitoes, and tsetse to deal with, some eighty men in six canoes threatened the flotilla from behind. The sound of musket fire and the sight of "shots skipping over the water" caused Stanley to reply in kind, which forced the pursuers, he said, "back in a panic with three or four killed."[116]

February 14 brought "the fight of fights" with the "Bangala," a name designating the traders who worked this section of the river. Despite overwhelming numbers and brave ferocity, the Bangala's weapons proved no match for the Sniders. When the battle finally ended after five hours, the expedition counted nary a casualty, while Stanley said the Bangala "suffered more severely than I ever supposed they were capable of bearing."[117] This constant need to fight baffled him. He didn't know that warfare had become endemic along the Congo, as various groups competed for control of the trade. Far better in such circumstances to attack than be attacked.

Despite a critical shortage of food, they dared not go ashore to search for it. By February 19, however, matters had become so desperate that no other choice existed than to risk a landing. Surprisingly, the villagers of Ikenge turned out to be friendly and readily sold food. As a result, Stanley called a three-day halt to stock up and find out about conditions downstream. With one exception, none of the place names mentioned by people appeared on the Sanford map of the Congo Stanley carried with him. He, therefore, felt confident about traveling through completely uncharted territory.

As had happened so often before, the mood of the residents changed quickly, for at Irebu, just downstream from Ikenge, bullets whizzed by. No harm was done, however, as the channels winding through the numerous islands lining this portion of the river provided avenues of escape. And the depth of the river, even in the channels, led Stanley to believe that large steamers would be able to pass without difficulty, a boon for trade prospects.

The people encountered at Bolobo proved to be a pleasant surprise: Though wary of the strangers, they showed no signs of hostility, and, indeed, some fishermen pointed out a place at which to make a comfortable camp. The next day their leader, Chumbiri, came to visit and said they could stay and make his village their home. This, of course, pleased everyone immensely, for it meant a chance to purchase food and get additional information about conditions downstream. The chief's wives caught Stanley's eye. He described them as "pretty . . . large-eyed, and finely formed, with a graceful curve of shoulder I had not often observed."[118] When it came time to leave on March 7, such pleasures and Chumbiri's offer to provide forty-five escorts had lightened Stanley's mood considerably. But a violent storm caused the escorts to fall behind, and before they caught up on March 9, six of the expedition's crew had been wounded during a surprise attack just downstream from where the Kwa River joins the Congo. It represented the thirty-second, though last, attack experienced on the river. Stanley asked Chumbiri's men to accompany him as far as the falls said to be up ahead. A demand of more brass wire in advance to do so convinced him to push on without them.

On March 12 the *Lady Alice* sailed into a quiet expanse of water some eighteen miles long by fourteen miles wide. Stanley claimed that Frank suggested the names Stanley Pool and Dover Cliffs for the surrounding white limestone bluffs on the northeast side. Today the pool is known as Malebo. Here they met a friendly Bateke chief by the name of Mankoneh, who said it would be impossible to navigate the falls ahead. Another chief, Itsi of Ntamo, offered supplies and a promise of friendship for one of the two remaining big goats from Umanyema that had survived the journey. Stanley at first refused, but not wishing to make an enemy of Itsi, he eventually agreed. An exchange of charms—Itsi gave Stanley a salty-tasting white powder said to provide lifelong protection, and Stanley handed over a vial of magnesia—and an act of blood brotherhood between the chief and Frank sealed the deal.

The journey resumed on March 16, with the river, not the people, now providing the opposition. It had become, in Stanley's words,

> no longer the stately stream whose mystic beauty, noble grandeur, and gentle uninterrupted flow along a course of nearly nine hundred miles, ever fascinated us . . . but a furious river, rushing down a steep bed obstructed by reefs of lava, projected barriers of rock, lines of immense boulders, winding in crooked course through deep chasms, and dropping down over terraces in a long series of falls, cataracts, and rapids.[119]

Frank took a contingent overland, while Stanley in the *Lady Alice* led the canoes around the first set of rapids known as "Mother." Beyond lay the roaring "Father" that Stanley claimed would make "the most powerful ocean steamer, going at full speed . . . be as helpless as a cockle-boat."[120] Consequently, everything now had to be hauled overland. Despite exercising great caution, the treacherous path produced numerous injuries from falls on slippery rocks and nasty encounters with tangled vegetation. At one point Stanley stumbled and fell nearly thirty feet. Luck again was on his side, as he walked away with no more than a few bruised ribs. Food regularly ran low, and, when available, it cost dearly, except cassava. Ten days were required to make this hazard history.

By staying close to the right bank, the expedition could once again use the river. Unfortunately, on March 28 a canoe strayed too far toward midstream and plunged down another falls. All five aboard, including Kalulu, drowned in the swirling water. In commemoration, Stanley named the place

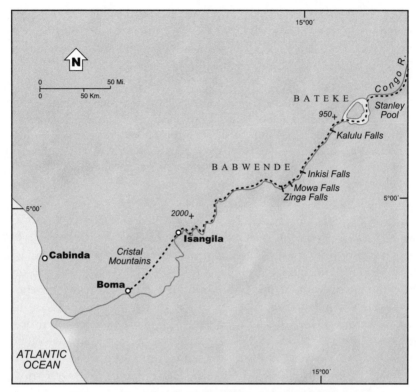

Map 5.6   From Stanley Pool to Boma, March–August 1877

Kalulu Falls. Then another canoe was swept over; this time the crew managed to make it to shore. A third was not so lucky, and three more men disappeared from view, although they reappeared unscathed several days later. Since the remaining nine canoes and the *Lady Alice* lacked sufficient space, from now on some of the expedition would have to proceed by land under Frank's command.

As often as not, the boat and canoes had to be lifted and lowered by cables in order to get around what looked like an endless succession of rapids and falls. It was slow, dangerous work, and both man and craft suffered. Stanley again had a brush with death when he fell into the water and nearly got swept away. And at one point the *Lady Alice* broke loose and catastrophe seemed imminent until it came to rest on a sandy beach. All told, Stanley felt nothing he had experienced before could compare to those last few weeks. Prospects looked "dismal." What he had left behind appeared an "Eden" compared to the current "watery hell."[121]

On April 21 they at last found a place to rest, having traveled a mere thirty-four miles in five weeks. The local inhabitants sent palm wine and cassava and said another falls stood in the way, a mighty one known as Inkisi. From the bluff above, Stanley recorded his thoughts:

> We are hemmed in with difficulties which daunt the boldest. Before us is the increasing roar and tumult of falling floods, increasing in number & violence to which our past experience can show no comparison. Ending in a narrow confined river hurried with awful speed between lofty wall of rock finally plunging down a great depth whence nothing mortal might escape intact and unbruised by the weight of the floods.[122]

He hoped it might be Tuckey's Cataract, named after Royal Navy Capt. James K. Tuckey, head of an ill-fated attempt to explore the Congo in 1816 as part of a broader effort to determine the river's possible relationship with the Niger. Well financed and supplied, it set off in two ships, carrying three natural scientists with intentions of measuring everything that could be measured. Physical exhaustion, illness, and low morale forced Tuckey to turn around before getting this far upstream. The effort cost seventeen of the fifty-four Europeans, including Tuckey, the three scientists, and two officers, their lives.[123] No major expedition along the Congo had since been mounted. With only canoe men as aides, Hungarian Lázló Magyar tried in 1848 without ever reaching cataract country. He did, however, produce a fairly detailed description of the lower reaches of the river. Unfortunately, it remained largely unknown because it was published in Pest by the Hungarian Academy of Sciences.[124]

Staying with the river for the next several miles would be impossible. Stanley considered crossing to the other side of the river, which presented a less daunting physical challenge. The people, however, looked threatening, and their numbers couldn't be estimated. Staying in place or going back weren't options, and thus they would have to climb a steep escarpment to reach the plateau above. Even with locals helping, it took three days of exhausting effort to complete the ascent. Markets in the area stocked a wide array of European products, especially cloth, and thus the expedition's trade goods had very little exchange value. Even Stanley could afford only such things as "cold cassava bread, ground-nuts, or pea-nuts, yams, and green bananas" to eat. Dysentery and ulcers produced pain and misery, and the state of both his and Frank's footwear concerned Stanley. He considered shoes and boots a necessity, for protection and to serve as symbols of European superiority, feeling that feet should never be exposed to the "vulgar gaze of the aborigines."[125] To many European travelers, displays of supposed dignity served to demonstrate the moral distance separating the civilized from the uncivilized. Stanley thus shaved every day and wore clean and neatly pressed clothes whenever possible.

The three-mile journey to a place where the river could be rejoined required ten days to complete. Along the way Stanley hit upon the idea of building replacement canoes from some of the taller forest trees: Workmen managed to fashion three of them. Fierce thunderstorms broke regularly and the river rose each day, bringing worries that their camp might soon be inundated. But that didn't happen, and on May 24 the next leg of the journey to Mowa Falls began. Thirteen of the men were too sick to help, and what started out as pimples on Frank's feet turned into ugly ulcers.

Along the way around Mowa Falls, the *Lady Alice* sustained some damage that necessitated stopping for repairs. During the lull, Stanley decided to check on the route to Zinga Falls, only about two miles away. Although the falls looked imposing, they didn't compare with the hazards posed by Inkisi. Frank provided a bigger cause of concern. His foot ulcers had become so bad that he could no longer lead the land party.

Stanley labeled June 3 "A Black Woeful Day!"[126] It started when whirlpools forced him to turn back from an attempt to take the *Lady Alice* to a point above Zinga Falls. Worried about the reception the expedition might receive from the people at Zinga, he made the trip by land instead, leaving instructions for some of the crew to see if canoes might be able to negotiate the whirlpools. Relieved at finding Zinga free of problems, Stanley climbed to a bluff above the river. The view revealed a capsized canoe being swept downstream. Eight of the occupants made it safely to shore, but three didn't. They included Frank, who, out of restlessness, had insisted upon going along. Stanley reported deep gloom engulfing everyone, and any hope that Frank might somehow have escaped drowning was dashed eight days later when a fisherman found "the upturned face of a white man" floating by him. No one bothered to take the body from the water, apparently because "they feared it."[127] The depth of Stanley's depression is evidenced by his journal entries, some of which over the next couple of days are either incoherent or undecipherable. At other times, however, the words are clear. One lamentation is written in biblical style:

> Alas, my brave honest, kindly-natured, good Frank, thy many faithful services to me have only found thee a grave in the wild waters of the Congo. Thy many years of travel and toil and danger borne so cheerfully have been but ill-rewarded. Thou Noble Son of Nature, would that I could have suffered instead of thee for I am weary, Oh so weary of this constant tale of woes and

death; and thy cheerful society, the influence of thy brave smile, the utterance of thy courageous heart I shall lack, and because I lack, I shall weep for my dear lost friend.[128]

Word of Frank's death fueled rumors that Stanley purposely saw to it that none of his European traveling companions would survive to tell their stories. True, he often made critical comments about them, and he may have been less than charitable on many occasions, but the evidence overwhelmingly supports a verdict of innocent in all five cases.

The expedition had come to a complete stop—part of it under Stanley at Zinga, another part at Mowa, and a third part in between. The men evinced no desire to go on, with some, in fact, "declaring that they would prefer living and hoeing for the heathen than follow the White man longer, for his wages were but the wages of death."[129] Slowly, however, they got back into action, and by June 19 all the canoes had been brought to Zinga. Still, many of the men remained unhappy with their situation, and thirty-one walked out the next morning. Two days later, they came back, thanks to help from Babwende chiefs and a promise not to be punished. Problems continued. Two of the new canoes and a carpenter were lost when they fell into the swirling river, and the remaining boats in the flotilla didn't make it past Zinga Falls until June 25. All told, only three miles had been covered in thirty days, and immediately ahead stood an imposing series of rapids. While being towed from shore, the *Lady Alice,* with Stanley and six others aboard, broke from its cables and hurtled downstream. Miraculously, it managed to avoid disaster. Four days of heavy toil brought the rest of the expedition forward without further incident.

Badly depleted food stores required making as much haste as possible. The river now proved to be less daunting, and the gorge in which it had been encased for so long gave way to a more sloping shoreline with only occasional tall cliffs. Still, along the way, the expedition lost two more men, one from dysentery, which caused fear of an impending epidemic. Furthermore, the Babwende in this area acted less friendly, for according to Stanley,

They did not seem to relish the idea of a white Mundelé [merchant] in a country which had hitherto been their market, and they shook their heads most solemnly, saying that the country was about to be ruined, and that they had never known a country but was injured by the presence of a white man.[130]

Despite such feelings, they didn't block the way, and neither did two other turbulent stretches of river, which were passed via side streams on July 13. The people at Ntombo Mataka, whom Stanley called the politest he had met in Africa, helped them around the next series of rapids.

Supposedly the last cataract on the river, it turned out not to be, and Stanley blamed the 1874 Sanford map for much of the expedition's difficulties during this segment of the journey. Looking back from here, Stanley penned a summary of events since leaving Nyangwe:

> We have attacked and destroyed 28 large towns and three or four score of villages, fought 32 battles on land and water, contended with 52 Falls and Rapids, constructed about 50 miles of tramway work through Forests, hauled our canoes and boat up a mountain 1,500 feet high, then over the mountains 6 miles, then lowered them down the slope to the river, lifted by rough mechanical skill our canoes up gigantic boulders 12, 15 and 20 feet high, then formed a tramway over these boulders to pass the falls of Massassa, Nzabi, and Zinga.[131]

With food becoming harder and harder to find, some of the men resorted to stealing, causing Stanley to have to buy back those caught in the act. On one occasion, however, he left a man behind. The asking price couldn't be afforded, and any attempt to free him by force seemed too risky. The precarious nature of their situation also led Stanley to refrain from doing any exploration, despite being in what he called a region of "beautiful and endless solitudes." They simply hadn't the strength. He reported,

> The freshness and ardour of feeling with which I had set out from the Indian Ocean had, by this time, been quite worn away. Fevers had sapped the frame; over-much trouble had strained the spirit; hunger had debilitated the body, anxiety preyed upon the mind. My people were groaning aloud; their sunken eyes and unfleshed bodies were a living reproach to me; their vigour was now gone, though their fidelity was unquestionable; their knees were bent with weakness, and their backs were no longer rigid with the vigour of youth, and life, and strength, and fire of devotion. Hollow-eyed, sallow, and gaunt, unspeakably miserable in aspect, we yielded at length to imperious nature, and had but one thought only—to trudge on for one look more at the blue ocean.[132]

During a conversation with a group of locals, Stanley heard shots coming from nearby. Once again, expedition members had been caught attempting to steal food. Six returned wounded, with three others taken captive. As in the previous instance, they were left to their fates.

At Isangila another series of rapids barred the way, with four more said to exist before the river reached Boma, where European traders operated. Convinced by now that the Congo-Lualaba connection had been established beyond doubt, Stanley considered his job of exploration completed and announced that they would finish the journey by land. Shouts of thanks to Allah rang out. Ceremoniously, the *Lady Alice,* having endured a journey of almost seven thousand miles, was lifted to a summit above the falls and left "to bleach and to rot to dust!"[133]

The march to Boma began on August 1, with all desperately hungry and some forty of the expedition's remaining 115 members sick from a variety of disorders. Stanley now knew firsthand the difficulties faced by Tuckey's men as they scrambled over the rugged Cristal Mountains. Little in the way of food could be purchased, as hardly any cloth remained and no one here wanted beads or brass wire. Exhausted, Stanley decided to stop three days later in order to send a letter ahead appealing for assistance. Just in case no English speakers could be found, he made copies in French and Spanish and appended a P.S. noting, "You may not know me by name; I therefore add, I am the person that discovered Livingstone in 1871."[134] Two days later the returning messengers met him on the trail, bringing a welcoming letter, food, and other supplies from Hatton & Cookson, a Liverpool-based firm operating in the Congo region since the 1840s. In a return letter, Stanley expressed his gratitude:

> Dear sirs, though strangers, I feel we shall be great friends, and it will be the study of my lifetime to remember my feelings of gratefulness when I first caught sight of your supplies, and my poor faithful and brave people cried out, 'Master, we are saved; food is coming', and the old and the young, men, women and children lifted up their wearied, wornout frames to chant lustily an extemporaneous song, in honour of the white people by the great sea [the Atlantic] who had listened to their prayers. I had to rush to my tent to hide the tears that would flow despite all my attempts at composure.[135]

With stomachs full and spirits lifted, the Anglo-American Expedition began the last leg of its journey, and reached Boma on August 9, exactly 999 days out from Zanzibar. After a midday banquet on the 11th, Stanley and the others boarded the *Kabinda* for the Portuguese enclave of the same name, where they remained until the 20th of the month. During the stay an unknown disease claimed the lives of four Wangwana, and four more died en route home.

Stanley used his time in Cabinda (modern spelling) to write a dispatch with recommendations for Central African development. The Congo Basin, he concluded, needed commerce first, with a depot at the limit of navigation on the lower stretch of the river staffed by freed slaves maybe the best way to begin. As for the lands around the Great Lakes, Stanley thought missionaries more crucial in order to help free people from prevailing despotic rule.[136]

Uledi - the bravest. Manwa Sera the Headman

Stanley. Nov 1877.

At admiralty House. Simon's Bay. Cape G^d Hope

En route to Zanzibar

Stanley with survivors of the 1874–77 expedition in Zanzibar, November 1877.
Courtesy of the Royal Museum of Central Africa

From Cabinda they all went to Luanda, with Stanley being put up by the Portuguese explorer Serpa Pinto. Here he penned his final dispatches describing the Congo journey. A statement in one would soon prove to be prescient: "I feel convinced," he said, "that the Congo question will become a political question in time."[137] At last, on September 27, Stanley, 114 men and women, and two children boarded HMS *Industry,* headed first for the British naval base of Simonstown at the Cape of Good Hope. The need to make repairs to the ship kept them there from October 21 to November 6. Cape Town's Chamber of Commerce put out the welcome mat for Stanley, and afterward he visited the Cape Dutch center of Stellenbosch. Twenty days at sea finally brought Zanzibar into view. Of those who left the island on November 15, 1874, 128 didn't make it back—seventy-seven died, forty-five deserted, and six were honorably discharged. Those who managed to survive rejoiced, Stanley said, at seeing familiar sights. The expressions on their faces caused him to feel pleasure and ask, "What had the poor fellows not suffered since 37 months before they had left their homes?"[138]

Festivities were few, and Stanley spent much of the time on the island seeking out the families of the dead to make sure they received the payments due to them. He left on December 13 aboard the British India steamer *Pachumba* for another long voyage to Europe. Although buoyed by letters and press releases praising him for what some called the century's single greatest feat of exploration, he also learned that Alice Pike had become Alice Barney in January of 1876.[139] She didn't even wait two years for him. In a note offering congratulations, she sheepishly explained,

> I have done what millions of women have done before me, not to be true to my promise. But you are so Great, so honored and sought after, that you will scarcely miss your *once* loved friend & *always* devoted admirer of your hero-ism. For indeed you are the hero of the day. That alone should console you from my loss. No doubt before long you will consider it a gain, for *Stanley* can easily find a wife all his heart could decree to grace his high position & deservedly great name. . . . If you *can* forgive me, tell me so, if not *do please* remain silent. Destroy my letters, as I have burnt all of yours. Adieu, Morton. I will not say farewell, for, I hope in some future time we may meet, shall it be as friends?[140]

Alice lived an eventful life until succumbing to a heart attack in October 1931. A letter to him dated December 26, 1886, and a portrait she later painted reveal that he did not vanish from her thoughts. As for Stanley, nary a word survives to show his feelings. But he never destroyed her letters, per-haps an indication that he felt more sadness and loss than anger.

CHAPTER 6

In the King's Employ

CREATING THE CONGO FREE STATE

F rom Suez, Stanley proceeded overland to Cairo for a meeting with
Khedive Ismail, who honored him with the Egyptian order of Medji-
dieh Grade Grand Officer on January 3, 1878. A meeting with former
president Ulysses S. Grant, then in the midst of a round-the-world trip with
his wife, took place two nights later. They conversed throughout dinner, and
during a round of toasts, Stanley proclaimed it "one of the proudest
moments of his life to find himself seated by our guest."[1] It's doubtful he
brought up his Civil War days to the commander of the Blue Coats at Shiloh
and later of the entire Union Army.

The next morning a steamer took Stanley to Brindisi, Italy, where he
caught a train for Marseilles to attend an honorary gala hosted by the city's
Geographical Society on January 14. A week's stay in Paris brought further
celebrations, and in London a regular round of lunches, dinners, and receptions continued into May. Despite all the socializing, Stanley managed to
find enough time and energy to finish the nearly 1,200-page manuscript of
Through the Dark Continent by the end of April. He also campaigned vigorously for a British presence in the Congo basin, stressing two interconnected
themes—the region's commercial potential and how its development would
bring the inhabitants into the civilized world. According to him, the river
could become the "grand highway of commerce to West Central Africa."[2]
And with commerce, civilization would naturally follow. Earlier, Cameron
had tried to drum up support for Central Africa by emphasizing the riches
awaiting developers, but his words fell on deaf ears. By the mid-1870s, offi-

cials and the public had grown wary about the high costs of overseas adventures, and with Livingstone gone from the scene and the slave trade no longer front-page news, Africa generated little interest.

Stanley was hardly the best person to act as the region's spokesman to those in power. Many still viewed him as a renegade American, and he made an easy target for detractors. They included his old nemesis John Kirk, who saw an opportunity to take several potshots. He called the survey description of the Rufiji "exaggerated and inaccurate" and criticized the way the expedition fought its way down the Congo.[3] As he stated in a letter to the Foreign Office,

> I have been led to form the opinion that the doings of Mr. Stanley in the Expedition were a disgrace to humanity and that his proceedings will prove one of the principal obstacles that future explorers and missionaries will have to meet when following his track.[4]

Although he may have been right about the "disgrace" allegation, the future would prove him wrong about the "obstacles" one. If anything, Stanley's appearance more often than not paved the way for others, even though not always those he wished for.

Kirk also seems to have been the source of two widely circulated rumors—that Stanley accepted a young female slave from Mutesa to serve as his mistress and that he kicked a man to death.[5] Given his temper, the kicking incident might have been believable, but there's no evidence to support it, or the mistress rumor. Stanley seems to have avoided sexual liaisons altogether while in Africa. It's doubtful that ambivalence or racism explains his behavior, for, as we've seen, women, including African women, constantly caught his eye. Rather, as with cursing and alcohol, Stanley's behavior more likely derived from his views about proper behavior and the need for Europeans to exhibit it in front of others in order to demonstrate their moral superiority.

Unlike Kirk, who operated behind the scenes, just as he did with complaints about Livingstone following the Zambezi expedition, others went public with criticisms of Stanley, especially over the attacks against the Wanyaturu and Bumbire Islanders. Things started heating up when the RGS praised Stanley for his Lake Victoria discoveries at its November 25, 1875, meeting. In an about-face from 1872, James Grant went so far as to call the journey "one of the most important and brilliant that has ever been made in Central Africa, or, indeed, in any other country."[6] In a letter to the *Pall Mall Gazette* someone identifying himself as F. R. G. S. (Fellow of the RGS) protested:

We had also the privilege of listening to Colonel Grant, Sir Samuel Baker, and Mr. Hutchinson, and to Mr. Arnold in praise of that stalwart missionary-journalist who is now vigorously engaged in extending the joint circulation of the Daily Telegraph and the New York Herald in Central Africa. Very interesting it all was. The more so, perhaps, that this, which may be called a representative assemblage of the educated, comfortable classes, condoned with 'effusion' the trifling offense of putting a few niggers out of the world. Sir Samuel Baker's jocular reference to the wholesale butcheries of which he and Mr. H. M. Stanley had been guilty in the cause of science and Christianity was received with laughter and cheers by this highly civilized audience. . . . I am decidedly of the opinion . . . that the unscrupulous slaughter of miserable negroes merely for the sake of getting more quickly from one part of the country to another is not altogether justifiable.

In comparing Stanley to past travelers and explorers, the letter went on to say:

their object hitherto has been to make friends with the natives. . . . Nowadays we spread Christianity and put down slavery by killing with improved weapons the very people whose interests, moral and physical, we proclaim ourselves so anxious to protect. Such conduct on the part of a Spaniard or a Turk would be generally condemned; but on the part of an Englishman or an American it is evidently considered by kid-gloved philanthropists as a heroism of the highest order.[7]

The Anti-Slavery and Aboriginal Protection Societies registered their complaints, and a member of the latter suggested that Stanley be sent back to Bumbire and hung.[8] Little else happened until RGS member Henry Mayers Hyndman got into the act. A member of a prominent family and a frequent critic of capitalism and imperialism, he informed the society of his intention to bring before its November 13, 1876, meeting a resolution stating:

That the Council and the Fellows of the Royal Geographical society, although they cordially appreciate the courage and determination shown by Mr. H. M. Stanley during his explorations in Central Africa, emphatically condemn his method of dealing with the natives not only as unjustifiable and cruel in itself, but as involving most serious danger to travellers who may follow in his footsteps.[9]

Told that it might cause "confusion" or "loss of time," Hyndman replied that he would modify the wording and then referred to the previous November's meeting, when Stanley's "shameful brutalities" were "sanctioned by a very distinguished assembly." He suggested that because the society had said nothing since then, "The impression . . . undoubtedly exists that the Royal Geographical Society did justify Mr. Stanley's acts."[10] As the meeting of the 13th convened, Hyndman rose and asked permission to introduce his resolution. The society's president, Rutherford Alcock, refused, saying the RGS had "no legitimate grounds for action."[11] That ended the discussion for the time being.

At the next meeting, on November 27, Hyndman changed tactics and requested time to read a few sentences from Stanley's letters and then ask the members to express their opinions about them. Col. Henry Yule, a member of the RGS council, supported Hyndman and told the society, "They had all shared in giving Mr. Stanley an ovation; let them now all share in expressing condemnation of his act." Rawlinson replied that the society did not get involved in matters unrelated to "any principles of practical geography" and noted that Stanley was not a member of the RGS, not even an Englishman.[12] The meeting moved on to its regular business. Still, according to the *Pall Mall Gazette,* Hyndman's efforts had been useful.[13] The RGS took a more or less neutral stance, and the concerns of the critics had received a public airing.

There the matter stood until the beginning of 1878, when the RGS congratulated Stanley on his safe return and asked if he would present a paper or narrative account of his discoveries in Central Africa on February 7. Anticipating a large crowd, they moved the event to James Hall, which could accommodate two thousand people. Stanley began by informing the audience (which fell a couple of hundred short of capacity) that he would tell the story "briefly and rapidly." Aware of his critics presence, he remarked, "it would be but mere affectation in me to pretend not to know that there are some here who do not agree with my treatment of the African" before getting on with the talk. At its completion, the Prince of Wales offered a cordial thank-you, and Baker concluded the evening by noting:

> He was sure that Mr. Stanley, as an American, would look back to this evening, and regard the welcome given to him not as a mere formality, but as coming from their hearts, and would feel that the kind words of encouragement and thanks which his Royal Highness has so graciously offered him expressed the voice and gratitude of England.[14]

The RGS council continued the celebration by holding a dinner for Stanley at the prestigious Willis' Rooms, with seating for three hundred, two days later.

Such an outpouring of adulation sent the critics into action. Even before the address, Yule had expressed his opposition, claiming Stanley's own statements indicted him. Regarding the description of the Bumbire incident, he said, "In now re-reading and transcribing it my impression is even stronger than at first that no scheme of slaughter was ever more astutely planned or more ruthlessly carried out."[15] Hyndman then said he would bring Stanley's "methods of exploration" up for RGS fellow consideration. He felt that by their actions to date, the society had committed itself "to a mode of discovery which, apart, from its inhumanity, will in my judgment tend in the long run to hinder rather than advance the progress of science, besides endangering the lives of other travellers."[16] Some segments of the press joined the fray. The *Pall Mall Gazette* accused the RGS of having compromised itself by celebrating Stanley and called his methods "exploration plus buccaneering."[17] In a lead article the *Standard* posed the question: "Is the opening of Africa to geographical science, not to speak of trade, missionary enterprise, and so forth, so important that any acts committed for its attainment are deprived of their ordinary moral character and become praiseworthy?"[18] Never one to back down from verbal assaults, Stanley responded to what happened to the Wanyaturu by noting in his February 7 speech, "I am happy to say we did not leave that place until we had perfectly sickened them."[19]

Critics never really had a chance. The sheer weight of what Stanley had accomplished buried them. As the RGS council put it,

> Mr. H. M. Stanley's discovery of the course of the Congo is the greatest geographical event of the year; and his name would undoubtedly have been proposed for the award of one of the Royal Medals of this year, had he not in 1873 received a Medal for the discovery and relief of Dr. Livingstone. In acknowledgement of Mr. H. M. Stanley's eminent services to Geography, it is unanimously resolved that he receive the thanks of the Council of the Royal Geographical Society, and be elected an Honorary Corresponding Member.[20]

And on the other side of the Atlantic, the president of the American Geographical Society proclaimed that "it may be truthfully said that no one man has ever, in explorations upon the land, done so much for the acquisition of geographical information."[21] Left unsaid was to what end such geographical information would be put.

Stanley did have one run-in with geographers, however. While noting that he "had it very much at heart to call the Congo River the Livingstone," the RGS wouldn't go along with "altering a name that had been current for the last 300 years." Stanley disagreed with their position, labeling the name a "fraud" unintentionally made by Portuguese explorer Diego Cão, who took the name for a country and applied it to a river. Now they could correct the mistake and in the process "honour themselves by honouring the name of Livingstone."[22] This round he lost.

The battle to convince England of the value of Central Africa was also being lost. As an article in the *Edinburgh Review* put it, the area contained far too many problems and uncertainties to warrant investment. These included:

1. rivers with too many rapids and waterfalls;
2. natural products that could be could be grown elsewhere with easier access;
3. minerals too distant from the coast;
4. the link between ivory and slavery;
5. few motives to encourage white settlement in the interior
6. "no rich and luxurious civilization . . . like Peru or India, to tempt commercial adventurers"; and
7. the need to choose workers carefully from "idle and clumsy" inhabitants.

It ended by cautioning that "The opinion that the interior of Africa has been thrown open to civilization and trade by Mr. Stanley's daring navigation and descent of the Congo River, is one which requires to be supported by much stronger evidence than we at present possess before it can be adopted."[23]

The evidence, however, had convinced someone, namely King Leopold II of Belgium. Born April 9, 1835, just four years after the country officially came into existence, he became convinced early on that his *petit pays* (little country) needed overseas possessions. They would provide wealth and prestige, help heal internal divisions over class and language, and secure the new dynasty's position.[24] Tangible evidence of his thinking survives in the form of a piece of Parthenon marble on which he had *Il faut à la Belgique une colonie* (Belgium must have a colony) inscribed in 1860, when he was the Duke of Brabant. Trips to British India and the Dutch East Indies made a vivid impression on him, and after ascending to the throne after the death of his father, Leopold I, in December 1865, he looked toward Asia and the Pacific, with China an especially inviting target. Like others with grand imperial designs, Leopold eyed its market potential and figured settlers could be lured to the parts of the country with climates similar to Europe. Other places he considered included New Guinea, Borneo, Formosa, and Sarawak, but ultimately his most intense efforts were directed at the Philippines, in

the belief that Spain, because of its ongoing political and economic problems, might be willing to sell or lease it. When by 1875 no deal with Spain
seemed in the offing, Leopold began looking more seriously at Africa. Earlier, he'd considered acquiring portions of Abyssinia and Mozambique, or
perhaps launching a commercial venture somewhere along the west coast.
The best bet at this time, however, appeared to be Central Africa. Unlike the
British, he put stock in the reports by Cameron and others emphasizing its
great store of wealth just waiting to be exploited.[25]

A conference of interested parties seemed a good way to begin, and following a visit to London during May 1876 to check on sentiments there,
Leopold decided to hold one in Brussels September 12–14. All the major
European geographical societies were invited, and many prominent members
came, including explorers Cameron, Grant, Gustav Nachtigal, Gerhard
Rohlfs, and Georg Schweinfurth. At the end of a sumptuous banquet, the
king made a brief statement stressing the need to lift the darkness enveloping
the people of Central Africa. He likened it to a crusade and said his only
desire was to serve as they instructed him to in achieving this goal. After
wishing everyone well in their discussions, he withdrew, leaving the meeting's chair, Russian geographer Pyote Semenov, in charge.[26]

The main item under discussion was the need to build a series of Euro-
pean-staffed stations across Central Africa for provisioning future explorers,
collecting information on such things as soils, climate, flora, and fauna, and
putting an end to the slave trade. In order to emphasize their supposedly
humanitarian purposes, the delegates agreed to call them *stations hospitalières,
scientifiques et pacificatrices* (stations for hospitality, science, and pacification).
For organizational and fund-raising purposes, they decided to form national
committees, whose activities would be coordinated by the Association International Africaine (AIA). Leopold was appointed president, his close friend
Baron Jules Greindl secretary general, and Brussels chosen as headquarters.
Commitments of support came from France, Italy, Holland, Switzerland,
Austria, Britain, Spain, Portugal, Russia, and Belgium. The United States
wasn't represented, although the AGS expressed interest. As a way of gaining
international support, Leopold liked to compare the association with the Red
Cross, a deception if there ever was one.[27]

The king knew government and public opinion would be against creating
a Belgian colony anywhere, not just Africa, and thus favored a territorial
concession open to investors of all nations. From the outset it is clear he
expected to be in control and that with time, as Greindl put it in a letter to
the king, "the enterprise will become, by force of things, Belgian in name

as in actual fact."[28] In the meantime, subscriptions raised by the national committees of the AIA would help to lessen the drain on the royal treasury.

Given what eventually happened, it's easy to see the king's actions as stemming entirely from a desire for profit. But at the time profit and progress were often thought to go hand-in-hand, with all parties the better for it. Only later did it become clear that more often than not someone's gain amounted to another's loss, and in the Congo the losers numbered in the thousands. Furthermore, despite all his enthusiasm, Leopold couldn't have known much about the region's economic potential. That would have to await future exploration.

By the time the AIA next met in Brussels, the following June, the British delegation had decided to go it alone under the aegis of the Royal Geographical Society's African Exploration Fund.[29] Its council did consider appointing a representative to the committee but concluded, "the Society was not authorized by its charter to take part in the political or commercial exploitation of territory." Furthermore, it felt that a society with "so pronounced a national character" should "concentrate its efforts on British enterprises and avoid any entangling alliances."[30] Interest about Africa in Britain, however, had reached another low point, and the fund's members never did much beyond planning exploration routes in East Africa and supporting the expedition in which Joseph Thomson eventually reached Lake Tanganyika. It was dissolved in 1880.

American Henry Shelton Sanford took over as the English-speaking representative on the AIA's executive committee. The son of a wealthy industrialist and land speculator from Connecticut, he was sometimes called General Sanford because of having been made a major general in the Minnesota Militia for giving its First Regiment a battery of steel guns. Sanford admired Leopold, having met him while he was serving as U.S. minister to Belgium during the Lincoln administration, and promised to do everything within his means to promote the interests of the association in the United States. Sanford represented the American Auxillary Society, the brainchild of Charles P. Daly, Chief Judge of the New York City Court of Common Pleas and at the time president of the AGS.

After much discussion, the delegates decided to play down the matter of ending slavery, feeling that commerce and winning people's confidence would accomplish this better than more direct tactics. As a result, *Pacificatrices* disappeared from the description of the stations. They also decided to make Zanzibar the base of operations and put the first Congo station somewhere in the vicinity of Nyangwe. Brussels would seek to establish a station on the eastern side of Lake Tanganyika.

With the AIA providing a cover of political legitimacy, Leopold needed someone to do his bidding. He'd been following Stanley in the papers and after making some inquiries to ascertain his reliability and character decided to approach him through his representative in London, Baron Henri Solvyns. Nothing, however, must be done to displease the British, for they could easily spoil, the king warned, *"une bonne occasion nous procurer une part de ce magnifique gâteau africain"* (a good occasion for us to procure a part of the magnificent African cake).[31] Stanley first learned of the AIA's existence in Cairo, and after the festivities in Marseilles, Sanford and Greindl spoke with him about going back to the Congo in the association's employ when freed from obligations to Bennett. Preferring Britain take the lead in Central Africa, Stanley said he played it cool by remarking, "I am so sick and weary that I can not think with patience that I should personally conduct it. Six months hence, perhaps, I should view things differently; but at present I cannot think of anything more than a long rest and sleep."[32] Undeterred, Leopold asked both men to stay in touch with Stanley, hoping to win him over. After seeing his *Through the Dark Continent* off to the publisher, Stanley relented and agreed to meet with the king at the palace in Brussels. Well aware of the value of pomp and circumstance and flattery, Leopold had a royal carriage waiting as Stanley stepped from the train on June 10. He made no commitments to the AIA during discussions over the next several days, but he did put forth two proposals for consideration. One involved creating a company to build a railway from the coast to the pool, and the other stressed the need for putting steamers on the upper Congo.[33] As for the near future, Stanley intended to relax and enjoy the "liberty" that came with regaining his health. Besides, he doubted the king's resources matched his ambitions.

Greindl sent Stanley several letters immediately afterward. They weren't of much importance, other than to keep him in tow. One, for example, asked about the availability of fresh water above Boma for steam engines and workmen and how much earthmoving would be required for a railroad.[34]

Stanley's frame of mind certainly got a big boost from reviews of *Through the Dark Continent*. According to the *Scotsman*, as a work of literature, it constituted "a decided advance on Mr. Stanley's previous books of travel," while the *Manchester Guardian* remarked,

> Mr. Stanley's eagerly looked for volumes will certainly not disappoint readers, and the narrative of his thousand days across the dark continent will ever be regarded as one of the most valuable contributions to our knowledge of geography, and one of the most exciting narratives of courageous enterprise, in an age singularly rich in stories of travel and records of exploration.

Even a skeptical *Pall Mall Gazette* joined in the praise, noting that "These two volumes contain a full account of the most remarkable discovery in the present century, and one which will entitle the hero of it to a high rank among great travellers in all ages."[35]

The "liberty" Stanley looked for took him to Antwerp and Paris for receptions by geographical societies, and on July 4 he met Bennett in Le Havre at the christening of the *Jeannette*, a ship specially designed to take Commodore George Washington De Long to the North Pole. Bennett was the expedition's sponsor, and before settling on De Long he asked Stanley about leading it. Not really interested and no longer a *Herald* employee, Stanley could refuse the offer without fear of consequences. The decision proved to be a wise one, as the ship sank and many died, including De Long. A dinner with Hettie Pike, the sister of Alice, whom Stanley recorded as "my former lady love," followed the next day. They'd met at that same function on May 13, 1874, and while he found her "good looking," she appeared "fast" and talked "disagreeably loud."[36] He didn't say if she'd changed or not.

By August, with the help of a vacation in Geneva, Stanley felt much better but was somewhat bored with the routine of receptions and dinners. Consequently, following further overtures from Greindl, he agreed to meet with several of Leopold's men in Paris for more serious discussions about the Congo. The outcome was a report to the king on matters ranging from whether the expedition would be primarily philanthropic, geographic, or commercial in nature, to cost considerations, to the requirements of a railway.[37]

The king's tactics were having their intended effect, and on October 3 Stanley provisionally agreed to a proposal that would have him lead a Congo expedition for five years and possibly five more at a salary of one thousand pounds per annum. An additional twenty thousand would be made available to cover expenses during the first year, with five thousand each for years two and three. If after that time Leopold judged the project unprofitable, he could terminate the contract. An amendment stipulated that should such a decision be made, 2,800 pounds would be provided to return African workers to their homes. Worried about an upcoming speaking tour of England and Scotland, the king warned Stanley "to say nothing to incite people to undertake something on the Congo." If leaks somehow occurred, Stanley could say that he'd been entrusted with "the philanthropic mission of establishing three hospitable & scientific stations between Boma and Stanley Pool" and that when completed they would serve "to benefit the European and American trade and industry." Assurances could be given that AIA spon-

His Majesty Leopold II. the King of the Belgians. at the time of my engagement by him. Nov. 1878.

King Leopold II of Belgium as Stanley would have first seen him in 1878. *Courtesy of the Royal Museum of Central Africa*

sorship meant only "peaceful means" would be employed to accomplish the task.[38]

During the lecture tour, from November 4 to December 7, Stanley followed instructions and did not tip things off by directing most of his remarks to the events of 1874–1877 and descriptions of interior Africa's geographical features and peoples. With no time to relax, he hurried to Brussels on December 9 for the next round of discussions. The first item of business involved finalizing the contract, not with the AIA but with the Comité d'Etudes du Haut-Congo, an organization cooked up by Leopold, with him as honorary president and Col. Maximilien Strauch as titular president. This one committed Stanley to a three-year term and two more at the discretion of the Comité. The financial arrangements remained as agreed to in October.[39] Stanley then received instructions "to devote from this moment the whole of your time and well known activity to the framing, studying, and drawing up of . . . plans, estimates, and suggestions" at the request of the Comité. These were to be submitted by the end of December, in time for the next scheduled meeting, on January 2, 1878.[40] The most important item on the agenda involved discussions with prospective financial backers, especially the Rotterdam-based firm Afrikaansche Handels-Vennootschap, which operated in Banana at the mouth of the Congo. Conflicts with its representatives led Stanley on two occasions to proffer his resignation. However, he stayed on, and the January 2 meeting went ahead as planned.

When the British rejected a request to recruit workers from their possessions in West Africa, Stanley decided to go back to Zanzibar for some of his "old followers."[41] While he did so, the Comité promised to find Europeans to be in charge of the stations and also hire Kru and so-called Cabinda boys. The Kru hailed from the coast between Sierra Leone and Liberia and, besides being excellent canoe men, had proven themselves willing porters. Workers from Cabinda were usually employed for lighter domestic tasks thus the appellation "boys." A letter from Stanley to Sanford reveals a plan to hire "15 American Negroes" between 22 and 27 years of age for terms of three years.[42] The use of and possible return of American blacks to Africa was one of the reasons for Sanford's abiding interests in Leopold's Congo project. He saw their "contact with the white races," combined with recent "emancipation and education and equality of political rights," as making "them by far the superiors of their parent race." As such, they would "excite a spirit of enterprise, ambitions and desires hitherto dormant" in Central Africa.[43] Although nothing ever came of the idea, Sanford continued to stress its desirability. As he told a *Herald* reporter many years later,

> It is the land of promise for our people of colored descent: perhaps some colored Moses may yet arise and show them the way back to their Fatherland; they would do there good missionary work for civilization, and find ample field for every worthy ambition and enterprise.[44]

The lofty language provided a smokescreen for Sanford's real interest, repatriating as many blacks as possible. He didn't see them fitting in a "white" America.

Stanley then went to London, where he chartered the *Albion* for the trip to Zanzibar. It sailed on January 31 with his newly appointed secretary, Anthony B. Swinburne, aboard. A year earlier, the young man had written Stanley saying he'd like to be among those to welcome the explorer home but he knew he couldn't as the gathering would be for the "Big, Rich & Powerful ones."[45] The show of initiative netted him a job. Stanley planned to join the *Albion* at Suez after another meeting with Leopold, whom he now considered a "statesman of the first order."[46] Traveling with him on the ship from Marseilles was Lt. Oswald C. Dutalis, whom the Comité had designated to lead an upcoming AIA expedition. To avoid detection, Stanley traveled under the name Monsieur Henri. During the stopover at Aden, he hired several Somalis, including Qualla (Dualla) Idris, who spoke excellent English as a result of having worked as a cabin boy on an American ship, to be his personal assistant.

Their arrival in Zanzibar, on March 18, caught everyone by surprise. No one had been forewarned, including the American consul William H. Hawthorne. Kirk, who'd resumed his duties as British consul general, suspected a commercial scheme might be in the works but couldn't really be sure.[47] Whether out of secrecy or dislike, Stanley never paid him a visit. Dutalis's presence deepened the mystery, and in the coming weeks Stanley kept people guessing. Two trips to the mainland proved especially puzzling to those trying to discover what he planned to do. One targeted the Wami River during the first ten days of April. Stanley still thought it might be useful in "shortening the route to the interior," but it proved not to be—in addition to the many rocks observed in 1874, the narrow channel had few straight stretches, and large numbers of hippos and crocodiles infested the waters. Then on April 26 he took the *Albion* to Mafia Island for a further check of its potential. A revisit of the Rufiji River dampened his earlier enthusiasm. The costs of developing the island seemed too high for saving only about one hundred miles of overland journey. In fact, later investigations showed the Rufiji to be navigable for fewer than seventy miles from its mouth, and to that point by small boats only. Serious, sometimes catastrophic, flooding also limited the river's usability.

Qualla Idris, who served Stanley faithfully while working in the Congo. *Courtesy of the Royal Museum of Central Africa*

Back in Zanzibar on May 7, Stanley sent a letter to Lt. Ernst Cambier, the leader of the Brussels AIA-sponsored expedition that had been held up by Mirmabo while attempting to establish a station at Karema on the east side of Lake Tanganyika. The expedition was set to leave when Stanley stopped in Zanzibar during December 1877 but couldn't because of the sudden deaths of two European members within ten days of each other. Their replacements fared only a little better. One succumbed to fever on the way to Unyanyembe in December 1878, and shortly thereafter the other decided to quit for health reasons. Stanley told Cambier to head for Karema and wait there for the arrival of a second expedition under Dutalis's command before doing anything more.[48] As it turned out, Dutalis never got to show his metal, as a severe fever forced him to return home after getting no farther than Mpwapwa.

Two additional AIA officers were also scheduled to appear in Zanzibar, Lt. Emile Popelin and Capt. Frederick Carter, on his way from India with four elephants to use for station and road building. Three of them died before reaching Lake Tanganyika, as did Carter, either in a skirmish with Mirambo's men or by suicide. The details are too fuzzy to say which. Mirambo passed away on December 2, 1884, probably from throat cancer. While a master strategist and diplomat, he never succeeded in overcoming the Arab and Waswahili traders, and his state died with him.[49]

In a letter to Popelin, Stanley urged caution, saying,

> Rush not into danger by any overweening confidence in your breech-loading rifles and military knowledge. Be not tempted to try your mettle against the native chiefs, for you will certainly gain no honour, but possibly you may rush to your own destruction. Be calm in all contentions with native chiefs; and one golden rule which you should remember is, "Do not fire the first shot," whatever may be the provocation.[50]

He wanted to stay to help with their arrangements, but noted "I am needed on the Congo, & I am impatient to begin my work."[51] Thus, on May 25, Stanley departed Zanzibar aboard the *Albion* with sixty-one men in tow, about three-quarters of them veterans of the previous expedition. Surprisingly, they included one of the men left behind in the Congo in 1877. He'd managed to escape his captors, reach the mouth of the river, and catch a ship home. The sultan stipulated that only freemen could be recruited, but a few slaves appear to have been among the ranks.[52] Susi, Livingstone's former headman, who, along with Chuma, had prepared and brought the doctor's body to Bagamoyo, also signed up.

Doubts now began to cross Stanley's mind about the project's success. The AIA would need a port somewhere on the east coast, but so far Barghash showed no inclination toward granting the required concession. At Aden a telegram awaited Stanley with news of the financial default of Handels-Vennootschap, and another at Suez instructed Stanley to come to Brussels for further discussions with the Comité. He refused, thinking delays might cause problems between his men and the ship's crew that could scuttle the whole project, and cabled Strauch asking that someone meet him in Gibraltar instead.[53]

By the time Stanley got there, on July 8, the financial crisis had passed, and so Strauch told him to go ahead as planned and said that more funds would be made available to cover expenses. Much to his surprise, Stanley also learned that Brussels wanted the stations to be the focal points for creating a "a powerful negro state" along the Congo. He demurred, noting that "It would be madness for one in my position to attempt it, except as one course might follow another in the natural sequence of things."[54] What Strauch doesn't seem to have revealed is that Europeans, not Africans, were to have absolute power in this new state. Another thing he kept from Stanley was the king's use of the financial crisis to dissolve the Comité and return all of the subscriptions, which hadn't totaled very much anyway. Correspondence makes it seem likely that Sanford initiated the idea.[55] In its stead Leopold formed his own Association Internationale du Congo (AIC). The emphasis needs to be placed on "his own," for in reality the king had no associates and didn't want any, even though that meant using personal wealth to finance the venture.[56]

Problems with the *Albion*'s boilers caused the voyage to take longer than expected, and a stop at Sierra Leone for repairs led Stanley to worry that all the Africans on board might arouse suspicion. As a further precaution, he asked the captain to keep his presence secret and turned down an offer to visit with the colony's governor on the grounds of not feeling well.[57] When it became clear that the delay would last more than a day, Stanley abandoned the secrecy and agreed to join a picnic lunch on shore. His worries were for nothing, and the stopover allowed for the purchase of much needed supplies, such as locks and bolts, that hadn't been loaded in England.

The extra time also led Stanley to ruminate on a number of things. He still had difficulty understanding why the British reacted so negatively to his efforts aimed at stirring up interest in Central Africa. As in so many other instances, he took it as a personal rebuff, noting that "Either they suspect me of some self-interest or do not believe me. My reward has been to be called a mere penney a liner." All told, Leopold and the Belgians seemed a

Stanley wearing the special cap he devised for work in the Congo. *Courtesy of the Royal Museum of Central Africa*

worthy alternative, even though he felt that the king "has not been so frank as to tell me outright what we are to strive for." It wasn't hard for Stanley to put two and two together, however, for, as he noted, it is "pretty evident that under the guise of an International Association he hopes to make a Belgian dependency of the Congo."[58]

On August 14, 1879, the *Albion* finally dropped anchor at Banana. A narrow sand-spit only six feet above high water and with few trees to provide shade from the tropical sun, it served as the break-in-bulk point for shipments headed up stream. A week later the expedition began its journey in a flotilla consisting of five steamers—the *Espérance,* the *Belgique,* the *Royal,* the *Jeune Africaine,* and the *En Avant*—a wooden whaleboat, and the *Albion,* which Stanley had scrapped and painted. Those aboard included the sixty-one from Zanzibar, thirty-seven Kru, eighteen from Cabinda, and eleven European agents, including Augustus Sparhawk, who'd come out to serve as superintendent in charge of supplies. Stanley considered it a skeleton workforce, and he asked Strauch to provide eighty more Kru, forty Cabinda natives, and additional Zanzibaris beyond the seven already on their way.[59]

Occasional clusters of factories provided the only signs of human activity as the boats worked their way along the mangrove-lined lower portion of the river to Ponta da Lenha, where they spent the night. Stanley admired the Dutch for the solidity of the factories they built but didn't think much of their penchant for imbibing strong spirits, which he considered dangerous to health in the tropics. Above Ponta da Lenha the river's current slows and the channel becomes choked with low-lying islands and sandbars that demanded charting a somewhat more circuitous route. Four hours of sailing brought Boma into view. Stanley described the town as consisting of "a congeries of factories," having a history "fraught with horror, and woe, and suffering" because of "the pitiless persecution of black men, by sordid whites." However, by 1879 its commerce had become, in his eyes, "innocent" trade involving "the butter of the oil-palm, rubber from the forests, kernels from oil-nuts, nuts from the ground, copal from old deposits, ivory spoils of the elephant, &c." Furthermore, he reported that in spite of past injustices, "we see that the natives do not seem embittered or soured, but, on the contrary, that a pleasant and confident bearing marks their behavior as they tread the river street of the town."[60] Trade was seemingly having its intended effect, or at least Stanley wanted readers of his book to think so. He doesn't seem to have asked the town's Africans what they thought.

The dry season gave the town a parched look, and African sunlight, Stanley said, only served to make the view less appealing. "It deepens the shadows, and darkens the dark-green foliage of the forest, while it imparts a wan appearance or a cold reflection of light to naked slopes and woodless hilltops. Its effect is a chill austerity—an indescribable solemnity, a repelling unsociability."[61] A characteristic that never changed in Stanley was his strong reaction to places and he let them be known.

For the next week, the boats shuttled back and forth between Boma and Banana, bringing supplies until enough were on hand to seek out a new lower base of operations. Wanting to keep his men away from "pernicious trade centers" with their gin and rum drinkers, Stanley chose Mussuko, four hours above Boma on the left bank of the river. From there he took the *Royal* to the rapids at Vivi, some three hours away, returning for a second look a few days later. The plan called for Vivi to be the first station, and fortunately the locals seemed pleased to see him, sensing this would bring traders to them rather than they having to take produce to Boma. Stanley returned to Vivi the last week of September to select the station site. The chiefs recommended a hill some three hundred feet above the river. At first glance the slope appeared to be too steep, but because of the "aimiable character of the natives," Stanley decided he'd look at it anyway. To his great delight the hill had a level top, plus a reasonably gentle slope to the riverbank. A stretch of rapids marked the way, but it looked like the *Esperance* could handle it without too much difficulty. The site would thus do, and he reached an agreement with the Vivi chiefs to begin developing it. In addition to the land, Stanley secured recognition as the *mundelé* of Vivi to white men, a promise of workers, and rights of passage for traders. For this he handed over fifty pieces of cloth; three boxes of gin; five each of military coats, knives, caps, cloth waist belts, and loincloths; and a monthly rent of two pounds worth of cloth.[62] Because the land stood unused, the chiefs probably thought the deal a pretty good one.

Construction began to "the inspiring sound of striking picks, ringing hoes, metallic strokes of crowbars, and dull thudding of sledge hammers" raised by the workforce.[63] Women did the clearing. As Stanley told it, during a demonstration for the Zanzibaris on how to use sledgehammers, one of the Vivi subchiefs proclaimed, "Stanley is too hard for us, let us all call him Bula Matari in future."[64] The proper rendering along this stretch of the Congo would have been Bula Matadi—the substitution of *r* for *d* is Kiswahili in origin. The term is usually translated as "breaker of rocks," and he took it as a compliment. In point of fact, it could also be rendered "break stones," and given the Congolese penchant for assigning names based on personalities rather than events, it might have had negative connotations, such as him being a "slave-driver," or "destroyer."[65] Whatever its origins or pronunciation, the stories about Bula Matari started spreading upriver, and it became his generally accepted name. Later, it served as a term of endearment among close friends.

Nearly four months of working six days a week from 6:00 to 11:00 A.M. and 1:00 to 6:00 P.M. were required to get the station in working order. In addition to staff houses, Vivi contained a headquarters building, which some claimed looked like a castle or church from the river, plus an array of stables and sheds. Rich valley bottom topsoil carted up the 340-foot slope supported newly planted vegetable gardens and a grove of fruit trees. Stanley thought a city of twenty thousand inhabitants could be accommodated on the site, with nearby valleys providing considerable room for expansion. With a road to the interior, trade could expand. A particularly enticing thought was the prospect of millions of Congolese someday wearing Europe's secondhand clothes, which at the time went mostly wasted. Like many travelers, Stanley found African dress and undress uncivilized. Of course, tidy profits awaited sellers.

Letters from Strauch arrived regularly, and in one he suggested that to protect the legality of the enterprise it might be necessary to form the stations into a "free state," a variant of the idea floated earlier. Stanley should begin obtaining concessions and plan for settlers. Stanley considered the idea unrealistic, given the number of men at his disposal. At the moment they totaled only thirteen Europeans, sixty-six Zanzibaris, seventy Kru, forty-six from Cabinda, Qualla, and six locals. This prompted a reaction to an earlier cable from Sanford urging economy. If that's what Brussels considered most important, maybe it would be better, Stanley replied, for the mission to be a surveying one only, or even terminated.[66]

Stanley decided to locate the next station at Isangila. Putting a nearly completed Vivi in Sparhawk's hands, he set off overland on February 21 to find the best route. At first, the prospects looked less than promising, but closer inspection suggested to him that a road could be built without undo effort. Two days later, he met with some thirty chiefs to get their approval for it and to obtain guides for the rest of the journey. According to Stanley,

> They expressed themselves very well pleased with our coming into the country. It would be a good thing to the country that a road should be made. No chief had any objection whatsoever to the idea. In their eyes the coming of the white man would be productive of good—good to chiefs and people. It meant trade and they were all traders.[67]

Gift exchanges followed the negotiations, and the next day Stanley left, traversing the same path as in 1877, although under far less trying circumstances.

During the journey Stanley learned that the *Lady Alice* had been "smashed for the sake of its iron & copper nails," and upon reaching Isangila on February 28 he discovered nature had obliterated all signs of his former camp.[68] As at Vivi, the locals put on a warm welcome and the chiefs agreed to allow a town to be built by the riverside in exchange for "an ample supply of fine clothes, funky coats, and tinsel-braided uniforms," along with an assortment of wares and rum. The site pleased Stanley, for it too seemed to have considerable growth potential. However, as he informed Strauch, the richness of the country between Vivi and Isangila would make it difficult to recruit workers. Poor people from elsewhere in the Congo or freed slaves might be needed to fill the roster.[69] And the road would by no means be easy to build, for after the first twelve miles

> begins the up-and-down work, the removing of great rocks, the filling up of hollows, until we come to a forest, which has to be cut through; we then come to a river, its bed filled with boulders, out of which we emerge to drag the waggon up a slope which has a rise of one foot in four. Then another bit of fair road, through stubborn bush and tall grass, takes us six or seven miles, when we come in presence of the worst of our difficulties—ravine after ravine, hill after hill, stream after stream, while the great river itself at this particular place is one narrow wild rapid, hemmed in by tall black cliffs impassable to anything.[70]

Upon returning to Vivi on March 9, Stanley discovered that four Europeans had tendered resignations. While two subsequently changed their minds, he blamed the Dutch at Banana for sowing discontent in an effort to derail the project. Nevertheless, everything seemed in order for constructing the road, and so work commenced on March 18. The opportunity to build one caused Stanley to proclaim buoyantly: "There is no pleasure in life equal to that enjoyed by one who makes a broad straight road for the first time through a wilderness."[71] The work went as well as could be expected, and after a week the road measured between nine and ten miles. Whenever possible Stanley continued the task started in 1877 of asking people their name for the Congo. All of them seemed to mean river. One, Zali or Zari, the Portuguese had rendered as Zaire.

By April 6 the road extended more than fifteen miles. Care had to be taken to avoid poisonous snakes, especially spitting cobras, and unfriendly buffalo herds regularly got in the way. Still, the work continued without interruption, and the road counted seven more miles by the time it reached the landing place at Manguba on April 21. From this point the Congo could

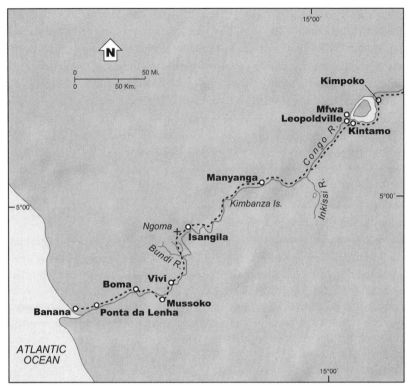

Map 6.1   Station Building on the Lower Congo

be used as far as the Bundi River, where an easy ascent to the plateau existed. Three days later, Stanley and the workmen set off for Vivi, "having for the first time the pleasure," he said, "of travelling on a road almost as good as an English turnpike—Indeed in many places it is better."[72]

Everyone needed a rest, including Stanley, before they could face the next task of hauling the disassembled *Royal* to Manguba. The quality of the road eased the task, and on May 11 the *Royal* was refloated. Back in Vivi, Stanley found things going far less smoothly with the Europeans. According to him, "they pine & fret, & complain of so many things that they are like children." By the end of May seven of them would be lost; two died, three resigned, one was discharged for not doing his job, and another had to leave because of illness. A Zanzibari's death bothered Stanley even more. They constituted the backbone of the whole project and he considered one to be "superior in proportion to his wages to 10 Europeans, be they English, Belgian, or American."[73]

Two tasks needed immediate attention—putting the final touches on the Vivi station and moving supplies first via road to Manguba and from there to the Bundi by using the *Royal* and the *En Avant.* Progress slowed when fever put Stanley out of commission for more than a week at the end of June. He continued to feel unwell for a while afterward and developed a painful ulcer on his foot. The by now chronic shortage of men also slowed work. As July drew to a close, Stanley could count only four Europeans and sixty-seven Zanzibaris, plus some locals for the heavy work ahead, while the staff at Vivi consisted of seven Europeans, seventy-four locals, and three Kru. In spite of everything, by August 4 the transfer to the Bundi had been completed. To reach Isangila, a road would be required virtually the whole way.

Each advance above the Bundi seemed to bring a new challenge to the workers. In some places they had to cut through dense forest, at others ten to fifteen foot high stands of grass stood in the way, whereas at still others it meant hammering the road out of exposed rock under a scorching sun. Fortunately, another short stretch of the Congo proved to be navigable, as Stanley considered the land thereabouts impassible to wagons. His main jobs were of marking the next day's route and shooting game for a regular supply of meat.

Six weeks of road building and hauling took them another sixteen miles and face-to-face with the imposing barrier of Ngoma, a high hill looking more like a mountain. Along the way, crocodiles devoured six workmen and two asses. Stanley detested the creatures, noting that "at every opportunity given me I never fail to try and avenge myself on them, & I suppose I have shot more crocodiles in Africa than any 4 Explorers."[74] Annoyingly, Strauch's letters expressed impatience with the pace of progress and urged "a dash for the pool" in order to get concession agreements signed. Stanley wrote back arguing against any precipitous actions that might provoke hostile responses from Africans or other Europeans. He considered it far better "to have one task finished before beginning another."[75] And the task requiring undivided attention right now was to complete construction of the stations. Furthermore, insufficient manpower prohibited moving more quickly. Strauch's idea of sending Chinese coolies didn't seem reasonable. Even if they were hired, Stanley figured they wouldn't make it to the Congo until after all the hard work had been finished.

On November 7 a messenger brought a note bearing the name Le Comte Savorgnan de Brazza, Enseigne de Vaisseau. An Italian by origin, de Brazza had made a name for himself by exploring along the Ogouwé River in 1875–1878.[76] An hour later he made an appearance, having come from Stanley Pool

The road around Ngoma. *Henry M. Stanley,* The Congo and the Founding of Its
Free State *(New York: Harper & Brothers, 1885).*

accompanied by a mixed contingent of Senegalese and Gabonese soldiers.
His going there in the employ of France was what prompted Strauch's messages to hurry. Stanley welcomed him, and although neither spoke the other's language very well, they spent that afternoon and evening in
conversation. According to Stanley, he mostly listened as de Brazza related
his experiences along the Ogouwé. While giving him credit "for a brave feat
of exploration," Stanley expressed some doubts about the truthfulness of his
accounts. He thought many of them exaggerated and, as a journal entry indicates, sensed not being told everything:

> Underneath the gay ebullience of his manner & his affected heartiness his
> speaking eyes betray that he has achieved a triumph of some kind other than
> that what personal magnitism may have obtained. What it is I cannot imag-
> ine, but there is a laughing mocking spirit in the visual glances I detect now &
> then, which makes me suspect that it has some connection with me.[77]

The following morning de Brazza left for Vivi, intending to catch a steamer
to Banana, where he could make a connection to Gabon. Stanley lent him
his own riding ass for the road, sending along a couple of Zanzibaris as

guides and a letter to the Vivi staff telling them to look after the count's needs.

Stanley now puzzled over what to do about Ngoma and its steep ravine-scarred slope, which de Brazza calculated would take six months to surmount with the small number of workers on hand. After another look, Stanley concurred and decided to go around Ngoma by building a rock causeway through the forest between its base and the river. Work began on November 12, and it took nearly a month of blasting and moving rocks at an average pace of forty-two yards per day for the bypass to be completed. From the new advance camp on the other side, the river could be used to get within a mile and a half of Isangila, thus saving some six weeks of roadwork. On December 24, Stanley selected a spot for a camp a little ways below the rapids, and four days later the transfer of goods began. Ninety-five men would have to see to the task of bringing more than five hundred sixty-pound loads plus two full wagons ahead. They did it by February 15, 1881, and three days later Stanley established a camp above the cataract to start construction on the station.

A full year had been consumed covering the distance between Vivi and Isangila, which Stanley estimated at 2,300 miles when all the comings and goings were added up. Twenty-two Africans and six Europeans lost their lives in the process. Stanley described it as "a year dark with trial and unusual toil." Still, he concluded, "Our little band of labourers are proud of the grand work their muscles have accomplished," and now they "are more hopeful of the future, inasmuch as their labours, by means of steamers will be greatly lightened."[78] We don't know what the workers actually thought, but prospects of a lighter workload must have cheered them.

The plan called for building the next station at Manyanga. With 118 workers, two Belgian military passengers, and more than fifty tons of baggage to transport, Stanley figured he would need seventy to eighty days to get there. It was less arduous work than required between Vivi and Isangila, but the many small rapids along the way suggested the likelihood of serious accidents. Reports from Strauch about hostile reactions from the Dutch and Portuguese provided another cause for concern. Stanley figured the former feared losing some of their profits to the Belgians, whereas the latter, he supposed, worried about infringements on their assumed river rights. So as not to provide either with opportunities to spread rumors that could be used against the association, he wanted to make sure none of his men misbehaved and that, in particular, they "refrain from punishing the natives or treating them otherwise than with patience & kindness."[79] Experience in Africa had taught Stanley quite a bit about life. One couldn't always be a Bula Matari.

The loading of the boats began on February 21, and five days later the camp had been cleared. At this time, Stanley wrote a most interesting passage, given his past concern for stiff-upper-lip-type dignity. It came from observing one of the Europeans having fun and shows another way Africa had changed Stanley:

> I love to see young men of my own colour take delight and enjoyment in life in Africa. Nothing so soon excites a general smile on everybody's face than to see young Albert racing like a young elephant over the beautiful pure sand, and showing to the astonishment of blackies that the white man has also a sense of fun, and can run, and leap, and race like themselves. The dark faces light up with friendly gleams, and a budding goodwill may perhaps date from this trivial scene. For far different is the reception of the white man whose dignity is so meaningless that it chills the native on-looker on coming within its presence. To such an impressionable being as an African native, the self-involved European, with his frigid, imperious, manners, and the pallid white face, and dead, lustreless eyes, is like a sealed book. The native views the form resembling his in figure; he hears him speak in veritable human tones; but the language is unintelligible, neither can he utter any sound that is familiar to him. But let the strange white man relax those stiff, pallid features; let there enter into those chill, icy eyes, the light of life and joy, of humour, friendship, pleasure, and the communication between man and man is electric in its suddenness.[80]

At the outset, the journey went as smoothly as could be hoped for. Then on March 6 Sudi, one of the "faithfuls," who'd survived Ituru in 1875 and Kalulu Falls in 1877, was gored by a buffalo and died. Relatively placid days followed, with curious locals showing up at each landing place, usually eager to trade. All the rapids were passed without incident, although to get around some required short stretches of portaging. On April 8 they reached Kimbanza Island, where Stanley decided to stop in order to let the men rest and make needed repairs on the boats. They stayed until the 19th of the month, and two forays upstream produced the first hostile encounters since returning to the Congo. Stanley said he diffused one by drawing a line in the sand and the other by firing shots overhead as a warning.[81] Trade also went less smoothly along this portion of the river, as the inhabitants only sold produce on scheduled market days. In comparative terms, these constituted minor impediments, and Stanley reached Manyanga before the month was out. While having made better time than earlier predicted, overall the work had moved at a "snail's pace," and Stanley Pool was still about ninety-five miles away.

Negotiations with the local chiefs were productive. According to Stanley, they told him "that there is no lack of space for you and your village and gardens—and that you are free to choose where you like, here by the river, or up on the hills."[82] He could also take his time making the decision, and payment details would be worked out later. On May 5 Stanley started feeling feverish and experienced a severe headache. He went to bed, but rest and ever larger doses of quinine brought no relief. Unconscious from May 12 to 19, he later recalled thinking death was at hand and summoning the Europeans and Zanzibaris to his bedside so that he "might bid them farewell." Struggling to get out "intelligible" words, he described being overcome by a "dark cloud" and drifting into "oblivion."[83] A full week passed after he regained consciousness before Stanley could muster enough strength to raise himself even slightly. Despite considerable weakness and weighing only about a hundred pounds, he felt well enough by June 2 to sit outside his tent in a chair.

Stanley's spirits soared when he heard that a contingent of new recruits from Zanzibar had reached the Congo, with an advance party led by German Otto Lindner already on its way upriver. On June 5 they arrived, bringing six months' worth of correspondence, which included letters from Strauch filled with more demands. One repeated earlier instructions to:

go to Stanley Pool as fast as possible,
make sure statins are established at Isangila, Manyanga, and Stanley Pool,
conclude commercial treaties to obtain territorial concessions,
leave at each point a few "faithful" men commanded by a European,
entrust the European with construction of the station,
enlist natives for transport, and
embark on the Upper Congo and establish new stations.[84]

Stanley immediately sent a reply with a series of questions about how such a thing could be accomplished even with the new laborers. He also responded to charges made in the *Journal of Loanda* about putting Africans in chains by noting,

It takes some time to drill and discipline a body of raw negroes, it generally takes a year, about the same time it takes to acclimatise them in another section of Africa—not their native land. Punishment must be in two forms only—the stick or whip—and irons. The first is repulsive if inflicted with severity; it wounds, disfigures and renders disgusting the very person in whom you wish to plant self-respect, and invest with a certain degree of dignity, and for whom you desire to entertain a certain degree of liking. . . . The best

punishment is that of irons, because without wounding, disfiguring or tortur-
ing the body, it inflicts shame and discomfort. Envy of the freedom their
friends enjoy causes regret for past foolishness; the person in irons constantly
hopes that before the period of sentence expires, the master will relent, but
pardon before expiration of the sentence can only be purchased by good
behaviour, readiness to work being the essential ingredient.[85]

Here Stanley revealed another dimension of his Calvinist upbringing. People
must work, and if they didn't punishment might be necessary to get them
to. The punishment, however, should not impair the person's future capacity
for work.

In better health, Stanley resumed making preparations for the next leg of
the journey. Three tasks needed immediate attention—getting a contract
with the Manyanga chiefs signed, starting station construction, and building
a road around the cataracts. With the help of two hundred locals, the latter
took only twenty-two days to complete. Nonetheless, doubts now crossed
his mind about the purposes of the stations. Why Brussels kept sending military men didn't make sense given the nature of the job at hand. While they
would be able to create "admirably kept, and well-ordered" stations, they
could not found and maintain ones for trading.[86] For Belgian personnel the
AIC had to rely on military types, as the country lacked civilian candidates.
These had to be sought from elsewhere.

The rest of the relief party, including three Europeans to take charge of
Manyanga, made its appearance July 14. Good news came along—Vivi was
progressing nicely, and a young Belgian lieutenant named Eugene Janssen
had taken over at Isangila. Six days later, after getting them situated, Stanley
left with a small party to locate the way to the pool. In the meantime, he
wanted Lindner to go by boat to the rapids at Mpakambendi and then start
building a road to the plateau. The party moved quickly, encountering
receptive people willing to trade and work. Despite occasional rough spots,
a wagon road could be built. Then on July 27, while camped at the village
ruled by Chief Bwa Njali, Stanley heard someone calling out *"Bonjour Bonjour."* The greeting came from Malamine Kamara, a Senegalese sergeant
employed by de Brazza, who had instructions to show any Europeans he
came across a treaty signed by a chief called Makoko ceding territory to
France on the north side of Stanley Pool. When he visited Stanley, de Brazza
had the treaty on him. They key portion dated October 3, 1880, read,

In the name of France and in virtue of the rights conferred on me on September 10th, 1880, by King Makoko, I have taken possession, on October 3rd,

1880, of the territory extending between the river Iné and Impila. In token of this taking possession, I have planted the French flag at Okila. . . . I have handed to each of the chiefs who occupy this part of the territory a French flag to be flown over their villages in witness of my having taken possession thereof in the name of France. . . . By the despatch to Makoko of this document, made in triplicate and bearing my signature and the marks of the chiefs, his vassals, I give Makoko formal notice of my taking possession of this part of his territory for the establishment of a French station.[87]

The nature of de Brazza's "triumph" became evident. It set in motion two competitions, one between Stanley and de Brazza, and the other the "scramble" for African territory that would become full-blown in just a few years' time.

The next day, Stanley led his men on a quick march to the ivory trading center at Mfwa. Since no food could be found there, he decided to leave and set up camp on the south side of the pool, hoping people would notice them and come to trade. When told by some youths that this was unlikely to happen, he headed for the village of a chief called Gamankono. The chief turned out to be the same person Stanley had known as Mankoneh four years earlier—the one who showed him where to camp. Asked if Makoko had sold any land, Gamankono replied that he knew of no such thing, and besides, he said, each village had its own king and lands. No one, therefore, could speak for others. Then Malamine appeared on the scene and took Gamankono aside for a brief word. At its conclusion, the chief informed Stanley that his presence was no longer welcome.

With circumstances showing no signs of improving—in fact they appeared to have worsened overnight—Stanley told Gamankono that he and his party would leave immediately. On the way out of the village, some men came to take them to a landing place to await the arrival of a chief named Ngaliema. Three days later he showed up, and much to Stanley's surprise, he proved to be none other than Itsi, Frank Pocock's blood brother from 1877. If they stayed put, Ngaliema said, canoes would come to take everyone to his village of Kintamo at the pool. That never happened. Instead, he returned with news that a meeting with other chiefs would first have to take place in order to decide about the best course of action to follow.

Meanwhile, a dangerous food shortage had arisen. No one came to trade, and some men sent to get food at Bwa Njali's returned empty handed after running into hostile threats. Because he was well armed, Stanley did not think an attack likely, and he blamed Malamine for stirring up trouble. On August 11 Ngaliema once again made an appearance, this time bringing five

chiefs with him. He told Stanley that "after a long palaver it had been concluded by all his people that they would not accept the white men as residents with them." A protracted discussion produced a compromise: ten men
bearing fifteen loads of gifts could proceed to Kintamo, while Stanley would
take the others back down river for a return along the south bank. By then
Ngaliema felt he could resolve the problems and have a "fine site" at the
Pool ready for their arrival.[88]

Stanley concluded two things from these meetings: He needed to secure
the goodwill of Ngaliema whom he credited with fending off de Brazza's
efforts to secure both sides of the Pool for France.[89] And dealing with leaders
like him required having a much larger stock of trade goods on hand. Consequently, he sent one of the European officers to Luanda to purchase such
items as silks, velvets, and fine flannels.

Stanley got back Mpakambendi on August 21 and was relieved to find
Lindner and all the supplies on hand. Consequently, he had the workers
begin their new round of road building immediately. By September 12 everything and everyone had been brought to a point opposite the Inkisi River. As
the *En Avant* could now be used for occasional stretches, the pace of advance
quickened and they reached the river crossing point on October 8. Once on
the left bank, though, progress would necessarily slow down, as the rest of
the journey to the pool required going by land.

On October 15 two gunshots echoed through the camp. The men returning from Kintamo had fired them, and the news they brought wasn't encouraging. Under pressure from local traders, the chiefs on the south side of the
pool had threatened Ngaliema with retaliation should Stanley ever reach
Kintamo. They reiterated that they didn't want white men in their midst
who could buy up everything with their large stocks of cheap cloth, and in
this way cause the country to "die," meaning no longer produce for them.[90]
Ngaliema, therefore, wanted road making stopped. As compensation, he
promised to send some ivory. Stanley ignored the message and pushed ahead
as planned.

For a change, he didn't mind the slow going promised by the succession
of gorges facing the workers, feeling it would help the people along the route
overcome their concerns about Europeans. And, indeed, they willingly
traded and joined on as laborers. The surrounding countryside also looked
promising. Surveying it from a 1,450-foot summit, Stanley claimed to see a
land "fair to look upon." Given proper amenities, he felt "a residence on the
best parts of this breezy ridge, with such a daily prospect, would by no means
be considered a privation."[91]

A meeting with Chief Makoko took place November 7. He impressed

Stanley as "a guileless & peacefully disposed person," and following the usual palaver, Makoko announced that he would allow a station to be built at some place convenient to both of them. Ngaliema, however, might pose a problem. According to Makoko, in order to stay in the good graces of the traders, he was on his way with a large contingent of armed men to turn Stanley back.[92]

The next morning Stanley began preparing for whatever Ngaliema might have in mind. He felt confident that an attack could be repulsed and also wanted to quash rumors of possible fights, as these only served to alarm people. His published account is a colorful one depicting a plan in which a few men were given instructions to stay in camp "and assume a listless and indifferent attitude" while everyone else hid from view. Upon hearing a gong they had instructions to rush out "yelling like madmen" and wave their "guns about wildly . . . like the Ruga-Ruga of Unyamwezi." At their meeting Ngaliema told Stanley he must go back downriver. War would result if he didn't. After exiting Stanley's tent, Ngaliema supposedly wanted to hear the gong hanging outside rung. Stanley called it a war fetish and said its sound "would raise fighting men from above & from below and from all around. The sight would be too awful." When Ngaliema persisted in his request, Stanley gave it several blows that unleashed "a stream of frantic infuriates." At their sight, many of Ngaliema's men dropped their weapons and fled panic stricken. Stanley said he then told the chief not to be afraid and ordered an end to the demonstrations. Half an hour later he reported that everyone "swore faithful brotherhood and everlasting peace" while drinking palm wine.[93]

How much of this story was true is difficult to say. But something of the sort does seem to have happened, for he told a brief version of it to Strauch in a letter he wrote shortly thereafter.[94] During the episode, Stanley learned that Ngaliema wasn't a true chief, rather a captive and former slave at Kinshasa. When freed after his owner's death, a common Central African custom, Ngaliema stayed on and became a successful ivory trader. Although he had built a large following, many considered him a "nobody" who could be ignored. By this time, Stanley knew the area around the pool to be a confederacy of chiefdoms in which none dominated. He thus concluded it would be wise to gain "the consent of every chief without distinction," even a pretender like Ngaliema.[95]

With Ngaliema out of the way, the journey resumed. Some tough roadwork remained to reach the pool. The addition of seventy-eight locals helped speed the effort, and on November 29, Stanley got there. Attention could now be directed at finding a site for the station. Stanley decided on one just above the cataracts and six hundred yards downstream from Kintamo. From there direct communications with Manyanga could be maintained without having to cross through land controlled by Ngaliema. The top of a hill rising two hundred feet above the river provided a good site to put the station chief's house. A pleasant breeze blew regularly, and it afforded an unob-structed view downstream. Groundwork began on December 1, and two days later the *En Avant* lay at anchor in a cove adjacent to the emerging village of Leopoldville. Work on the settlement progressed without interrup-tion, save repeated visits by Ngaliema, whose hostility had resurfaced. A meeting with him and the key chiefs on December 24 apparently cleared the air, for afterward Stanley reported that "The country all around is in a gra-cious & aimiable mood." Even news about de Brazza's signing treaties and giving out French flags on the north side of the pool failed to deflate Stan-ley's mood. As a matter of fact, he viewed this as a good thing, since it seemed to have provoked Leopold into providing more money for expenses. As a result, he figured rivalry with France would serve to hasten the coming of civilization to "Old Africa."[96]

On the negative side, Sparhawk had resigned his post and left the Congo without warning. This puzzled Stanley, since they'd been friends for a dozen years. His replacement at Vivi would be Lindner, whom Stanley considered the "most capable man" among the officers, and to soften the blow, a hun-dred fresh Zanzibaris had reached Vivi to replace those scheduled to go home at the end of their three-year contract period on May 16, 1882. Stanley insisted that no attempt be made to lure them into staying longer and that "Whatever is good for their comfort must be done." Were the replacements already at the pool, he felt the four additional stations Strauch asked for could be built by August. At the moment, the priority must be to secure the present site; it had to be strong enough to deter any attempts at "plunder & violence," for Stanley felt that "the shedding of one drop of blood would be ruin to our future prospects. Peace & commerce would be impossible."[97]

Twenty-two additional Zanzibaris arrived on January 19, bringing the number of African laborers at Leopoldville to 153. While the pace of work picked up, providing enough to eat for all became burdensome and expen-sive. As the economy of the pool area shifted to a greater reliance on trade, fewer and fewer people farmed and fished, creating a situation where food shortages were becoming common. By March preparations had reached the point where crops could be planted at the station, which hopefully someday would free it from relying on others for food. Stanley considered the soil of the pool area to be "the richest alluvium it would be possible to find in any part of the world!" If properly developed, he estimated "half a million tons of rice annually, and wheat, sugar, yams, sweet potatoes, millet, Indian corn *ad infinitum*" could be produced annually. In addition, the lower slopes "would permit the remunerative growth of tea, coffee, cocoa, sago, and other spices."[98] Even with the good progress, Stanley fretted. He'd lost ten Europeans to death or departure, and the remaining Zanzibaris were still nowhere in sight. Yet Strauch kept urging more rapid progress. Concerned about French activities and recent concession agreements obtained by the Dutch and Portuguese, he told Stanley to hurry on, buy ivory, and build more stations.

A clipping from an English newspaper accused Stanley of working "several gangs of slaves in chains." This he denied, but did admit occasionally using "light foot chains & neck collars" on the Kru for disciplinary purposes. It seemed to him more humane than the fetters and handcuffs used by the British military and it "allowed locals to see who were troublemakers." Besides, nothing requiring their use had taken place since reaching Stanley Pool.[99]

Depressing news from Manyanga didn't help his disposition. For the second time, a fire consumed lives and property, and taking advantage of an unguarded *Royal,* some locals lifted its whistle and some screw bolts. An attack on the station that killed four villagers and wounded three others followed. Stanley realized he couldn't do anything about the situation from such a distance. He attributed the problem to the quality of officers Brussels sent him. "They do not know how to be sociable with the natives; they know nothing of the language, and they never care to acquire it by trying to talk with them, they know nothing of business and practical life—they are continually at the military pose," he complained to Strauch.[100] By way of contrast, April 8 and 9 proved to be good days. The new recruits finally showed up, and Stanley and Ngaliema made a brotherhood pact that supposedly bound them together forever.

Given Leopoldville's satisfactory condition—water was handy, fuel easy to come by, the locals friendly, and connections with Manyanga established—on April 19 Stanley loaded forty-nine men aboard the *En Avant,* the whaleboat, and two canoes for a sortie to the Upper Congo. Somewhat reluctantly, he left Lt. Charles Braconnier, a man who'd been briefly dismissed from service for failing to make enough progress in road building and for taking offense too easily, in charge.[101] While uncertain what the coming months might bring, Stanley envisioned that by Christmas three more stations would be operable. Mswata looked to be the most likely place for the next one, and although Stanley was cordially greeted by the area's chiefs, it took eleven days of negotiations to reach an agreement about where to build. The delay stemmed largely from having to convince some women to relinquish a prized cassava field. The chiefs also agreed to give the association exclusive trade rights from the Kwango River toward Stanley Pool. After putting Janssen in charge, Stanley returned to Leopoldville and, to his satisfaction, found more supplies on hand and, in general, everything progressing nicely. On May 14 he went back to Mswata, where Janssen had made considerable progress in getting the station built and in securing the cooperation of the locals. This, Stanley said, showed that "A little common sense & good nature are all that is needed to ensure prosperity to our enterprise. Quarrels most naturally occur now & then, but with a little patience & tact, these need not mar the cordial relations that have been established."[102] Years later, one of his officers, Charles Liebrechts, described Stanley's patience with the Congolese as "*évangéligue,*" noting that this gained him enduring prestige in their eyes.[103]

Sensing it would be at least a month before the next European could reach the pool, Stanley decided to explore the Kwa River to see what it might have to offer. He intended to travel about two hundred miles, expecting the round-trip to take nine days from its inception on May 19. Although the lower part of the river was narrow, it soon widened more than two miles. At the junction with the Fimi, Stanley met Queen Ngankabi, whom he described as a "gracious and hospitable" friend and resembling Martha Washington with her "austere, fixed, resolute, and earnest-eyed" appearance.[104] She wasn't actually a queen, rather the mother of a chief among the matrilineal Baboma, which therefore gave her great prestige and authority.[105] When informed about his intention to follow the Fimi, Ngankabi told Stanley not to because his party might be killed by hostile peoples upriver. He paid her no heed, concluding that this was a scare tactic designed to protect a trade monopoly. When she left to retrieve some belongings, he steamed on. Encountering none of the predicted opposition, the *En Avant* entered a wide lake with pitch-black water on May 27. Already gone almost nine days, and facing at least a three-day return trip to Mswata, Stanley had to decide whether to explore it. Thinking such a chance might not present itself again anytime soon, he figured the risk was worth taking, even with food running low and fuel in short supply.

A wild nighttime thunderstorm greeted their arrival, and the next day at the head of the lake any thoughts about landing were quickly dispelled by men from a large village who made threatening gestures with spears and bows and arrows. Further hostile demonstrations followed at other villages, which convinced Stanley to turn back and wait to make contacts some other time. He named the lake Leopold II (now Mai Ndombe), and during the night of May 31 he recorded feeling a "deathly languor" indicative of a "grievous illness" on the way. The premonition proved to be accurate, for the next day found him wracked by fever. So bad did it get, that he was literally too sick to move during the return to Leopoldville.

Overcome by weakness and helplessness, Stanley concluded the time had arrived to leave the Congo, and thus on June 24 he and Qualla boarded the *Belgique* for the first leg of the journey home. A meeting with his successor, German naturalist and geologist Dr. Eduard Peschuel-Lösche, took place at Vivi. The two had had a run-in during the December 1878 discussions about financing the project, when Peschuel-Lösche expressed doubts about the likelihood of success. That he would be the new chief of operations came as a complete surprise. Still, Stanley was glad to have an official replacement already on hand, as it relieved him of further duties and the worries that went with them. Following a quick visit to Boma, he and Qualla set off for Ambriz, intending to catch the July 17 mail boat to Europe. Missing it by just a few hours, and with little or nothing to keep them there, they went to Luanda, with Stanley now worried about his badly swollen legs. He could barely move and feared the cause might be elephantiasis. A diagnosis of anemia came as a great relief. The ship bound for Lisbon finally called, and on August 17 they boarded it for what turned out to be a more than a month-long voyage to Lisbon. From there Stanley took an overland route to Brussels for a meeting with AIC officials on the last day of September.

The meeting started with congratulations for the work accomplished so far. Stanley reacted by claiming "that the Congo was not worth a two-shilling piece in its present state." He emphasized the need for a railway to connect the lower and upper reaches of the river, cautioning that it "will not be remunerative unless commercial men and settlers" were induced into developing the river basin's riches. Furthermore, they must have "absolute immunity from oppressive tariffs," and not be subjected to the "blackmailing tricks of officials who have no interest in anything save their own pecuniary advantages."[106] Free trade and only free trade would be beneficial for all involved, including Africans. Ivory seemed a good starting point, and he urged that substantial quantities of trade goods be sent to the Congo in order to buy as much as possible. Strauch informed Stanley that they expected him to return to the Congo as soon as possible. Surprised, he first resisted the idea, claiming to be no longer a "hardy pioneer." In fact, during the trip downriver, he'd said good-bye to the Congo, intending not to return.[107] When Leopold responded with "surely, Mr. Stanley you cannot think of leaving me just when I most need you," his resistance faded. "Devoured with a desire to do something for Africa," he put health considerations aside.[108]

Certain conditions had to be met, however. These included putting an end to "contradictory orders," such as simultaneously trying to get territorial concessions, buy large amounts of ivory, and make a dash to the upper reaches of the Congo. Do one thing at a time, he reiterated. More Europeans, preferably ones like Janssen, were required to handle growing political and commercial activities. And Stanley again pressed the need for an assistant to take charge of things on the lower Congo. The man, he emphasized, must be "of rank & influence besides intellect to curb the unruly, to direct political affairs, & control matters wisely," so that when Stanley returned from long up-river journeys he "would not find everything topsy-turvy." Could they possibly get Col. "Chinese" Gordon, he asked, or, if not, appoint Strauch's assistant, Captain Albert Thys?[109] The king had wanted Gordon for quite some time and tried to hire him in March 1880, when it looked as though Stanley was spending much to accomplish little. Negotiations broke down over the colonel's desire to involve the Sultan of Zanzibar in the battle to suppress the Congo's slave trade. Leopold wanted no interference from anyone in authority, much less an Arab sultan.

After a two-week stay in London, Stanley went to Paris to speak at a Stanley Club banquet on October 19. He knew that de Brazza was also in town and planned to use the occasion to disillusion those in France "who attribute to him an apostolic character." It would also provide an opportunity to attack French plans to ratify the Makoko treaty. While the two met before the banquet, questions remain about where and how. In Stanley's version, de Brazza came to see him at his room in the Hôtel Meurice, where they chatted pleasantly. In a jocular tone, he promised to administer de Brazza a *"coup mortel"* (mortal blow). Another version, seemingly spread by de Brazza, had them meeting on the street by chance.[110]

That evening, as planned, Stanley went on the offensive by spending the first half of his talk criticizing de Brazza for such things as having been shoeless and ragged in appearance when they first met and wasting money on fruitless activities. He disputed the count's assertion that he'd freed hundreds of slaves, said he'd tricked Makoko into ceding territory, called him an "ingrate," and said he was duplicitous for representing France while being paid by the association.[111] At the end of the talk, de Brazza entered the room. After the two men shook hands, de Brazza delivered a prepared speech in English without rancor that emphasized the need for international cooperation in the Congo. Naturally enough the next day's editions of the French papers attacked Stanley for his remarks, prompting him to record, "What a vocabulary of abuse this polite nation has! Of all men the French excel in beastliness." Still, he didn't think it "worthy of much thought," noting that

"But for Africa, which has been a corrective for crude opinions of my youth, I should feel myself annihilated today."[112]

Returning to the Congo and securing the upper portion of the river before de Brazza was a far more important concern than engaging in a profitless argument. And it would have been profitless, since the French government ratified the treaty and, in addition, funded a third Congo trip by de Brazza. In order to beat him there, Stanley hatched a plan to leave secretly from Cadiz. During the dinner soup course before catching the November 12 night train from Paris to Madrid, he nearly passed out from excruciating stomach pains. A recent threatening letter led him to fear he had been poisoned. Instead, it turned out to be the recurrence of a gastric disorder that first appeared in Manyanga the previous July. It would flare up many times in years to come. Several doses of morphine calmed the pain and allowed him to continue the journey to Madrid, where he remained under a doctor's care for a week.

Still not fully recovered, Stanley ignored advice and joined fourteen officers and six hundred tons of goods aboard the steamer *Harkaway* on November 23, 1882, bound for the Congo. Immediately upon disembarking at Banana exactly three weeks later, he heard one horror story after another about conditions at the stations. The litany included the sudden departures of the two German chiefs, Lindner and Peschuel-Lösche, numerous desertions, plus "wars, quarrels, and misgovernment." The situation at Vivi was said to be particularly bad, and so following a quick stop in Boma, Stanley went there to see for himself. He found it "in a ruinous state," and the upstream supply system looked to be in total chaos.[113] Nothing further could be accomplished until the Vivi mess was taken care of. The arrival of 224 fresh Zanzibaris on December 31 proved a godsend. They allowed him to send a caravan with boards and planks to repair the boats at Stanley Pool and to form an expedition destined for the Kouilou-Niari River in hopes of securing the area between it and the Congo before the French could. With these things accomplished and Vivi functioning again, Stanley set out on January 22, 1883, with ninety-five Zanzibaris and twenty-three Kru to inspect the other stations.

No major problems existed at Isangila, where Stanley sent a second expedition to Kouilou-Niari, this one told to proceed upriver from its mouth. Yet a third he dispatched from Manyanga and instructed another to hurry along the south side of the Congo in order to sign treaties with chiefs between there and Leopoldville. In the meantime, Stanley oversaw the hauling of the *Royal* along the right-bank road. It went through the Mowa district, where several months earlier Captain Eugène Hanssens, then stationed at Manyanga, had destroyed a number of villages during a dispute with the locals. Since then the villages had been re-built and tempers cooled. While admitting that Hanssens's actions "improved the manners of the Mowa natives," Stanley once again voiced concern about the use of force, noting that it would be wise not "to press this method of civilizing the black man, lest every cocky young officer adopt it."[114]

On February 27 Stanley received a note from Braconnier describing a state of near starvation at Leopoldville, and a week later another note from him proclaimed that those at the station had "nothing to live on." Given the friendly receptions, plus what appeared to be an abundance of food all along the route, Stanley thought this impossible. When he got there on March 21, almost nine months after his previous visit, Braconnier's words proved all too true. A trivial dispute between the Europeans and the locals had led to supplies being cut off. Furthermore, instead of the "fair land of order and plenty" Stanley had hoped to see, the scene before him exhibited "disgraceful poverty." Grass grew where productive gardens were supposed to be. The *En Avant* and the whaleboat lay rusted from sitting in the water for nearly a year and a half, and he could detect almost no progress in getting the new steamer *AIA* (*Association Internationale Africaine*) readied for service. And almost no money remained in the treasury. In a long letter to Strauch, Stanley lamented, "Oh dear you will never believe how little your chiefs at station know of looking after things. The revenue of Belgium is not sufficient to maintain the enterprise from total collapse, when conducted so carelessly & unsystematically." He went on to say, that "Were it possible for me to have known in Brussels, what the state of things would be, on reaching Leopoldville I certainly should not have entered upon such a desperate job as to attempt to restore this ruin into order."[115]

Restore it he must, and a little more than a week later, in a letter to the king, Stanley said that the boats would soon be sailing again and once they were, their motto would be "forward & forward without pause."[116] A few days later a meeting with the chiefs at Leopoldville produced a treaty ceding to the AIC "fullest powers to deal with everything that is not domestic."[117] The chief at Kinshasa also signed on, as did a somewhat recalcitrant Ngaliema. The process of restoring Leopoldville then began in earnest. It included establishing a marketplace, something Stanley felt essential for any "aspiring town" along the Congo. By and large, the work went smoothly, except for some political meddling by missionaries and problems with the *AIA*—its top speed proved to be only five knots, a rate that would require eighty days to reach Stanley Falls. Frustrated by what he thought to be yet another miscalculation by the people in Brussels that would threaten the success of the mission, Stanley vowed to make do in spite of them. Consequently, on May 9 he started the *AIA*, the *En Avant*, the *Royal*, and the whaleboat upstream, taking along seven Europeans and seventy-three Africans, six tons of goods, plus a Krupp cannon and several machine guns.

Nothing needed doing at Mswata because of Lieutenant Janssen's diligence. The next important stop was Bolobo, a five-to-six-mile-long series of villages in one of the mostly densely populated parts of the river region. Stanley discovered an inflamed situation at the station, which Hanssens had established in November 1882. The problem started when the Zanzibaris expelled a chief named Gatula for what they took to be his threatening gestures in an incident involving a young female slave. Her regular visits to the station suggested to Gatula the presence of a lover, a gross violation of expected behavior, not only by the woman but also the man and thereby those associated with him. In retaliation, he ordered an ambush on a party of Zanzibaris out cutting wood that killed two of them and wounded two others. The next day, a Zanzibari shot and killed one of Gatula's followers, and the men at the station wanted to exact further revenge. Stanley found their argument compelling and figured a fight might be necessary if Gatula didn't pay blood money. But he had second thoughts, recording in a notebook that

> To fight & conquer was easy enough and to wreck the murderer's fortune was possible, but war victorious or otherwise leaves its stings to the backsides. On my side it would quadruple the difficulties of any further settlement above, on which we are now bound. Rumor would have magnified its terrors until it would appear that I was the aggressor, and Gatula the unfortunate. And it is also certain that being so strong I had similar designs against the whole country, first to embroil & disturb, then to kill.[118]

Still, to give in too easily wouldn't be an appropriate response either because it might allow Africans to value "our people's lives too low & tempt them to try on another occasion to murder a few more, perhaps a European or two." Negotiations seemed a better course to pursue, although he must appear as "being ready at any moment to wreak revenge."[119] A week went by before everyone felt satisfied with the arrangements, and when Stanley asked the chiefs at Bolobo if they wanted the association to stay or go elsewhere, they all agreed that it should stay.

With the matter settled, Stanley resumed heading upriver on May 28 in hopes of establishing two more stations. Lack of manpower precluded building them from scratch, and so they would have to be located at or near existing villages. Immediately above Bolobo, the Congo broadens into wide channels laced with numerous small islands. Stanley thought the views were unmatched by any other river in the world, although at the moment the slow steamer pace of two and a half knots per hour and cramped spaces created a sense of "weariness" among everyone. At Lukolela they came upon a large settlement extending some five miles along the left bank of the river. At first suspicious of strangers in strange boats, the people quickly got over their fears and brought large quantities of food to trade. To Stanley it seemed "a capital position for a station," and so he hinted he would return for further discussions about the possibility of building one.[120]

Above Lukolela, the welcome became ever more exuberant, and on June 4 Stanley said he encountered "the best & kindliest natives we had yet seen." They urged him to build a station on the spot, a fact he attributed to "our long residence at Leopoldville, Mswata, and Bolobo, & to returning caravans conveying the news of some rich man called Bula Matari who was building at various places, & would undoubtedly come up." He didn't consider the site strategically enough located to warrant a station, however. Upon further reflection, Stanley decided against Lukolela as well, concluding that while being a good place for one, it was not yet "ripe" for an "aimiable welcome of whites."[121]

An hour's journey brought the expedition to Irebu, whose traders knew the river's course for the roughly six hundred miles between Stanley Pool and Upoto. Once part of a wider Bobangi federation, Irebu by this time had gone its own way.[122] Greeted enthusiastically by the subjects of Chief Mangombo, Stanley agreed to a blood brotherhood ceremony, as long as he would be the sole *mundele*. Mangombo then told of an internecine war among the three factions comprising Irebu. Concerned that it would consume them all and thus put an end to their dominance along the river, he asked Stanley to serve as a mediator. Stanley replied that he couldn't spare the estimated ten days it would take just then but agreed to see what might be done later. At the moment he wanted to find a large tributary he remembered from passing this way in 1877, and so the journey up the Congo resumed. It turned up nothing more substantial than the Ikelemba (Mohindu), with a mouth a mere fifty feet wide. Following the river proved to be even more disappointing. The first village didn't come into view until the second day, and its people Stanley described as being "frantic and armed with bows and arrows which they seemed much disposed to use."[123] Sensing conditions unfavorable to further exploration, and with negotiations highly unlikely to improve them, he turned the *En Avant* around at the eighty-mile mark.

Where to locate the station became the next concern. With no great confluence anywhere in sight, it would be a matter of choosing among lesser

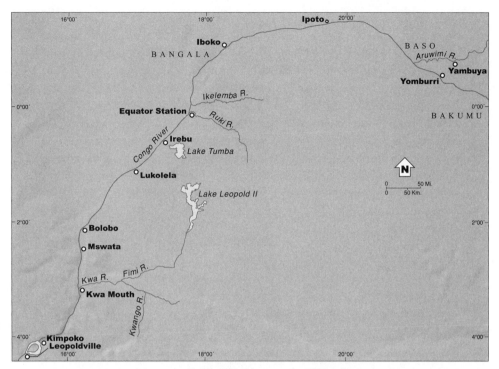

Map 6.2   Station Building on the Upper Congo

advantages. After weighing the options, Stanley selected Wangata, largely for
its "good view upriver." Located at 0° 1′ 0″ N, it received the name Equator-
ville, or Equator Station (later Coquilhatville, now Mbandaka). He then
headed back to Irebu, where the crisis still raged. Native wars, Stanley
observed, tended to be "prolonged affairs" and ended "often in the total
ruin & dispersion of powerful communities."[124] Given Irebu's strategic location, he agreed to see what might be done to end hostilities. Adopting a form
of shuttle diplomacy, Stanley convinced all the chiefs and headmen to attend
a palaver. The discussions produced a peace agreement on June 22, one he
hoped would spare Irebu "from the horrors of internal strife, for many long
years."[125] This particular episode ended, but "horrors" of a different kind
would soon be upon the people.

An exploration of Lake Tumba followed. Along its shores Stanley saw a
population so dense that he calculated "were it uniform throughout the
Congo Basin we should have about 49,000,000 souls or about fifty-five to
the square mile." In addition, he claimed to "have never seen such keen trad-

ers . . . everything is marketable, and all their thoughts are directed to turn an honest penny by trade." Figuring the distance to Lake Leopold II only thirty miles, Stanley thought the two bodies of water might turn into one during the rainy season, which would facilitate trade even more.[126] The actual distance between them is about forty miles, and they do not connect. Next, he returned to Lukolela to sign a treaty of agreement. The required blood brotherhood ceremony with the chief prompted Stanley to say: "My arm gets very well marked. I lose much blood in these affairs, but what will man not sacrifice for peace."[127] The chief persisted in wanting a station built, and Stanley said he would endeavor to do so during the next visit.

A report of a canoe wreck nearby reached Stanley just prior to the scheduled departure from Lukolela. Taking the whaleboat to see what could be done, he found the stranded party to be that of Chief Miyongo of Usinde, a familiar figure from an earlier meeting. Miyongo requested that he, his wife, and six others be dropped off at Bolobo. Aware that a little generosity now could pay dividends later, Stanley quickly agreed, and upon depositing the party at Bolobo, he sweetened the deal by giving Miyongo enough brass rods to buy supplies for forty days. After short stops at Mswata and Kimpoko, the boats reached Leopoldville in the late afternoon of July 4. Its head, Lt. Louis Valcke, whom Stanley had derided earlier for being ineffective, seemed to have control of the situation. The change in Valcke confirmed his belief "that a white man during his first year in Africa has only a copper value, the second year that of silver, the third year that of gold, the fourth year that of a diamond."[128]

Letters from Strauch awaited Stanley's attention. One spoke of de Brazza leading a contingent of men to the Congo, and because of this Strauch recommended fortifying the stations. To strengthen them further, he said, the association would be sending twelve Krupp cannons, two thousand percussion rifles, plus eight new officers, fifty Kru, one hundred Hausa, and five hundred Chinese coolies. Strauch also reported a favorable climate of public opinion in Europe and America, and urged making every effort to sign as many concessions as possible in order to "prepare the creation of an Independent State." It would be necessary, he noted, "to give confidence & security to trade," and ought to be large, so as "to facilitate the exploitation of natural products."[129] In order for the state to be recognized, three conditions were necessary: The members must possess their own land, they must be able to defend the land, and each must have some kind of social organization. The committee had decided to call the state "New Confederacy."[130]

Stanley wrote back saying such a thing would be impossible just now. He had insufficient time, plus each district cherished its independence and nothing bound them together except the road. However, citing the progress around Stanley Pool, where eighteen chiefs seemed "united by one common idea," he thought such an entity might be possible in two years.[131] Irebu also showed promise. He'd called the inhabitants "infuriates" in *Through the Dark Continent*, but now felt "My dearly beloved" might be more fitting.[132]

In another letter to Strauch, Stanley reiterated the need for an assistant who could take over in case of an emergency. He'd already decided to leave the Congo in March. Stanley also informed Strauch about a recent disaster. Thirteen people had drowned when their boat capsized during a sudden gale. They included Lt. Janssen, Stanley's model chief of station. Only three months had remained of his tour of duty when the accident happened.[133]

More as an impediment to de Brazza's plans than anything else, Stanley sent a mission under a young officer named Sanderson to see about establishing a station at Bwa Njali's. When days passed without hearing from him, Qualla went to see what had happened. Just after crossing the river, he found Sanderson lying on ground, bound hand and foot and guarded by several Zanzibaris. When asked what happened, Sanderson claimed the Zanzibaris and Bwa Njali's men had tried to steal rifles and planned to kill him. He said he managed to loosen his bonds and escape, only to be caught and re-bound. The Zanzibaris told a different story. According to them, one morning Sanderson unaccountably started beating his servant and threatened to kill him and others, including Bwa Njali. During the ensuing scuffle, a Zanzibari was wounded, which prompted the others to disarm and bind Sanderson. They were in the process of bringing him to Leopoldville when Qualla appeared. Further investigation confirmed the Zanzibaris' version, and Sanderson was dismissed from service. Stanley abandoned plans for the station because of "the natives being so much frightened at the terrible scene, that they refuse to look at a European anymore."[134]

The next problem involved Kimpoko. A letter from there reported an incident in which six natives were killed and one wounded. Stanley set off immediately with a contingent of Hausa troops and Zanzibaris to get the details. The scene was puzzling—an intact station but no villagers anywhere in sight. Inquiries produced information about a dispute over a dead hippo. The station chief wanted the corpse removed because of the stench. The villagers refused and a fight erupted, producing the casualties. Only the arrival of boats prevented a full-scale attack in retaliation. Stanley couldn't find a way to resolve the situation and therefore opted to abandon the station and burn it to the ground.

A letter from Leopold required immediate attention. The king wanted

Bolobo Mission Station on the Upper Congo. *Courtesy of the Royal Museum of Central Africa*

more concession agreements signed on the Upper Congo forthwith. Further station building could be put off until afterward. He hoped to augment the association's forces with a thousand Hausa troops, although he reported no luck getting Chinese laborers.[135] The king continued trying and later thought the impending United States ban on Oriental immigration might make it more feasible.[136] Stanley replied that he had only twenty-seven Zanzibaris left from the number available in January. The rest were dead, sick, employed by other expeditions, or being used as servants by Europeans. He thought a workable supply line might be formed from native carriers, but getting enough of them would require more time and additional experienced officers to serve as commanders. Inexperienced ones, he observed, usually had difficulty with Africans, as they lacked the necessary qualities of cordiality, kindness, and forbearance, mixed with a "spice of generosity" the job required. Instead, they often treated the Congulese like conquered subjects, or slaves. "This is all wrong. They are neither subjects or slaves—it is we who are their tennants," he emphasized. Steamers posed another impediment to meeting the request to hurry to the Upper Congo. Those he had carried only enough loads for provisioning the stations between Equator and Leopold-ville. Stanley wanted one like the Baptist mission's *Peace,* with a capacity greater than all his boats put together.[137]

In the midst of preparations to go to Stanley Falls, word arrived that a fire at Bolobo had consumed the station, along with 138 loads of goods and fifty-eight rifles. Hurrying as fast as possible aboard the *En Avant,* Stanley got there on August 29 and discovered the report true. Both the *Royal* and the *AIA* were following, and just outside Bolobo, gunfire from the shore halted their progress. Apprised of the situation, Stanley immediately set the *En Avant* on course to help out and it, too, came under attack. Since nothing like this had happened in the past four years, the crews were caught off guard. Return fire freed the boats, and all three made it safely to the station landing point. Sporadic exchanges of gunfire continued for the next several days, and the accidental killings of two Bobangi traders during one of the fights complicated attempts to diffuse the situation. So, too, did the fever that struck Stanley on September 2, which delayed negotiations until the 14th. Backed by a demonstration of Krupp cannon fire and a threat by Stanley to withdraw from Bolobo for good, they finally brought matters to a peaceful conclusion.

Two days later the flotilla headed for Lukolela. The destination presented mixed prospects. A luxurious forest, including teak and mahogany, promised a bountiful supply of timber for building boats and an array of furniture. Hard pan soils, however, dimmed prospects for productive gardens. Stanley left a young Englishman, Edward James Glave, in charge of a twenty-five-man garrison, and the river journey resumed on September 25.

At Bolobo, Miyonga and his family had come aboard for the trip home. After dropping them there, Stanley went to Equator Station. The jobs done by lieutenants Alphonse Vangele and Camille Coquilhat in building and stocking it with food elated him. Moreover, as both men had yet to get sick after more than four months' residence, the site looked to be an exceptionally healthy one. It would become Stanley's favorite Congo station.

Bowing to requests from Brussels, Stanley departed on October 16 to found settlements and make treaties at Stanley Falls. Four Europeans and sixty-eight Africans accompanied him. Five days later, the boats reached Iboko, home to the Bangala who'd fought so fiercely in 1877. He thought the inhabitants might be "too vindictive to be friendly." That would be a shame, for their bravery had won his deepest respect, and he believed "that if their confidence can be won Congo civilization will owe much to them."[138] Instead of showing resentment, they welcomed him, even after the paramount chief Mata Buike learned that Bula Matari and Tandaley, as they remembered Stanley here, were one and the same. Although now elderly, Stanley considered that the chief, who stood more than six feet tall, "must have been at one time the grandest type of physical manhood to be found in equatorial Africa." He called him "an ancient Milo, an aged Hercules, an old Samson—a really grand-looking old man."[139] The two became blood brothers, with Mata Buike reportedly telling his people to accept Tandaley as one of their own and Stanley promising to build a station among the Bangala sometime in the near future.

This portion of the Congo looked highly promising for commercial activity. Stanley described the islands as being "blessed with a celestial bounty of florid and leafy beauty, a fulness of vegetable life that cannot be matched elsewhere save where soil with warm and abundant moisture and gracious sunshine are equally to be found in the same perfection." And the forests and river seemed to teem with products just waiting to be developed. As for the people, they could be looked upon "with much of the same regard that an agriculturist views his strong-limbed child; he is a future recruit to the ranks of soldier-labourers." Given enough of them, he felt the Congo Basin could "become a vast productive garden" to enrich both its inhabitants and those of Europe.[140] Sadly, in years to come, the riches mainly benefited the latter.

Friendly receptions continued to be the norm, and a nearly uninterrupted string of blood brotherhood ceremonies gave Stanley a sore arm that prompted him to worry about blood poisoning from powders placed on the cuts. He was spared this particular malady. The behavior of the Zanzibaris and Hausas also caused concern. The women went virtually naked, and since Stanley's men assumed this meant looseness, they often became the objects of sexual advances. As a result, people sometimes fled the expedition's approach. Stanley wanted to punish the offenders but concluded he couldn't because so many of the men were involved.[141]

As an area newly opened to external trade, almost every village offered ivory at very low prices. Lack of space forced Stanley to refrain from buying any, even at the risk of giving offense. He hoped future steamer trips would make up for the slight. Fear of the steamers, though, might pose a problem, at least initially. Few had ventured that far upstream, and the noise and smoke caused people to think a dreaded spirit called *Itanga* lurked inside them. As expected, repeated exposure soon allayed people's fears.

On November 15 the boats reached the Aruwimi. Stanley recalled the battle in 1877, noting, "Had the natives but held on a few seconds longer we should have been sunk by their weight!" He ordered his men to prepare for any challenges the Baso might offer. At one point a fight seemed likely. The river banks, Stanley said, "were alive with dancing, & boisterous warriors who defied us with the full power of their healthy lungs, while drums made a deafening clamour and the long ivory horns boomed out afar their mellow notes."[142] The expedition's guide and interpreter called out that they had come to trade and meant no harm. At first the Baso kept their distance. Persistent entreaties, however, eventually brought them around, and later that day another blood brotherhood ceremony marked the beginning of peaceful trade relations between Bula Matari and the Baso.

Stanley wanted to explore the Aruwimi but was urged not to because of the likelihood of encountering hostile peoples along the way. This only heightened his curiosity, and he set off to follow it on November 17, anticipating that the Aruwimi would lead to the upper portion of the Uele River. Instead, the Aruwimi ran mostly parallel to the Congo. Although numerous villages lined its banks, they appeared empty, the people having fled at the sound of the boats. After four days and ninety-six miles, with no clear evidence of the river's course and without having made any contacts, they reached a series of rapids near Yambuya. Even though they weren't overly treacherous ones, Stanley decided the time had come to turn back and resume the journey to Stanley Falls.

Because of the numerous battles fought along this portion of the Congo in 1877, the men stood at close alert. Concern mounted when a long column of canoes was seen approaching. Stanley estimated their number at a thousand (an unlikely total) and worried that they might belong to raiders called the Bahunga, who were said to be responsible for attacks that had caused the villagers in the neighborhood to flee for their lives. Seeking to avoid conflict, especially with a vastly superior force, he kept the flotilla speeding ahead. The next day presented scenes of utter desolation—villages burned to the ground, acres of fields leveled, and huge canoes mysteriously set on end. From a forlorn group of people crouched by the shore, Stanley heard of the attackers having come from upriver. When asked about their appearance, he was told, "'They are like your people in your boats and wear white clothes.'"[143]

There seemed no end to the horror, which included two dead women bound together floating downstream. From the references to white clothes, Stanley surmised that the perpetrators must be Arab-led and that they couldn't be far away. Thoughts about intervening crossed his mind, but he resisted the idea because this was not association territory and he didn't represent a recognized government. Furthermore, it occurred to him that "The invaders also were subjects of Sayed Barghash & countrymen of my crews,

who would be aghast at the idea of fighting the Arabs." A little farther on a
large village came into view, and Stanley counted two hundred men with
guns lining the shore as a lone canoe came toward the *En Avant*. He longed
for an excuse to attack, but instead

> before any excuse was offered, the men in the canoe had ranged alongside and
> involved us in a kind of friendliness. Having given our hands to these ruffians,
> we could do no more than assume the appearance of curious and disinterested
> visitors, though I felt more inclined to pray for forgiveness that I had to play
> such a mean politic part; and to vow that some day I would root out such a
> horribly wicked set of people.[144]

The canoe's crew reported that they had departed Nyangwe sixteen
months earlier, raiding across an area Stanley calculated to be slightly larger
than Ireland before settling at their present site of Yomburri. A then "too
awful" scene presented itself—about 2,300 captives, most kept in sheds
housing about two hundred each.

> There are lines or groups of naked forms upright, standing, or moving about
> listlessly; naked bodies are stretched . . . in all positions; naked legs innumera-
> ble are seen in the perspective of prostrate sleepers; there are countless naked
> children, many mere infants, forms of boyhood and girlhood, and occasion-
> ally a drove of absolutely naked old women bending under a basket of fuel,
> or cassava tubers, or bananas, who are driven through the group by two or
> three musketeers. On paying more attention to details, I observe that mostly
> all are fettered; youths with iron rings around their necks, through which a
> chain, like one of our boat-anchor chains, is rove, securing the captives by
> twenties. The children over ten are secured by three copper rings, each ringed
> leg brought together by the central ring. . . . The mothers are secured by
> shorter chains, around whom with their respective progeny of infants are
> grouped, hiding the cruel iron links that fall in loops or festoons over their
> mammas' breasts. There is not one adult man-captive amongst them.

He wanted to free them and "massacre the fiends who have been the guilty
authors of the indescribable inhumanity," but didn't see how under the circumstances. At the very least, he thought the flotilla's arrival probably put
an end to this particular bout of slaving violence.[145]

Anxious to leave, Stanley put the boats back on course for Stanley Falls
the next morning. Both banks of the river were unoccupied, as was an island
he remembered as fertile and populated in 1877. Given these circumstances,
a nearby level terrace some eight miles long and two hundred feet above

the river struck him as "a charming field for European agriculturists."[146] On December 1 Stanley talked with Wawenya chiefs about locating a settlement just below the lower falls. Because of their navigational skills, the Arabs had made allies of the Wawenya instead of enslaving them. This relationship assured Stanley that a station could be built, as both parties would see the profit in it. And once it was up and running, he felt the station would block Arab influence from spreading downstream. Negotiations resulted in the chiefs conceding to Stanley and other white men bearing the gold star on blue background flag of the AIC "the sole right to build on any of the islands below the Falls."[147] He then secured a source of food by coming to terms with Chief Siwa-Siwa of the Bakumu on the adjacent mainland. The two men got on famously, with Stanley feeling that "Good Fortune certainly seemed to have prepared for me pleasant places in the wilderness!" Since the intended station chief had been complaining for weeks about being ill and wished to return to the coast, Stanley put the Scottish engineer Andrew Binnie in charge, leaving him thirty Hausa soldiers for protection. When the flotilla headed back down the Congo on December 10, totting a load of ivory, time seemed ripe for consolidating the association's gains. Instead of a state, Stanley recommended creating a "Protectorship" as the way to "become masters of one uninterrupted and consecutive territory from Vivi Station to the Falls."[148] Brussels, of course, harbored other plans.

Ten Arabs went along to purchase supplies, a good thing Stanley felt because they would serve as security for Binnie and his men. During the journey, the boats made numerous stops on both sides of the river to arrange agreements and plant the flag. The only inconveniences were a two-day layover to repair the *Royal* after it ran into a snag, some bouts of sickness Stanley attributed to chilling winds, and a run-in with thieves at Ipoto. One of those apprehended turned out to be the grandson of Mata Buike. The chief sent an ivory tusk and a slave as ransom. When he didn't appear at the designated time to negotiate the full conditions of release, Stanley decided to take the grandson and several others with him. As a journal entry shows, he meant for this to be an example. The entry also illustrates his continuing view of Africans being like children and thereby in need of the same kind of treatment:

> Mata bwiki, will I fancy have to be taught a lesson, before he stoops from his proud reserve. We are dealing with grownup-children & if we let children have their own way in everything they will become unmanageable. We have so far been giving them sweeties repeatedly, because they have been good children, but a fit of naughtiness has overtaken the Bangalas now, & they must

be made aware that when naughty the sweeties must be stopped. If they get fierce, they must be firmly met.[149]

Continued enthusiastic greeting by villagers convinced Stanley that others all along the upper portion of the Congo would act in a similar fashion. It just took a few visits. "The first visit paves the way, which is tedious, the second the natives troop out for a closer inspection & do a little trading, at the third—they shout glad cries, and troop out spontaneously."[150]

Stanley discovered a crisis brewing at Equator Station. A series of disagreements had produced an exchange of gunfire that resulted in the death of Chief Ikenge ten days earlier, and only the arrival of the boats staved off a retaliatory attack on the station. Stanley placed much of the blame on Vangele, claiming his handling of the situation "has a suggestion of murder in it—but I cannot tell him so." The other chiefs wanted payment made to Ikenge's mother. Stanley claimed they told him "We are your women & you have punished us, but will you not relent now, & rejoice our hearts with gifts? A husband does not always bear malice against his wife. When angered he strikes, but when his anger has flown, he gives her something to make her smile, and be happy again." Some cloth, beads, and "jew jaws," seemed to meet with everyone's satisfaction.[151]

Stanley left Equator Station for Bangala on New Year's Day, taking Coquilhat along in hopes of establishing a station at Iboko. Before this the Mata Buike situation would have to be resolved. Though feverish, Stanley continued negotiating and reached an agreement to hand over the hostages. Nevertheless, the events raised serious doubts in his mind about leaving men behind. Were the Bangala "naturally vicious, or simply insolent because of numbers?" he asked himself. Their fighting skills would definitely be of value in the "work of bringing civilization in the Congo basin"; however, at the moment the situation looked unpromising. Stanley thus steamed off to see about the prospects for establishing a station somewhere in the vicinity. This, too, came to naught because of concerns over the killing of Ikenge. As a result, upon getting back to Equator Station, Stanley decided to pay blood money in hopes of cooling inflamed tempers.[152]

Vangele told a gruesome story about an event in October. An important chief had died, and as part of the funeral ceremony his relatives intended to sacrifice a number of slaves. After Vangele said no, they took fourteen captives from peoples inland and, with the Europeans looking on, beheaded them. The heads, Vangele claimed, were then boiled and the skulls placed on polls to decorate the chief's grave and the blood-soaked soil buried with him. Stanley felt the decision not to intervene a wise one, as any attempt to do so "would simply have been to make them victims instead, and to depopulate the land."[153]

The journey downstream resumed on January 13, 1884. Glave had Lukolela in tip-top condition and the people acted "extremely friendly." There was bad news about Bolobo, however. Another fire had broken out, this one due to a sick, lonely man who, wanting a glorious funeral, had torched the station's houses. Once again it would need rebuilding. Thankfully, Kwa Mouth Station seemed to be in good shape, as did Leopoldville when he pulled up the boats on January 20. In addition to the Arabs, Stanley had also taken along eighteen children from Yomburri. He turned one over to the Livingstone mission and another to the Baptists. The remaining sixteen were to be taught how to speak Kiswahili and sent back home to help win over their peoples to the work of the association. What became of them remains an untold story.

Stanley's exhausting schedule triggered a week's spell of fever. Upon recovering, he faced the daunting task of catching up on correspondence. A letter from Leopold requested that Stanley forbid friends from publishing excerpts from his letters, because "Every time you write a letter, or make a speech, it is said there is an attack by you on some other power, and it causes great trouble."[154] The king expressed particular concern over statements made by Harry Johnston before the British Association based on a letter Stanley wrote him regarding a proposed Anglo-Portuguese treaty that would, in affect, give Portugal control of the Congo. The key portion stated,

> Despite every prognostication to the contrary, this river will yet redeem the lost continent. By itself it forms a sufficient prospect, but when you consider its magnificent tributaries which flow on each side of it giving access to civilisation to what appeared hopelessly impenetrable a few years ago, the reality of the general utility and benefit to the Dark tribes and nations fills the sense with admiration. . . . Such an ample basin, with such mileage of navigation, with its unmeasured resources, would you bestow as a dower upon such a people as the Portuguese who would but seal it to the silence of the coming centuries? Would you rob the natural birthright of millions of Englishmen yet to issue, seeking homes similar to these which their forefathers built in the Americas and the Indies? For what? Is the robust Empire called the British in its wane that you will put a limit to its growth? Such an idea is simply self-murder, and a personal confession of impotence.[155]

"I earnestly beg of you," Leopold pleaded, "to desist writing in this manner to anybody, because it can only produce much harm. Your official position in our service causes everything you say or write to be scanned most minutely." He went on to point out that

> Our stations are free ports & our districts free districts. Their union & their confederation with the tribal chiefs, constitute the guarantee of the freedom of the Congo, & which will be most beneficial to the African people & to all the Europeans & which will endow your name with most glorious fame & secure the success of my efforts.[156]

To himself Stanley mused that the king "believes me activated by a desire for fame, but I really am as much interested in securing fair play for traders & the future of the Congo Region as he is."[157] A recurrent dilemma for him emerges from the exchange, that of serving multiple clients, in this instance himself, Leopold, Britain, and the Congo. Not all could be satisfied.

The king also told of plans to send a paddle wheel steamer to the Upper Congo larger than the Baptist's *Peace.* Stanley wished he already had it, as such a vessel would allow "great work" to be done. The benefit would be someone else's, since he intended to be gone by March or April at the latest. He made this clear in his reply to Leopold, saying,

> Your majesty must please forgive me for taking this step. But as I cannot undertake the impossible, the step is unavoidable. When Mr. Gordon Bennett offered me the North Pole Expedition, I declined it because the means he was willing to devote to it were not sufficient to command success in the way this Expedition is conducted. For no sooner have we urgent work to do, but the means to do it are frittered away, and we are obliged to look in blank dismay, and to listen to a din of reprobation at our lack of energy. . . . Not for the fortune of a Rothschild would I undertake to go through the same experiences I endured in 1880, 81–82. I perceive these looming up again in 1884. Gigantic work—endless contradictory orders—with insufficient means in my 6th year of service to haul a 30 ton steamer with 200 men! While the garrisons of 30 stations are crying out for food! The committee sending series after series of impossible orders, interminable correspondence to conduct & the young chiefs of Vivi putting everything in a muddle, and hastening home as soon as I turn my back.

In a more apologetic tone, he blamed illness for feeling so despondent, telling Leopold, "it is certain that I am not the man I was in 1879 when I began the Congo work." He concluded the letter by advising the association, "do not run too far, or too fast. Consolidate what has been obtained below the

Kwilu & Stanley Pool, & do not go on scattering over Africa with only a few hundred men, leaving the main purpose to starve for want of support."[158]

In another letter, Leopold mentioned that Gordon had entered the service of the association. He would be leaving for the Congo on February 5.[159] Both men shared an interest in the southern provinces of the Sudan. Gordon wanted them protected from the Mahdist revolt then sweeping the northern half of the country. It had begun in 1881 when a mystic named Muhammed Ahmed declared himself Mahdi, a widely held Islamic belief in the appearance of an "expected one," or "deliverer," to drive out infidels and restore purity to the faith. The target in this instance was Sudan's Egyptian rulers, and Ahmed found enthusiastic support among common people and wealthy slave traders, whom the Egyptian government was attempting to put out of business.[160] Gordon felt he could secure the provinces not yet under the Mahdi's control and hand them over to Leopold. This fit the king's plan of gaining a foothold on the Nile.

Stanley now wondered about Gordon's qualifications, as he talked about wanting to "kill the slavers in their haunt." Which slavers did he mean and, if along the Congo, how could this be done? The Zanzibaris wouldn't fight against Arabs, and there were too few Hausa troops for the task. Besides, Stanley thought, any such action would divert efforts away from consolidating the association's gains and probably allow de Brazza to expand French influence. "Fighting slave raiders & peaceful expansion of an international state are incompatible," he noted. This matter would have to be sorted out when the two men met at Vivi.[161]

Stanley set off on March 21 amid reports that the station was again experiencing problems. Despite ample food supplies, comfortable houses, and pleasant surroundings, no chief since Sparhawk had lasted long. Maybe this resulted from poor sanitary conditions, as sickness seemed to be a constant problem. Stanley planned to investigate.

The well-traveled road led through country inhabited by people now favorably disposed toward signing treaties, even though just two years ago some of them seemed ready to contest the appearance of outsiders. As a general rule, these treaties assigned sovereignty to the AIC and included promises by the African signatories to keep trade open, not to impose tariffs and taxes, and to resist forcible intrusion by foreigners of all kinds. In return, the chiefs would be paid a monthly stipend in merchandise, usually cloth, plus guarantees by the AIC not to take occupied lands, to promote the country's prosperity, to provide protection, and to settle disputes.

Conditions at several other stations proved disturbing. Despite the roughly ten thousand pounds sterling expended on it, he described North

Manyanga (a second called South had since been erected) as being "without any order or design," and thus had it torn down and rebuilt, while at Isangila many needed improvements remained undone. Overall, the scene looked "disheartening."[162] As expected, Vivi provided the real shock. Stanley first glimpsed it from the crest of a hill above Yelala Falls on April 22, but he didn't look for long, wishing he "could sponge out the history of this unhappy place from [his] tablet of facts."[163]

The house and surroundings of a Livingstone Mission station that Stanley had seen a few days earlier stood in sharp contrast. Stanley credited the order and attractiveness to a missionary's "delicate-looking" wife, who brought a "rich gift of taste, inherited from far-away England." Her cheerful presence seemed to bode well for Europeans being able to endure the Congo's climate.[164] Why, then, the mess at Vivi? A concern with life's luxuries and excessive alcohol consumption seemed the likely explanation. Upon close inspection it looked even worse than described. The station housed twenty-two Europeans, more than twice the number Stanley thought suitable. Yet he could see no signs of work having been done. Indeed, everything seemed in shambles. Concluding Vivi needed a new beginning, he reorganized the staff and ordered headquarters rebuilt at a higher elevation.

There would be no meeting with Gordon—he'd been sent to Sudan to deal with the Mahdist uprising and by all accounts was trapped in Khartoum. In some ways Stanley felt relieved, as he considered Gordon unrealistic, and there'd now be no need to worry about some harebrained scheme "to kill the slavers in their haunt." Stanley did get a replacement, Col. Francis de Winton, who reached Vivi on May 8. He'd been hired to take over as administrator general of the area between Vivi and Stanley Pool, and the king hoped this might induce Stanley to stay on longer. De Winton looked like a good choice. He'd served Britain admirably in Canada and counted the Royal Family among friends. Stanley didn't change his mind about leaving and de Winton assumed the post of *adminstrateur général*, holding it for two years.

What bothered Stanley most at this point was the position of the AIC. As he told Strauch,

> So long as our status & character are not recognized by European Governments De Brazza with his walking stick, a French flag, and a few words spoken in the presence of the Europeans at Leopoldville is in reality stronger than Stanley with all his Krupps & war material, faithful adherents, natives, etc.[165]

In his last letter to Strauch, written on June 2, he warned of the possibility of having to fight de Brazza at the pool.[166] The degree to which the Italian cum Frenchman had become an obsession with him can be seen in several long notebook entries. They include references to de Brazza being a "dissembler," of having engaged in "scandalous artifices with natives," of not considering " breach of trust . . . an immoral act," and for going "about the country without shoes, and in ragged clothes." All the adoration bestowed on him by the French was particularly galling:

> It is this odd & shallow man that the Parisian Press with their usual want of discernment have found their model patriot, it is out of this coaster that the President of the Paris Geographical society has proclaimed the discovery of a second Livingstone, it is out of this extravagant & spend thrift that the French Economists have sought a pattern for their government, it is of this disciple of Niccolo Machiavelli that the French have sought their ideal hero, it is in this scoffing cynic that we are told we must look for the Apostle of Africa.[167]

Yet Stanley had bested de Brazza along the Congo, leaving him with only some land on the north side of the pool for building Brazzaville. The only explanation for his thoughts is that he didn't know this at the time.

Stanley left Vivi on June 6 and four days later boarded the steamer *Kinsembo* at Banana for the journey home. Qualla and a Baso boy named Baruti accompanied him. The sailing schedule called for a number of stops along the way, which pleased Stanley, since it would provide an opportunity for him to learn more about West Africa. One stop allowed for a brief exploration of the Cross River. Impressed by the wealth oil palm brought to Africans in Duke Town and Creek Town, Stanley envisioned much the same taking place along the Congo once the civilizing influences of "fair trade" were established. Upon being informed about a white man having been sentenced to eighteen months' imprisonment for whipping an African, he wondered "what some of our young officers on the Congo would say to that."[168]

Stanley went directly to London immediately upon disembarking at Plymouth on July 28. There he received a letter saying that Leopold wanted to see him as soon as possible. To keep the matter secret he was instructed to cable the day and hour of arrival using the format "I will see John on the . . . . At . . . [morning or evening]."[169] Just prior to leaving on August 2, Stanley assured a London *Times* correspondent that the goals of the association had been accomplished, pointing out that its aims are "entirely benevolent; they are not anxious to make any profit out of their operation." He went on to proclaim the richness of the country—it contained ivory and a range of other valuable natural products. Once past the coast and its problems with fevers, the interior could support settlers in a healthy fashion. To be successful, he emphasized that the natives must be treated with "proper tact."[170]

In Ostend, Stanley and the king spent five days in intense discussions about the Congo and the status of the AIC. So far, despite twenty-two stations and more than three hundred treaties, it had only two confirmed supporters. The United States came on board first, thanks largely to the persistent lobbying efforts of Sanford, who served as Leopold's private envoy in Washington. A pronouncement from President Chester Arthur on December 1, 1883, set the public side of the process in motion. He told Congress that

> The rich and populous valley of the Congo is being opened to commerce by a society called the International African Association, of which the King of the Belgians is the president, and a citizen of the United States is the chief executive officer. . . . The objects of the society are philanthropic. It does not aim at permanent political control but seeks the neutrality of the valley. The United States cannot be indifferent to this work nor to interests of their citizens involved in it. It may become advisable for us to cooperate with other commercial powers in promoting the right of trade and residence in the Congo Valley free from the interference or political control of any nation.[171]

After failing to agree on several earlier resolutions of support for the president's position, the U.S. Senate finally did so on April 10, 1884, and urged recognition of the association's flag. This action and a letter from Sanford brought about the following proclamation on April 22:

> Frederick T. Freylinghuysen, Secretary of State, duly empowered therefore by the President of the United States of America, and pursuant to the advice and consent of the Senate, heretofore given, acknowledges the receipt of the foregoing notification from the International Association of the Congo and declares that, in harmony with the traditional policy of the United States, which enjoins a proper regard for commercial interests of their citizens, while at the same time avoiding interference with controversies between other Powers as well as alliances with foreign nations: the Government of the United States announces its sympathy with, and approval of the humane and benevolent purposes of the International Association of the Congo, administering as it does, the interests of the Free States there established, and will order the officers of the United States, both on land and sea, to recognize the flag of the International African Association as the flag of a friendly government.[172]

Note the statement's use of both the International Association of the Congo and the International African Association. Did Sanford use them interchangeably in private conversations so as to leave the impression that the two were one and the same? A canny politician, he probably did. Before the end of the month, the French also signed on under the provision that they would have the option of "first refusal" should Leopold give up his Congo claims.[173]

With talks concluded, Stanley went to Paris for ten days before returning to London in hopes of securing British recognition for the association. The mood had become somewhat more receptive to Africa than it had been in 1878. The *Banner*, for example, criticized the country's lack of response, proclaiming that "The establishment of commercial intercourse with the interior of Africa . . . would be the most effectual preventitive of wars and slavery, and the shortest and surest road to civilization and Christianity." The article also noted that England would profit as well, since the country, especially the Lancashire area, was currently manufacturing more than it sold.[174] Discussions with the likes of lords Granville and Wolseley, while cordial, produced no concrete results.

Stanley, nonetheless, felt hopeful. After a well-received presentation to the London Chamber of Commerce about the Congo's potential and the work of the association, he told Sanford, "The public is uncommonly enthusiastic. I could raise 5.000.000 for any work on the Congo. These people are thoroughly in earnest and I find that I have touched their hearts by the respectful manner they treat me. So different from the old days."[175] Another project involved working up a plan for his pet railway project. It needed two segments, one from Vivi to Isangila and the other from Manyanga to Stanley Pool. Brussels wanted him to look for financial backers in England, and Stanley figured he could count on two for sure, as, with Leopold's urgings, they'd agreed to form a company for that purpose the year before. For various reasons, the company never got off the ground.

One of the men was William Mackinnon. Born into poverty in Scotland, he'd become a millionaire as the head of the British India Steamship Navigation Company. Deeply religious and generous with his fortune, Mackinnon had attended the 1876 Brussels conference and came away a strong supporter of Leopold's proclaimed philanthropy. He recruited workers in Britain for him, was the one who negotiated the deal with Gordon, and spoke often in support of British recognition of the AIC, seeing it as the necessary vehicle for maintaining free trade in the region. James F. Hutton was the other. A friend of Mackinnon's and Sanford's, he'd long been involved in West African commerce, and at the moment served as president of the Manchester Chamber of Commerce. Both subscribed to the Comité, making them the only ones in Britain to do so, and both had become admirers of Stanley and now his colleagues in working for Leopold.

Besides the railway, the three men shared deep concerns about the Anglo-Portuguese Treaty that had been tentatively agreed to on February 26, 1884. Neither wanted it to become official, and each said so on many occasions. They were aided in their efforts by John Kirk, who saw the potential of the Congo Basin and feared that French and Portuguese dominance might close it off to British commercial interests. He frequently wrote Mackinnon about the matter, expressing the opinion that doing business with Leopold seemed the best option to keep this from happening.[176] Longtime foes, Kirk and Stanley suddenly found themselves allies.

Stanley turned down an offer from Bennett to go to the Sudan and instead spent much of September writing letters and working on his Congo book. Instructions from Brussels said to hold off on publishing it because negotiations over the new state's boundaries were at a critical stage. Nothing could appear under his name that might jeopardize their successful completion. In fact, Stanley knew that every word he wrote would need the king's approval.

The beginning of October saw Stanley preparing for a lecture tour, with three presentations in Manchester, on October 21, 22, and 23 to the Chamber of Commerce, the Geographical Society, and the Anti-Slavery Society.[177] These, too, had to be cleared by the king, who struck some statements from the drafts and changed words here and there. Stanley also received warning that there must be no "direct allusions" to the Anglo-Portuguese treaty and nothing said about Manchester having a trade monopoly, as Germany intends "to come in for a considerable portion of it."[178] He should, however, stress the trade advantages to the city that would come with recognition of the AIC. To reduce any concerns about conflict of interest, they agreed that the speeches would be delivered in Stanley's name, not the association's. Stanley at times came close to stepping across the line, especially with critical comments about Portugal, but overall the speeches struck the right chords with audiences and stirred no controversy. The one to the Chamber of Commerce generated a resolution supporting "the earnest efforts of His Majesty the King of the Belgians to establish civilization and free trade on the Upper Congo" and hoping all nations would recognize "the independent state or states proposed to be founded there."[179]

Events, however, had moved beyond what mere speeches could influence.

1885
At Balnakill. Loch Tarbert.

Sir W. Mackinnon,   Lady Mackinnon.   Stanley
Miss E. Jamieson.   Col Jamieson   J F Hutton.

Stanley in Scotland with friends in 1885. On his right are Sir and Lady William Mackinnon. *Courtesy of the Royal Museum of Central Africa*

These centered on Germany and Chancellor Bismarck, who, drawing on an earlier Portuguese idea, called for a November conference in Berlin to address a number of issues associated with increasing European involvement in Africa. By this time Germany had become a player through the *Gesellschaft für Deutsche Kolonization,* headed by Carl Peters, who at the very moment was busy signing treaties between Bagamoyo and Tabora. Bismarck had no real interest in securing colonies, but he wanted to make sure that territories remained open to German commercial ventures.[180] To not profit while rivals did would disadvantage Germany.

Stanley hoped to participate in the conference but couldn't do so on behalf of the AIC because it still lacked official recognition by enough states. Thanks to the strenuous lobbying efforts of Sanford and John A. Kasson, the country's minister in Berlin and head of the American delegation, Stanley became one of its "experts," providing testimony on so-called technical matters. Leopold definitely wanted Stanley involved, but as usual he worried about his tendency to create controversy. He thus warned him "to be prudent in what you say" and "to consult with and be guided by Mr. Sanford."[181]

Accompanied by Sanford and a recently hired sixteen-year-old German-speaking manservant named William Hoffmann, Stanley reached Berlin two days before the opening session of the conference at the Reich Chancellery on November 15, 1884. Fourteen countries sent representatives. Stanley's first presentation came five days later as part of depositions given by experts. In it, he objected to using only the drainage pattern to determine the geographical extent of the Congo Basin because the lack of a delta would leave the territory only twenty miles wide at the river's mouth. Instead, he proposed a "Commercial Basin" with a "Commercial Delta" extending between 1°25' S. and 7°50' S. as more realistic. The definition extended the free trade zone east to Zanzibar and south to the Zambezi River. For official purposes, "Conventional" replaced "Commercial."[182] According to Baron Alphonse de Courcel of the French delegation, the "speech produced a great impression."[183]

In the session on November 27, Stanley jumped in to support a proposal by Sanford that whoever controlled the larger share of the Congo Basin should have the right to build a railway or be allowed to designate a company to do so on its behalf.[184] His only other direct contribution was a brief presentation about religion and missionary activities on the last day of November. After that, Stanley left Berlin for a series of speaking engagements in Scotland, including giving the inaugural address to the Royal Scottish Geographical Society in Edinburgh. In it, he expressed the wish that more cities in Britain would follow Edinburgh's example, for to him knowledge of geography was essential to commercial success. Ship owners and manufacturers needed to study it. So, too, did all their employees. In fact, he emphasized, geography should "be studied by every resident, male or female, in the country."[185]

During Stanley's stay in Edinburgh, a "private and confidential" letter from Leopold's *chef du cabinet,* Count Paul de Borchgrave, arrived, saying that sources reported England was ready to recognize the AIC. They wanted Stanley to take "every opportunity to explain to the British public the great importance of the New Free State of Central Africa, and how much it concerns them to support our work. It is to their political & commercial interest." Mentioning the French had to be avoided. "We must on no account," de Borchgrave cautioned, "hurt their pride & make it impossible for them to become again friendly to us."[186] On December 16, Great Britain signed an agreement recognizing the association's flag in return for the right of its subjects to enter the country freely, be exempt from import duties, and, should it be necessary, be tried in courts under British consular authority. Stanley's contributions to this were slight at best, as internal political considerations had taken a backseat to the machinations of kings, chancellors, presidents, and prime ministers.[187]

Stanley spent the Christmas season in London. While there, he received invitations to attend banquets and give speeches in Cologne, Frankfurt, and Wiesbaden on January 7, 8, and 9, 1885. Brussels granted permission as long as he didn't discuss de Brazza. Every attack on him, the letter of approval said, resulted in his friends appealing to national pride, which caused problems for the association. The speeches, instead, should emphasize

> the share which the Germans are beginning to take in the manufacture of articles suitable to the natives of Africa. Show them that this share will day by day increase. That it will supply work to Germans, who now are obliged to go & seek for some in America, & that it will enable them to remain in their country, which is surely large enough to maintain all her children.[188]

Stanley did as he was told and returned to Berlin on January 19, 1885, to attend the final days of the second half of the conference, which had reconvened two weeks earlier. He gave no formal presentations this time although discussions about Portugal's claims drew his attention. With Britain prohibiting the export of East Africans to the Congo, Cabinda's role of providing a reliable supply of labor had become more important. And should Portuguese control of the Lower Congo be recognized, he felt it would ruin trade with Isangila and effectively put an end to the new state's existence.[189] Although Portugal wound up in possession of nearly a thousand miles of coastline, including Cabinda, it didn't get the mouth of the Congo. That went to Leopold, along with recognition in the General Act of Berlin (February 26) for a nascent state more than seventy-five times the size of Belgium and larger than the one he and Bismarck had discussed during the months preceding the conference. A series of protocols and articles supposedly bound Leopold to maintain a free trade zone open to all countries and to take care of the welfare of the state's inhabitants. Freedom of religious propagation was also part of the guarantee, thus keeping the "commerce and Christianity" connection.[190] All the parties recognized him as the true authority, the Congo's "proprietor," to use his word, not the A.I.C., which now faded into history.[191] A more widely used title for him was *le Roi Souverain*. Interestingly, the United States never ratified the General Act. Newly elected president Grover Cleveland, however, did reaffirm the country's position of support for the state's purported objectives.

It is important to stress that, contrary to what is often claimed, Africa was not formally partitioned in Berlin. Nonetheless, the negotiations, often informal and behind-the-scenes, pretty much set the rules that guided what happened.[192] Within twenty years, only Ethiopia, Liberia, Morocco, and a portion of the Sahara now split between Libya and Egypt, would remain unclaimed.

In spite of the coup, Stanley's forthcoming book still worried the king. Writing on his behalf, de Borchgrave cautioned,

> Your book coming after the close of the conference must be written in a peaceful spirit towards everybody. You must not allow a single sentence, nay a single word to be written that would hurt the legitimate pride of any Power. There is no sense to point out that the Portuguese had no claim to the Mouth of the Congo, or that England had changed her policy about it. All that belongs to the past, to difficulties which have been overcome, and which we must, on no account, bring on ourselves.[193]

With these words in mind, Stanley set about completing *The Congo and the Founding of Its Free State,* by this time officially known as l'Etat Indépendent du Congo. After reading through the manuscript, Leopold sent it back, saying he wanted the language softened, especially when discussing the officers. Harsh words, he thought, would make future recruitment efforts difficult. The king also expressed concern about the dedication. It should be, he said, to "All the friends of Africa, to all those, great & small who have contributed to open Africa to trade & civilization."[194]

Stanley put the finishing touches on the book during April while visiting his old friends the Webbs in Newstead Abbey. Criticisms of European officers he handled by referring to general characteristics, such as those with "physical weakness," ones who "had simply mistaken their vocation," and the "malingerer" without revealing actual identities. In contrast, those considered to have performed exemplary service were named. As for the dedication, it came out:

THIS NARRATIVE
of
LABOUR, EXPLORATION AND DISCOVERY
and
HISTORY
of a great and successful
POLITICAL AND DIPLOMATIC ACHIEVEMENT,
is, by special permission,
Most respectfully Dedicated to
HIS MAJESTY LEOPOLD II.,
The King of the Belgians,
The Generous Monarch Who So Nobly Conceived, Ably Conducted, And Munificently Sustained
the Enterprise Which Has Obtained The Recognition Of All the Great Powers Of The World,
and Has Ended In The Establishment Of
THE CONGO STATE;
And Also To All Those Gentlemen Who Assisted Him By Their Zealous Service, Talents, Means,
And Sympathy, To Realize The Unique Project Of Forming A Free Commercial State In Equatorial
Africa, By Their Humble And Obedient Servant,
THE AUTHOR.

Stanley told readers he knew the secret to European survival in the tropics. It was not the climate per se but rather ignorance of its requirements that caused so much suffering and even death. Most important, one must take every precaution to avoid chills, which meant being sure not to work up a heavy sweat in the sun and then quickly retreating to the cool shade of trees or indoors while still wet. It also meant that settlements should not be located at sites prone to chilling winds, such as happened at Vivi, Manyanga, and Leopoldville. And perhaps above all else, one must avoid drinking too much alcohol in any form, and it should never be consumed during the day unless prescribed by a doctor. Following these and a variety of other recommendations, such as returning to Europe for three months after eighteen on duty, would, he concluded, quell, the "silly fear" of the Congo's climate and "prevent at least three-fourths of the maladies that have punished our imprudent youths."[195]

He then proceeded to spell out "the Kernel of the Argument" for the Congo Basin. This time his estimate settled on about 43,000,000 people (a substantial overestimate by later counts) in a territory arrayed with resources—oil palm, rubber trees, gums, hardwoods, numerous plants for fibers and medicines, a wide array of food crops, skins, ivory, iron ore, copper, and some gold. Due to such bounty Stanley told readers the basin presented far greater potential than the Mississippi basin when first seen by De Soto. As elsewhere in the world, including Europe, the stimulus of outsiders would be required to realize the potential. These he called the "missionaries of commerce," and prophesied "But let the Vivi and Stanley Pool railroad be constructed, and it would require an army of Grenadiers to prevent the traders from moving on to secure the places in the commercial El Dorado of Africa." Given subsequent events in the Free State, Stanley's closing remarks are intriguing:

> All men who sympathise with good and noble works . . . will unite with the author in hoping that King Léopold II, the Royal Founder of this unique humanitarian and political enterprise, whose wisdom rightly guided it, and whose moral courage bravely sustained it amid varying vicissitudes to a happy and successful issue, will long live to behold his Free State expand and flourish to be a fruitful blessing to a region that was until lately as dark as its own deep sunless forest shades.[196]

Accurately subtitled *A Story of Work and Exploration,* with few discoveries and hardly any battles, the book's story line was far less compelling than its predecessors. Yet, because it came from Stanley's pen, it, too, became a bestseller.

United States laws provided no copyright protection for noncitizens, so to head off financial losses from pirated versions of the book, Stanley made a quick trip to Washington, D.C., to file for naturalization. Receiving it would end once and for all the question that continued to vex him. As he frustratingly noted to yet another inquiry:

> I answer that I have given the affirmative so often in public and private that it appears to me the fact is known all over the world. In my work How I Found Livingstone, in chapter "Life in Unyanyembe," I have shadowed that right. I am undoubtedly a citizen of the United States. I travel under American passports and always have. I claim and possess all rights of an American citizen . . . I always have with me the emblem of nationality—in civilized countries the passport—in savage countries the flag of the United States of America, and never sought the protection, aid, or consul of any other than the American, conformably with my right as an American citizen. All legal documents are drawn with me as an American citizen and no other ever has

been and never will be. I have sacrificed honours and distinctions because I am an American citizen for having done deeds worthy of honour.[197]

Stanley received the certificate of naturalization on May 15 and immediately returned to London expecting to find a call to service from Leopold. None existed, and with still no word out of Brussels as the end of May approached, he reminded de Borchgrave of an earlier promise about being ready for Africa by spring. In anticipation of going back, Stanley had purchased a personal "Congo kit" good for three years.[198] The king, de Borchgrave replied, was out of town, but in any event, "The government of the Independent State of the Congo is not yet officially constituted, nor will it be for some time to come. I am therefore quite unable to give you any instructions at present."[199] Upon hearing this, Stanley and Mackinnon canceled their impending trip to Brussels. Leopold, bowing to French and Portuguese concerns, had decided to keep Stanley in Europe *"comme une seconde corde à notre arc"* (basically meaning a second string in one's bow). He would stay until circumstances dictated otherwise.[200]

To keep busy and hopefully stimulate a more positive response, Stanley returned to the railway project. He claimed a line would raise Congo revenues from their current twenty thousand pounds per year to one hundred thousand in the first year of operation, and half a million a few years later. While the king would benefit the most, Britain could also profit. To stress his readiness to get started, he informed de Borchgrave about having hired an Arab boy (Qualla had left in order to marry) and even buying a donkey from Zanzibar.[201] When a few weeks went by without getting a reply, he wrote again. This time de Borchgrave responded, saying that the precise time of his going back couldn't be determined. Everything must be guided by "the interest of our enterprise" and right now this demanded his presence in Europe.[202] Stanley interpreted this as giving him an indefinite leave of absence.

A letter from Leopold finally came on July 19. It contained a thank-you for the book and an expression of gratitude for all Stanley's efforts on behalf of the Congo. While he would continue with efforts to build a railway, the king said it must wait "until I have the support of first class firms." He promised to write again as soon as he had "good news" about Africa.[203] Just a few days earlier Stanley had written to Sanford expressing concern about the lack of candor coming from Brussels:

> The friends of the Association are gradually cooling here because of this indirectness which is almost perverse but certainly intentional, I think. But why

they should be treated so I cannot imagine. If it is necessary for the sake of patriotic interest to concentrate Belgian influence upon the Congo instead of International, all will agree that Belgium, on account of the King's munificence, deserves the lion's share—say: all if necessary—but why not say so. Such explicit frankness would make less enemies than this indirectness. It is necessary for the honor of Belgium that the chief officer of the State [Congo] should be a Belgian, why not say so and let there be an end of this suspense to me, that I may seek other fields. The State would make as many friends as she has lost. If the King is striving to effect a railway alone on the Continent and does not wish to any assistance from here, why not say so to put an end to the suspense of friends like Hutton and Mackinnon.[204]

Heeding Sanford's advice, Stanley went to Switzerland at the beginning of September for a vacation. While his health improved during the stay, he didn't make the acquaintance of any of the "pretty girls" Sanford said would be there.[205] The lack of a wife continued to be a sore spot, and Stanley was fussy about looks. A handsome figure, not too thin, nor too plump, ranked at the top of his list.

The first encouraging word about Africa for quite some time came in a letter from Edmund van Eetvelde, the administrator general of foreign affairs of the Congo State, in late September. He mentioned granting a concession to a commercial company for building a narrow-gauge railway to link Vivi with Banana.[206] Stanley immediately contacted Mackinnon and Hutton, and they quickly raised four hundred thousand pounds from twenty-six shareholders. The agreement to form the Royal Congo State Railway and Navigation Company was reached in Brussels during discussions from the middle of December to Christmas Eve.[207] The three men hoped this meant the beginning of a larger company that would save East Africa from the Germans.

Other information from Africa proved less encouraging. Stanley told Mackinnon about receiving "a number of letters from the Congo, which say fearful things about the state of affairs. My best friends have been harried, & their villages burnt. One of eight years standing has had his property utterly destroyed & three of his women drowned while prisoners." His former colleague van de Velde confirmed the disorder and expressed hope that Stanley would return soon as governor general. The chiefs at Vivi, in particular, wished he would come back.[208] There's no doubt Stanley desperately wanted to go.

A flare-up of gastritis had been plaguing Stanley since mid-November. He blamed it on lack of exercise and fresh air due to reading and writing so many letters and to anxiety about the future. In a long letter to Leopold he expressed concerns about declining in the king's favor. The press repeatedly implied as much, and he wanted something with authority behind it to dispel the notion.[209] In reply, de Borchgrave said the king wished to extend his contract for several more years, which should show the world how much his services were valued by him. Stanley could anticipate going back to Africa soon. Meanwhile, the king needed his services in Europe and de Borchgrave said he would receive the Grand Officier de l'Ordre de Leopold II. Although pleased to receive the honor, Stanley worried that a future assignment might put him second in command to whoever replaced de Winton. Such a thing couldn't happen to Bula Matari! Furthermore, he didn't want to spend the one-thousand-pound retainer on such things as food and drink, as they would make him "unfit" for the Congo. And he couldn't let "old Africa sink back to its former slothful state." He wanted "to be in it, to rouse it to life, to have the pleasure of seeing it move responsive to my wishes, & feel the exultation rising from it."[210] The king, however, had written him off in terms of administrative duties. For details on how to run the state, he turned to Britain's Sir Travers Twist and a Prussian émigré, Egide-Rudolphe Arntz.[211]

Because of continuing poor health, Stanley's doctors suggested he take a long vacation in the south of France. Just after departing for Nice with Mackinnon, he began feeling worse and returned to London for treatment. The famous physician Sir William Jenner took charge of his case and recommended both a strict milk-based diet and a long rest at St. Lawrence-on-Sea in Ramsgate. During his recuperation de Borchgrave asked Stanley for an important favor. Gordon had been killed at the fall of Khartoum on January 26, 1885, and the Mahdi's forces controlled all but the extreme south of the country. He thus wanted Stanley to

> write a letter to His Majesty [Leopold] saying that if the Egyptian Government were to grant the Independent State of the Congo a lease of the Soudan, together with an annual subsidy of 20,000£ the Independent State might, by way of the Bahr-el-Ghazal which borders on its territories, try to restore peace and order in the Soudan and set the province to produce a revenue once more, which would be duly remitted to Egypt. This revenue in 1878 amounted to 600,000£.

Egypt would supply the army, with Belgium providing officers. The "letter should be so written that H. M. could show it to Ministers of the British Crown as information given by a highly competent man on a subject of actual interest."[212]

The idea of using the Congo route to rescue Egyptian forces trapped there can be traced to early 1884, when Strauch suggested to Stanley that "You could perhaps send one of your agents to lend them assistance by the Aruwimi. Should you rescue them by taking them down to the Congo, it would be a worthy counterpart of the fact of having found Livingstone."[213] Stanley responded to the new request enthusiastically. The Congo route was as close to Europe as that along the Nile and would avoid the mass of swamps comprising the Sudd. In addition, instead of encountering "religious fanatics," it traversed country inhabited by people "to whom religion is unknown, and whose only motive to violence would be apprehension of harm from strangers." He urged the king to pursue the idea, especially since the Free State had a number of officers and a flotilla of steamers at its disposal. With financial assistance funneled through Egypt from Britain, a force of five thousand Belgians and ten thousand Egyptians would easily do the trick. An initial subsidy of two hundred thousand pounds would be matched, he felt, by revenue within a few years.[214]

Aided by the milk diet, Stanley recovered sufficiently to resume his trip to Nice on March 23, and from there he went on an extensive tour of Italy, visiting Florence, Rome, Naples, Milan, and Lake Como, that lasted until April 28. During the trip he corresponded regularly with Dorothy (Dolly) Tennant. The two had met the previous June at a dinner party in London hosted by her mother, Gertrude. A wealthy widow, she was a London legend for sumptuous parties attended by the rich and famous in the family home at 2 Richmond Terrace. After the party, Dorothy invited Stanley to come to tea, telling him to choose his "*own day*" and "*own hour*."[215] He thanked her for such a generous offer, and added,

> I owe very many for the abundant pleasantries of the evening before last. I consider the incidents forming on the whole one of the most charming evenings I ever passed, which is not likely to be forgotten by me, and I feel sure that I am indebted to you for the honor and pleasure derived from it.[216]

Regular get-togethers followed, and she convinced him to sit for a portrait to be presented to Edward Arnold. Dolly had become famous, in some quarters infamous, for paintings of ragamuffins. Their deepening friendship and his ever improving health led Stanley to tell Mackinnon that he felt the "dark days of illness were fast receding & a brighter future of more or less duration dawning."[217]

Stanley passed most of May, June, and July by attending meetings and social gatherings, hoping to hear something positive from Brussels. In anticipation, he rehired Hoffmann to serve as "general servant, messenger boy, or otherwise at the sum of two pounds eight shillings per month." A clause stipulated that any suspicion of dishonesty or indifference would result in a prompt discharge.[218] It would later be invoked, although in a modified form.

On August 2 Stanley left with Dolly and her mother for Glasgow to join sixty-five others in a weeklong cruise of the Scottish isles aboard the *Juma,* a new steamer of Mackinnon's British India Line. During the voyage, his affection for Dolly grew, and after saying good-bye to the Tennants on August 11, he returned to London and mailed a six-page letter to her on the 16th. It contained an offer of "an unqualified love, earnest, sincere, pure," and if she accepted it he promised to be "father, brother, friend, best companion through life—a perfect husband." Hoping for the best but prepared for the worst, Stanley went on to say that "If my love is unacceptable to you, merely close this letter in another envelope and return it to me."[219] She chose to keep the letter and pen her rejection instead. Her note has never been found and he left no reference to it anywhere. Neither seems to have written the other after this, although Gertrude sent a couple of notes inviting him to tea or dinner. He ignored the offers.

The rebuff helped to refocus Stanley's thoughts on the Congo. He spelled out his ideas in a letter to Sanford: The king could send him back as administrator of the Upper Congo or use his services to explore new territories where valuable resources might exist.[220] One thing that wouldn't be happening just now was the railway. An official letter from Brussels claimed that the state was unable to grant a concession to the syndicate and that there were no plans to build a railway currently under consideration. Should, however, a plan materialize, it went on to say that "we will not fail to inform you, so as to enable you and our English friends to take part in it, in case it would be agreeable to you and them."[221] The combination of frustrations led Stanley to tell Mackinnon, who'd by now become a personal confidant, that

> I have been living ever since the book left my hands last year in a fool's paradise. That woman entrapped me with her gush & her fulsome adulation, her nick-knacks inscribed with "Remember Me," her sweet scented notes written with a certain literary touch which seemed to me to be a cunning compliment—to myself—as I detected a certain kind of effort, her pointed attentions to use te te te on leaving her presence. I was bouyed up with love letter or despatch from Brussels, which kept me on the stretch of expectation. "We do not know exactly when we shall need you, but we shall let you know—My dear Mr. Stanley in ample time to prepare. . . . So I lived constantly, hoping, hoping here, hoping there, and after all both have come to nothing. I look

back therefore with regret that nearly 16 months of my life have been lost through these artful people.[222]

Left facing an increasingly uncertain future, Stanley signed a contract to present fifty lectures in the United States at one hundred dollars per lecture plus expenses. Leopold approved on the condition that he return if needed. In an effort to avoid the disaster of 1872, Stanley gave several presentations in England before departing on November 17. The practice must have worked, since his agent described the first lecture given in New York City as "thrilling and interesting in the extreme."[223] When stops in Hartford and Boston proved equally successful, the number of lectures was increased to one hundred. A handsome profit thus seemed in the offing, and a tour in Australia loomed as a possibility as well. Then, during preparations for an engagement in St. Johnsbury, Vermont, on December 11, a cable from Mackinnon brought an abrupt end to the tour. It read, "Your plan and offer accepted. Authorities approve. Funds provided. Business urgent. Come promptly. Reply."[224] The matter at hand was to lead an expedition to relieve Emin Pasha, governor of Equatoria province, Egypt's last bastion in the Sudan. Mackinnon considered Stanley ideal for the job and asked him to rough out a strategy before leaving for America. Despite serious reservations about being able to raise enough money to be successful, Stanley produced a plan of action in early November. Furthermore, he told Mackinnon that should the necessary money be found, he would agree to lead an expedition "without hope of fee or reward" and be available "at a moment's notice." True to his word, he sent a return cable stating, "tell authorities prepare Holmwood, Zanzibar, and Seyyid Barghash."[225] By Christmas Eve, Stanley was back in London ready to go to Africa yet again.

CHAPTER 7

In Relief of Emin Pasha

PHILANTHROPY AND COMMERCE GONE AWRY

S ince the time of the pharaohs, Egypt had periodically looked southward for lands to conquer. In the 1820s Khedive Muhammed Ali
launched a new effort in an attempt to make the country a serious
world power. His successor Ismail continued the project, and by the 1860s
the upper reaches of the White Nile basin looked like a plum ripe for the
picking. It was a region of considerable strategic importance, as yet
unclaimed by others, and exploratory expeditions revealed the potential for
a lucrative ivory trade. On April 1, 1869, Ismail, backed by the British government, reached an agreement with veteran traveler-explorer Samuel Baker
to command the operation for four years. His charge included ending the
slave trade, replacing it with "regular" commerce, establishing navigation on
the Great Lakes, and building a string of interconnected military posts some
three days march apart.[1] A series of delays, including festivities associated
with the opening of the Suez Canal, postponed Baker's departure from Khartoum until February 1870, and the first attempt to get his boats through the
swampy mass of the Sudd failed. A second succeeded, and on April 15, 1871,
he, his wife, staff members, and twelve hundred Egyptian and Nubian soldiers reached Gondokoro, the site chosen as headquarters for Equatorial
Province, or Equatoria as it became more commonly known.[2]

Baker spent the first months building additional administrative and military posts among the area's Nilotic-speaking Bari and Madi (not to be con-
fused with the Mahdi) inhabitants. Both resented the Egyptian presence and
failed to cooperate. Baker, however, had a bigger concern: Bunyoro, which

stood between Equatoria and the headwaters of the Nile. Intent on annexing it, he led his army south on March 18, 1872. When neither force nor negotiation worked with Kabarega, Baker withdrew to concentrate on pacifying Equatoria. His lack of tact and statesmanship turned a difficult task into a virtually impossible one. When Baker left his post on May 26, 1873, little had been accomplished beyond freeing some slaves and driving a few dealers out of business. The trade continued unabated, and the region's inhabitants remained, for the most part, openly hostile. Lacking regular supplies from Khartoum, Baker's people lived off the land. The constant raiding and plundering this entailed only served to heighten local opposition.

The Egyptians next turned to "Chinese" Gordon, who assumed the post of governor, or pasha, on April 16, 1874. He found only two stations still functioning, Gondokoro, and Fatiko, a small one located east of the Nile in what is now northern Uganda. Even more than before, the ragtag troops and their dependents preyed on the surrounding countryside. With characteristic dispatch, Gordon went about setting things right. He moved the headquarters to Lado, extended the network of stations along the river to near Lake Albert, established posts away from the river, launched two steamers, and oversaw considerable surveying and mapping. He also made the ivory trade a government monopoly, prohibited the import of ammunition, and banned all private military forces.[3] Despite these efforts, when Gordon left Equatoria for good in October 1876, the slave trade still hadn't been crushed, and away from the stations and posts, the province existed in name only.

Working for Gordon during his last months was a curious, frail, and extremely far-sighted man known as Emin Effendi. Born in Silesia to Jewish parents who'd converted to Lutheranism and baptized Eduard Karl Oskar Theodor Schnitzer, he earned a medical degree in Berlin in 1864. Due to a mix up, Eduard missed the state certification exam, and instead of waiting for the next one, he went to Vienna and then to Turkey, where he managed to secure an appointment as quarantine medical officer for the port city of Antavari in Albania. A talented linguist, Schnitzer learned to speak Turkish and Arabic and dressed according to local fashion. To further his cultural immersion, he called himself Dr. Hairollah Effendi. Whether the name change also involved a formal conversion to Islam remains unresolved. Most likely it didn't. From 1870 to 1874, Effendi worked for the governor of northern Albania. After the governor's unexpected death, he willingly assumed care of his widow and children and in August 1875 brought them home to Niesse. The widow later claimed they married, although no documents exist to prove a ceremony ever took place. A month later Effendi did another disappearing act, eventually showing up in Khartoum on December 3. Speculation had it that a desire to get away from the widow prompted the departure. With no means of support, he lived off the largesse of the city's small German community until Gordon hired him to be the chief of sanitary services for Equatoria. By the time he reached Lado, on May 7, 1876, he sported a new name: Mehmet Emin Effendi, with the emphasis on Emin.

With staff in short supply, Gordon gave Emin the task of negotiating the release of some Equatorian troops held by Mutesa. They'd mistakenly entered Buganda while searching for prospective station sites closer to Lake Victoria, and suspecting hostile intentions, the *kabaka* ordered their capture. Impressed by Emin's affable personality and his knowledge of religion, Mutesa agreed to let the prisoners go. In appreciation of Emin's efforts, Gordon turned over more responsibilities to him. He visited Bunyoro, did some exploration, and began a natural history collection that became his true passion.

The Egyptian government had fallen deeply in debt from its attempts at modernization and territorial expansion and suffered a profound psychological blow when Abyssinians routed its invading army in 1875–1876. Equatoria was thus of low priority, and, in protest over lack of support, Gordon left the service in 1877. He came back to fill his obligations only because of British pressure. Meanwhile, hard work and devotion to duty landed Emin the post of governor of Equatoria in July 1878, a promotion that entitled him to be called Emin Bey. The pasha designation came later.

Once in charge, Emin expanded the network of administrative stations and introduced innovations that made the province self-sufficient in food. Ivory paid for most things, including troop salaries. For the world outside, Equatoria hardly existed. Only two steamers per year made the round-trip from Khartoum, and few people entered via overland routes. Its isolation became complete with the Mahdi's rise to power. No steamer could get through after April 1883, and by May 1884, only Equatoria and Khartoum, with Gordon at the helm, still remained under nominal Egyptian control. Suspecting an invasion from neighboring Bahr el Ghazal at any moment, Emin puzzled over whether to surrender or make a stand. The situation looked especially desperate when news of Gordon's death and Khartoum's fall reached Equatoria. Ordered to evacuate the city, in a typical display of arrogance, Gordon figured his presence could save the day. After further deliberation, Emin decided to hold out as long as possible. To improve their chances of survival, he consolidated his troops and followers into the stations that could be connected by steamer and made Wadelai the new capital. Those who remained at the stations north of the rapids at Dufile had to fend for themselves. While no invasion ever occurred, Emin and the ten thousand

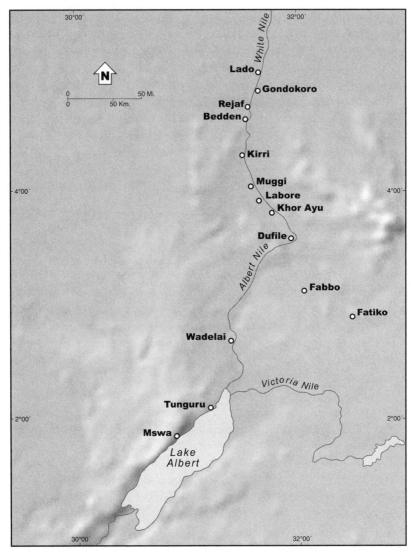

Map 7.1 Egyptian Stations of Equatoria

or so people under him were effectively cut off from outside contact. Nothing came in and nothing went out for nearly two years.

Wilhelm Junker finally broke the silence. An experienced African traveler and naturalist, at Emin's request he left Bahr el Ghazal in January 1884 for the greater security of Equatoria. A year later, Junker began a journey to the east coast, hoping to get word out about the province's plight. Delayed for a long time in Bunyoro, he didn't reach Zanzibar until December 1, 1886. While en route, however, Junker sent Emin's letters ahead, and their arrival in England during late October created quite a stir. As related by historian and prominent RGS member J. Scott Keltie,

> People began to realize what a remarkable man was shut up in this little corner of Africa, barred on the north by the hordes of the Mahdi, and on the south by that merciless young royalty, Mwanga, the son of Stanley's old friend, Mtesa. The excitement rapidly grew; the heroism of Emin's conduct—for he could have easily got away by himself—and the crucially critical nature of his position, took possession of the public mind, and especially that of England. It was realized that to a considerable extent England was to blame for what had happened, and the general verdict was that England was bound to rescue Emin and his fellow prisoners, for such they were.[4]

Dr. Robert W. Felkin, who'd stayed with Emin from July 23 to September 18, 1879, took the lead in drumming up support. He published a letter from him in the *Scottish Geographical Magazine* and followed that with an article called "The Position of Dr. Emin Bey," designed to prompt the British government into action.[5] At his urging, the council of the Scottish Geographical Society passed a resolution in support of Emin and sent it to the secretary of state for foreign affairs. An accompanying letter carried the suggestion that Joseph Thomson lead a "pacific relief expedition" from Zanzibar to Lake Albert.[6] Thomson had added to his fame by leading a highly successful RGS-sponsored mission of discovery across Masaailand in 1883–1884, and Stanley in fact mentioned him as a possible leader before agreeing to take the position himself.[7] The government resisted the pressure, saying it couldn't undertake such a responsibility.[8] Then Prime Minister Salisbury felt Germany should go to his aid, and he didn't want to risk a confrontation by doing anything that might cause diplomatic problems. Any rescue attempt, therefore, would have to be in private hands, a task to which Mackinnon now directed his considerable energies and monies.

As long ago as 1877, Mackinnon and Kirk had tried to form a chartered company to tap the supposed riches of the eastern African interior, especially Africa's "pearl," Uganda. To do so meant getting a concession from Sultan Barghash and Britain's approval. Although Barghash seemed agreeable to the idea, nothing ever came of the negotiations with the British government, and the idea faded away.[9] Playing on recent German advances under Carl Peters's

Gesellschaft für Deutsche Kolonization, Mackinnon made another attempt in 1885 but failed again because the government refused to accede to his demands for acting on its behalf. Urged on by Kirk, he resurrected the idea after the collapse of the Congo Railway Committee.

While Uganda still constituted the main prize, its luster had dulled after Mwanga came to the throne following Mutesa's death on October 9, 1884, from gonorrhea. Mwanga viewed the growing number of Christians as undermining his authority—they served another master—and to prove the point ordered the capture and subsequent killing in October 1885 of James Hannington, the Church Missionary Society's first bishop of East Equatorial Africa. Hannington wanted to visit the CMS station in Buganda and chose the direct route from Mombasa through Busoga. The resident missionary Alexander Mackay tried to warn him of the danger and said to come via Tabora instead. The letter never reached Hannington. In endeavoring to escape, all but four of the fifty Zanzibaris in the caravan met a fate similar to the bishop's.[10] The following May, Mwanga upped the pressure on his Christian subjects and in a fit of rage had some thirty court pages who refused to recant their newfound religious beliefs burned alive. Equatoria looked like an attractive alternative. Seemingly abandoned by Egypt, it was reputed to have an orderly administration in place and bright prospects for profit, especially from ivory. Furthermore, getting there could be presented as a humanitarian effort to aid Emin and his followers. One rescue attempt had already been made with financing from Junker's brother. Led by Dr. G. A. Fischer, it had managed to reach Kavirondo in December 1885 but went no farther due to Mwanga's open hostility and the likely prospect of being attacked in Busoga.

Mackinnon decided to pursue the familiar strategy of building stations and gaining concessions from chiefs along a route designed to stretch from Mombasa to Wadelai. The Anglo-German Boundary Agreement negotiated in October and November 1886 opened the way by putting the intervening country within the British sphere of influence. Mackinnon's umbrella would be a company modeled on the lines of the Royal Niger Company, which had government support, if not direct backing. This way a large area, including Equatoria and Uganda, could be secured against future German advances.

As the year wound down, Emin's plight and his determined stand had reached mythic proportions. According to the *Glasgow Herald,*

> Certainly no incident in the history of European enterprise in the Dark Continent has been so interesting since the search for Livingstone and the fate of Gordon. Emin Bey's figure stands out now prominently on the African roll as

one of the noblest and bravest on the list. The wonderful work he achieved in his isolated province, his endurance and fortitude, his gallant stand, and his submergence of personal considerations of the claims and interests of the people he was sent to help, are features of one of the most brilliant exploits of our generation.[11]

The committee considered four routes during a meeting on December 29. Stanley pushed for the Congo option, arguing that it was safer and less likely to tempt the six hundred or so Zanzibaris he planned on hiring to desert. Consensus, however, favored a route going from Bagamoyo to Lake Victoria through Karagwe and Acholi to Lake Albert. Of the fifteen hundred land miles, only two hundred would traverse unknown territory. Still technically in Leopold's employ, Stanley met with him the very next day. They, too, discussed routes, with the king obviously wanting the expedition to follow the Congo, as it might provide an opportunity to gain his long-desired foothold on the Nile. Stanley doubted the committee could be induced to change its mind. Without being specific, Leopold made reference to another mission he had in mind for him of more importance than relieving Emin. He would, however, postpone it for eighteen months as a gesture of support for the committee.[12]

A letter from Leopold ultimately proved decisive. Among other things, he threatened to activate the claim on Stanley's services, which would preclude his leading the expedition. This could be avoided if the committee agreed to the Congo route, and as an inducement he urged Stanley to write Mackinnon immediately with an offer to make the entire Free State flotilla, except those steamers needed for administrative duties, available for transporting the expedition upriver.[13] Mackinnon told Stanley he'd go along if the king agreed "that no work for the Congo State should be required from you until the work of the Expedition was completed and you had returned with your men to the East Coast."[14] On January 12, 1887, the committee fell in line with the king's wishes. Its official rationale centered on the Congo route lessening the likelihood of misfortune befalling missionaries, the greater ease of evacuating women and children, and opening a new avenue up the Aruwimi River for future relief activities within equatorial Africa.[15] Other factors involving imperial designs also seem to have come into play. Peters didn't want a British-sponsored expedition passing through territory his company sought to control, and the French feared that if Stanley entered Uganda he might provoke attacks against the White Fathers stationed there. Furthermore, since Stanley planned on returning via an eastern route, he could do business for Mackinnon then. Overall, there seems to be little doubt that if any conflict arose regarding which man's interests to serve, Mackinnon would get the nod over Leopold.

An Egyptian pledge of ten thousand pounds sterling cinched the financial side of the plan, now formally under the aegis of the Emin Pasha Relief Committee. The money had originally been allocated to support an expedition led by Junker that failed to get off the ground. In any event, the Egyptians anticipated being reimbursed from ivory, estimated to be as much as seventy-five tons, Emin had stored at Wadelai, and thus in the end it would cost the treasury nothing.[16] With a thousand pounds from the Royal Geographical Society, five hundred from the *Times*, and 9,600 from thirteen individual subscribers, the money pledged met the twenty thousand Stanley estimated the expedition would need. One of the subscribers was Angela-Burdett Coutts (her husband was on the committee). She was widely admired because of her generous philanthropy that counted Livingstone among its recipients, and her association helped to validate the humanitarian nature of the committee's objectives.[17] Mackinnon provided additional support by offering ships from his British-India fleet to carry men and materials. Besides forfeiting the income from the lecture series, Stanley turned over rights of publication of his letters, which eventually totaled 2,200 pounds sterling. A second subscription boosted the total budget of the committee to 29,800 pounds after Egypt decided to keep a thousand for future use in helping meet its costs.[18]

The job of hiring Zanzibaris fell to George Mackenzie. Mackinnon's friend since their days in school together, he now served as his right-hand man in Smith, Mackenzie and Company, a trading firm headquartered in Zanzibar since 1877.[19] Stanley selected Yambuya, where he turned back in 1883, to be the base camp on the Aruwimi for the trip to Lake Albert and a presumed meeting with Emin. A decision about whether the pasha would stay in Equatoria or come out could be made then. In either event, the plan called for the women and children of the Egyptians who wished to leave to be escorted to Yambuya and then to the mouth of the Congo, where the Egyptian government was to have a ship waiting to take them home. Stanley, his men, and any others would proceed to either Mombasa or Bagamoyo, signing treaties en route.

Back in London, Stanley undertook the all-important task of finding European officers to assist him. Letters from people who wanted to join an expedition that promised excitement and career advancement literally poured in, eighty coming in a single day. One from the Societa D'Esplorazione in Milano offered "young Italian Representatives . . . who would be at your service entirely at our own expense."[20] As usual, Stanley found serious flaws in just about all the applicants but eventually settled upon three active military officers, Maj. Edmund M. Barttelot, Capt. Robert H. Nelson, and Lt. W. Grant Stairs. He also hired William Bonny, a former sergeant with some medical training, and John Rose Troup, who had served in the Congo for three years, including a nine-month stint as chief of the Vivi station. Two others, Arthur J. Mounteney-Jephson and James S. Jameson, were added on condition that each pay the committee a thousand pounds for the privilege of going along. Jameson came from the Irish whiskey family of the same name and had traveled widely on hunting excursions. A less experienced young man, Mounteney-Jephson needed something to do after serving a short stint with the Pacific & Orient steamship line. Stanley required all of them to sign similar contracts stipulating that

1. I, . . . agree to accompany the Emin Pasha Relief Expedition, and to place myself under the command of Mr. H. M. Stanley, the leader of the Expedition, and to accept any post or position in that Expedition to which he may appoint me.
2. I further agree to serve him loyally and devotedly, to obey all his orders, and to follow him by whatsoever route he may choose, and to use my utmost endeavours to bring the Expedition to a successful issue.
3. Should I leave the Expedition without his orders, I agree to forfeit all claim to pay due to me, to return passage-money, and to become liable to a refund of all moneys advanced to me for passage to Zanzibar and outfit.
4. Mr. Stanley also agrees to give £40 [forty pounds] as an allowance for outfit, and to pay my passage to Zanzibar, and my return to England, provided I continue during the whole period of the Expedition.
5. I undertake not to publish anything connected with the Expedition, or to send any account to the newspapers for six months after the issue of the official publication of the Expedition by the leader or his representative.
6. In addition to the outfit, Mr. Stanley will supply the following: tent, one Winchester rifle, one revolver, ammunition for the same, canteen, a due share of European provisions taken for the party, besides such provisions as the country can provide.[21]

Dr. Rolf Leslie, known to Stanley from his Congo days, had originally agreed to be the expedition's medical officer but insisted that the "all" be struck from the contract when it came to obeying Stanley's orders. Given that he'd also "split hairs" about other conditions in the contract, the committee members decided to break off negotiations with him in hopes another doctor could be found later on.[22]

Stanley made the Congo route public during a short speech after he had been awarded the Freedom of London on January 13, making him the first journalist to receive the honor. The city's newspapers gave their bravos, praising him as the perfect leader of the expedition. As one put it the next day's edition,

> Success might be deemed almost a miracle; but Mr. Stanley has made his reputation by performing miracles—by proving that what is impossible to the "arm-chair" geographer and the pessimist is the proper duty and function of the man of faith and action. His latest African achievement, for instance, is of a kind to confound the unbeliever and to put shame the doubter in the power there is in one heroic will to work a miracle.[23]

Stanley then crossed the Channel for another meeting with Leopold. Barttelot went with him as far as Dover on the way to Egypt in advance of the others. Much of the discussion between the two men centered on what to do about the Arabs of Umanyema. They had attacked the station at Stanley Falls in August 1886 after its new commander, Walter Deane, provided sanctuary for a woman reportedly fleeing physical abuse. This seems to have been the final straw in a relationship that had been strained from the beginning of Deane's tenure. For protection he had three Krupp cannons, thirty-two Hausa troops, and forty Bangala with the *Stanley* slated to bring up reinforcements. When it arrived, all Deane got was Lt. Eugene Dubois to be second in command. A few days under siege convinced the two of them that it wouldn't be possible to hold out. Seven Hausa had been killed and ammunition was running low. During preparations to abandon the station, all but four of the remaining Hausa fled. They and a few Bangala workers who stayed helped Deane and Dubois put the station to the torch, and together the remaining men stole away under cover of darkness. Dubois drowned attempting to cross the river, and the others retreated into the forest in hopes of avoiding detection. The crew of the *AIA,* commanded by Capt. Camille Coquilhat, found them all alive at the village of Yarukombe exactly thirty days later.[24]

Leopold saw the Emin expedition as a vehicle to reclaim the station for the Free State. Stanley argued that this could wait until later. At the moment they needed the Arabs on their side. They had the upper hand in the region and could easily doom the Congo route. In addition to his own forces, Tippu Tip could count on support of the Wawenya, who controlled the left bank of the river between Stanley Falls and the Luama River. To secure Arab cooperation, they discussed the possibility of making Tippu Tip governor at Stanley Falls for a nominal fee. Later, when the state became strong enough, it "could throw off the mask of compromise & boldly take the opposition."[25] According to the king's sources, Tippu Tip was in Zanzibar and in need of money. Stanley should check with him when he got there. If he proved agreeable and didn't want too much in return, a five-year term might be possible. To keep the matter secret, Stanley was to refer to Tippu Tip as "No. I" in all communications.[26]

Mackinnon hosted a farewell banquet on January 19. A reporter described the mood as one of "jovial enthusiasm," with Stanley confidently predicting:

> Give us five days to go up the Congo and establish our camp. We will be able to march 17 days more to Stanley Pool; and then we could embark for 30 or 35 days, steaming up the Congo, and establish an entrenched camp. In 117 days we arrive at the southern end of Lake Albert; we launch our boat, taking 40 minutes to screw it up; and in four days we come across probably one of Emin Pasha's steamers. Imagine Emin Pasha's men looking at the Egyptian flag! (Cheers) Imagine the joy of those beleagured people—(Cheers)—on being told that the boat they saw was but a forerunner of a great and costly expedition brought together by a number of English sympathisers. (Cheers).[27]

The boat was the steel *Advance*, twenty-eight feet long and six feet abeam. Made in sections for ease of assembly and disassembly, it could carry twenty-two men and a thousand pounds of cargo. Much of Stanley's confidence hinged on having it, plus an expectation that there'd be a well-trod path connecting villages in the forest beyond Yambuya.

The next day Stanley supervised loading of the British India's old and painfully slow *Navarino*. Jephson, Nelson, Stairs, and Bonny were slated to sail with it. The latter had charge of Baruti, who'd be serving as an interpreter once the expedition reached the Aruwimi. Both missed the sailing because Bonny left the boy at the railway station and didn't get back in time to catch the train. Much later Bonny revealed that he'd stepped away to avoid detection by a former wife. Stanley felt like firing him on the spot but refrained because he needed someone with medical experience. Bonny was allowed to take another ship to Suez. Jameson planned to meet up with the others in Aden, while Troup went directly to the Congo to oversee logistical arrangements and secure porters for the overland trek between Manyanga and Stanley Pool. Multiple groups would be required, as locals only worked between certain points. A trip theoretically possible to complete in two

Tippu Tip as governor at Stanley Falls. H. M. Stanley: Explorzteur au service du Roi *(Tervuren: Musée royal de l'Afrique Centrale, 1991). Courtesy of the Royal Museum of Central Africa.*

weeks, it often took two to three months because of many delays. Troup needed to make sure this didn't happen.

The next evening, Stanley, accompanied by Hoffman (by now he'd dropped the final *n* to conform to the English spelling) and Baruti, took the train to Brindisi to catch a ship for Alexandria. Interest remained high. As one commentator noted, "All the newspapers had articles both on the MAN and his expedition, and many thousands of English people gave a kindly God-speed to Stanley in their thoughts, and compared his readiness to depart on this errand to that of Gordon when he went to the Soudan."[28]

From Alexandria, Stanley proceeded to Cairo to see Evelyn Baring, the British consul general, who passed along some troubling news. Junker and old Africa hand George Schweinfurth were doubtful about the Congo route and had expressed this to Egypt's prime minister, Nubar Pasha. Baring also had reservations. Stanley defended the choice, reiterating his view that it presented fewer obstacles than a march from the east coast. With a little arm twisting, Baring and Nubar Pasha came around to his position.

Stanley also pressed the case at a meeting with Junker and Schweinfurth. While noting his "repute" for getting through hostile country, he stressed the need for as bloodless a relief of Emin as possible. Still, it might be necessary to repel attacks along the Aruwimi, and consequently he wanted to have a Maxim gun and in excess of five hundred Remington rifles to overcome any opposition. And if using the weapons meant that

a few score natives are hurt, surely the saving of Emin & his hundreds or thousands as the case may be are well worth the cost. The greater good of the greatest number ought to be considered first, and whatever faddists may say, no nation has been redeemed, without some bloodshed, and I fancy the posterity of the present wild Aruwimi tribes will have reason to rejoice that the unreasoning portion of their ancestors had to retire before our rifles. But after all it is only such as are unreasoningly murderous [who] will have cause to regret our march through these gloomy haunts. Otherwise we are not likely to abuse authority.[29]

Junker brought up other concerns. Emin would be surprised if ordered to leave; he wanted to be resupplied and remain in Equatoria. His determination at this stage to do so was clearly revealed in a letter written in October 1887. Responding to the prospect of Egypt abandoning the province, he stated, "I will not leave it, that is not to be thought of & therefore I should have to say goodbye to Egypt and stand on my own feet."[30] As for Emin's followers, Junker estimated that about six hundred Egyptians and northern

Sudanese might want to leave, but the troops, mostly from Equatoria, would choose to stay. Furthermore, information indicated that some garrisons had lost faith in Emin and were in revolt. As for the ivory in Emin's possession, Junker thought that the porters would be able to carry only an amount worth six thousand pounds, not the ten thousand Egypt expected.[31]

More meetings took place over the next several days, two of which were with Khedive Tewfik, who'd replaced a deposed Ismail. At their completion Stanley went to Port Said to join the *Navarino,* carrying official Egyptian orders for the evacuation of Equatoria. He also had a letter from Nubar Pasha informing Emin that the object of the expedition "is to bring you, your officers, and soldiers back to Egypt by the way which Mr. Stanley shall think most suitable." Those wishing to remain in Equatoria could do so, "but at their own risk and by their own expense."[32] In Cairo, Stanley filled two more expedition needs by hiring Surgeon-Maj. Thomas H. Parke, then attached to the army medical staff in Alexandria, and Syrian Assad Farran to serve as Arabic interpreter. In addition, Baring had secured the services of sixty-three Nubian troops. As arranged, Jameson awaited Stanley in Aden along with Barttelot, who'd signed up thirteen Somalis. On February 12, they all boarded the *Oriental* for the voyage to Zanzibar. Another of Mackinnon's "old tubs," it was infested by vermin and so hot that everyone slept on the deck most nights.[33] Along the way, one of the Nubians came down with smallpox. Prepared for such an eventuality, Parke vaccinated all those who needed it, and no outbreak occurred.

After short calls at Lamu and Mombasa, the *Oriental* reached Zanzibar around noon on February 22. Stanley immediately swung into action, first checking with the acting British consul general, Frederick Holmwood, about the status of porters and supplies. He then went to pay respects to Sultan Barghash and gave him a letter from Mackinnon with a request to reopen discussions about trade concessions for his proposed company. Next came the crucial meeting with Tippu Tip, who was fortunately still in the city. Nominally a subject of the Sultan of Zanzibar, he headed a virtual Manyema state in the Congo that included agents, mostly relatives, seeing to the maintenance of order and the conduct of the ivory and slave trades. Tippu Tip initially balked at the proposal. He didn't like the Belgians and had no desire to work for, in his mind, an inferior power. Stanley told his "old friend" to talk things over with others before rejecting the offer.[34] Bowing to Barghash's wishes, Tippu Tip agreed to accept the position of governor of Stanley Falls at a symbolic salary of thirty pounds per year. The contract contained the following conditions:

1. Tippu-Tip is to hoist the flag of the Congo State at its station near Stanley Falls, and to maintain the authority of the State on the Congo, and all its affluents at the said station downwards to the Bujine or Aruwimi River, and to prevent the tribes thereon, as well as the Arabs and others, from engaging in the slave-trade.
2. Tippu-Tip is to receive a resident officer of the Congo State, who will act as his secretary in all his communications with the Administrator-General.
3. Tippu-Tip is to be at full liberty to carry on his legitimate private trade in any direction, and to send his caravans to and from any place he may desire.
4. Tippu-Tip shall nominate a *locum tenens*, to whom in case of his temporary absence his powers shall be delegated, and who in the event of his death shall become his successor in the Waliship; but his Majesty the King of the Belgians shall have the power of veto should there be any serious objection to Tippu-Tip's nominee.
5. This agreement shall only be binding so long as Tippu-Tip or his representative fulfils the conditions embodied in this agreement.[35]

Tippu Tip signed a second agreement dreamed up by Stanley that required him to provide armed porters to carry supplies from Yambuya to Lake Albert and to transport the many tons of ivory presumed to be in Emin's possession. Porter compensation would be thirty dollars plus food per person, with Tippu-Tip guaranteed a thousand-dollar bonus for each round-trip made by a caravan. It was up to Stanley to supply gunpowder and firing caps.[36] As per an agreement, George Mackenzie had hired 620 Zanzibaris. Whether known to him or not, a goodly number appear to have been slaves working off obligations to their masters. With these essential tasks taken care of, Stanley sent a letter to Emin telling of their plans. He expected little trouble along the way and asked Emin to leave word of his whereabouts at Kavalli's village near Lake Albert. Kavalli was the name of a leader of one of the several Bahima groups occupying the area on the western side of the lake, and in common fashion, his village bore his name. He also asked Mackenzie to see to it that two hundred loads of goods for purchasing food on the return trip to the coast be shipped to Msalala near Lake Victoria.

Early in the morning of February 25 a large gathering of wives and children assembled at the dock to say their good-byes as the expedition began its journey on the newer and faster *Madura*. It carried 808 people, including Tippu Tip and ninety-six of his followers, who received free passage as a part of the deal. An array of goats, sheep, and donkeys also crowded the decks.

Two hours out to sea, a fight over space between the Sudanese and Zanzibaris almost caused the ship to turn around. As Jephson described it,

> On going forward with Stanley it seemed as if hell itself was let loose—sticks, iron bars, coal and every sort of moveable thing were flying though the air, an indescribable scene of confusion and noise was going on—our men seemed transformed into devils and many were bleeding in their heads and arms. We went about the deck disarming the men and throwing their sticks etc. overboard, several of them were using spears. On seeing Stanley the Soudanese crowded around him, each man screaming out the cause of their quarrel and appealing to him to save them from being killed by the Zanzibaris, whilst the Zanzibaris on the other side, shouted out curses at the Soudanese as being the cause of the fight. Stanley's action in the midst of the babel of noises was theatrical and effective and much amused me. Placing his hand on his breast he told them to look at him and be reassured, he would protect them and see justice done, was he not their chief and protector! The quieting effect on them was wonderful and ordering the Soudanese into a separate place between decks aft, he soon restored order and quiet. The Soudanese were certainly the aggressors, and I was glad to see them get a beating for they are much too big for their boots and they require to be taught manners and have the conceit taken out of them.[37]

This would not be the last time Nubians and Zanzibaris clashed.

Stanley's musings aboard the ship illustrate some uncertainty about the outcome of the expedition. It all hinged on Emin's intentions, whether to stay in Africa, accept Mackinnon's offer, or join with the Free State. Whatever happened, he would do what must be done, from resupplying him, to finding a new place to settle, to providing escort to the coast.[38]

With plenty of time on their hands and no other crises to attend to, Stanley set about organizing the expedition. He divided the men into seven companies, each commanded by one of the European officers, who would be responsible for behavior and supplies. He cautioned them to remember "that the men's labour is severe" and that "punishments should be judicious, to prevent straining the patience of the men; nevertheless, discipline must be taught, and, when necessary, enforced for the general well-being of the Expedition."[39] The nature of the project made it more like the search for Livingstone and the crossing of Africa than working for Leopold.

On March 5 the *Madura* pulled in to Simon's Bay at the Cape of Good Hope, and four days later it stopped in Table Bay to take on coal, ammunition, and provisions before steaming on to the Congo. A new member joined the expedition, John Walker, an engineer, whose job it would be to keep the steamers afloat. More uneventful days at sea followed until two Zanzibaris died, one from dysentery and the other from pneumonia, just before the *Madura* dropped anchor off Banana on March 18. Its sudden arrival came as a surprise. Troup, then at Manyanga, had estimated the 25th of the month as the most likely date, and a break in the cable line meant that word of the ship's quicker-than-expected progress hadn't been received. As a result, none of the Free State's boats were waiting for them. Frustrated by this unexpected turn of events, Stanley quickly secured two steamers from Dutch and British concerns, plus a paddleboat and a small gunboat from the Portuguese consul to take most of the expedition over the 108 miles of river between Banana and Matadi. Located across the river from Vivi, Matadi had developed into the Congo's major seaport. The state's *Heron*, freed of duties, soon showed up to provide additional transport.

At Boma Stanley heard more bad news. Severe food shortages existed upstream, and he shouldn't count on the Free State's flotilla at Stanley Pool being available. Due to shoddy maintenance, several boats were reportedly out of commission. It might be possible, however, to lease the *Florida*, a steamer being assembled at the pool for use by the Sanford Exploring Expedition. Leopold had recently granted his longtime friend a concession to trade along the Upper Congo, with ivory as the principal lure. Like virtually all Sanford's financial adventures, this one eventually proved ruinous. He died in 1891 deeply in debt and disillusioned with Leopold's imposition of import duties and the corruption among many Free State officers.[40] Stanley knew that two other steamers, the *Henry Reed* of the Livingstone Inland Mission and the American Baptist Society's *Peace,* operated at the pool. He hoped to get them as well.

A more immediate concern existed—the grueling overland trek across the Cristal Mountains immediately ahead. The Europeans had donkeys to ride, but the men, out of shape from their long sea voyage, would have to negotiate the narrow, winding paths by foot. Four had already been buried at Banana, and twelve were too sick to travel.[41] The first stretch beyond Matadi was especially difficult, as it required a rapid ascent of about a thousand feet across sun-scorched rocks and clay. Stanley considered the so-called road the "worst" one in Africa and called the hills the "Heart Breakers."[42] There were many difficult streams to cross and day after day of oppressive humidity to endure. As it turned out, the journey to the pool, which took from March 25 to April 19 to complete, proved to be even more taxing than Stanley had envisioned, and from the first day illnesses, exhaustion, and painful foot ulcers caused men to fall by the wayside. The leader suffered an early attack of debilitating diarrhea. Many members failed to ration their food carefully, and as predicted, little could be purchased along the way. Hunger thus added its share to the ordeal. By journey's end, twenty-seven men had died or deserted, with more felled by one disorder or another. Some were left behind to recover or not.

Under such pressure, morale took a beating. Rows between Stanley, the officers, and the men erupted almost daily. Barttelot regularly expressed his discontent about having to oversee the Sudanese. Soldiers by training and attitude, they refused to carry loads, continued to scuffle with the Zanzibaris, and on several occasions nearly mutinied over food. Barttelot claimed that Stanley blamed him for their misbehavior and then threatened to ruin his reputation "if the Soudanese revolted, and had to be shot down."[43] For Mounteney-Jephson the main problem involved having to endure John Walker. He found him "hopelessly wanting . . . in sense of decency" and his laziness, he said, made it "hard to get natives to work & be sharp." Despite annoyance at having been sent to help Troup bring up supplies from Many-anga, Mounteney-Jephson got on well with Stanley, and even went so far as to describe him as "one of the kindest hearted men possible."[44] Jameson seems to have been the least happy of the lot. He considered the work required as "not fit for any white men." It ought, he remarked, "be given to slave-drivers," since it involved doing "nothing all day but kick lazy carriers, and put the loads on to the heads of those who choose to fling them down."[45] Stanley's harsh language and frequent criticisms also got under his skin. It all came to a head when Stanley lectured him after his company lost a box of ammunition. Told he would be dismissed if it happened again, Jameson felt that "If this thing is to go on, and he speaks to me again as he did to-day, I should not be sorry if we did part, for I certainly will not keep my temper again."[46]

Stairs took most things in stride. Even Stanley's outbursts didn't bother him much, although he did worry about the "tremendous leverage" the expedition's leader exerted on everyone.[47] Constant wetness from rain and crossing streams bothered Parke, and he expressed concern about the men's proneness to "straggling and pilfering." The doctor thus supported Stanley's enforcement of stricter discipline involving lashes and chains. According to him,

Whatever may be said or thought at home by members of philanthropic African societies, who are so anxious about the extension of the rights of humanity, there is no getting an expedition of Zanzibari carriers across this country without use of a fair amount of physical persuasion. In its absence they become utterly reckless, and soon forget all discipline.[48]

A few days beyond Matadi, the expedition acquired another European, Herbert Ward, a three-year Congo veteran employed by both the Free State and the Sanford Exploring Expedition. On his way to the coast in anticipation of going home, Ward met Charles Ingham, a missionary hiring porters for the expedition, who told him about Stanley being nearby. The two had met in 1884, and afterward Stanley passed Ward's name along to Leopold as someone worthy of consideration for employment by the Free State. The thought of joining "the little band who were bound for far regions of Equatorial Africa, to carry relief to a brave and devoted man" seemed too good an opportunity to pass up, and Ward immediately wrote to Stanley asking to be accepted as a volunteer.[49] Aware of the expedition's labor needs, Ward rounded up three hundred porters, hoping they would serve as an entry ticket. Duly impressed, Stanley welcomed the prospect of adding "a young man of great promise" and instructed him to help Troup bring up the loads from Manyanga after finishing his business in Matadi.[50] Other Europeans tried to join, but with this addition, Stanley felt enough officers were already on hand. In general he found Europeans too demanding and wanted only as many as absolutely necessary.

Although everyone was glad about having reached the pool—Mounteney-Jephson described its sighting as "lovely"—conditions there didn't improve matters.[51] The markets carried little food, certainly not enough to feed the hungry stomachs of so many newcomers. The previous growing season had been a poor one, which only intensified the usual shortages. According to Stairs, "Acres of bananas and manioc could have been planted, but no, everything is ivory from morning to night; all are concerned with getting down the greatest quantity of ivory."[52] Jameson shot some hippos, but the meat wasn't enough to placate Stanley's concerns about a "breach of order" taking place if food shortages continued.[53] To obviate such an eventuality, he wanted to get under way as quickly as possible. Once again the dilemma of not having enough steamers for the job crimped his plans. Of the Free State's four on the Upper River, only the *Stanley* was ready and able. The *En Avant* lacked both engine and boiler, the *Royal* lay rotting on the shore, and the *AIA* had gone on assignment to Bangala.

As a way to lessen the immediate food problem, Stanley sent 153 of the men under Barttelot and Parke to Mswata. He figured they would be able to find food there and cut a supply of wood for future use by the steamers. Stanley then set about requisitioning the other boats at the pool. As luck would have it, his former secretary Anthony Swinburne served as Sanford's Kinshasa agent and he offered to loan the expedition the still unfinished *Florida*. Without an engine, it, like the *En Avant*, would have to be towed like a barge. Both missionary societies steadfastly refused to turn over their steamers, with the head of the Baptists declaring that he had consulted the Bible and found a "command" not to assist the expedition in this way.[54] Under pressure he finally gave in and agreed to loan the *Peace*. Some strong-arm tactics eventually secured the *Henry Reed* as well—the Free State simply seized it for a fee of one hundred pounds per month, Stanley's original offer. On May 1 the hodgepodge flotilla finally set off for Yambuya. Troup and Ward had hurried from Manyanga so as not to miss the departure. An unpleasant surprise, however, awaited Troup. With space at a premium, Stanley ordered him to stay at the pool to look after the supplies that couldn't be loaded and to wait for any stragglers who might show up. The *Stanley* would come back for him later. Because they had been badly packed the first time, Troup spent much of his time re-packing supplies.

Problems with the boats surfaced almost immediately. The *Peace* nearly capsized when its rudder snapped just after getting under way. Even when fixed, she moved at a snail's pace. On May 7, the *Stanley*, with the *Florida* in tow, struck a reef. Her "steel crumpled up like paper," and two days were needed to repair the holes with pieces fashioned from oil drums.[55] A daily task involved cutting massive quantities of wood to feed the steamers' hungry boilers. Luckily, the river cooperated. The water level didn't fluctuate like it could, the hippos and crocodiles stayed clear, and few insects bothered the passengers. Furthermore, as expected, the food problem vanished at Mswata. To conserve space, Stanley told Barttelot and Parke to take their men overland to the next stopping place at Bolobo. Two things of significance happened there. First, Ward and Bonny were instructed to stay and look after the 125 men determined least fit to travel. They could catch up later, along with Troup's men and supplies. Stanley also informed Barttelot of his future plans. Concerned that they might not reach Emin in time, he decided to lead a lightly supplied contingent on a quick march from Yambuya to Lake Albert, while the major, as second in command, stayed there with the others to await porters from Tippu Tip. If they came in time, catching up would be easy because of the opportunity to follow a well-marked path. When asked about whom he wished to be next in command, a clearly unhappy Barttelot chose Jameson, since the two had become fast friends. Troup, Ward, and Bonny would eventually join them to complete Yambuya's staff of Europeans.[56]

Above Bolobo, the steamers often lost contact with one another, and, therefore, at Equator Station, Stanley ordered them to stay in sight from then on, which slowed progress to the pace of the *Peace*. Edward Glave, now in the employ of the Sanford Exploring Expedition, greeted them. His robust health reinforced Stanley's opinion about the superiority of the site compared to the other stations along the Congo. As for Stanley, Glave described him as being "exceedingly jolly" during the stopover.[57] Six days later the boats reached Bangala. Prosperous and well fortified, it served as the Free State's farthest station up river at that time. By previous agreement Tippu Tip and his party left for their settlement at Stanley Falls, known as Kisingitini to the Arabs. Stanley provided the *Henry Reed*, the most reliable of the steamers, sending Barttelot with forty Sudanese to act as escorts. After dropping them off and inquiring about porters, Barttelot was told to head straight for Yambuya. Stanley said he and Tippu Tip parted as friends and promised to meet in England someday.[58] A problem, however, had developed over the promised gunpowder and firing caps. Tippu Tip wanted them immediately, whereas Stanley claimed to have only enough for his own needs at the moment. The *Stanley* would bring the rest later. In the meantime, Tippu Tip could buy powder and caps from the Belgians at Stanley Falls.[59]

Stanley continued to explode every so often. Even the usually unflappable Stairs started to have serious doubts about him after a run-in over the punishments he and Mounteney-Jephson handed out to some Zanzibaris for looting food from a friendly village. Stanley jumped in on the side of the Zanzibaris and unleashed a verbal assault that prompted Stairs to record that never in his life had he "stood more swearing at, heard more degrading things, and swallowed more intemperate language."[60] As he had on other occasions, such as the remarks made about Kirk in Paris, Stanley regretted his words almost immediately, noting privately that "To be carried away by a petty outbreak of this kind . . . is to make one feel almost hopeless of ever overcoming natural infirmities."[61]

On the other hand, conditions along this portion of the river pleased the leader. Cannibalism, ordeals by poison, and the sacrifice of slaves all seemed to have vanished, and if the killing of twins and their mothers still existed, it must be limited and done in private. Stanley recorded feeling "a great inward satisfaction" at having been "the instrument chosen to initiate the civilization of the Congo basin" and hoped that someday people would credit him for it.[62] The passage of time would lead to a rather different judgment being rendered.

The remaining boats started for the Aruwimi on June 2. In Upoto a large number of canoes came out to meet them. Their crews seemed suspicious and maybe hostile; however, long palavers and gifts of many beads, cowries, and lengths of cloth brought an agreement to trade for much needed food. Nonetheless, over the course of the next days, villagers frequently greeted them with shouts, shaking spears, and occasional throat-slashing signs. The sight of a recently burned village suggested the presence of "accomplished raiders" having done their work, and a little farther upstream armed men decorated with face paint stared down from the banks above the river. As they entered the Aruwimi on June 12, Baso scouts kept a close watch on their progress. One of them just happened to be Baruti's older brother, and through him concerns about the expedition's intentions were allayed, allowing vigorous trade to get under way. Without further incident, the boats reached a point on the right bank of the Aruwimi, directly across from Yambuya, three days later.

Early the next morning Stanley took the *Peace* across the river in hopes of negotiating for a place to build a fortified camp. When three hours of talks produced no progress, he signaled for the *Stanley* to come over as well. Both boats repeatedly sounded their whistles, and when the men scurried up the banks, they entered an abandoned village from which virtually everything had been removed.[63] The *Henry Reed* had yet to arrive, and Stanley began worrying that something untoward might have happened. The thought crossed his mind that the Arabs could be holding the men captive, but he didn't think Tippu Tip capable of such treachery. Perhaps the Sudanese had mutinied, or the boat may have run aground. In the meantime, Baruti stole away to rejoin his kin downriver, taking two rifles and one of Stanley's revolvers with him. When June 22 came and went with no sign of or word from Barttelot, Stanley ordered Stairs to take about a hundred men and head back toward the Congo to see what could possibly have happened. If necessary, they could use the Maxim gun. Then, just as the party was preparing to depart, the *Henry Read* pulled into view, with all safely aboard.

As reported by the men, Tippu Tip and the others at Kisingitini had treated the Barttelot party extremely well. The major delay in reaching Yambuya involved the burned village seen earlier. A dispute over food occasioned a fight in which several of Tippu Tip's people suffered wounds. They retaliated by burning the village. Tippu Tip asked Barttelot for help, but the major refused to let the Nubians join the fray. Episodes of fog, the need to cut wood for fuel, and boiler problems also contributed to the delay. During his short stay at the Falls, Barttelot discovered the expedition's plans might be in jeopardy. Tippu-Tip claimed Stanley was in breach of their contract because he had failed to provide the gunpowder and firing caps. As a result, he felt under no obligation to find porters. Barttelot claimed to have "effected a sort of compromise by making him [Tippu Tip] half promise to supply . . . 200 men with ammunition, to be repaid" at an unspecified later date.[64] He never seems to have revealed the nature of the compromise.

On June 24 Stanley gave Barttelot a letter of instructions about what to do after he left for Lake Albert. The key portion stated:

We will endeavor, by blazing trees and cutting saplings along our road, to leave sufficient traces of the route taken by us. We shall always take by preference tracks leading eastward at all crossways where paths intersect. We shall hoe up and make a hole a few inches deep across all the paths not used by us, besides blazing trees when possible. It may happen, that should Tippu Tib have sent the full number of adults promised by him to me—viz., 600 men able to carry loads—and the *Stanley* has arrived in safety with the 125 men left by me at Bolobo, that you will feel yourself sufficiently competent to march the column, with all the goods brought by the *Stanley* and those left by me at Yambuya, along the road pursued by me. In that event, which would be desirable, you will follow closely our route, and before many days we should most assuredly meet. No doubt you would find our bomas intact and standing, and you should endeavor to make your marches so that you could utilize these as you marched. Better guides than these bomas of our route could not be made. If you do not meet them in the course of two days' march, you may rest assured that you are not in our route.

It may happen also that, though Tippu Tib has sent some men, he has not sent enough to carry the goods with your own force. In that case you will, of course, use your discretion as to what goods you can dispense with to enable you to march. For this purpose you should study your list attentively—viz.:

1st. Ammunition, especially fixed, is important.
2nd. Beads, brass wire, and cowries rank next.
3rd. Private baggage.
4th. Powder and caps.
5th. European provisions.
6th. Brass rods as used in the Congo.
7th. Provisions (rice, beans, peas, matamas, biscuit).

Therefore, you must consider after those sacking tools, such as shovels (never discard an axe or a billhook), how many sacks of provisions you can distribute among your men to enable you to march, whether half the brass rods in your boxes couldn't go also, and there stop. If you still cannot march, then it would be better to make marches of six miles twice over, if you prefer marching to staying for our arrival, than throw too many things away.

The letter went on to say, "There is only one chief, which is yourself; but should any vital steps be proposed to be taken, I beg of you to take the voice of Mr. Jameson; and when Messrs. Troup and Ward are here, pray admit them to your confidence, and let them speak freely their opinions."[65] Bonny wasn't considered equal to the others, a situation he resented.

Worried that the instructions were less than perfectly clear, Stanley said he told Barttelot several times the next day to make two or three short marches daily if for some reason Tippu Tip failed to send porters. Nevertheless, plenty of time remained, since the *Stanley* wouldn't be bringing supplies and the men until around August 10. Stanley remained confident about Tippu Tip living up to his end of the bargain and providing at least a "fair number" of men. Arabs just tended to be slow in such matters, he explained.[66] A letter to Troup contained instructions about which stores to sell and which to take to Yambuya. A PS noted, "On arriving here place yourself under the Major, for he will no doubt, when you join, push on after me with you all."[67] The evidence suggests that Stanley expected the rear column to move out in some fashion. Later this issue would become a major point of contention.

Yambuya looked promising. A stockade surrounded by a ditch containing sharpened stakes was near completion. There seemed to be plenty of food in the vicinity. The previous inhabitants had established a new village on the other side of the river, and Barttelot underwent a blood brotherhood ceremony with the chief to establish good trade relations. Food could also be obtained from a large cassava field that surrounded the settlement. In any event, Stanley didn't plan on being gone long. Based on an average march of six miles per day, he planned to reach Lake Albert by the end of September. A quicker return trip should bring him back to Yambuya sometime in November, if the rear column hadn't already been met on the way.

Stanley organized the 389 most fit men in four units for the journey. That left 129 at Yambuya to await those coming with supplies from the pool and Bolobo. A problem existed with Stairs. He was seriously ill and couldn't walk. Stanley considered leaving him at Yambuya but decided to have him brought along by litter, figuring that if he were destined to die, it might as well happen along the road.

On June 28 the advance began, following a narrow trail that after five miles forced the men to crawl to avoid low-hanging creepers. Later that afternoon, a large group of women and children stared at them from a string of islands, while armed men waited in canoes and war drums sounded. A little farther on, a wide path leading to a large village suddenly appeared. Thick bush blocked each side, and sharply pointed stakes designed to impale intruders lined the way. As Stanley led his unit carefully along it, he noticed smoke rising from the village. The inhabitants had set it ablaze before coming out to fire a barrage of arrows at presumed attackers. None struck a target. A real fight took place on the other side of the village. After another volley of arrows produced two wounded, Stanley ordered twenty men to open fire. They continued firing as the villagers fled to their canoes, killing an estimated thirty of them and wounding many more.[68]

The route took the column away from the river and into a section of forest containing numerous villages. Rather than offering resistance, the inhabitants simply melted away. Sharpened stakes along paths occasionally did some damage to barefoot men. If deep enough, their wounds became gangrenous. Additional hazards included pits designed to ensnare animals, mazes of felled trees, and swamps deep enough to swallow donkeys. Because of all the obstacles, the column managed to cover only sixteen miles in six days, less than half of what Stanley thought could be accomplished. And with no villagers with whom to trade, food started to become a worry.

In light of the conditions, Stanley decided to head back to the Aruwimi, where he had the *Advance* reassembled to carry the loads of forty-four men on a rotational basis. The rest of the space went to the sick, who included Stairs. The *Advance* could go no farther on a given day, however, than those hacking out a path along the shore. As for Stanley, he generally traveled in one of the canoes they managed to find or pilfer along the way.

The next day the river party came upon a totally abandoned village from which even "the fowls had taken to flight."[69] Luckily a cassava field provided some badly needed food. Mounteney-Jephson and the land party then spied the fleeing villagers unloading their goods at a riverside encampment. As he and a group of scouts approached in an effort to make contact, the people quickly scampered away, leaving their belongings, including more cassava, behind. Hearing gunfire from the forest, Mounteney-Jephson hurried in that direction and discovered one of the scouts had shot two of the villagers. He described himself as being "awfully angry with the man for shooting men who were merely taking the liberty of running away from us in their own forest." They seemed to be bleeding to death, but he left them where they lay in hopes that "their people would find them & do the do the best they could for the poor fellows."[70]

Constant wet and somber grayness marked each day's passage, as did work at cutting through overhanging lianas and crossing swollen creeks. The men showed the strain, and Stanley wished he had the fifteen steel boats he had asked for but were refused by Mackinnon.[71] Ants caused more discomfort. According to Parke:

> They travel in army corps; with their commissariat, pioneers, intelligence, and other departments thoroughly organized. They frequently pass in a continuous stream for several hours by our tents, sometimes even through them. If not molested, they go along quietly; but once disturbed, and their line broken,

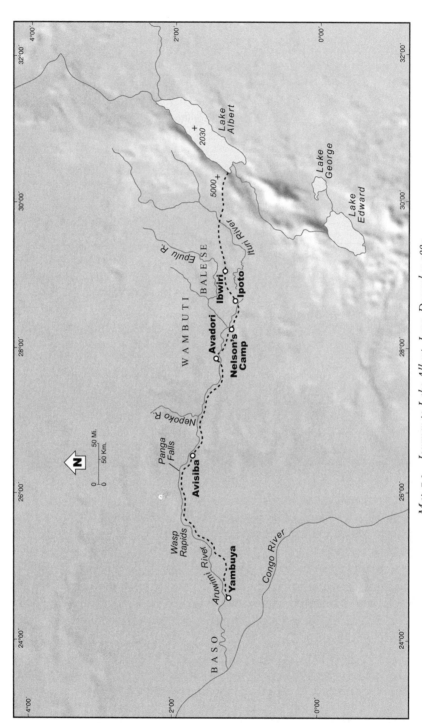

Map 7.2 Journey to Lake Albert, June–December 1887

they become vicious and revengeful. The majority are small and red, but a certain proportion of large black ones are to be seen among the crowd. We are obliged to strap our knickerbockers very tightly round the leg; petticoats would never do in this country.[72]

Although numerous villages lined the banks of the river, none contained any inhabitants by the time the column reached them. This, though, had its upside—easy pickings for food, meat excluded. Few, if any, livestock were ever left behind, and frightened by the noise of men slashing away at vegetation, whatever game may have been in the vicinity disappeared from view.

When, on rare occasions, the land party came across villagers, they would be taken to Stanley for questioning. Not much of value was ever learned from them. However, a fifteen-year-old boy who voluntarily came aboard the *Advance* on July 12 proved useful by serving as a translator for a discussion with some men in a canoe. They sold a couple of fowls and went to get three more. The sale proved a good omen, as for the first time, the Aruwimi people showed themselves willing to barter, and in subsequent days, empty cans and cartridge shells bought maize, sugarcane, and tobacco, while chickens were had for cotton handkerchiefs. This convinced Stanley to stay with the river route.

Despite a steady stream of sickness and injuries, the column had so far experienced only one fatality, a Zanzibari who bled to death from an arrow wound to the thigh. Two others were missing. They either deserted or became lost. Overall, the Somalis suffered the most. To Stanley's way of thinking, they proved themselves "perfectly useless in humid regions."[73]

Thankfully, mosquitoes were few, but the forest's small, stingless bees annoyed everyone by crawling into mouths, eyes, and ears. One day, while following a narrow channel around a stretch of rapids, some men in the *Advance* reached for branches to steady their progress. This unleashed "an army of fierce spiteful wasps" that Stanley said "settled on our faces, hands, and bodies, every vulnerable spot, and stung us with the venom of fiends."[74] Noticing the attack, the canoes following crossed to the other side, but the Somalis and Nubians on land couldn't cross and suffered the same fate as those in the *Advance*. In memory of the event, Stanley named the place Wasp Rapids, and he ordered a day's rest for those most severely stung to recover.

Although the people thereabouts also proved willing to trade, they demanded unheard-of prices—a brass rod bought only three ears of maize, and a chicken cost four rods. With food supplies dwindling rapidly, the men began bartering away their cartridge pouches, ammunition, billhooks, and axes. Stanley reacted by ordering the seizure of one of the chief's slaves and said he would not be returned unless an agreement was reached on more equitable terms of trade. When nothing changed, he gave up bargaining and sent out a group of "foragers" who located enough food to last ten days. Foraging had two meanings—finding food in the forest and stealing it. In most cases, the latter proved to be the easier option.

A second death occurred on August 2, and the deteriorating state of the men signaled the need for another rest. But the journey continued when it proved impossible to find a convenient place to stop. Every so often someone attempted to desert; those who were caught or voluntarily returned felt the sting of the rod. Like the men, the donkeys found little to eat and began dying, and the capsizing of several canoes resulted in the loss of supplies, including rifles. One capsizing occurred at Panga Falls, a mile-long stretch of water that posed the first serious obstacle to river transport so far. Foraging here yielded too little food to stay long, and so the wearying job of portaging around the rapids went on without a break. More accidents occurred on water and land, and seven others joined the growing list of the dead. Only the occasional capture of goats buoyed the men's spirits. As the following journal entry shows, Stanley grew ever more worried about the expedition's fate:

The people are ravenously hungry, and it is a marvel how well they bear this meagre food which we have been able to obtain. There is naturally a good bit of stealing, but punishment would have no deterrent effect at such a time. Matters may become worse unless we can reach somewhere where we can get a bounteous supply. We have several living skeletons with us already.[75]

Despite now having fourteen canoes, so many men were debilitated that on most days it became hard to find enough paddlers.

At about noon on August 13 Stanley led his party into an abandoned village called Avisiba. During an investigation into the circumstances surrounding the killing of a Zanzibari the day before, shots were heard from the direction of the river. Stairs, now recovered from his illness, and a group of riflemen hurried to the scene and discovered some of the men collecting food under attack. A fierce battle ensued, during which Stairs took an arrow just below the heart. The shaft broke off, and fearing poison Parke sucked out the point, applied carbolic acid to the wound, and injected a heavy dose of morphine that sent Stairs into a deep sleep. Continuing fire drove the attackers off, and the next day, Stanley ordered all villages in the vicinity burned in retaliation. Over the course of two days' intermittent fighting, nine of the column suffered arrow wounds and Parke did his best to treat them. While Stairs eventually recovered, the others died in agonizing pain, not from poison but tetanus. Somehow a story started circulating about Stanley having been killed during the battle. Similar rumors followed. For example, one rumor supposedly based on intelligence contended "that M. Stanley has been massacred, together with all members of his escort, with the exception of two men who escaped."[76]

Another bout with misfortune started when the land party under Mounteney-Jephson, Parke, and Nelson didn't show up at a designated meeting place on time. Stanley figured they must have become lost, and a small group of scouts went back to try to find them. Looking at the many sick and wounded strewn about that camp, he despaired:

> It is scarcely possible daylight will ever appear again, at least so I judge from the human faces steeped in misery. Their owners appear stupefied by terror, woe, sickness, loss of friends, hunger, rain and thunder, and general wretchedness. They may be seen crouching under plantain-leaf sheds, native shields, cotton shelters, straw mats, earthen and copper pots above their heads, even saddles, tent canvass covers, blankets, each body wreathed in blue-vapour, self-absorbed with speechless anguish.[77]

A driving all-day rain hardly helped his mood, and with only eighteen able-bodied men for defense, Stanley worried about an attack. Should one come, he figured they would all be annihilated. At last, the land party dragged into camp, having been found by the scouts. Three of its members died during skirmishes on the way back, while Stanley also lost three at the camp. Their current state shook his self-confidence to the core.

> The . . . passion of my life has been I think to succeed in what I undertake, but these last few days have begun to fill me with doubt of this Expedition. We are not yet half way to the Albert. The people are fading away. Every march must be attended with a loss of life. We have nothing with us save a few brass rods for barter money.[78]

Along this stretch of the Aruwimi, more people lived inland than on the banks. Nevertheless, the column stayed with the river route because it afforded opportunities for finding at least some food, mostly small bananas and plantains, which Stairs described as "green wizened things 40 of which would not make a square meal for a man."[79] Sickness continued unabated.

Leg ulcers were especially common, and they made the burdens of cutting paths and carrying loads more difficult to bear. A measure of relief came on August 26 where the Nepoko enters the Aruwimi. The site contained a large number of villages and food in quantities unsurpassed since Yambuya. In spite of their apparent formidable numbers, the inhabitants had chosen to flee, which allowed "the people to get a real food feed," including fowls, without struggle or having to pay.[80] A huge canoe had also been left behind, and it served to transport those too sick to paddle or walk.

From a longitude reading on August 30, Stanley concluded that the half-way point to Lake Albert had been reached. It had taken sixty-four days, and the poor state of the men suggested that they couldn't possibly cover the remaining distance in an equivalent amount of time. The next afternoon, just after setting up camp, Hoffman hurried toward Stanley claiming to have seen Emin Pasha, or at least a canoe bearing the Egyptian red flag. Instead, the nine men aboard proved to be part of a contingent under a chief from Umanyema called Ugarrowwa out exploring the river to see if it led toward Stanley Falls. They left after about an hour, having reported Ugarrowwa's village, Avadori, to be about twenty days away and the forest extending for another twenty days' march farther on. The presence of Arab-led slavers explained all the burned villages they had seen recently, and it also caused Stanley to worry about desertions. One of the reasons he had chosen the Aruwimi route was to lessen the likelihood of encountering Arab settlements. His worries became reality, for over the next couple of days, fourteen carriers disappeared, taking supplies with them. To discourage further disappearances, Stanley seized the mainsprings from the rifles and the ammunition of some sixty men deemed most likely to steal away.

Nothing now seemed to favor the column's progress: More rapids and waterfalls blocked the way, and paths could not be found, requiring those on land to cut, cut, and cut some more. And all the while, the men's condition worsened. By September 12 sixteen of them had died, with fifty-eight on the sick list. Four couldn't go any farther and were left behind with little food and water. Everyone knew they wouldn't survive for very long. Hunger worsened, and yet the loads became heavier, as only three donkeys remained alive, and one of them soon disappeared into the forest's depths. Stairs became angry about the conditions of the Europeans:

> The way in which we are fed and looked after in this Expedition is simply disgraceful. Stanley does not care a jot about our food as long as he is well fed. He never by any chance interests himself in his officers' behalf in any way. We come in wet after a long march as yesterday and then have to pitch our

tents in the dark and rain, when all this time his men have been in camp, having come by river.[81]

Stairs would continue recording his discontent about the inadequacy of supplies without, it appears, ever having said anything to Stanley.

More burned villages, dead bodies, and some infants bearing gunshot wounds testified to recent visits by slavers. Few locals, therefore, showed themselves, and the ones who did spoke unfamiliar languages. Then, on September 16, three canoes filled with Kiswahili speakers showed up, bringing a welcome from their leader Ugarrowwa, whose village lay just upstream. Ugarrowwa's real name was Uledi Balyuz, a Zanzibari who had worked for Speke and Grant in an 1864 expedition as a tent boy. Ugarrowwa mentioned to Stanley that two other Arab stations were situated in the Ituri and it was likely that the column would encounter resistance from people who'd recently borne the brunt of slave and ivory hunting. The open country Stanley sought lay a month away, according to informants.

The three days spent at Avadori reinvigorated most of the men—they had plenty to eat and an opportunity to rest. Stanley made arrangements to leave the fifty-six still too weak to travel there at five dollars per head per month. He expected Barttelot to collect them. Those ready for the march totaled 292, including six Europeans, eleven boys, and two cooks.[82] In exchange for much needed gunpowder Ugarrowwa agreed to see that a letter from Stanley reached Yambuya. With an accompanying sketch map, it outlined the column's progress to date, instructed Barttelot not to believe what deserters said, and told him to "Follow the river closely, & do not lose sight of our track."[83] Ugarrowwa kept his word, although attacks forced the men carrying the letter to turn back before completing their mission.

Three more men deserted just before the scheduled departure on September 19. Caught by Ugarrowwa, they received floggings before being handed back. To Stanley the time had come "to try the severest punishment," for he considered "running away with . . . rifles and ammunition, as equal to open war."[84] He told the men as much and then had the three runaways draw straws to determine who would be executed on the spot and who on subsequent days. The loser was hung almost instantly, and the other two were spared in a scheme Stanley had concocted to make him look magnanimous. Once again, he displayed mastery at distancing himself from punishments administered to Africans. Councils were held, and Africans called on to mete out punishments. Sometimes he jumped in to soften the verdicts.

Although a land route from here seemed possible, Ugarrowwa convinced

Stanley to stay with the river, claiming passage would become much easier than it had been. Rapids, however, continued to get in the way, and some required repeated trips to get everything safely to the other side. The men often did this on empty stomachs, for the countryside yielded little or nothing to eat. The seriousness of their plight led Stanley to record, "How we shall pull through this wide devastated district—God only knows. It would appear we had not one chance in a hundred." Parke described the situation as one of "grim starvation, grim despair."[85] The next afternoon some Zanzibaris located just enough plantains to ward off starvation, and a woman told them that many more existed nearby. They never found the plantations, and the forest continued to be a desert as regards food. To Parke it appeared

an utter wilderness—huge gloomy trees and dense thick bush beneath—there is no chance of shooting anything in it; one can never see more than a few yards ahead. If any person loses consciousness of the exact direction in which he started . . . he has no means whatever of guiding him back except he has a compass to steer with. No visible or tangible trace is left in the dense undergrowth; and, accordingly, it is most dangerous for the men to wander from the line of march, or from the camping-place, even for any trifling distance. Of all the scenes of desolation for any human to be left alone in! I could not have fancied it before I came here. Snowed in at the North Pole, launched in a canoe in the middle of the Pacific Ocean, hardly either could compare with it.[86]

Desperation led to a massacre on September 28. Stairs seems to have been the instigator, for in his own words:

About 3:30 we heard the natives pounding their cloth and bananas, and shortly after this we caught sight of some huts and saw the natives peacefully at work. We had no canoe nor could we find one. Stanley was far behind us and could not get up by dark. If the natives saw us they would bolt taking everything with them; we had thus no means of cutting off their retreat from the opposite side of the island. What could we do?

I sent word to Stanley to send a canoe if possible quickly up the eastern channel to attack. The natives would thus rush out on our side with their goats and everything while we, hidden in the under growth, would grab everything. For three hours we waited till darkness was coming on and something must be done. At last, seeing no canoes could reach us to-day, I decided to fire on the village from three places, one at the top of the island to sweep the other channel, one at the bottom for the same purpose, and one directly where we were hidden. I opened the game by shooting one chap through the chest, he fell like a stone and was seen the next day, stiff as mutton. Immediately a volley was poured on the village. At first the natives ran, but rallying, they peppered us with their iron-tipped arrows but without effect. For some minutes we took pot shots at the heads as they appeared above the grass and huts and managed to drop a few more and gradually they made off one by one till all was quiet. At the bottom of the island the doctor managed to drop two as they were making off in a canoe—above also some were knocked over. After all was quiet, some men swam across the channel, say 75 yards wide, and ransacked the place. The only things they found were some spears, dried bananas and smoked elephant meat.[87]

Stanley made no mention of the incident. He arrived in camp late and may not have been told about it, although that's difficult to believe. The diaries of Mounteney-Jephson and Parke confirmed what happened.

The luxury of traveling regularly by river ended on October 5, when the column came face to face with a narrow gorge through which the river, now called the Ituri, ran "wild and furious." Stanley thus ordered the canoes abandoned and the *Advance* disassembled so that it could be carried to the next suitable stretch of water. Another critical decision needed to be made. Nelson and fifty-six of the men were so weakened that they couldn't continue. Stanley decided to leave them at the junction with the Epulu River (Stanley's Ihuru) along with eighty loads and press on. Six scouts went ahead to look for a settlement and bring back food. Parke described leaving Nelson and the others as

altogether the most heart rending good-bye I have ever experienced or witnessed. I cannot fancy a more trying position than that of abandoning, in this wilderness of hunger and desolation our white companion and so many faithful men; every one of whom has risked his life dozens of times for the relief of hypothetical friend, Emin Pasha.[88]

Dark as prospects seemed to be, Stanley said he "entertained a lively hope that we could save them."[89] Still, he proclaimed he had never been in a worse predicament. It surpassed even Ituru, Bumbiri, and the Congo in 1875–1877.

Things didn't improve, as each day became an uncertain adventure in finding something to eat. Though warthogs, buffalo, and antelope left signs of their presence, none showed themselves. A wild bean pounded into flour for porridge, supplemented by grubs, caterpillars, white ants, and some occasional maize kernels found at deserted settlements, made up meals on most days. It wasn't nearly enough food, and between October 6 and 9, eleven carriers died or deserted. With rations all but gone, stealing became rampant.

The culprits included Hoffman, who, like others, received a flogging for it. And all the while, more desertions and deaths occurred. Sometimes the famished and ill simply dropped by the wayside, knowing full well what awaited them.

On October 15 another division of the column occurred. With the location of Ipoto still uncertain and not having yet heard from the scouts, Stanley wanted to abandon the *Advance*, which required all of Mounteney-Jephson's forty-two men to carry the pieces. Uledi proposed another plan—he and a few others would oversee movement of the boat, while everyone else went ahead. Rugged terrain only made the going more difficult for men who could barely walk, much less carry loads. They got some relief from hunger when a recently abandoned camp yielded a little leftover maize and beans. Stanley also killed his all-but-expired donkey, and Parke said the men "struggled like pariah dogs for the blood, hide, and hoofs" after the meat had been distributed.[90] Then, around noon the next day, they came upon a heavily trodden path, suggesting that the Arab settlement might be fairly close. But could the men make it? According to Stanley,

> Over fifty were yet in fair condition: 150 were skeletons covered with ashy grey skins, jaded and worn out, with every sign of wretchedness printed deep in their eyes, in the bodies and movements. These could hardly do more than creep on and moan, and shed tears and sigh.[91]

Mounteney-Jephson described the leader as having "frightful" anxiety over the future of the expedition, talking "about it all in a very hopeless manner."[92] The path, though, eased travel, and spirits rose as night fell on 17th, when sounds of singing reached the camp. Gunshots in the morning gave further proof of people being nearby. A short while later they became visible and beckoned the strangers "with friendly hails." Looking right and left, Stanley saw "thriving fields of Indian corn, rice, sweet potatoes and beans."[93] Ipoto had at last been found.

The village was on the north bank of the river, and its headman turned out to be a former slave from Zanzibar named Kilonga-longa. Away at the moment, he'd brought a group of Wamanyema to this point about five months earlier, having come from the direction of the Lualaba hunting for slaves to exchange for ivory. Since they controlled the situation for many miles in all directions, Stanley knew he'd have to deal with them like it or not.

Problems with food put the relationship to an immediate test. The Wamanyema demanded payment, but the column carried little they valued.

Some of the men resorted to stealing, and when this was stopped, others began selling "shirts, caps, waist cloths, belts, & knives, & every article of personal property to satisfy their inordinate hunger."[94] The situation worsened when a muster on October 21 revealed nine rifles and sixteen hundred rounds of ammunition missing. Each man who couldn't produce his rifle received twenty-five lashes and was ordered to get the rifle back. Two days later a Zanzibari caught stealing bananas received two hundred "cuts with a cane," and a cook who'd stolen two rifles for purposes of trading was summarily hung. While Stanley wanted to fight the Wamanyema, he couldn't because it would be foolhardy to "leave enemies between himself & Nelson & Barttelot." Despite telling his men to "Be patient. Avoid giving offense," he was on the verge of losing control when Uledi showed up to calm him down and negotiate a truce with the Wamanyema.[95] Uledi also found the missing scouts just four miles downstream. They'd become hopelessly lost, and only good fortune saved them from starvation.

The situation led Stairs to complain in a note meant for Jameson that

> Stanley's true character came out here in full force; we had no monies, food was in plenty, we were all skin & bones & a man dying every second day or so from starvation, yet he would not sell a single rifle though we carried over 40 which were of no use to us as there were no men for them. To save ourselves from starvation, Jephson, Parke & I had to sell nearly all our clothes.[96]

Stanley fumed when he found about the note, which was never delivered, and said that he, himself, parted with virtually all his personal effects to buy food.[97] Stairs apologized for his actions and matter was forgotten.

Stanley debated about whether to continue on this route, double back and find another one, or return to Yambuya and then head home. Stairs thought the second option made the most sense, as they could collect the rear column and find a way through country not yet ravaged by Arabs.[98] It would, however, add months to the Lake Albert journey, which was already taking far longer than expected. Stanley stuck to the original plan.

One thing after another delayed the departure of men to relieve Nelson's party until October 26. Commanded by Mounteney-Jephson, the unit contained forty Zanzibaris and thirty Wamanyema. Stanley instructed them to come ahead as fast as possible after bringing Nelson and any survivors to Ipoto, where they were to be housed according to a deal worked out to pay for their keep at a later date. Parke also received instructions to remain at Ipoto to care for twenty-nine others considered too sick to travel. The prospect hardly pleased him. "Everywhere, all around the village," he said, "the ground is covered with filth."[99] Ticks bored into nostrils, and the huts harbored lice and rats in profusion. The thought crossed his mind that more than likely he would be left alone, since Nelson had likely already died or gone downriver. As regards Stanley's actions, while calling him "rather hard," he couldn't

> see how else he could have dealt with these barbarous people—how he has made two ends meet is a mystery. He is different from any other man. There is no change in his expression or behaviour; he will never be found to sacrifice all in attempting to save one. His policy rather is to sacrifice one and save the remainder.[100]

Of the Europeans, only Stairs and Hoffman accompanied Stanley on the October 27 march from Ipoto. In addition to his regulars, Stanley had bargained for the services of forty-three Wamanyema to carry loads for fifteen camps. They would be paid with cloth when Barttelot arrived. The route took them away from the river, and proved to be treacherous, as each clearing made by Balesse cultivators required negotiating fallen tree trunks in stacks that rose many feet above the ground. A small misstep, rendered more likely by humidity and perspiration, could mean death or serious injury. Indeed, one man died from just such a fall. On the last day of the month, the first of many Wambuti pygmy encampments came into view, and over the course of the next few days, the travelers made much better time, even as much as two miles per hour. Food posed less of a problem than it had before, and upon entering a place on November 10 called Ibwiri, they came across a bounty of food surpassing even that at Nepoko. Famished men indulged themselves on bananas, plantains, potatoes, yams, beans, and, to their great delight, goats and fowls. Even Stairs stopped complaining about rations. The circumstances resolved any doubts about where to wait for Mounteney-Jephson and his Zanzibaris. It would be Ibwiri.

Stanley's attitude about his men softened during the stay. Prone to cursing them for stupidity and greed to their faces and in journals, he now recorded, "I do not know any other men in the world, white or black who could have shown the same endurance with such little complaint." They might easily have killed him and the other Europeans and left them "in the woods to rot." As a result, he decided not to hand out punishment for stealing food. The chief would receive compensation for whatever the Zanzibaris took.[101]

Mounteney-Jephson reached Ibwiri on November 16. He'd found Nelson nearly three weeks earlier with only four men at his side, the others having

Negotiating a treacherous clearing in the Ituri Forest. *Henry M. Stanley,* In Darkest Africa. *(New York: Charles Scribner's Sons, 1890).*

died, deserted, or come up missing. When Parke saw Nelson, he described him as "a living skeleton, with hollow cheeks, sunken eyes, and bearing every trait of the extremest physical depression."[102] Nelson thus stayed with the doctor and those men still unable to travel. Only 175 men marched out of Ibwiri on November 24. As usual, Stanley went at the head of the column, with Stairs and Mounteney-Jephson looking after the rear. Fortunately, the long rest with plenty of food had restored almost everyone to a robust state of health. They looked forward to leaving the forest behind. Furthermore, they'd grown tired of all the fleas, cockroaches, ants, and rats sharing their huts. An easily traversed path brought more cheer, as did the departure of the hated Wamanyema, even though they hadn't fulfilled the fifteen camps agreement.

Numerous pygmy encampments dotted the countryside, but no residents showed their faces. Huge clearings for maize and plantains, some as large as two miles by one and a half miles, marked the way, their number augmented by the Lese habit of cultivating a plot for only one year. They, too, left their villages before the column arrived.

The view from a summit on November 30 revealed "an altogether different region of grassy meads and plains and hills, freely sprinkled with groves, clusters, and thin lines of trees" to the east.[103] Stairs described it as resem-

bling Kent from this distance and concluded it must be Equatoria. To commemorate "our first view of the land of promise and plenty," Stanley named
the summit Mount Pisgah, after the mountain at the north end of the Dead
Sea from which Moses reported seeing the Promised Land.[104] More stretches
of forest, however, still had to be negotiated, although conical roofed huts
thatched with grass surrounded by fields of bananas, plantains, maize,
tobacco, castor, tomatoes, sweet potatoes, and yams gave hope that end of
the "green hell" must be fairly near. The happy day came on December 4,
when the men drank in "a joy that was simply indescribable"—an open
plain, "green as an English lawn." As they rushed ahead, the dark of the
previous months gave way to bright sunlight and open country as far as the
eye could see. Ever the journalist, Stanley told readers, "We were like men
out of durance and the dungeon free and unfettered, having exchanged foul-
ness and damp for sweetness and purity, darkness and gloom for divine light
and wholesome air."[105]

Fields rich with grains and sweet potatoes greeted their eyes, and succumbing to temptation, some of the men attempted to loot what looked like
an abandoned village. Unlike in the forest it wasn't, and a shower of arrows
from villagers hidden behind rows of millet and sorghum greeted their
advance. A quick burst of rifle fire ended the affair before either side sustained serious casualties. The night brought sporadic attacks that did little
damage other than cause loss of sleep.

Attempts to elicit information proved difficult. The people met weren't
very forthcoming and spoke a language unlike any the men had heard so far.
One mentioned a large *nyanza*—a widespread Bantu word designating a
large body of water—three days away, but where exactly couldn't be deciph-
ered. And Stanley had difficulty making sense of what he heard about the
Ituri. It suggested to him two rivers, the one they had followed and another
flowing into the lake.

Tracking southeastward, the column encountered no opposition for the
next couple of days. The first sign of trouble came on December 8, when
they entered the most densely populated area seen since Bangala. Large
groups of menacing people looked down on them from the crests of hills
some eight hundred feet above the plain, and their numbers grew larger as
the column continued on its way. Spying what looked like two defensible
hill sites, Stanley ordered them fortified because out in the open his men
would stand little chance against such a large force. Sharpshooters kept
potential attackers at bay while the site was being prepared. Stanley wondered why a fight should be necessary, seeing that neither party knew the

other. The next day brought prospects for peace. One of the men understood the language a bit and learned that the country was called Undusuma and had two chiefs. Negotiations with one named Mazamboni seemed promising, and after being given two yards of scarlet cloth, he promised to bring some cattle in return. When the sun broke through the clouds and mist on December 10, Stanley looked about and wondered "when such a beautiful land would become the homestead of civilized settlers."[106]

This sense of serenity, however, didn't last. The interpreter came back from a meeting saying he had made a mistake—the words heard meant war not peace. They then told him "we don't want your friendship, we are coming down to you presently to drive you away with sticks, for such as you are not worth throwing spears at."[107] Stanley decided to strike first and sent out three companies in different directions. With spears no match for rifles, the warriors retreated, only to re-form and come back again and then again. As evening fell, fighting ceased. Stanley felt, however, that the lesson "was not completed." That for future's sake, "it was . . . far more merciful to finish the affair thoroughly before leaving behind a tribe in unwhipped insolence in our rear."[108] Thus, in the morning, Stairs, Mounteney-Jephson, and Uledi took their men to finish the job, which included burning villages they came across.

Neither sound nor person greeted the breaking of camp on December 12. Soon though the warriors returned, shouting that the column would not survive the day. They followed the shouts with forays at the rear guards, but in each instance were driven back. Later a full-fledged engagement took place at a crossing point of the Ituri, It ended as the others, with the warriors in retreat and villages abandoned. Harassing actions continued the next morning and at one stage Stanley estimated fifteen hundred people assembled on both the left and right flanks. Another exchange occurred, with spears and arrows again no match for bullets.

The trail led upward to a point some 5,200 feet above sea level. From a precipice, Stanley thought he saw a gray cloud on the horizon. Looking northeast, it proved to be haze surrounding a large body of water, the long sought after Lake Albert, lying more than three thousand feet beneath them. At its sight, Mounteney-Jephson said, "one felt a warm glow, almost a feeling of triumph & mixed up with it a feeling of thankfullness & gratitude, it was as if one had wakened out of a bad dream—& the waking was very pleasant."[109] The "bad dream," however, hadn't ended, as the descent to the shore resulted in what Stairs called "our worst piece of fighting ever since we landed in Africa. Every inch down the desperately steep hill the natives pushed us. From behind the huge granite boulders they would shoot out, rush down to shooting distance and let fly their arrows."[110] Not until evening did the attackers break off. Amazingly, the column, down to 169 men, sustained only one injury.

Stanley hoped to find canoes for the journey to Wadelai, figuring Emin must have come to the south end of the lake to make arrangements for ones to be there waiting for him. None could be seen, nor trees suitable for their construction, just scrawny acacias, mimosas, and tamarinds. An attempt to procure canoes from villagers failed. While civil, Stanley said, "They would not accept our friendship, nor make blood-brotherhood, nor accept even a gift."[111] And the information provided by them could hardly be considered encouraging. People all along the lake used only small fishing canoes, did little farming, and weren't accepting of strangers. Furthermore, they'd never seen a white man on the lake, even though their fishermen went out on it every day.

A serious dilemma had to be faced. Of the forty-seven cases of cartridges still in their possession, Stanley figured twenty-five would be used going to Wadelai by land, leaving the rest to be split between Emin, should he still be there, and the return trip to Yambuya. He thus concluded,

> there is but one way left to us, and that is to turn right back to Ibwiri, establish a defensive position there, & bring our boat from Ipoto there, and also all convalescents from Ugarrowa's and Ipoto, send messengers to seek the rear column, & send letters to the officers, with news of all we have done & are doing—& hurry the column up. When sufficient men of our stragglers & sick have been collected, we can leave all superflous baggage at Ibwiri to enable the advance column to start on a second search for the Pasha with the steel boat, which would make us independent of every native. If we find on our second search that the Pasha has gone to Zanzibar or homeward as he threatened to do, why then we shall have to decide what is best for us to do. Whether to march back by way of Ibwiri to the Congo or proceed by ourselves overland to the East Coast. On that point we can make no decision until we know what has become of Barttelot.[112]

Mounteney-Jephson and Stairs expressed "shock" at the thought of having to retreat. To placate them, Stanley agreed to continue trying to find canoes for a few more days. The two also devised a plan to reach the other side of the lake in order to contact a European said to be residing in Unyoro. They knew him to be Capt. Gaetano Casati, who some eight years earlier had been sent by the Milan Geographical Society to map the Bahr el Ghazal province. Left in a precarious position there, Emin rescued him. For the last year and a half he'd been serving as Equatoria's agent to Kabarega. Unbeknownst to

Mounteney-Jephson and Stairs, Casati had recently escaped with his life after having been tied to a tree and left to die. Kabarega apparently thought him part of an invasion plan involving the Emin Pasha expedition and Egypt. In any event, Stanley declined to seek out Casati as a way of getting information to Emin, feeling that too many lives would be lost in the process. Thus, on December 16, the column did an about-face for Ibwiri.

Hard upon a miserable night of rain and cold, the men faced the excruciating task of scrambling back up the slope under the glare of a blazing sun. An advance group of forty went to secure the top, with Stanley leading a second group and Stairs and Mounteney-Jephson in charge of a third bringing up the rear. Once again the villagers attacked, spearing to death two porters. To halt the pursuers and exact a measure of revenge, Stanley sent a party of five to set an ambush, which killed one and wounded another. This caused the attackers to retreat, allowing the others in the unit to escape unharmed.

Why the hostility? Stanley later offered two reasons. First, the people on this side of the lake considered Kabarega their enemy because of frequent cattle raids by his heavily armed troops called Warasura. Not knowing this, Stanley had proclaimed Kabarega and Bunyoro friends. Second, great suspicion existed about anyone coming from the direction of the Ituri forest. As one man reportedly said when hearing from whence the column had come, "Ah! That proves you to be wicked people. Who ever heard of good people coming from that direction."[113]

After confiscating a five-day supply of grain and beans from the stores of a village, the march resumed, again in three groups. Within a few hours another attack occurred, taking the life of a Zanzibari, who'd strayed or become too weak to go on. During a rest stop, Stanley puzzled over the continuous attacks and the next morning sent out eighty men to " 'bring away every cow, sheep, and goat you can find' and take prisoners so 'that I may have some of their own people to send to them with my words.' " The latter didn't happen, but enough cattle were confiscated to provide a welcomed feast and create a herd to take back to Ibwiri. To Stanley recent events symbolized life in Africa—"a series of varied sufferings with intervals of short pleasure."[114]

This time during the journey through Undusuma, the enemy warriors kept their distance, even in the area where all the villages had been burned just a little more than a week earlier. With no opposition to slow travel, the column reached the main channel of the Ituri River on December 23, only to discover all the canoes gone and the suspension bridges cut down. A quick repair of one of the bridges and an ingeniously constructed banana-leaf raft allowed the crossing to be made. Save one additional death, the column covered the rest of the distance to Ibwiri by January 7, 1888, without suffering serious incident or privation. Indeed, the forty-five days of the round-trip to Lake Albert produced fewer deaths—five—than any comparable span of time since the column left Yambuya. And the survivors hadn't been in as good a condition since then, either. With optimism renewed, Stanley set about overseeing the construction of an edifice christened Fort Bodo.

On January 19 Stairs and ninety-six men left for Ipoto to collect Nelson, Parke, and the others. Should the *Advance* still be usable, Stanley instructed the lieutenant to bring it along as well. Everyone else continued to work on the fort, and before the end of the month, tents gave way to more comfortable quarters built of wood. For security reasons, a ten-foot-wide by six-foot-deep trench surrounded the fort. Beyond that a space cleared for maize provided an unobstructed line of sight for revealing potential attackers or others bent on mischief. When a patrol found several Wambuti camps about a mile away, they put the inhabitants to flight and leveled the camps, to discourage the locals from coming too close to the fort.

Parke, Nelson, and their remaining men arrived February 8, telling a story of misery and despair.[115] The Wamanyema headmen at Ipoto claimed Stanley hadn't made any arrangements for provisioning the men, and so they were required to sell virtually everything for tiny quantities of food. Wild greens mixed with fungus often served for meals, and toward the end, after Kilonga-longa arrived with some four hundred followers, food became very scarce. On many days the Zanzibaris subsisted on little more than banana and plantain roots. "A continuous torment by the shoals of flies, fleas, lice, ants, and all sorts of abominable creeping things" encouraged by growing squalor and filth added to their sufferings.[116] In such circumstances, illness, especially ulcers and various fevers, became chronic. It was little wonder that Parke described Stairs's appearance as "a moment of excitement, a reprieve from the death sentence which we had so long felt pressing over and around us."[117] For fourteen Zanzibaris with Parke and Nelson, the reprieve came too late.

Stairs and a group of bearers brought the *Advance* to Fort Bodo on February 12. Amazingly, it had survived Ipoto almost unscathed. A discussion among the Europeans took place about what to do next. Stanley favored a second attempt to find Emin, but the others thought seeing to the rear guard and the men at Ugarrowwa's should come first. They agreed on a compromise. Stairs would go to Ugarrowwa's to fetch the men and send twenty couriers from there to Barttelot with information and a map about how to proceed to Fort Bodo by the fastest and safest route. Should, however, Tippu

Tip's men be with them, Stanley advised building a strong camp and waiting for help to come because the "column will break up with Arab influences around Ugarrowas."[118] In the meantime, he intended to take a contingent back to Lake Albert. They'd wait until the third week of March to allow Stairs to participate in the relief of Emin. If for some reason Stairs didn't appear by then, Stanley figured he could still catch up, as his men would be slowed by carrying the steel boat. Stairs had his doubts about the enterprise, noting,

1. I don't believe that twenty men can be trusted to make their way down the river even as far as Yambuya;
2. I don't think Ugarrowwa will give over the men and rifles *to me*;
3. I don't think that a month's delay is worth the few men we will get from Ugarrowwa. Really fifty-six, but only thirty of them would be fit to fight.[119]

Stairs departed on February 16, and two days later Stanley developed a large, painful abscess on his left arm and became ill with a severe case of gastritis. Sometimes drifting into unconsciousness because of the morphine administered by Parke, he seemed on several occasions ready to expire, and it was the middle of March before he could walk even a few yards. All the while, work continued on the fort, and lush fields of maize and beans grew up around it. Despite precautions, arrows shot from the cover of the forest killed two of the men.

Stanley finally left for Lake Albert on April 2, accompanied by Hoffman, Mounteney-Jephson, Parke, and 126 men. Nelson stayed put with forty-nine others to wait for Stairs. Parke described them as invalids, none weighing more than one hundred pounds and most suffering from debilitating ulcers.[120] Sharply pointed stakes once again littered the way, although by now they knew how to find them without too much difficulty. The path needed widening for the boat, and constant rain slowed things down. A brief encounter with a group of Wambuti took place at the crossing point of the Ituri. They quickly dispersed, according to Mounteney-Jephson, when Stanley wounded two with a single shot. Then, while preparing camp at the end of the first day in open country, Lese villagers launched a bow-and-arrow attack that wounded one of the Zanzibaris. Rifle fire drove them off before any additional damage could be inflicted, and the wounded man recovered under Parke's care. Upset by some of the men's behavior during and after the attack, Stanley shot at two of them, grazing the heel of one and taking a piece of skin from the other.[121] In Undusuma, instead of opposition, the people welcomed them with a guarantee of unhindered passage to Lake Albert. By now the Bahima inhabitants between the forest and the lake knew the strangers weren't allies of Kabarega. A blood brotherhood ceremony sealed a pact of friendship between Mazamboni and the expedition.

The march to Lake Albert resumed on April 16, with twelve guides, more than one hundred new carriers provided by Mazamboni, and many others trailing the column. All along the way to Kavalli's, people called out greetings, and their chief Gavira asked the group to stop for a day. Gavira informed Stanley that a white man called *Malleju*, or "Bearded One," had been seen on the lake in an iron canoe several months ago.[122] He'd left a packet for Stanley at Kavalli's. It turned out to be a letter from Emin dated March 25, 1888, which instructed Stanley "to rest where you are" and wait for the pasha's steamer. Stanley gave orders to get the *Advance* down the escarpment and into the water without further delay. Mounteney-Jephson was put in command and instructed to find Emin. He carried a letter for him recounting the contents of the one sent from Zanzibar and briefly explaining the circumstances of their first visit to Lake Albert. Stanley also asked Emin to bring as much food as possible, including all his cattle, and if "already resolved on leaving Africa . . . every native willing to follow."[123] Emin had never received the earlier letter, although he did know via another from Holmwood of the relief expedition coming his way via the Congo route.

Stanley enjoyed the break at Kavalli's and felt grateful for having made new friends. He owed Mazamboni, Gavira, and Kavalli "debts of gratitude" and noted that "if they are ever troubled by enemies while I am here I promise to give each protection, as one friend may give another when attacked by raiders."[124]

After waiting a week, Stanley took the rest of the column down the escarpment to be on hand for Emin's arrival. In the early morning of April 29, as they prepared to march to the lake shore, a guide brought a note from Mounteney-Jephson saying he had reached Mswa, and that as soon as Emin got there they would be on their way. Later that day, while looking upon the lake, Stanley said he "saw a dark object loom up on the north-east horizon." As it moved closer, he could make out a steamer towing a couple of boats. It turned out to be Emin's *Khedive*, one of Baker's old steamers, and at 8:00 P.M. the two men finally met. Capt. Casati was also part of the party. The pasha's appearance proved something of a surprise. Stanley had

expected to see a tall thin military-looking figure, in faded Egyptian uniform, but instead . . . saw a small spare figure in a well-kept fez and clean suit of snowy cotton drilling, well-ironed and of perfect fit. A dark grizzled beard bordered a face of a Magyar cast, though a pair of spectacles lent it somewhat an Italian or Spanish appearance. There was not a trace on it of ill-health or anxiety; it rather indicated good condition of body and peace of mind.[125]

They spent the next couple of hours conversing and finished the evening by polishing off five bottles of Stanley's champagne that had somehow managed to survive the Congo's heat for more than a year.

The next morning Stanley marched his men the two miles to where the *Khedive* sat anchored. When compared to Emin's smartly dressed and well drilled Sudanese, the Zanzibaris "seemed altogether a beggarly troop, and more naked then ever." Still, Stanley noted, "It was by their aid . . . that we had triumphed over countless difficulties" and compared to them "the best of these Soudanese soldiers were but children . . . for the needs of a Relief Expedition."[126] At the completion of required formalities, Stanley handed over thirty-one boxes of ammunition, some clothing, and a bundle of letters, the sole material items of the "relief," and then went aboard the *Khedive* for breakfast. Afterward he asked Emin about evacuation plans but didn't get a clear response. They spoke again the next day, and although Stanley said Emin told him "that it is best we should retire from Africa," the pasha didn't think many of his people, other than the Egyptians, would agree.[127] The Sudanese wanted to stay, and besides, most had wives and children, who could hardly be expected to walk all the way to the coast. Still, he declared himself "perfectly ready to put in execution the Khedive's order to retire to Egypt, provided my people wanted to go."[128] On May 2 the *Khedive* sailed back north to find out just that. Emin, Casati, and twenty soldiers stayed behind to help construct a camp at Nsabe, choosing a small hill overlooking the lake. They wanted it strong enough to withstand possible attacks by Banyoro and Baganda troops.

There's little evidence that Emin had changed his mind about leaving Equatoria. In a letter to his friend Felkin dated April 17, 1887, he stated, "I should indeed consider it shameful to desert my post just now. . . . There is no question about it; I shall remain here." In the case of Equatoria being abandoned to its mercies he later told Felkin, "I should have to say goodbye to Egypt and stand on my own two feet." And after reading Stanley's letter, he jotted in his diary, "my resolution is fixed. Go, I will not."[129] Some Egyptians confirmed this, telling Stanley, "The Pasha does not wish to return, he is happy with his travels about the country, bird studies and such things."[130]

Although Emin had brought a substantial quantity of food with him, shortages started to appear as the days passed. Little existed in the immediate vicinity, and on one occasion some Zanzibaris raided a village. Hearing that one had been killed and another captured, Stanley told Parke to take forty-two soldiers to bring him and the others back. They burned some huts and took food during the search, which prompted the villagers to retaliate. Getting back to Nsabe safely required taking a circuitous route. Storms, often violent, broke virtually every day. One Stanley described as being particularly bad:

> The sound of the wind as it approached was like that made by the bursting of a dam. The rain fell in torrents & was blown with such force, that it pierced through everything. . . . The darkness was as black pitch, & the uproar was so deafening that all we could do was to hear it in silence & with closed lips.[131]

During the wait for the *Khedive*, Stanley presented Emin with the two other options for him and his people. One involved Leopold's offer to take over Equatoria. Emin could stay as the general in charge. The other was to relocate in the vicinity of Kavirondo on the eastern side of Lake Victoria under the auspices of Mackinnon's company. Once established, they could serve "as a colony of men amenable to law and discipline" to govern and civilize a territory for the IBEAC stretching as far as Mount Kilimanjaro.[132] Stanley admitted he hadn't been authorized to make such an offer, but he felt it would be granted once he reached the coast and spoke with the authorities. In fact, the company existed in name only. While numerous influential subscribers came on board following Barghash's granting the concession on May 24, 1887, it didn't receive its official charter from the British government until September 3, 1888. Emin rejected the first option outright but responded enthusiastically to the second, calling it "extraordinarily practical and easy of execution." He also saw it as a place from which to launch an attempt to enter Uganda and reclaim lost territory.[133]

The *Khedive* returned May 14 carrying several of Emin's officers. The news they brought, however, wasn't much help in reaching a decision about which course of action to follow. Whatever the choice, Stanley figured he would have to bring up Barttelot and the rear column first. Consequently, the *Khedive*, with Casati in charge, headed north to secure replacements for porters lost since Yambuya. It and another steamer, the *Nyanza*, brought 130 Madi recruits and eighty soldiers on the 22nd of the month. Emin now faced the task of canvassing his people at the various posts about their wishes and felt that the presence of one of the expedition's officers would help convince skeptics about its origin and true intent. Many seemed to doubt that it had Egypt's blessing. Stanley chose Mounteney-Jephson, who much preferred going to Yambuya but didn't protest. It would be his job to see to the reading of the letter from the khedive, as well as one from Stanley, which concluded with

> I go back to collect my people and goods, and bring them on to the Nyanza, and after a few months I shall come back here to hear what you have to say. If you say, Let us go to Egypt, I will then show you a safe road. If you say, We shall not leave this country, then I will bid you farewell and return to Egypt with my own people.[134]

Emin translated it into Arabic and felt two passages might prove to be stumbling blocks. One read, "If you stay here, you are no longer his [the Khedive's] soldiers," and the other, "Your pay continues until you arrive in Egypt."[135] He couldn't, however, delete them. When the tour of the posts was finished, Stanley told Mounteney-Jephson to select about twenty men and hurry to Fort Bodo. Jephson felt he could do all this in a little more than two months' time.[136]

With Mounteney-Jephson on his way, Stanley's party started off for Fort Bodo. After they had gone only going a short distance, a boy pointed to "a mountain said to be covered by salt." At first glance Stanley thought it might be an advancing storm, but then realized he must be looking at the fabled Mountains of the Moon. He wondered why others, including Baker and Emin, hadn't seen such an imposing mass and blamed the haze that always seemed to block the view. Baker's "Blue Mountains" were most likely the highlands to the west of the lake that reach above eight thousand feet. Romolo Gessi, who circumnavigated Lake Albert in 1876, may have caught a glimpse but made no mention of it.[137] There's no doubt, however, that Parke and Mounteney-Jephson saw the mountains on April 20. They reported this to Stanley, whom Parke described as being "a good deal interested."[138] Stanley, however, willingly took credit and accepted Emin's congratulations on the "most splendid discovery of a snow-clad mountain."[139] He called it Ruwenzori, using the name he had heard earlier, which in Lunyoro means "the place from whence the rain comes."[140] It was the same mountain seen in 1876.

Stanley recorded the existence of two peaks and called one Gordon Bennett and the other Mackinnon.[141] Later observation showed him to be wrong, and the names for the peaks were rejected. There are actually six discernable massifs, with the central and highest, at 16,795 feet, given the name it bears today, Mount Stanley. The other five massifs also retain their European names, due in large measure to their location along an international boundary. That explains the persistence of Lake Victoria, as well.

The first day also brought an en masse desertion by the new porters, apparently in response to rumors that Stanley planned to kill them after they had served their purpose.[142] When informed about this, Emin sent Stanley a note apologizing for their actions and said that a new supply of porters had arrived at Mswa and he would send a boat to bring them up immediately. They numbered eighty-two, and to make sure none disappeared, Emin assigned twenty-five troops to take them to Stanley.[143] Refurbished, the party set off again, only to hear that a chief called Msiri planned to carry out an earlier threat to attack if it came his way again. He backed down after learning that Stanley was accompanied by some fifteen hundred of Mazamboni's and Gavira's warriors. A celebration ensued, and Stanley called the singing and dancing "certainly one of the best & most exciting exhibitions" he'd ever witnessed in Africa. As icing on the cake, Msiri sent word that since everyone else had made peace with Stanley, he, too, wanted to be counted a friend and would demonstrate his intention the next time with gifts of food.[144]

Stanley grew confident of his tactics. In a letter to Col. Grant a few months later, he stated,

> My idea has been all along to fight as little as possible, but, when compelled to do so, to set about the job as efficiently as possible, so that there will remain no doubt in native minds what we propose doing when we tell them. By this policy we have won a large section in our favor—at least have compelled them to pay ready obedience.[145]

The march to Fort Bodo resumed June 1. Arriving a week later, Stanley found Stairs with Nelson. He'd come April 26, having spent seventy-one days on the trip to and from Ugarrowwa's. Of the fifty-six men still there, only thirty could make the trip, and half of them died along the way. With no news about the rear column's situation, Stanley decided to lead a relief force in the direction of Yambuya. His only European companion would be Hoffman. He considered asking Stairs to do the job but felt two arduous trips were enough. Parke had the task of taking a small team to Ipoto to collect the supplies stashed there and bring them to the fort, where he would stay with Nelson and Stairs. Stanley admitted that the men left with them weren't the best, but he felt they had ample rifles and plenty of ammunition to be secure. And he told Stairs, "My principal reliance is of the commandant [Stairs] himself. If the chief is active, watchful & wary, our fort is safe, and no combination of natives can oust the garrison from its shelter. I need not tell you that I leave you with confidence."[146] Upon Mounteney-Jephson's return, Fort Bodo could be evacuated, with everybody going to Lake Albert. As for his own journey, Stanley surmised that it probably would take until sometime in December to complete the thirteen-hundred-mile round-trip.

The group that left on June 16 consisted of 113 Zanzibaris, ninety-five Madis, and four of Emin's soldiers. Each carried twenty-five days of rations. Familiar now with the hazards of forest travel—red ants, skewers, pitfalls, thorns, creepers, nettles, mud—they moved quickly and reached Ipoto in six days. Parke, trailing behind, arrived two days later and headed back to Fort Bodo the next afternoon with thirteen loads of goods. He got there on July 6, having lost one of his fourteen men along the way. Another died later at the fort from an arrow wound suffered en route.

This time at the head of a superior force, Stanley wanted to exact retribution for the way his people had been treated at Ipoto. Circumstances, however, dictated otherwise. Kilonga-longa apologized and turned over the rifles and ammunition the men had traded for food. As an extra show of goodwill, he presented gifts of rice and goats and furnished ten guides for the journey.

Able to maintain a quick pace, Stanley made it to Nelson's former camp at the confluence of the Ituri and Epulu Rivers on June 28. Remarkably, 80 percent of the goods, including much needed ammunition that had been stowed in the ground, proved usable. At this point they left the river and followed a forest route in order to bypass the killer stretch of river to Avadori. The decision slowed progress considerably. A few Madi deserted, and others died, sometimes from indeterminate causes, and nearly three days were lost when some local women serving as guides unintentionally led them in a circle. Hopes of getting news about Yambuya and picking up some of Stairs's men at Avadori were dashed when they reached the village on July 13 and found it abandoned. No food could be found, either, as Ugarrowwa's people had picked the area clean.

The party moved on, following the river again. A looming food crisis was avoided when some men ventured inland and discovered an abundant supply of plantains. Stanley called a halt for two days so that an ample quantity of porridge could be prepared for the road ahead. Even when better fed, the Madi porters continued dropping by the wayside. Some canoes were found to help transport the weak, but two of them capsized, taking the life of a Zanzibari and a boy of one of Emin's men. On July 25 Stanley counted thirty more Madi among those about to expire. "Almost every individual among them," he said, "was the victim of some hideous disease, and tumours, scorched backs, foetid ulcers, were common; while others were afflicted with chronic dysentery and wretched debility caused by insufficient food." Stanley felt unwell and admitted having a short temper that exploded at every inconvenience. Fortunately, they did find some badly needed food, including three fowl. After eating meat for the first time in a long while and feeling better as a result, Stanley figured its lack had caused the Madi's suffering. By now enough canoes had been collected to carry all of them, the loads, and half the Zanzibaris.[147]

The journey downriver passed through old sites, including Avisiba, the scene of the arrow attack that had wounded Stairs the previous year. Quite unexpectedly a naked young girl speaking Kiswahili walked into camp. She belonged to Ugarrowwa's party and had been left behind with five women ten days earlier because of illness. When villagers attacked and killed the women, apparently in retaliation for having lost many of their own to Ugarrowwa, the girl fled into the forest to escape detection. She lived off wild fruits and plantains taken from fields during the night. The party, with its new addition, pressed ahead and reached Panga Falls on August 3. The trip proved costly, as several canoe accidents resulted in the deaths of another Zanzibari and five Madi.

The villagers at Panga Falls had gone to an island near the other side of the river leaving some fishing nets behind that the men put to good use. Heavy rains and the need to forage kept the party in place until August 7. Although the river and the adjacent forest yielded a reasonable amount to eat, accidents and disease continued to thin the ranks. Signs, however, indicated that Ugarrowwa was nearby. A gruesome sight appeared: a dead woman "washed, laid out on the bank close to the river, and near by three bunches of bananas, two cooking pots, and a canoe capable of carrying five people." Stanley concluded they'd interrupted plans for a feast.[148] Impatient to reach Ugarrowwa in order to find out about the rear column, Stanley took several canoes downstream on August 10, ordering the men to paddle as fast as possible. Less than five hours later, they found their quarry at Wasp Rapids, along with some of Stairs's couriers. Four had been killed in a fight at this very spot, and the rest, all but one of whom suffered wounds, turned back when it became clear that they wouldn't be able to reach Yambuya. Ugarrowwa professed he'd heard nothing of the men there.

Two days later the journey resumed, this time with everyone in canoes. In contrast to the Madi porters, the Zanzibaris had borne up well, and only three having been lost. On August 16 the canoes reached Bungangeta Island. However, the closer Stanley got to Yambuya, the less confident he felt. Even with as few as a hundred porters, the rear column should have advanced at least this far. He could only conclude that something must have happened to cause many, perhaps all, of the Zanzibaris to desert. Barttelot's temper might have been responsible. Hoffman described it as "very lusty . . . often time very nasty."[149] From Bungangeta they headed for Banalia, and during the approach an Egyptian flag and a European were seen at the shore. Stanley said he cried out "The Major Boys. There is the Major!" Instead it turned out to be Bonny, who told of the disaster that had befallen the rear column. Stanley couldn't at first believe what he heard, thinking that Bonny "was painting the scenes blacker than the facts warranted."[150]

In general outline, here is what seems to have happened.[151] On August 14, 1887, the *Stanley* brought Troup, Bonny, and Ward to Yambuya, along with 668 loads and 187 men. Walker then took the steamer back down the river, his last job for the expedition. Since no additional porters had shown up, the officers agreed to wait for Tippu Tip to supply them before leaving. Repeated visits to Kisingitini yielded no guarantees about when this might happen.

Life in the camp started out on a favorable note. Bonny thought it "a very healthy place": Most of the sick had improved and food seemed adequate in supply, thanks in large measure to friendly locals.[152] Within a short while, however, things had changed for the worse, largely because of an increasing Wamanyema presence. They didn't hunt elephants themselves but captured women and children to ransom for ivory. Many villagers fled deeper into the forest to escape their depredations, whereas others, under threats from the Wamanyema, refrained from trading with the camp. As a result, food became harder and harder to come by, a situation made more difficult by the area's having been virtually hunted out of game. For the Europeans this produced a boring but ample diet based on boiled rice, fried plantains, and tea, occasionally spiced with a little fish, honey, pumpkins, eggs, and palm wine.[153] They, too, sometimes captured women to use as ransom for food, and every so often the Arabs sent gifts of goats and fowls. In mid-September, Jameson could still report that "Our evenings are very pleasant; we all dine together and yarn about old times and future prospects."[154] Each one of them, though, endured moments of serious illness. Ward nearly died from a bout with dysentery that lasted from early September to the middle of October.

The Africans in camp fared far less well. They had little to eat other than cassava leaves and tubers, which the Zanzibaris often consumed raw. Unfamiliar with how to prepare the bitter varieties that contain lethal prussic acid, they slowly poisoned themselves. Most also had only rags for clothes and slept on the ground without blankets. Covered with ulcers and reduced to skin and bones, men died almost daily. Troup counted fourteen graves on September 22. By December 5, the number had grown to thirty-one, and on February 3, 1888, it reached fifty. He stopped counting on May 23, when the graves passed the one hundred mark. Ward despaired that "almost as many lives will be lost over this philanthropic mission as there are lives to save of Emin's people."[155] Breaking out the reserve supplies probably would have saved many lives, but per instructions from Stanley, Barttelot held them back for future use.

Deteriorating conditions made discipline harder to maintain without recourse to floggings. The usual number of lashes seems to have been twenty-five, but on some occasions more were administered.[156] The whip, called a chicotte, was made from hippo hide and drew blood after just a couple of lashes. Given the conditions, William Davy, the chief engineer of the Sanford Exploring expedition who'd called at Yambuya, later wondered why Barttelot had never asked him for help. His boats could have made a show of force to Tippu Tip and brought supplies, especially medicines.[157]

What to do became a regular topic of discussion among the officers. Jameson and Barttelot reached an agreement that if some kind of disaster befell Stanley, they would pay Tippu Tip five thousand pounds for men and hurry toward Lake Albert, taking only bare necessities.[158] Earlier, as many as five hundred Wamanyema porters had been dispatched from Kisingitini to find the camp. On the way they ran afoul of natives and turned back after suffering some casualties. Facing a quandary, Barttelot decided to cable the committee, summarizing their situation and asking for its "advice and opinion." Barttelot instructed Ward to hurry downriver and send the cable from either São Tomé or Luanda. In a longer letter to Mackinnon, he explained that lacking news from Stanley and with aid from Tippu Tip seeming "as remote as ever," the time had come "to act." Tippu Tip, in fact, had gone to Kasongo to look for recruits. Both Jameson and Farran went with him, hoping to speed things up. In a second letter, Barttelot asked for four hundred fighting men, as "it is useless to try and relieve Mr. Stanley, if he be in a fix with a force as small as the one he started with."[159] Ward doubted the wisdom of making the trip, but per orders left on March 28, choosing to start just below Stanley Falls in order to avoid the more dangerous Aruwimi. Troup accompanied him to the Lomami in order to get some canoes and goats from the large Arab encampment there.

At Bangala, Ward sent most of the thirty Zanzibaris and five Sudanese with him back to Yambuya. He then boarded the *Stanley* at Equator Station with twenty-five new porters for the journey to the pool. They'd be needed for the overland journey to Luanda, which he reached on May 1. The reply from the committee to his cable came May 6, saying, in essence, to follow Stanley's instructions. The lack of an available steamer and the need to wait for carriers kept Ward put for ten more days. When he reached Leopoldville, a letter from Barttelot awaited with instructions to proceed to Bangala and "report yourself to the chief of station and take over the stores from him belonging to the expedition." The letter also stipulated that he must stay at Bangala pending further orders. Barttelot didn't care much for Ward and may have seen this as an opportunity to keep him at a distance. Disappointed to the point of calling this "the unkindest act" he had so far experienced on the expedition, Ward felt like quitting but in the end complied.[160]

On the way to Bangala, Ward ran across Troup coming downriver on the *Stanley*. He'd taken a bad fall on April 15: The wound ulcerated and then a fever came on that wouldn't quit. After six weeks in bed, Bonny advised Troup to go home, giving a diagnosis of "general debility consequent of his long residence on the Congo" that couldn't be treated at Yambuya.[161] Troup submitted the necessary formal request to Barttelot, who signed off without hesitation. The two had stopped speaking to one another, and his departure didn't bother him at all. In fact, he told Troup to go directly home and "not to stay at any place along the road longer than is absolutely necessary."[162] When Troup boarded the *Stanley* on June 9, he discovered that Farran would be a traveling companion. Suffering from foot ulcers that prevented him from walking, he, too, was leaving the Congo. This further gladdened Barttelot, who loathed the Syrian.

When the *AIA* showed up, Barttelot took it to Stanley Falls to make final arrangements for the porters, leaving Bonny in charge of Yambuya. Tippu Tip provided four hundred of them on Barttelot's guaranteeing payment and providing an advance of cloth and gunpowder. The overseer, Muni Somai, secured the other thirty and received half his one-thousand-pound fee. About a hundred wives and slaves would also be coming along. A hitch involved the size of the loads. Unused to being porters, the Basongo recruits balked at the normal sixty-four pounds, and after several heated arguments Barttelot agreed to reduce it to forty. Some carried only twenty pounds. He intended to follow Stanley's route to Lake Albert and adapt his strategy according to conditions. Everything hinged on the advance column's whereabouts and circumstances and Emin's desires.[163] If Stanley wasn't found, Barttelot planned to head for the east coast. A letter sent to his sister, however, expressed some doubts about their prospects. "We leave," he said, "for abomination, desolation, and vexation, but I hope in the end success. Perhaps I may not come back, perhaps I may; but while there is life there is hope, and God rules all."[164]

Of the original 271 men left behind at Yambuya, only 132 marched out on June 11, and that number dropped to 101, mostly from desertions, on the way to Banalia, the farthest upstream settlement of Tippu Tip's followers. With groups frequently losing the way and loads disappearing, forty-three days passed before everyone covered the ninety-five miles. During that time, Barttelot made several trips to Kisingitini to straighten things out, and according to Bonny, the whole affair had worn him down. Matters reached the breaking point early in the morning of July 19 over some loud singing and drumming. Barttelot told his boy Sudi to order the music to stop, and when it continued, he went to confront the revelers, revolver in hand. On his way through the camp, a bullet struck him just below the heart, bringing instant death. It came from the gun of a Wamanyema headmen named Sanga. Chaos and looting followed almost immediately. Bonny feared a massacre, but by rallying some of the men he managed to restore a semblance of order and get the major buried. Meanwhile, Muni Somai fled the scene, leaving his men leaderless. Bonny then sent Jameson, still en route from the falls, a note, simply saying, "Major shot dead this morning. Push on quickly. I have written to S. F." Bonny also took time to write a short note to Barttelot's father.[165]

Upon reaching Banalia and helping Bonny reorganize the loads, Jameson went to Kisingitini to make sure Sanga received due punishment. In quick order he was court-martialed and shot. Jameson then left to consult with Ward about a proposition made by Tippu Tip to go to Lake Albert for a payment of twenty thousand pounds. He then planned to cable Brussels from Banana about the offer. During the canoe journey Jameson developed a fever, probably the black water version, and by the time he reached Bangala on August 16, Ward said, "His eyes were half-closed and his skin a ghastly yellow." At 7:32 the next evening, Jameson died. Ward buried him in two Union Jacks and then wrote Bonny to tell him what had happened and to say that he'd be going to the coast to telegraph the committee about their predicament. In the meantime, Bonny should keep his "spirits up" until help came.[166]

The news broke months of silence about the status of the Emin Pasha expedition and created a stir in the papers. Then just as quickly the subject dropped from public view. The relief committee drew up a withdrawal plan that involved Ward and Bonny bringing the men to Banana for embarkation home and selling the leftover goods. No further expedition would be sent up the Congo. Ward stayed on a while longer and made a visit to Stanley Falls. He then departed for England, taking along the twelve Zanzibaris still under his command. On July 4, 1889, Ward bade them farewell as they boarded a ship for home.

Banalia reminded Stanley of a "charnel yard," and it left a vivid impression on Hoffman, who years later said,

> We found the camp in a dreadful condition. Lying on the ground, unburied and rotting, were the bodies of dead men. Close by, too weak to stand, crawled the sick, some obviously dying, their flesh eaten away by disease and dysentery, their bodies bearing ulcers as large as saucers. The whole place seemed to me like one gigantic graveyard; the stench was unbearable; the sights were worse.[167]

Though "stupified" by the sight and what Bonny had told him, Stanley quickly set about readying the return to Lake Albert. The most immediate problem involved porters. Only about sixty of the Zanzibaris from Yambuya seemed fit enough to travel, and not wanting their number to fall even further, Stanley decided to get everyone out of Banalia. Those too ill to move he left in the care of the chief. When sufficiently recovered they could go to Stanley Falls and wait for further assistance. The survivors were the ones Ward took to England. Everyone else had orders to assemble at Bungangeta Island, a process that took three days to complete. Stanley hoped he might be able to convince Tippu Tip to make the trip to Lake Albert. He told him,

> I am waiting to hear your words. If you go with me, it is well. I leave it to you. I will stay here ten days, and then I go on slowly. . . . Whatever you have to say to me, my ears will be open with a good heart, as it has always been towards you.[168]

Not yet knowing Jameson's fate, Stanley waited for him to show up as well. But they couldn't stay put much longer, with some five hundred people packed together on a small island. And, in contrast to 1887, the region lacked food, for, as Stanley said in a letter to the Royal Geographical Society, "the Arabs have followed my track . . . and destroyed villages and plantations, and what the Arabs spare, the elephant herds complete."[169] Furthermore, he intended to keep his word about reaching the vicinity of Fort Bodo before Christmas and Lake Albert by mid-January 1889. Consequently, on August 30 the expedition started on its way again without Jameson and Tippu Tip. The ranks included:

Zanzibari carriers	165
Madi carriers	57

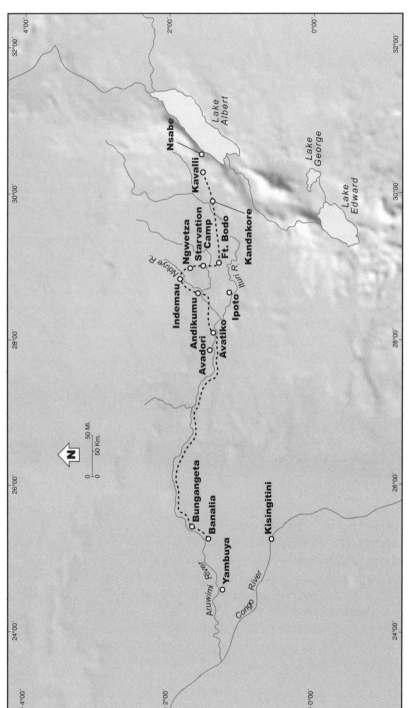

Map 7.3   From Banalia to Kavalli, August 1888–January 1889

Manyema carriers	61
Sudanese	21
Sick	45
Somali	1
Emin's soldiers	4
Other Manyema	108 (women and children)
Officers	2
Personal servant	1

Stanley anticipated losing carriers and thus had 283 of them for the 230 loads Bonny had managed to save of the 473 that had left Yambuya.

As so often in the past, one party with Stanley in command traveled by water, while another, this time led by Bonny, went via land. Within less than a week some of the remaining Madi came down with smallpox. Unprotected, they had apparently gotten it from the Wamanyema who seemed to have introduced the disease to this part of the Congo.[170] The addition of twenty-one recovered Zanzibari deserters helped compensate for the loss, but not for long, as others disappeared in spite of Bonny's warning that those caught would be shot or hung on the spot.[171] Another problem involved people straying from the ranks, especially while foraging for food. Attacks on them produced a dozen deaths within the first two weeks, and Stanley felt that "there would be scores of unresisting victims" if a serious conflict occurred. "We trust to chance mainly," he noted.[172] No direct confrontations occurred, however, and as in the past, the inhabitants abandoned their villages before the column reached them. When, on occasion some women and children were accidentally encountered, the Sudanese and Zanzibaris usually seized them to be servants.

At the end of thirty days, the death toll reached fourteen, and it continued to rise from bow-and-arrow attacks, drowning, and disease. By October 18 the number had climbed to forty-four, and ahead lay an unpopulated region largely devoid of food. Avatiko, reportedly about seven days away, looked like the next place to locate something to eat. Stanley couldn't be sure about it, and he ordered the men to find and prepare enough rations, mostly plantains, for ten days on the road.

Rain poured down in torrents, and beyond abandoned Avadori the land party faced the Ituri and its tributaries in full flood. On October 28 they left the seemingly foodless banks of the river and found Avatiko just a few hours later. A relative abundance of food did indeed exist there, and prospects brightened even more when a Mbuti man said large stands of huge plantains could be found inland just a day or two farther on. Although not all as large as he said, they provided hope that the days of hunger had been left behind. Such hopes were dashed when another foodless stretch exhausted the stocks, including the last goat, within five days. This and the many wounds suffered by the men forced Stanley to call a halt on November 6 so that the sickest could rest while others looked for something to eat. Given their circumstances, he felt thankful not to have to worry about Europeans other than Hoffman and Bonny. Their needs just couldn't be met. For the Africans, daily rations had shrunk to a cup of meal per five people, and when foragers failed to return on the morning of the 9th, Stanley envisioned the expedition on the verge of becoming a "total wreck." He couldn't see how they could last more than three days before the lack of food "would end us all."[173] Shortly after Stanley recorded those thoughts, the foragers turned up, having found enough food to allow the trek to begin again.

The next day brought them close to Ipoto, and despite the earlier apology Stanley thought about going "to settle some accounts" with Kilonga-longa.[174] Instead, he took the column north from the river, hoping to reach open country more quickly. The path through country filled with Wambuti camps seemed like a highway compared to earlier ones, but despite easier going, hunger and disease continued thinning the ranks of porters. Relief came November 14 at the village of Andikumu, for around it stood plantain groves to rival those at Ibwiri. At their sight, Stanley said, "Every face in the caravan is now illuminated by a joyful anticipation."[175] For four days the men ate their fills, some to such an extent that they felt the effects long afterward. The Madi continued to suffer the most, and by November 21 Stanley counted their dead at thirty-two. Two more died the next day, along with a Zanzibari, following a cold, demoralizing rain.

At Indemau Stanley decided to change course and head for Fort Bodo instead. The discovery of some rifle cartridges similar to their own in a passing native caravan caused him to have doubts about whether those at the fort had left for Lake Albert, so he decided to see for himself. The column stayed put for five days in order to stock up on plantains. Appearing to have housed about fifteen hundred people, Indemau, like so many other villages, had been abandoned because of attacks by Kilonga-longa. The men also used the downtime to build a bridge across the Nduye River, and after getting to the other side, on December 1, Stanley called a muster. By then two more Madi had died and fourteen of the Zanzibaris from Yambuya appeared to have little hope of surviving. The toll of Zanazibaris from Fort Bodo was two deaths and two sick. Three days later they reached Ngwetza and Stanley ordered everyone to prepare five days' rations for the final leg of the journey. Once on the road again, many of the men jettisoned their food loads after a

Mbuti claimed that an abundant supply of plantains was only a short distance away. When informed of this, Stanley called a halt in order to send the most able-bodied back to Ngwetza to find or replace the discarded loads. About two hundred started off, while the rest bedded down to await their return.

Thus began the ordeal called "starvation camp." Few rations remained, and the forest yielded only meager pickings, mostly berries and fungi. In despair, Stanley said he "pictured the entire column perished here in this camp, and the Pasha wondering month after month what had become of us, and we corrupting and decaying in this unknown corner of great forest . . . and our burial-place remaining unknown until the end of time."[176] Bonny agreed, noting that unless food came soon, "few will arrive at the Lakes to tell of our suffering and misery." Why Stanley had chosen to come this way didn't make any sense to him.[177]

Concerned that further delay would lead to their demise, Stanley ordered most of those who could walk—sixty-six men, twelve women, and a few children—to start back toward Ngwetza on December 15. Bonny agreed to stay with the loads if Stanley provided at least ten fit men and enough food for ten days, which meant all the rations on hand. The deal was made. Nothing could be spared for the twenty-six too sick and feeble to move. Stanley felt that without anything to eat, they had only twenty-four hours to live. Contemplating his own dim prospects, he decided that a quick death by pistol shot or poison was preferable to a slow one by starvation.[178] Before having to make such a decision they ran into the others laden with plantains and bananas and even leading a few goats. Later that afternoon, starvation camp ceased to exist, although not before claiming twenty lives.

In an effort to make up for lost time, Stanley had the party back on the road to Fort Bodo on December 17. Given the small number of available porters, Bonny stayed a few days longer to bury the extra loads and allow some of the people a little more time to recover. The Epulu River proved to be less than three hours away, and on the 20th of the month they reached the outer limits of the fields that had been established the previous year. When some Zanzibaris on patrol appeared on the scene, it became clear that Fort Bodo was still occupied.

The state of the rear column's men shocked Parke. They seemed to him in "a miserable state from debility and hunger" and "eaten up . . . with enormous ulcers."[179] It's no wonder that Stanley found conditions at the fort bordering on luxurious. In fact, they had improved, especially with regard to food. His concerns now shifted to Mounteney-Jephson's fate. Why hadn't he come as expected? A quick trip to Lake Albert would be needed to find the answer. A muster produced 412 people. This meant that 106 had perished between Banalia and the fort, thirty-eight of them members of the rear column. With loads now exceeding carriers by fifty-five, some double marches would be needed to get them all to a camp Stanley planned to establish at Kandakore, just across the Ituri. Promises of extra cloth netted an ample number of volunteers to make the extra trips.

By January 9, 1889, the move had been completed. With speed of essence, Stanley decided that Bonny would be the only European to leave with him. Stairs, Parke, Nelson, and Hoffman were instructed to stay at Kandakore, along with 136 people judged too sick and injured to go any farther. Parke called Kandakore "a large Hospital," noting that "Almost every man gets treatment and some of the worst cases have to be fed on their backs as they are too weak to sit up. They are simply reduced to skin and bone."[180] To Stanley the end of the ordeal seemed near; all that remained was "to deliver the ammunition into the pasha's hands, and escort a few Egyptians home." Both emotionally and physically, he reported feeling great, better than he had in a long while, with every muscle "as firm as steel wire."[181] However, his spirits sagged when messengers from Kavalli's brought letters from Emin and Mounteney-Jephson that painted a very different picture of their impending future. Emin no longer controlled the situation in Equatoria and both he and Mounteney-Jephson had taken refuge at Tunguru. The latter advised Stanley to stay at Kavalli's, as he would face "a difficult & dangerous task . . . dealing with the Pasha's people."[182]

The decline began with a rebellion by the battalion stationed at Rejaf that effectively removed the northern portion of Equatoria from the pasha's control.[183] The Egyptians stationed there no longer trusted him and wanted to stay put or return home via Khartoum, not believing it had fallen to the Mahdi. They even hatched a plot to capture Emin and bring him to Rejaf in chains. Emin hoped Stanley's arrival would convince the rebels to return to the fold; however, it seems to have had the opposite effect by fueling suspicions about a forced evacuation to the east coast. Indeed, the rebellion had spread more widely, and when Emin and Mounteney-Jephson went to Dufile on August 20 to check on reports of a mutiny in progress, they and their small entourage were surrounded by an angry mob and put under arrest and confined to a compound. No one was harmed, and following a hearing by a council that included officers from Rejaf, Mounteney-Jephson was allowed to leave on September 3. Rumors spoke of Stanley's return, and the council appointed a delegation to bring him to Dufile on the pretense of having discussions. Mounteney-Jephson insisted that he must be included, saying that otherwise Stanley would never accept the offer. After balking for a while, the officers in charge agreed to the request. At Tunguru, Moun-teney-Jephson discovered that Stanley had not yet returned, and he soon went back to Dufile, taking Casati with him. Another hearing by the council took place to consider a range of charges against Emin, including that of conspiring with Stanley.[184] With the cards stacked against him, Emin signed a statement that effectively removed him as governor of Equatoria. Although no longer officially a prisoner, he still could not leave Dufile and worried about being taken to Rejaf under force of arms. According to Mounteney-Jephson, Emin insisted he would shoot himself first.[185]

The situation in Equatoria deteriorated even further when a Mahdist army reached Lado. Joined by the Bari, the invaders easily overran Rejaf and a number of other stations during October and November. This convinced the rebels that Khartoum had fallen. Some opted for the Mahdist side, whereas others professed a desire to rejoin Emin. Fearing an attack, people began leaving Dufile for Wadelai.

Freed on November 17, Emin immediately joined Mounteney-Jephson and Casati. They stayed in Wadelai until December 5, then evacuated the station and headed overland with about four hundred followers to better fortified Tunguru. A dismantled *Advance* was left behind, along with virtu-ally all supplies, Emin's books, instruments, and natural history collections. About halfway to Tunguru one of the steamers came by, and all boarded it for the remainder of the trip. As 1888 turned into 1889, Mounteney-Jephson wanted to move to Mswa, but Emin insisted on staying put until receiving word from Stanley.

Stanley drafted his replies to Emin's and Mounteney-Jephson's letters during a stop at Gavira's and sent thirty men with rifles to take them to Lake Albert for forwarding. One letter to Mounteney-Jephson expressed frustra-tion with the situation, particularly the lack of progress during the last eight months. Although "perfectly willing to assist" Emin, Stanley said he needed clear instructions about his plans. Most important, did Emin intend to stay or leave? In a second letter, he urged Mounteney-Jephson to come quickly to Kavalli's. Stanley considered the site secure, as a war call would bring "2000 warriors to assist to repel any force disposed for violence." He ended the letter with "Let him who wants to come out of the devouring circle come—I am ready to lend all my strength & wit to assist him. But this time there must be no hesitation—but positive Yea or Nay—& home we go."[186] The letter to Emin had a more official tone. Stanley wanted a receipt for goods tendered and suggested that all those who wished to leave should set up camp along the lake and bring enough food to last a month. He set a twenty-day limit for receiving a reply from him or Mounteney-Jephson.[187]

The climb from Lake Albert to the plateau above. *Henry M. Stanley,* In Darkest Africa. *(New York: Charles Scribner's Sons, 1890).*

Stanley then resumed his journey to Kavalli's, where he received a warm welcome from allies, who often brought gifts of food. In return, he sent sixty of his men to join in a battle with the Baregga. The successful conclusion of the campaign solidified his position among the Bahima and netted the victors many cattle. On the occasion of his forty-eighth birthday, Stanley wrote,

> If I were asked whether the privations of the last two years had affected permanently my physical vigor & elasticity, I should feel bound to say that at present I am not conscious of it. The rest has enabled me to feel better than I have for some years, & I am in the utmost nicety of condition.[188]

Upon receipt of the letters, Mounteney-Jephson started for Kavalli's aboard the *Khedive*. At Mswa, the captain inexplicably steamed back toward Wadelai, leaving Mounteney-Jephson to hunt up canoes to complete the trip. He arrived on February 6 and presented Stanley with a letter from Emin containing the pasha's thanks for everything Stanley had done on his behalf and noting that he and Stanley would most likely not see one another again. He ended with "May God protect you and your party, and give you a happy and speedy homeward march."[189] Puzzled by Emin's "melancholy" and hoping to encourage him, Stanley sent a reply that praised his efforts. It seems to have worked, for a letter dated February 13 from Emin said he, Casati, twelve officers, and forty soldiers would be arriving soon to discuss departure arrangements.[190] Stanley sent Mounteney-Jephson and more than one hundred Zanzibaris and local carriers to escort them from the lake. While waiting, Emin composed a letter telling Stanley, "I hope sincerely that the great difficulties which you have had to undergo, and the great sacrifices made by your Expedition in its way to assist us, may be rewarded by a full success in bringing my people out."[191] A decision seemed to have finally been made.

Escorts collected Emin on February 17, and the next day he and Stanley discussed ways to bring all those who wanted to leave to Nsabe. Events took another positive turn when the party from Kandakore arrived, uniting the expedition for the first time in nearly a year and a half. Save three Madi and two Zanzibaris who died, the men recovered their strength at Kandakore, thanks in large measure to abundant food obtained from raids on nearby villages. This caused Stairs to write,

> I often wonder what English people would say if they knew of the way in which we "go for" these natives. Friendship we don't want as then we should get very little meat and probably have to pay for the bananas. Every male native capable of using the bow is shot, this of course we must do. All the

women and children are taken as slaves by our men to do work in the camps.[192]

Using a common practice in the Congo, severed hands served as proof of killings, something Free State officers had also learned by this time.

Emin went back to the camp at Nsabe to check on reports of an impending Banyoro attack. It turned out to be a false alarm, and when he returned to Kavalli's on February 27, 144 followers, including his young daughter Ferida, accompanied him. Emin's wife, an Ethiopian, had died two years earlier during the birth of a son. The boy had survived only a short while. Emin felt that it would take an additional twenty days for all his people to make the journey, whereas Stanley thought two months a more reasonable period of time, which turned out to be closer to the truth.[193] Despite warnings not to bring much in the way of personal possessions with them, many did anyway. Their loads often included bedsteads and even grindstones. The carriers soon grew weary of lugging heavy burdens from the lakeshore to the plateau above (a three-day round-trip of eighteen miles), and on March 10 some of them refused to do it anymore. The Egyptian penchant for using *abid*, or slave, as a term of reference didn't help their dispositions. Stanley reacted quickly by calling a muster and treating the situation like a mutiny. He ordered those in charge of the action flogged and put under arrest, after which the others quietly went back to work. To Parke, this provided yet another example of the "extraordinary influence which Mr. Stanley exercises over the men, and of the great respect and confidence with which they invariably treat him."[194]

A shortage of potable water at Kavalli's kept Parke busy with intestinal disorders. Cases of syphilis among the Egyptians and Sudanese added to his burden of work. Stealing, or at least attempts to steal, occurred regularly. Given the circumstances, Stanley wanted to leave on March 30, Emin on April 10. Growing more frustrated, Stanley exploded on April 5 after Emin's people refused to heed the call for everyone to assemble for an inquiry into an accusation of rifle stealing. He ordered armed Zanzibaris to bring them to the camp square, where some were flogged and others put in irons.[195] Stanley said in no uncertain terms that the departure day would be April 10. If the people remaining at Wadelai didn't show up by this date, so be it. By now he considered the Lake Victoria option off the table: all those able and willing would have to march to the coast or fend for themselves as best they could. Casati described Emin as "pale with rage and indignation" but resigned to the fact that they must make the long trip.[196] Mounteney-Jephson agreed with Stanley about any hopes of Emin's people settling near Lake

Victoria having vanished. Indeed, he felt this was fortunate, claiming, "They would soon have turned any beautiful country into a hell upon earth."[197]

The extra loads required additional carriers. About 550 were coerced or enticed to join, and when added to the 230 expedition members, 130 Wamanyema, and about six hundred of Emin's people, the column that filed from Kavalli's on April 10 numbered around fifteen hundred. The sprawling train also included herds of cattle, sheep, and goats. Only forty-two tusks from Emin's store had been secured, and these were needed to pay the Wamanyema porters. Egypt would get none.

Whereas the prospect of going home brought an air of cheer with it, the sorry condition of the Egyptians meant moving at a snail's pace. Everything then came to a complete stop at Mazamboni's because of a flare-up of Stanley's gastritis. A nearly fatal episode of fever followed, keeping Stanley bedridden until April 29. At one stretch Parke stayed with him for six nights running, and then he became ill, as did Mounteney-Jephson, seriously so.

During lucid moments Stanley worried about all the problems that could beset them. Would Kabarega attack? This seemed more than likely given the need to pass through so much territory that was directly or indirectly under his control. At one time he'd thought his force would be large enough to teach Kabarega a lesson, but now doubted this. What would happen when crossing Unyankole? How many would be lost during ambushes there? On top of such thoughts came rumors of plotting and scheming among Emin's people. A Sudanese absconded, taking twenty-two others and some rifles with him. After being tracked down, he was hanged for stealing and inciting men to desert.[198]

Just before they started again, one of Emin's men brought twenty-eight captives to use as slaves. Stanley recognized them as coming from friendly villages and ordered their release, commenting, "I am getting pretty sick of these Egyptians. I would rather they themselves should perish than that they should harm these people who have been so loyal & good to us."[199] A mistakenly delivered letter indicating that officers in Wadelai might be plotting the caravan's downfall added another incentive to get going without further delay. During the halt, porters drifted away, and now without enough of them, Stanley ordered some of the ammunition boxes buried to keep them from falling into enemy hands. Emin wanted to wait longer for others to appear but agreed that no more time could be spent doing so. Mazamboni had provided little in the way of food, and Emin worried that the constant raids to secure enough to feed everybody might soon head to retaliations.[200] Casati attributed the fact that they didn't to Stanley's orders to refrain from stealing livestock goats and never stoop to violence.[201]

The need to carry Stanley and Mounteney-Jephson, the poor condition-
ing of the Egyptians, and the large numbers of livestock kept the pace slow.
Despite this, many lagged behind, stretching the caravan to some three
miles. Worried about misbehavior, Stanley informed the officers that

> They will permit no straggling by the wayside, no looting of villages, no indis-
> criminate pillaging of plantations, no marauding upon any excuse; and upon
> any insolence, whether from Egyptian officer, private soldier, or follower, the
> officer in charge will call his guard and bind the offender, and bring him to
> me for punishment. If any violence is offered it must be met by such violence
> as will instantly crush it.[202]

The first conflict in quite a while occurred on May 10, when a small contingent of Warasura attacked a group of Sudanese taking baths. Armed Zanzibaris came to their rescue, forcing the attackers to flee. The death toll was
one Sudanese and three Banyoro.

Not long after leaving Kavalli's, Ruwenzori came into full view for a short
time. Earlier in April the massifs had been visible for three days, a rather rare
occurrence. They provided a beacon for the first leg of the trip, during which
Stanley had hoped to put the final pieces of the Nile puzzle in place. Between
the column and the mountains lay the deeply incised Semliki River, another
geographical name traceable to Stanley, although where he got it has never
been determined. It had to be crossed, and during the attempt on May 17,
about fifty Warasura opened fire from the other side. Return volleys forced
them to retreat, and by midafternoon on the 19th, the crossing was completed. The road now led through a dense stretch of forest. To Stanley, the
heat and high humidity made him feel as though they were inside "a great
fermenting vat." This and the mud slowed progress to about five miles per
day. By May 25 Stanley was in a sour mood, no doubt exacerbated by continuing stomach pains and occasional bouts of fever. In his estimation, the
Egyptians "had descended far below zero."[203] They complained constantly,
and "reason could not penetrate their dense heads." Reports of some of them
abandoning their children lowered their stock even more. Emin's penchant
for stopping to collect bird, reptile, and insect specimens had also become
an irritant. Stanley put the latter in the context of what he perceived as Africa's needs:

> Every man I saw, giant or dwarf, only deepened the belief that Africa had
> other claims on man, and every feature of the glorious land only impressed
> me the more that there was a crying need for immediate relief and assistance
> from civilization; that first of all, roads of iron must be built, and that fire and

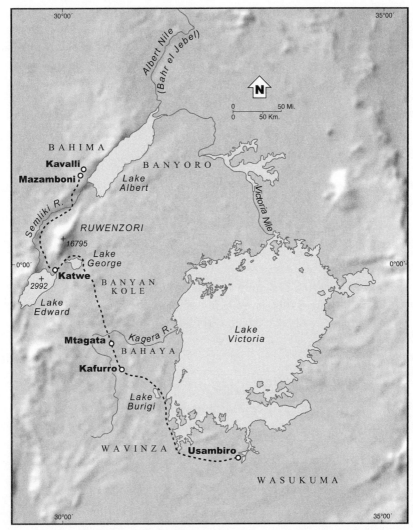

Map 7.4   From Lake Albert to Lake Victoria, April–August 1889

water were essential agencies for transport; more especially on this long troubled continent than on any other.

To him, "the Maker . . . intended that it should be reserved until the fulness of time for something higher than a nursery for birds and a store-place for reptiles."[204]

More stretches of forest, glades of sharp cane-grass, incessant rain, and deep ravines made it impossible to pick up the pace. Illnesses continued unabated and took the lives of several Wamanyema carriers. On a positive note the area's Baamba inhabitants were friendly and food so abundant that it surpassed Buganda in Stanley's eyes. He felt that the needs of a caravan ten times the size of the current one could easily be accommodated. Travel conditions slowly improved as they left the forest and traveled a decent road along a terrace of the Ruwenzori. Suddenly, without warning, part of the column came under rifle fire that killed two and wounded four. The perpetrators turned out to be a party of Kilonga-longa's ivory hunters who mistook them for Warasura. When they found otherwise, they called off the attack, and that night others from their party came to exchange peace offerings.

For many days the Ruwenzori range showed itself only fleetingly, just enough, Stanley said, to "fill the gazer with a feeling as though a glimpse of celestial splendour was obtained."[205] To find out more about the mountain, Stanley called for volunteers to try an ascent. Among the Europeans, only Stairs and Emin were fit or motivated enough to make the climb, and Emin turned back after ascending only about a thousand feet. Stairs and forty Zanzibaris eventually made it to slightly above 10,600 feet and afterward Stairs wrote a report for Stanley about what they'd seen.[206] Perhaps history should record him as the "discoverer," along with Frank Pocock, who was the first non-African to see it.

The road then traversed another stretch of deep forest on the way to Ukonjo, where the spearing of a Madi on June 9 caused concern about having to fight their way across one of the most densely populated areas they had seen so far. The appearance of a hostile crowd the next day made such a possibility seem even more likely. Armed skirmishers, however, quickly dispersed it and for good measure took some prisoners. During the afternoon, their chief offered to make peace if Stanley would return them. He also said that the expedition would be welcome in Itoro and Unyankole, both foes of Bunyoro.

Egyptians continued to fall by the wayside. "Helplessness may compel abandonment, but does not diminish its horrors," remarked Casati.[207] The nerves of the Europeans also suffered from the burdens of the journey, as illustrated by an exchange between Stanley and Emin on June 13 over a change in rear guard assignments. Mounteney-Jephson described both men as being in a "towering rage," with Emin saying, "I think you had better leave me here, I wish you had never come to help me," and Stanley replying, "You are a most thankless & ungrateful man."[208] Several days later Nelson reported Bonny for slacking off while in charge of the cattle. Bonny took umbrage and went after Nelson, but others stepped in to separate them before punches could do any damage.

Cooler uplands helped calm tempers a bit, as did news of a large lake being close by. A herder reported that one of Kabarega's generals, Rukara, had occupied the town Katwe at the north end of the lake and said that by hurrying there they might capture some of the cattle that had been stolen by the Warasura. Stanley sent fifty men with rifles to check things out, and they came back with twenty-five head. When the expedition got to Katwe the next day, no Warasura were anywhere in sight. Judged by the large amount of grain left behind, they'd cleared out in a hurry. Stanley called the lake Edward Albert, "out of respect to the first British Prince who has shown an interest in African Geography."[209]

Since little time could be spared for exploration, Stanley paused only long enough to make a few measurements and take a short canoe trip. He also visited two nearby saline bodies of water, the larger one about three miles long and three-quarters of a mile wide and the smaller some half-mile round, which provided salt for people for many miles in each direction. They were what made Katwe a strategic place to control.

A march of more than eighteen miles on June 20 led to a Bahima village. Its occupants had departed with their cattle to avoid losing them to Rukara, leaving large ornate houses to shelter the expedition's members. From there, they picked up a trail made by the Warasura across the former lakebed on the north side of the channel connecting Lake Edward Albert with Lake George. Stanley named it Beatrice Gulf, after Queen Victoria's fifth daughter, Princess Beatrice. The name didn't stick, and today it's known as the Kazinga Channel.

Signs showed the gap separating them from the Warasura closing, and on the 22nd of June those out in front, mostly Wasongoro and Wakonju who'd joined on as porters, came under heavy fire. Many jumped in the water to avoid being hit. A charge of the brake from which the shots came quickly put the Warasura to flight, and the expedition continued on its way. Two days later the Wasongoro and Wakonju volunteers decided to go home, producing another shortage of porters. Having made comparatively good time since Katwe and with abundant food, Stanley considered it wise to halt for a couple of days, particularly as reports described the stretch of country ahead as wilderness. Unfortunately, the site proved to be malarial and the water brackish to the point of being virtually undrinkable. Stanley called it the worst water he'd ever tasted.

Harassment by some Warasura proved no more than a nuisance. Of much greater concern was an outbreak of stomach illness from drinking the brackish water. By June 26, some two hundred people had become seriously ill, and a few days later the figure included nearly half the expedition's members. Of the Europeans only Nelson remained fit for duty. The symptoms included shivering, fever, and nausea lasting three or four days. Still, on they went, following a circuitous route to almost the exact spot on Lake George where Stanley had camped in 1876. Lacking a boat or canoes, and with so many people in train, they missed another chance to do some exploring. Near the Unyankole border, Stanley put three alternative routes to the coast before his officers. The shortest would be to go through Buganda to secure canoes at Dumo for a crossing of the lake to pick up the trail to Mombasa. With Mutesa dead and Mwanga still thought to be *kabaka*, Stanley doubted their ability to pass through Buganda peacefully. Fighting also loomed as a distinct possibility if they continued through Unyankole and Antari, his nemesis from Bumbire, could muster enough Bahaya troops to stop them if he wished. It might be safer to go through Rwanda and then head for Ujiji, but the country was unknown and the distance by far the greatest. After a vigorous discussion, they decided to stay with the Unyankole route.

It seemed like a wise choice, as villagers greeted them with surprising enthusiasm. On July 6 Stanley noted that

> All along the line of march today the herdsmen and their families gave us an ovation so that we begin to feel like heroes. If it were merely lip praise it would still be appreciated, but when at every resting place we receive unstinted hospitality, little mountains of bananas, piles of potatoes, numerous pots full of pombe & milk, we cannot doubt the sincerity of their gratitude.[210]

The cause was the sudden withdrawal of Kabarega's Warasura, seemingly in panic after run-ins with Stanley's troops. On a negative note, fever continued to run rampant, and since it was the height of the dry season, little potable water existed to quench parched throats.

On July 11 Stanley heard about recent turbulence in Buganda, with Mwanga, now supposedly a Christian, attempting to regain the throne from Karema, who'd seized power with the help of the Muslims. A deputy of the Christians asked Stanley to help them. Stanley said he would need to think about it for a while. They would get an answer before the caravan crossed the Kagera River. His reluctance stemmed from doubts about Mwanga's sincerity and distrust of the Basanda in general.

The trek across Unyankole's many valleys and gorges exhausted people already weakened by recurring sickness. At one point Bonny collapsed unnoticed by the others. He might have died but for the help of a local villager who revived him with a gourd of fresh milk. The large number of sufferers, including Stanley, required several halts to allow them to recover enough to continue. During one of the halts four Egyptian officers decided to stay put with their families. On July 21, Prince Buchunku of Unyankole greeted them. A blood brotherhood ceremony followed, which, according to Stanley, gave him right of residence and "free access to every plantation in the kingdom."[211] By now Stanley had decided not to aid Mwanga, and he led the struggling expedition across the Kagera and into Karagwe during the last week of July. All the while, Emin's people kept disappearing, including a woman who was carried off by a leopard.

A stop at Mtagata allowed everyone the luxury of a cleansing hot water bath. Although once again in familiar country, Stanley discovered conditions much changed since 1876. An unstable, bloody period followed Rumanika's death in 1878, and it hadn't ended until his teenage son Ndagara took over the throne. Still, tensions remained high because of recent invasions by the Baganda. Ndagara gave permission for the expedition to pass through the country and said food would be available as long as there was no trouble. After spending four days in Kafurro, the column started up again on August 7, leaving twenty-six seriously ill Egyptians behind. Five others died after a cold, soaking rain. So many had become sick that it became necessary to leave loads, including boxes of ammunition, behind in order to carry them. According to Nelson, the people were so thickly strewn on the ground inert & apparently lifeless, that it resembled a battlefield.[212] Stanley thus called a halt in order to slaughter some cattle for meat. He also formed an officer's "Inquiry into the Conduct of William Hoffman." Discharged from duty four times before for lying and stealing, he'd not been on the payroll since leaving Mazamboni's. This latest incident of theft led to his formal dismissal from the expedition and a warning "that he must not come near the Europeans again." Hoffman would, however, be allowed officer's rations for the rest of the journey.[213]

Lake Burigi marked Karagwe's southern boundary and the end of free food. To pay for needs from then on, each person received an assortment of beads. Some Sudanese reacted to the change by raiding a village for food, killing one inhabitant and wounding another. A deputation came to camp asking that the man responsible for the shootings be handed over to them. After they refused an offer of cattle as compensation, Stanley complied, saying that "He was marched away, and we never knew what became of him." Of course, Stanley did know. The man, as he noted in a letter, was handed over "according to the law 'blood for blood.' "[214] The others involved in the incident received floggings.

The road from Lake Burigi led toward Lake Victoria, which came into view on August 17. Five days of travel showed that the lake extended farther to the southwest and had more bays than was previously thought. The map would, therefore, have to be redrawn. Friendly villagers traded bananas, sweet potatoes, and sorghum for beads, but as the expedition turned east, conditions changed. Signs of recent Baganda and Wangoni raids became visible, and Stanley thought the Wangoni in particular had "done their work of destruction pretty thoroughly."[215] Understandably wary of such a large number of armed strangers in their midst, the inhabitants treated them with extreme caution.

The expedition reached a recently completed French mission station on August 27. Only a few converts still occupied the well-constructed and fortified site; the missionaries had departed because of local opposition and the lack of a nearby water supply. The next day brought them to the Church Missionary Society station at Usambiro, headed by Alexander Mackay, who'd left the chaos of Buganda. He and his associate David Deekes set out the welcome mat for a stay from August 28 to September 17. As planned, supplies for the long journey to the coast had been dropped off earlier by Charles Stokes, a former CMS lay missionary married to the daughter of a Nyamwezi chief and a successful ivory and arms trader. Pack donkeys and riding asses were purchased, and, thanks to priests at a nearby Catholic mission station, the Europeans had new clothing so as to be dressed in a presentable way for the remainder of the journey.[216]

Stanley urged Mackay, whom he considered a "modern Livingstone," to leave with him, feeling the missionary needed a break after many years in the field. Furthermore, the area didn't seem all that suitable for a station. He predicted that its large population would inevitably produce onerous "taxes, demands, and blackmail," and it also appeared an unhealthy place. Several missionaries had already lost their lives, perhaps because of the foul water of a nearby swamp. "It may be liquid sewage for all we know," Stanley said.[217] Mackay declined the invitation and died the following February. Two Catholic priests, however, asked to come along, as one needed to reach the coast for treatment of cataracts.

The three weeks at Usambiro revealed a number of things to Stanley. He heard that the IBEAC had received its charter and stories about Arabs and Africans contesting the rule of the German East Africa Company, headed by Carl Peters. Called the Abushiri uprising after its most prominent leader,

Abushiri ibn Salim al-Harthi, it began on the coast in August 1888 with protests over German abuses and then flared into open conflict threatening European property and lives. The situation became so serious that only Dar es Salaam remained securely under German control. Stanley and his officers also learned from newspaper cuttings that Europe was in total confusion about the fate of the expedition. After reading them, Jephson commented,

> One paper says we are completely Annihilated & another sends us off with Emin Pasha to fight the Mahdi; a third sends us to found a state East of the Niger, a fourth to found a state in Masai land; a fifth marches us off to Ujiji; a sixth leaves us sticking in a morass somewhere in a forest, & so on.[218]

Edwin Marston blamed the French for the misinformation, noting to Stanley that they had recently claimed Leopold "had known of your death for a long time but was keeping it back on account of financial considerations in connection with the *Congo State*."[219] The uncertainty did not go away until letters written by Stanley between Banalia and Fort Bodo reached London in late March and early April 1889.

At Usimbiro Stanley first received word of Jameson's death, and he also heard about a second Emin rescue attempt, commanded by Frederick J. Jackson. Mackinnon had instructed Jackson to establish a chain of stations in the direction of Lake Baringo, in present-day Kenya, and once there build a secure base for storing ivory. After that he was to go to Wadelai and find Emin, on the assumption that Stanley hadn't. When Stanley's success became known, Jackson received orders to alter his course and try for a meeting with him at Lake Victoria. It never took place, because Stanley decided to keep going as planned. He felt he didn't need Jackson's help, and he certainly wanted nothing to do with any scheme to enter Uganda or deal with the Mahdists in Equatoria, which seemed to be part of the plan.[220]

Emin still harbored thoughts about the Kavirondo resettlement option, and expectation of Jackson's arrival in Usambiro caused him to bring up the matter again. Given their earlier discussion, Stanley thought he must be joking and replied that to leave them there with the limited force he now possessed "would be to surrender you to the first native who chose to lift a spear against you." Responding to Stanley's usual blunt style, Emin labeled him "impatient, disobliging, pretentious, stubborn and lacking in knowledge."[221] Despite these feelings, he wrote a letter of appreciation to Mackinnon stating that until they could meet in person,

I beg to ask you to transmit to all subscribers of the fund the sincerest thanks of a handful of forlorn people, who, through your instrumentality, have been saved from destruction, and now hope to embrace their relatives. . . . To speak here of Mr. Stanley and his officers' merits would be inadequate. If I live to return I shall make my acknowledgments.[222]

As in so many other instances, Emin's behavior seems inscrutable.

A muster on September 12 produced 181 loads and 559 people. Some slaves of the Egyptians were left in Mackay's care. Stanley hoped to recruit a hundred carriers to take the place of those lost along the way but managed to get only eighteen by the time the remnants of the column marched out on September 17. From Usambiro they had two travel options: take the route to Mombasa and go through territory designated within Britain's sphere of influence or follow a longer one to Bagamoyo and traverse country under German jurisdiction. Stanley chose the latter for unspecified reasons. Emin's nationality may have been why.

Spirits soared at the thought of the journey's end being near. Mounteney-Jephson described himself as "fat as a pig" and "better than I have ever been before in Africa."[223] The first day passed peacefully enough, and the villagers sold cassava, sweet potatoes, groundnuts, bananas, and milk. Suddenly, though, conditions deteriorated. The downhill slide started with a boisterous challenge from a group of young men, and when one of Emin's people fell a little behind, he was hit on the head and robbed. Then came five days of fighting on a sun-scorched plain with little water. On one occasion Stanley would have been killed had not two Zanzibaris intervened. After that he ordered the Maxim brought into play to drive attackers back. They persisted in coming, and at the cessation of one encounter Mounteney-Jephson said his companions left "a great many dead on the field" and that the men "cut off their all heads & made a pile of them in camp."[224] In line with customary practice, burning of villages marked the end of successful engagements as well. Such actions helped earn Stanley and the officers the appellation *wazungu wakali*, vicious white men.[225]

Hostilities ended at Shinyanga, which put on a cordial welcome. The people there said that travelers always encountered problems in the area through which the expedition had just passed. Stanley attributed the change in Usukuma from fifteen years ago to caravans bound for Lake Victoria. They made the people greedy and prone to violence.[226] The next stop was at Stokes's encampment. He'd left earlier to take guns and ammunition to the Christians in Buganda. Stokes would make a career of gunrunning, and his summary execution by a Free State officer in 1895 for this and smuggling ivory

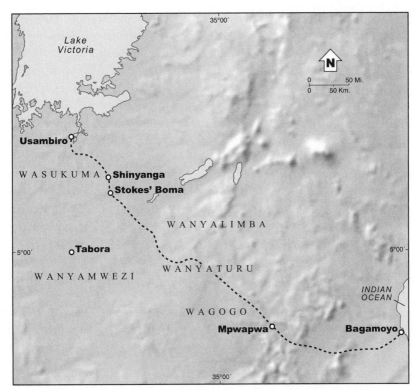

Map 7.5   The Return to Bagamoyo, September–December, 1889

led to an international incident between Britain and Belgium. The camp's strong fortifications and a friendly Nyamwezi chief provided an opportunity to resupply and rest. To bolster his position in an expected war with a rival, the chief had enlisted a large number of Masaai warriors, and he wanted assistance from the expedition's soldiers as well. Feeling that this was none of their concern, Stanley said no.

More porters were needed to carry the mounting numbers of infirm Egyptians. When travel began again on October 9, only a dozen or so new ones had signed on. Few villages existed in the area immediately beyond Stokes's, and for one three-day stretch they crossed through a classic marenga mkali. At a village on the other side, the sight of hundreds of human skulls led Stanley to believe a great battle must have been fought there not too long ago. Instead, he learned the skulls belonged to Wanyaturu who had died from starvation after fleeing a drought in Ituru, the scene of the notorious battle in 1875. The chief said he still had some refugee children, and Stanley asked for a boy to take to Zanzibar for a Christian education. He named him Sungoro and speculated that "the little one may turn out a shining light among African heathen some day."[227] His fate is unknown.

The French missionaries joined up during the stop. They'd missed the expedition's departure but didn't have too much difficulty learning its route. In addition, a caravan belonging to Tippu Tip passed by. When it left, the remaining Wamanyema went along for the journey home, further reducing the number of porters. The road again meandered through mostly unpopulated country covered by thorn scrub and scattered baobab trees to the borders of Ugogo. Stanley dreaded the days needed to cross a country that promised numerous *honga* negotiations and thefts. Halfway through, a large caravan going west brought news of Germans troops under Col. Hermann von Wissmann having crushed the Abushiri uprising. Wissmann was well known. He'd crossed Africa from west to east in 1880–1883 and received a Royal Geographical Society medal for explorations of Congo River tributaries. Bismarck was now in charge of Tanganyika, not the German East Africa Company.

Near the eastern boundary of Ugogo, Stanley realized that a long-held goal would never be achieved. Despite all the invectives, he wanted to be part of the area's future. But this was now German-controlled territory, and there'd be no place for him. As he said,

> Nineteen years ago I looked at this land and people with desiring eyes. I saw in it a field worth some effort to reclaim. In six months I felt sure Ugogo could be made lovely and orderly, a blessing to the inhabitants and to strangers, without any very great expense or trouble; it would become a pleasant highway of human intercourse with far-away peoples, productive of wealth to the natives, and comfort to caravans. I learned on arrival in Ugogo that I was ever debarred from the hope. It is to be the destiny of the Germans to carry out this work, and I envy them. It is the worst news of all that I shall never be able to drain this cesspool of iniquitous passion, and extinguish the insolence of Wagogo chiefs, and make the land clean, healthy, and even beautiful of view. While my best wishes accompany the German efforts, my mind is clouded with a doubt that it ever will be that fair land of rest and welcome I had dreamed of making it.[228]

Only one incident of note occurred, when some Maasai tried to steal the few head of cattle that remained. Sudanese guards drove them off, killing two.[229]

On November 10 the column straggled into Mpwapwa. Emin received a hero's welcome from Lt. Rochus Schmidt and the twenty-five Sudanese and one hundred Zulu soldiers recruited from Mozambique who were stationed there. After a few days' rest, the journey began again, with Schmidt coming along for good measure. People had recently been attaching themselves to the column for protection, swelling the number to about a thousand. One of the French priests described it as a "strange melange" of Africans, English, Americans, Italians, French, Germans, Greeks, and Turks.[230] As it had previously, Usagara seemed a veritable paradise compared with Ugogo, and more and more familiar sights greeted Stanley as they crossed the valleys of the Mkondoa and Mkata Rivers before passing a rebuilt Simbawenni.

Two reporters, Thomas Stevens of the *New York World* and Edmund Vizetelly of the *New York Herald*, came calling during one of the stopovers. Stevens had been looking for Stanley for six months, expecting him to cross Masaailand. He learned of the Tanganyika route while in Zanzibar and hurried to catch the expedition before it reached Bagamoyo, despite a German ban on travel by civilians. He got there ahead of Vizetelly, who'd received official permission and didn't expect any rivals. The *Herald* lost to a rival this time. When asked by Stevens if this would be his last African trip, Stanley replied, "Well you know, we always say so every time we leave Africa, but we always come back again, till we die, if there is anything left to be done. Look at Livingstone."[231]

Two large caravans of the Imperial British East African Company trekking toward the interior dropped off much needed supplies, including fresh clothing for the Europeans. At the Kingani River crossing, horses awaited Stanley and Emin to take them the rest of the way to Bagamoyo. The German officers, including Wissmann, laid out a lunch that Stanley said rivaled those in Parisian restaurants, and later in the afternoon of December 4, the first of the other members of the column arrived, having completed the fourteen hundred–mile walk from Lake Albert. That night Stanley and Emin made short speeches at a banquet, after which Emin went into an adjoining room and managed to fall from the second story to the street below. Theories abounded as to why—too much alcohol, severe near-sightedness that led him to mistake a window for a balcony door, a suicide attempt. No one knows for sure to this day. Taken to the German hospital, he lay unconscious until the next morning. Parke stayed by his side, and within a few days he reported that Emin was feeling much better and wanting the other officers to come for a visit.[232]

Fairly detailed letters from Stanley to Mackinnon and Marston appeared in the papers during late November, and the information they contained prompted an outpouring of editorials full of praise. According to London's *Times*, "Hardly anything, even in the heroic annals of African exploration is on a par with Mr. STANLEY's march back from Yambuya."[233] Though expressing skepticism over calling it an "Emin Relief Expedition," the *St. James's Gazette,* still concluded,

> But apart from the geographical significance of the journey it is memorable as a magnificent victory of human courage over the resistance of nature. Neither famine or fever, neither marsh nor forest, neither the slackness of disheartened followers, nor the violence and treachery of countless enemies could turn this indomitable leader of men from doing what he had pledged his word that he could and would do.[234]

On December 6 a mixed flotilla set off for Zanzibar. Only 246 of the 703 who left the island in February 1887 had managed to make it back. A large, enthusiastic crowd welcomed them, and on December 11 all the survivors, Africans included, attended a banquet in their honor. The men also received bonuses from the *khedive,* Mackinnon, and Sultan Seyyid. Barghash had died on March 27, 1888. Congratulatory telegrams from dignitaries came by the score.[235] The Queen's read,

> My thoughts are often with you and your brave followers whose dangers and hardships are now at an end once more. I heartily congratulate all including the survivors of the gallant Zanzibarees who displayed such devotion and fortitude during your marvellous expedition trust Emin Pasha progresses favorably.[236]

Between lunches, dinners, and other activities, Stanley wrote a fifty-seven-page report for submission to London. It contained a biting indictment of ivory trading:

> Slave-trading becomes innocence when compared with ivory-raiding. The latter has become literally a most bloody business. Bands consisting of from 300 to 600 Manyema, armed with Enfield carbines, and officered by Zanzibari Arabs and Swahili, range over that immense forest land east of the upper Congo, destroying every district they discover, and driving such natives as escape the sudden fusillades into the deepest recesses of the forest.
> In the midst of a vast circle described by several days' march in every direction, the ivory-raiders select a locality wherein plantains are abundant, prepare a few acres for rice, and, while the crop is growing, sally out out by the twenties or forties to destroy every village within the circle and to hunt up the miserable natives who have escaped their first secret and sudden onslaughts. . . . Thus the land becomes thoroughly denuded of ivory, but unfortunately, also, it becomes a wild waste.[237]

To stop it, he wanted a ban placed on the importation of arms and ammunition and a railway built from Mombasa to Lake Victoria without delay.[238]

Stanley also filed a ten thousand–pound breach-of-contract lawsuit on behalf of the EPRC against Tippu Tip for causing the demise of the rear column by failing to provide porters in a timely fashion. Stanley said he took the action in the "interest of subscribers to the fund, and on behalf of those [the members of the expedition] who suffered by the breach of contract."[239] Both he and Bonny gave depositions. The court ruled that Tippu Tip must be present for the trial to go forward. Various factors, including a serious outbreak of dysentery in Tabora, delayed his arrival until July 20, 1891. He immediately hired a lawyer to file a countersuit over the failure by Stanley as the committee's representative to live up to the terms of the contract. Although the promised powder eventually reached Kisingitini, the caps never did. Most, in fact, had rotted aboard the *Madura*, and Tippu Tip wound up buying them from the Belgians. He also disputed the charge about porters. Given all the ambiguities surrounding the case, the counsels for both parties agreed to a dismissal, which formally came on October 2, 1891.[240] Tippu Tip and Stanley would never have their friendly get-together in London.

Stanley's host, Col. Euan Smith described him as looking "dreadfully *usé* and done up" when he arrived in Zanzibar and credited a couple of weeks of "rest and good living" with working "a wonderful change for the better in his appearance."[241] The HMS *Somali* ferried Stanley to Mombasa, where he boarded the *Katoria* for Suez on January 1, 1890. Parke, now recovered from a case of black water fever that nearly took his life, Mounteny-Jephson, Stairs, Nelson, and Bonny joined him, while Hoffman stayed in Mombasa. Despite everything, including the formal discharge, Stanley helped him land a job with the IBEAC. Hoffman raised the idea, feeling he needed time to get his "character up again." When that happened, he hoped to work for Stanley again.[242]

Emin's people had left without him on December 19. He would never see Egypt again, preferring to enter the service of German East Africa after recovering from his injuries. Whether dislike for Stanley, as some have suggested, played a significant role in this decision can't be determined. The position eventually took him back to Equatoria and a reunion with some of his old followers and to a death at the hands of slavers near Lubutu about one hundred miles southeast of Stanley Falls during October 1892.

Enroute to Aden, Stanley suffered a bout of depression. He badly wanted rest and relaxation, not all the engagements looming on the horizon. And second thoughts about the expedition began entering his mind. He wrote:

The gradually deepening impression that we have striven too hard for an object that has much deteriorated in value has subdued my spirits, and affected my health. I am subject to conflicting emotions of pity for Emin, pity for ourselves, pity for the waste of life, & efforts, & money in a worthless cause, & they often send me to bed sickened in mind & body.[243]

The lone Somali survivor departed at Aden, and Stanley saw to it that the families of the others received the pay due them. At Suez, a large, cheering crowd awaited the *Katoria*'s arrival on January 13, 1890, and in the morning a special train whisked the Europeans off to Cairo, where a carriage waited its arrival to take Stanley to see the *khedive*. Unusually, it had been raining hard since the previous evening, turning the streets into torrents.

Sensing he would not be able to finish his still untitled book under the glare of London's spotlight, Stanley decided to stay in Cairo to write it. As in the past, he took quarters at the Shepheard's Hotel in the center of town. E. M. Merrick had been commissioned to do his portrait. During one of the

Stanley with his Emin Pasha Expedition officers in Cairo, February 1890. From left to right, Parke, Nelson, Stairs, and Mounteney-Jephson. *Courtesy of the Royal Museum of Central Africa*

sittings she heard him tell a Belgian reporter who had raised personal questions that "If people would only try and discover what Stanley has done and not who Stanley is, they would be saving themselves much time and trouble."[244] He probably should have added that they would have also saved him "much time and trouble."

When the Shepheard's proved to be too noisy and public a place for work, Stanley moved into a suite at the quieter, more elegant Hotel Villa Victoria on February 1. Most days involved feverish work from early morning until late at night, with only a secretary named Leonard Wilson allowed entry to the room. In addition to the book, Stanley had to attend to a massive correspondence. One instance involved a letter from Leopold marked "private." The king thanked him and wished he could be at the antislavery conference taking place in Brussels. He also hinted at future plans, saying, "you may feel assured of one thing & that is, that I will never submit to you any plan not entirely worthy of your acceptance & efforts . . . I do not want to add to the chapters of your glorious history, new chapters of lesser magnitude." Then came a request to see if "good soldiers can be engaged in Egypt, for what price and in what number." Stanley called it a typical Leopold letter, one full of compliments but also containing the "usual want of feeling for employees," as the request for a favor indicated.[245]

Toward the end of February, Stanley wrote Mackinnon, saying, "I shall have one more month to finish up or die."[246] The writing took seven weeks, a period during which Stanley said sometimes the pen "would fairly race over the paper at the rate of nine folios an hour, [while] at other time it could scarcely frame 100 words." The result was a 903-page manuscript titled *In Darkest Africa or the Quest, Rescue, and Retreat of Emin Governor of Equatoria*. Stanley had considered some fifty others before settling on this one as most appropriate. According to Marston, "probably no book has ever been more eagerly looked for in every part of the civilized world." In the United States, others tried to capitalize on the excitement by rushing bogus books into print. As a warning, Stanley sent a "Notice to the American Public" about being careful to avoid forgeries.[247] With nothing else to keep him in Cairo, he packed his bags for the trip home.

CHAPTER 8

Winding Down

YEARS OF HAPPINESS AND PAIN

With Parke at his side, Stanley left Cairo on April 7 in a state of near exhaustion, knowing that the weeks ahead offered little time to rest. A meeting with Mackinnon, then in Cannes vacationing aboard his yacht *Cornelia,* was the first item of business. German advances in East Africa dominated their conversations, with the current effort by Carl Peters to reach Buganda a cause of special concern. Originally conceived as a German Emin Pasha expedition when it looked as though Stanley's attempt had failed, the many delays caused by conditions in Germany and East Africa resulted in a change of plans. Strategic and unclaimed, Buganda became the new objective. Should Peters make it there and convince Mwanga to sign a treaty of protection, the IBEAC might well be doomed. Next came a rather cool reception for Stanley in Paris. The French press had never gotten over his criticisms of de Brazza, and continuing loyalty to British interests in Africa added to their dislike of him.

Things warmed up considerably in Belgium. A special train met Stanley at the border, and an honor guard and royal carriage waited at the Brussels station to take him past a large throng of cheering admirers to the most sumptuous apartment in the palace. The cream of high society attended honorary receptions. Mounteney-Jephson, Nelson, and Stairs joined Parke to share in the festivities.

Business, not celebration, was the main reason for the visit, and over the course of the next week Leopold and Stanley met regularly to discuss a range of issues related to the Free State. Once again we have to depend on Stanley to tell us what transpired. The narrative is contained in the final volume of the three journals purported to be the "true" history of the Congo.[1] The account starts with the setting—the reception room with a large marble desk over which the two men had faced one another many times previously, the last more than three years earlier. Nothing had changed since then, Stanley noted, except both of them. The king's formerly brown beard was now "white from ear to ear," and his own hair gone from gray to white. Leopold started by asking about the forest. Stanley replied that it could continue to supply ivory, provided an elephant sanctuary was established, and both gums and rubber-bearing vines existed in plentitude. Timber, though, constituted the forest's real value, according to him. Once sawmills were built, hardwoods could be shipped to Europe and enough timber cut to meet much of the Free State's needs. Except for the pygmies, he thought that all the people could be brought around to serve as laborers. "Good roads through the forest and gentle treatment of the natives" would ensure this happened.

When the subject of Emin came up, Stanley went on at length about the man's deficiencies. Rather than the person advertised, he found him to be "a little, pettish, conceited capricious, tiresome fellow, who was only a collector of bugs & beetles, and who had amused himself at everybody's expense by writing fictitious tales of adventures, discoveries, and heroic doings that had no foundation except in intentions that were never realized." Stanley said he learned in Cairo that a lawsuit by the Turkish woman Emin abandoned explained why he refused to go home. Showing up would have cost him money and pride. Maybe the fall in Bagamoyo hadn't been an accident after all, he speculated.

Leopold asked if any of Emin's former troops might be of value to the Free State, as he wanted to send an expedition to Lake Albert, using the Uele River as the route. They could be useful, Stanley said, if carefully supervised by Belgian officers. The troublemakers within their ranks needed weeding out. He advised the king that the Arabs and Waswahili needed attention first. There should be no delay in dealing with them and no stoppage "until every Arab settlement between Stanley Falls & the Tanganyika is in ashes," Stanley stressed. To reinforce the point he added, "Every man they kill, every woman & child they kidnap from their homes, every village they burn is a pecuniary loss to the State." He was referring, of course, to the labor and markets lost. With the slavers gone, the king could then safely look to expand toward Lake Albert.

The railway came up for brief discussion. The king told Stanley that his writings about the Congo and his current visit had generated great enthusiasm within the country for one to be built. Construction began the following year, although with Belgians at the helm, thanks to the fund-raising efforts of Albert Thys, one of the men Stanley had suggested as his replacement in the Congo.

Next Leopold revealed the "great mission" he had alluded to earlier. It involved leading an army to take Khartoum. Although he was startled by the suggestion, Stanley said that with twelve thousand white troops it could be done. The king, however, wanted to use Africans from the Free State, which caused Stanley to launch into a long discussion about how many would be needed, the time required to recruit and train them, and the costs involved. It all added up to the goal being, in reality, impossible to attain. Furthermore, the thought of working for Leopold didn't have much appeal at the moment. As he told Mackinnon in January, "I do not feel like forgiving him for imprisoning me in my room for two years waiting orders, when I might have had good health & made a fortune by some other work. I am not going to place myself in that predicament again for any king."[2] Leopold thanked Stanley for his remarks and promised not to do anything "rashly."

The last thing they talked about was where put the boundary between the Free State and the IBEAC spheres of influence. Stanley had already agreed with Mackinnon about the Semliki River being used as a divide, which would leave the entire Ruwenzori region to the company. Discussions continued afterward, laying the groundwork for an agreement between Mackinnon and Leopold on May 24, with Stanley signing on behalf of the Free State. The line ran through the middle of Lake Albert, followed the Semliki to Albert Edward to divide it in half, and ended at the northern tip of Lake Tanganyika.[3] Mackinnon couldn't have been more pleased, as the agreement provided a corridor for the Cape-to-Cairo route to which he had become committed as much as Cecil Rhodes. Both men envisioned the map of Africa colored red from end to end. Things didn't work out as intended, for despite tacit approval from Prime Minister Salisbury, Her Majesty's Government never ratified the agreement.

Stanley spent one afternoon addressing the antislavery conference. His main point centered on the arms trade. If it continued, he told delegates, "tribes who have hitherto warred against each other with bow & spear will now proceed with rifles, & they will end in mutual annihilation." The European powers must pass laws against importation and then actively work to prevent the trade and thereby "starve out the Arabs & others who lived upon warfare & plunder." This is another example of Stanley's conflation of humanitarianism with free, "legitimate" trade. The former simply couldn't happen without the latter. The conference, which lasted from November 18,

1889 to July 2, 1890, produced more than one hundred articles designed to remove Africa's slavery burden forever. Most resulted from compromises and lacked teeth. In a separate document, Leopold got an agreement to allow the Free State to impose duties to raise money for antislavery activities. Shortly afterward, the king also received a twenty-five million franc interest free loan from the Belgian government for agreeing to put in his will the right of the country to take over the Free State after ten years if it wished to. Each year costs were exceeding revenues, and he needed every possible franc to keep the enterprise going.

From Brussels Stanley went to Ostend to catch a boat for Dover. Parke, Nelson, and Mounteney-Jephson went with him. Chaos greeted their arrival on April 26. So pushy did the crowd become that a phalanx of constables was needed to make sure they reached the train waiting to take them to Victoria Station uninjured. The large gathering of friends and admirers there proved sedate by comparison.

The days ahead included two major events. First came a reception at St. James's Hall on May 2, attended by members of the Royal Family and other dignitaries. Three days later, the Royal Geographical Society put on a huge gala. Some 6,200 people, including the Prince and Princess of Wales, the Duke of Edinburgh, important people from all walks of life, and representatives from major geographical societies, packed Albert Hall. Greeted by loud, sustained cheering, Stanley delivered a speech titled "Geographical Results of the Emin Pasha Relief Expedition" that dealt mostly with the Ituri forest, Ruwenzori, and ethnographic observations and not Emin.[4] He claimed that treaties signed on the return from Lake Albert had secured a large swath of territory for the IBEAC and Britain. In fact, most of these were only oral understandings, and the six written documents he turned over to Mackinnon read more like memoranda of friendship than treaties. They thus carried little legal weight and were historically inconsequential.[5]

As an honor, the society created a Stanley Medal to record its

> sense of the skill and energy shown in his last journey across Africa, and of the importance of the geographical results obtained in the linking of the old Equatorial Province of Egypt and the territories of the Congo State, the discovery of the new source of the Nile, the restoration to their true place in maps of the legendary snow-capped Mountains of the Moon, and the enlargement of the Victoria Nyanza by a new bay.[6]

Stanley would receive a gold version, with bronze ones going to the officers. The surviving Zanzibaris were to be sent silver stars. The next day included dinner with Queen Victoria in Windsor Castle, and during a speech afterward Stanley tried to rally support for East Africa by telling the gathering "that the part of the country he had explored was very healthy, and would be a splendid place for emigration."[7]

To express its gratitude, the Relief Committee gave the officers honoraria. Stairs, Parke, Mounteney-Jephson, and Nelson each received four hundred pounds sterling and Bonny two hundred. Mounteney-Jephson got an additional 105 to reimburse his passage to the Congo and return from Zanzibar.[8]

The spotlight never seemed to dim. As one observer noted, "Stanley was the hero of the hour, and his name was on every tongue."[9] People could buy a maze game to find Emin, and poems were written to commemorate Stanley's accomplishments. A "welcome home" verse set to music graced a banquet held by the London Chamber of Commerce on May 21, and earlier the London *Herald* held a contest that generated an enthusiastic response, including a poem from a nine-year-old called Bluebell:

> Hail! Traveller, hail!
> The "Herald" come before thee,
> His silver trumpet echoes o'er the sea,
> "Stanley is coming home."
> Is coming home in glory,
>   And in Victory.
> Three years he looked through darkness unto Light
> Hoping for Liberty, longing for the Right,
> And like a monarch now he reigns o'er Africa's sands,
> "Emin is rescued from the Arabs' hands."
> He disappeared in darkness—no tidings of him more—
> Like Gordon, England thought him dead on Africa's lonely shore.
> Full half his followers who trod the forest path
> Were killed by fever, swept away by Death;
> Who, with a sickle in his bony hand,
> Called many a soldier from the faithful band.
> But still he stood as brave and bold
> (In Stanley's bosom is a heart of fire-tried gold).
> He longed to set his foot again on England's home and land.
> But first to rescue Emin from the Arab band.
> He cheered his brave men on, and on they went—
> From God and Queen Victoria on noble mission sent.
> At length they came to where the Pasha lay,
> Circled by savage warriors night and day.
> Full many a danger run, full many a hard-fought fight,
> Gave Emin back to liberty; gone was the gloomy night!

They locked their hands together—
Bound by no earthly tie—
And to the perils of that Unknown land
Said for a time "Good-bye."
Crown him the world's own traveller
With roses without a thorn.
Welcome the noble hero;
Hail Stanley! Welcome Home![10]

Edinburgh, Oxford, Cambridge, and Durham awarded him honorary degrees, and since March 24, the *Stanley and African Exhibition* had been running at the Victoria Gallery in London. It didn't feature Stanley so much as use his name and picture on the catalog's cover as enticements. Once inside, visitors could walk through five sections of displays of African material culture, discovery since Ptolemy, portraits of prominent explorers, missionaries, and other Europeans involved with the continent, the slave trade, and an array of pictures and photographs. There were even two young orphan boys in African regalia on display. Formed by a committee that included Mackinnon, Richard Burton, Samuel Baker, the RGS, the Anthropological Society, the CMS, the Colonial Service, and the Anti-Slavery Society, it conveyed a clear message that meshed well with Stanley's view that Africans needed Europeans to overcome the "dark" forces holding them back.[11]

Quite suddenly, Stanley's life took an unforeseen turn, one that played a major role in making the Emin Pasha expedition his last. Regretting her earlier decision, Dolly sought to rekindle their romance. She started by sending a congratulatory note to Stanley in Cairo, which elicited a polite thank-you from him. Encouraged by this small gesture, when he reached London, Dolly asked him to come see her "the very day after you receive the letter."[12] When Stanley failed to reply or show up, she wrote essentially the same letter two days later, proclaiming, "I do not want to see you for the first time at some crowded evening party, some great Banquet or public meeting. No, I want to see you *here*, at home."[13] Contrary to Dolly's wishes, their first meeting took place in public, the gathering at St. James's, and Stanley agreed to see her the following day. When he didn't follow through, she tried again, this time saying, "I only want to say goodbye to you, so do not mind coming. I also want to give you back something you gave to me. . . . I don't want to make anything different. I only want to see you quietly and then Bula Matari . . . good bye."[14]

In the meantime, Stanley had written her, saying "I must decline the pleasure of approaching you." He thought she looked regal at the party and said it was the picture he wished to retain of her.[15] Dolly responded by apologizing for her actions in 1886:

> When you were gone—when you were out of reach—I slowly realized what you had become to me, and then a great anguish filled me. I then made myself a vow that I would train myself, strive to become wiser, stronger, better, gentler. And then when you came back I would see you, and tell you quite simply, and say "Truly I never cared for another but you. I didn't not know when you wrote to me, for till you wrote the possibility of your caring for me had never even occurred to me, but at that time I was not worthy of your love— now I believe I am. Let me help you and take care of you and be everything in this world to you." But there was vanity in this, for it presupposed you still caring for me. Well dear Mr. Stanley, goodbye, God keep and bless you for ever. I will never again pass across or disturb your life.[16]

He obviously did care and, after chastising her for the rejection, urged her to meet him right away, claiming she represented to him "the highest grandeur of womanhood."[17] Events moved rapidly, and a week later they became engaged. Dolly was in seventh heaven. She told Mackinnon, "I am so unspeakably happy. I am to be Stanley's wife. My dear Sir William I don't know how to express my joy. I will make him gloriously happy, and God will bless us and keep us."[18] For Stanley, the long quest for a wife had finally ended. As he later remarked,

> I have had nine affairs of the heart. Each might have become full grown love, but there was a drawback to each. One was disdainful through excess of pride, another did not know English, another was too short, and in the future certain to become fat if she lived, another was married, another was a born coquette, another lacked refinement, another was too plain, and was too gushing.
> The one finally I chose was perfection, she was accomplished, amiable, wise, good, with loveliness and grace sufficient to enhance each natural gift, and gentlewoman writ all over her form and manner.[19]

On the day of the engagement, Stanley gave an address to the London Guildhall in which he lashed out at Quaker criticisms of the IBEAC for making profits from goods carried by slaves. Noting that the company had contributed twelve hundred pounds for the release of three thousand slaves, he asked the audience, "Have the Quakers of England contributed 12,000 pence to rescuing their dark relatives from slavery?" It was, of course, a rhetorical question, to which he immediately answered,

No: but if you and I proceed to their mansions in the north of England I could show you visible and substantial proofs that the purchases they annually make of ivory-handled table knives and forks, tooth, clothes, and hair brushes, ivory paper-cutters, ivory-backed hand mirrors, penholders, billiard balls, and such trifles have contributed more than anything else to enrich the Arabs, who have obtained the raw ivory by murder of countless thousands and devastation of the most fertile regions on the face of the globe.

A passionate defense of capitalists of the so-called philanthropic stripe followed. "Their purpose," he said,

is to create roads into the fastness of cruelty and ignorance, to extinguish the devastating slave trade, to arrest the Arab kidnapper and man-destroyer by making his trade an impossibility and his profession wholly unnecessary, and substitute railways for slave caravans, and lawful barter in lieu of robbery; to carry the merchant and the missionary securely and safely into the heart of the wasted regions, to redeem those still surviving from all fear of death and woe.[20]

Stanley's dislike for Quakers never subsided. In later jotting, he noted,

I would as soon be called a devil as a quaker. If I were called the first I would be supposed to be constantly wicked, professing evil and doing it, but to be called a Quaker means that under guise of righteousness and peace I can slander and villify my neighbours under cover of a reputation for being humane and peaceful.[21]

Because the gold medal hadn't been ready for the May 5 gala, the RGS held another function on July 3 to present it. Grand visions of empire stirred the crowd. The chair, Mountstuart E. Grant Duff, singled out Stanley's observations about the uplands of equatorial Africa as particularly noteworthy. They have, he remarked, "given us a hope" about districts having been found "where some of our descendants may find one more much-needed refuge from the overcrowding which seems likely to be the sad fate of the United States when she has 250 millions, and of these islands when they have 50 millions of inhabitants." Stanley urged further investigation of the Congo watershed to "see what can be made of the British possessions in that part of Africa." The extent to which he and the society had healed their differences and shared common political and social objectives is revealed by his telling its members that upon meeting with them next time, "I shall then hope to repeat the most amiable words which I have delivered this evening. They are full of love towards every member of the Geographical Society, which I hope may live in itself and a thousand branches growing out of it."[22]

Adding to the moment, *In Darkest Africa* reached the bookstores on June 28, and within just a few weeks 150,000 copies were sold, bearing out Marston's earlier assessment about people waiting in "eager anticipation" for it to appear. Few came away disappointed, and some, like the reviewer for the *Edinburgh Review,* were ecstatic in their praise. "Taken as a whole," the writer proclaimed, "there is nothing in the narratives of ancient and modern travel which surpasses it in courage, in perseverance, and in resource under circumstances the most wild and exceptional ever encountered by man." He also praised Stanley's literary ability, noting that "no traveller has ever described his wanderings and adventures in a more perspicuous narrative or in a captivating style."[23] Although calling most of the book journalistic in nature, the reviewer for the *Saturday Review* thought the parts dealing with the forest, pygmies, and the Ruwenzori region of special merit and deserved "preservation permanently" on their own. He also said that "it has been Mr. STANLEY'S good fortune and his good deed, at the very nick of time, at once to stir the English people up to demand, and to give English statesmen reason to insist, that no other nation shall enter into the fruit of these English labours."[24] His enthusiasm proved to be premature.

Stanley was paying a price for all the activity. "Those who have had the opportunity of seeing him at close quarters," a reporter observed, "are struck by the wearied expression on his features; they wear a pathetic appealing look which seems to ask for a slight respite from this interminable round of gaiety [!]"[25] He didn't get the respite, and just two days before the wedding, on Saturday, July 12, Stanley experienced another severe attack of gastritis. It caused him to miss a bachelor party planned by his Emin expedition colleagues and threatened the wedding. Round-the-clock care by Parke, however, allowed him to muster enough strength to show up at Westminster Abbey on time. One in attendance remembered Stanley looking like "almost a dying man," and without a chair to sit in occasionally, he probably wouldn't have made it through the ceremony.[26]

Crowds waited outside the cathedral and lined the route the carriage took to the Tennant home in Richmond Terrace, where guests gathered for the reception. The bride and groom stayed only long enough to say thank-yous before catching a train for their honeymoon quarters at fashionable Melchet Court in the New Forest. Sali went along, and Mounteney-Jephson, Nelson, and Parke visited during subsequent days. While convalescing, Stanley declined an offer to become more actively involved in the affairs of the IBEAC, citing as reasons a long list of upcoming engagements and the fact that the company's charter prohibited him, as an American citizen, from taking an active role. Still, he told Mackinnon, "If there is any other way that I could help you, you know that you have but to indicate what it is. I am on furlough now and my ears are open."[27] The ears-open remark could have referred to an idea he'd revealed to Mackenzie in December 1889 about leading a large expedition to Uganda on behalf of the IBEAC.[28]

Nearly a month passed before Stanley recovered sufficiently to return to Richmond Terrace, from where on August 14 he and Dolly set off for a real honeymoon in Maloja, Switzerland. Just before leaving, Stanley wrote a "Prefatory Letter" to Mounteney-Jephson's book *Emin Pasha and the Rebellion at the Equator,* calling it a "true tale of work manfully and nobly done and so modestly told."[29] It didn't hurt that Mounteney-Jephson confirmed most of his own conclusions about Emin.

Not too long after reaching Maloja, Stanley's fever returned, causing him to ruminate, "It will be long before I am free of Africa's spell."[30] In fact, he would never be free of "Africa's spell," health-wise or otherwise.

On August 19 Sir Richard and Lady Isabel Burton paid a visit. Stanley called Burton a "grand man," whose penchant for cynicism kept him from being among England's "great ones." At the time he appeared "much broken in health" compared with when last they met in 1886.[31] Stanley wasn't wrong and Burton died at home in Trieste just two months later.

By the time September rolled around, Stanley felt well enough to begin preparing for a lecture tour in the United States and Canada scheduled to begin later in the year. Major James B. Pond, America's most successful booking agent and arranger of the 1886 tour, was in charge of arranging the itinerary. Meanwhile, Leopold wanted the couple to call at Ostend on the way back to London, but as Stanley informed Mackinnon, "We do not know as yet of any fixed period for returning. We propose not to hurry but to enjoy this holiday in a lazy fashion with no other purpose than to establish health." As for Africa, he went on to say, "I have no immediate purpose of going . . . as I am bound by my lecture tour, but there might come a time when having fulfilled all my engagements I might think European life too dreary to be endured."[32] Stanley knew, however, that any future trip to Africa would meet with Dolly's strong disapproval, as the very thought of such a thing made her, he said, "shiver." Although they did stop at Ostend to see Leopold, apparently nothing about going to Africa came up during four days of socializing. Stanley enjoyed the vacation, and by the time they returned home on October 8, he recorded being "much improved."[33]

Until this point in time, the most serious criticisms of the Emin expedition centered on Stanley's relationships with slavers, most notably Tippu

Tip, and reports of slavery being sanctioned in the Free State. The latter had been sparked by an anonymous letter noting "that some of the Congo Free State officials, while professing to put down slavery, have become allies and . . . employers of men who trade in slaves."[34] As before, concerns were also sometimes voiced about Stanley's methods. As one reviewer of *In Darkest Africa* put it,

> The wondrous success which has attended his career has made him intolerant of failure, and perhaps incapable of judging of his own contributions towards it. Taking his own narrative and his own exposition of his feelings, we are obliged to recognise a relentlessness—we may say ruthlessness—of purpose underlying his plans, which can scarcely fail to damp the enthusiasm that his courage, endurance, and resource so freely kindle.[35]

Of lesser note, Stanley's handling of Emin didn't sit well with many Germans, and in Britain Felkin defended the pasha in a letter published in the London *Times* of February 11, 1890.

As fall rolled around, concerns over what had happened to the rear column, especially its officers, started grabbing attention. Stanley's views first came to light in a letter to the Relief Committee dated August 28, 1888, in which he claimed instructions about moving out from Yambuya were "explicit" and by the officers' admissions "intelligible."[36] And while his official report cited Tippu Tip's failure to provide supplies as the primary cause of the rear column's fate, the "indifference manifested by Barttelot and the others to the letters of instruction" ranked second to it.[37] Walter Barttelot responded with a letter to the London *Times* claiming his brother had faithfully followed instructions given, and it was their imprecision that produced the disaster.[38] Not much more happened until *In Darkest Africa* came out. Stanley dedicated the book to Mackinnon and the "Prefatory Letter" addressed to him carried indictments of the officers for waiting so long to move out and for a decision to send some of Stanley's supplies down river. An earlier letter to Barttelot's father didn't help matters. After expressing his grief over the loss of a son, Stanley made a series of statements about what the major "ought" and "ought not" to have done.[39]

Seeking justice, the families of Barttelot and Jameson fought back, their principal weapons being books based on diaries and letters that sought to shift the blame to Stanley for giving unclear instructions and not coming back to Yambuya when promised. Barttelot's reached stores in October, and when asked by a reporter to respond to it. Stanley replied that he had published only half the truth out of respect for the family and that the real facts were "black." If known, they would show that the major had been killed, not murdered and, furthermore, that no jury in England would have found the man charged of the crime guilty.[40] In another venue, he remarked, "If I have refrained in my book . . . from giving the *whole* history of the Rear Column, it has been solely out of consideration for the feelings of others."[41] In the preface to the Jameson book that appeared a few weeks later, Jameson's wife accused Stanley of only being concerned with protecting his reputation and thus stroving "to destroy that of others who are powerless to reply."[42]

Letters to the editor and editorials flew fast and furious. Initially, most opinion went against Stanley. The *Saturday Review* accused him of using Barttelot as a "scapegoat" and "whipping boy," while a *Daily Telegraph* editorial commented that "he repeats the malignant gossip of anonymous and irresponsible natives" at the expense of the honour of English gentlemen."[43] According to some, Stanley's conduct demanded the formation of an official commission of inquiry. After months of basking in adulation, he now felt that "throughout the length of Great Britain no name is more reviled than mine."[44]

With revelation of the "black" facts, especially his supposed cruelty and hatred of Africans, Barttelot's name quickly supplanted Stanley's as the "reviled" one. A book by Troup served as a catalyst. Written in 1889, its publication was delayed by a court injunction upholding the terms of the contract he'd signed upon joining the expedition not to publish until after Stanley had. Troup described Barttelot as having "had an intense hatred of anything in the shape of a black man" and doing nothing to conceal it.[45] In a subsequent interview, he confirmed reports of the major's having ordered many beatings, including one of three hundred lashes on an interpreter named John Henry for stealing. A day later John Henry died.[46] Troup said he'd warned Barttelot many times about possible retaliation and cautioned him never to go into the bush alone.[47] Barttelot figured he might be shot some day.

Bonny told pretty much the same story, noting that every African in the camp hated Barttelot.[48] He also related how the major would stand in front of his boy Sudi and "show his big teeth, work himself into a rage, & overwhelm him with all the vile names he could think of." Then just prior to the shooting, Bonny claimed Barttelot kicked Sudi in the shin so severely that it opened a deep gash, which subsequently festered and made walking impossible. Despite being carried during the march from Bungangeta and receiving regular care from Stanley, Sudi died from the infection.[49] *In Darkest Africa* contained no accusations, merely the notation about Sudi having a wound

that exposed four inches of shinbone. According to Harry Johnston, Barttelot's brother should never have released the diaries, as they brought shame on
both the major and the country. He felt Stanley's only blame resided in making a bad decision about putting Barttelot in charge of Yambuya.[50] A *Speaker*
editorial agreed:

> To us it seems (and we confess that the conclusion is in direct opposition to
> our own expectations) that Mr. Stanley has come out of his squabble with
> Major Barttelot's family with flying colours. . . . He spoke when it had become
> absolutely necessary that he should do so, and not a day sooner. That the facts
> which he brought to light cast a cloud over the whole story of the Emin Pasha
> Relief Expedition, and have sent a thrill of horror and disgust throughout the
> civilized world cannot be denied; but his is not the shame of the story, nor
> can he be blamed for having at the last moment, and under the strongest com-
> pulsion, withdrawn the veil by which temporarily those hateful incidents had
> been hidden from public view.[51]

Publication of Jameson's journal rekindled earlier charges of his having
been involved in an instance of cannibalism. Farran opened what proved to
be a Pandora's box with comments made to the chief Free State officer at
Stanley Falls that were published in the September 18, 1888, edition of the
Standard. He claimed that while coming back from Kasongo with Tippu
Tip, Jameson got into a discussion about cannibalism, saying he'd heard of
but never seen it. Some Arabs supposedly replied that they would show it to
be true if he purchased a young slave girl for six cotton handkerchiefs and
turned her over to some "cannibals" in the camp. After that, Farran said,
they killed the girl and began carving her body into parts for eating, with
Jameson making six sketches of the events.[52] When word of Farran's allegation reached him, Jameson told Mackinnon that the killing did indeed happen but denied having any part in it. He said he came upon the act in
progress and later drew the sketches from memory.[53] The sketches haven't
survived, but Troup, Bonny, and Alphonse Vangele all claimed to have seen
them.

Jameson's journal words were more explicit. He noted that during a conversation on May 11, Tippu Tip related a story about cannibalism. Jameson
responded that people at home believed such accusations to be "traveller's
tales," after which

> Tippu Tib then said something to an Arab called Ali, seated next to him, who
> turned round to me and said "Give me a bit of cloth and see." I sent my boy
> for six handkerchiefs, thinking it was all a joke, and that they were not in

earnest, but presently a man appeared, leading a young girl about ten years old by the hand, and I then witnessed the most horribly sickening sight I am ever likely to see in my life. He plunged a knife quickly into her breast twice, and she fell on her face, turning over on her side. Three men then ran forward, and began to cut up the body of the girl, finally her head was cut off, and not a particle remained, each man taking his piece away down to the river to wash it. The most extraordinary thing was that the girl never uttered a sound, nor struggled until she fell. Until the last moment, I could not believe that they were in earnest. I have heard many stories of this kind since I have been in this country, but never could I believe them, and I never would have been such a beast to witness this, but I could not bring myself to believe that it was anything save a ruse to get money out of me, until the last moment.

The girl was a slave captured from a village close to this town, and the cannibals were Wacusu slaves, and natives of this place called Mclusi. When I went home I tried to make some small sketches of the scene while still fresh in my memory, not that it is ever likely to fade from it. No one here seemed to be in the least astonished at it.[54]

The incident faded into the background until Farran's story started to leak. The first hole occurred immediately upon his return to England when he told the army sergeant sent to meet him at the railway station that Jameson hadn't bought the girl and had come across her dismemberment by chance. As regards the earlier version, he blamed a missionary for it. Afraid of possible punishment, Farran said he wanted to talk with the Relief Committee to clear things up.[55] At the meeting, he confessed to lying, claiming he had done it out of hatred for Barttelot and Jameson, and then signed a retraction.[56] Later Farran performed another about-face during a visit with Stanley in Cairo. This time he said he was forced into the retraction under threat of losing the pay due him and proceeded to give an even more detailed account of what had happened in front of three witnesses.[57] Stanley initially dismissed all the talk about cannibalism as nothing more than "a sensational canard."[58] In Darkest Africa contained nothing about the incident, perhaps because Jameson's family had threatened to bring an injunction if it did. Upon being informed of their intention Stanley told de Winton,

What or who could have put that idea into their heads? Well now, a very little may make this case a serious one for the Jameson family, if they at all have any regard for his memory. To the Lawyers it will matter nothing of course, but the family as connected with Jameson and to Jameson's memory much. The very least thing will explode the whole secret which I have wished to keep down. You are yourself aware of what Assad Ferran had to say & what he did say I am firmly persuaded is true and can be proved at a very small expense.[59]

His words turned out to be prophetic, for in the end Jameson emerged as the villain, not Stanley.

No commission of inquiry was ever formed, although many felt that all the confusing and conflicting evidence required Stanley to step forth and clear things up. He didn't have to, for by the end of the year the issue had pretty much run its course. Yet a fourth book about the rear column, this one by Herbert Ward, made little impact.[60] He said little about Barttelot and Jameson, and like Troup, he wrote to clear his name from responsibility for acts detrimental to the column and Stanley. An editorial in the London *Times* best summarized feelings in Britain by this time. It called the whole affair "a story of failure, of sickness, of despondency, of barbarities, and severities which if necessary are a condemnation in themselves of the expedition, of which the Rear Column was an essential part, and if unnecessary are a disgrace to the English name."[61]

Those who still wanted to attack Stanley shifted attention to the conduct of the expedition. One labeled it as "filibustering" and mounted "in the mixed guise of commerce, religion, geography and Imperialism, under which names any and every atrocity is regarded as permissible."[62] Another wrote a book called *The Other Side of the Emin Pasha Relief Expedition* that brought into question virtually everything Stanley had done or said from the very beginning. At the end, the author asked, "Is it too much to hope that the civilized world will take some warning by the disasters and misdeeds of the Emin Pasha Relief Expedition, and never again allow so much mischief to be done in the name of philanthropy?"[63] The author of an article purporting to demonstrate that the expedition was by legal definition "piratical," concurred. He claimed,

> Neither philanthropists nor explorers ought to be allowed to engage in military ventures, no matter how laudable the object, without far greater care than marked the inception of the Emin expedition, particularly when such ventures are likely to be attended with loss of life, damage to property, and the presentation of civilization and Christianity in an odious and fearful light.[64]

The editor of the satirical *Punch* took Stanley to task on more than one occasion, not just in the magazine but in books as well. One had the not subtle title *A New Light Thrown Across the Keep It Quite Darkest Africa,* and he titled a chapter in another "Across the Keep-It-Dark Continent: or, How I Found Stanley."[65] Both parodied Stanley's style of writing, and in the fashion of *Punch* they contained numerous cartoons, many portraying Africans in ways that by today's standards would be considered racist. At the end of the day, though, such efforts produced few waves of any note. Stanley was back on top.

In the midst of the rear column fuss, Stanley left for the speaking tour of the United States and Canada, accompanied by Dolly, Jephson, and Sali. Rough seas and four electrical fires aboard the *Teutonic* hardly helped to soothe his jangled nerves. A packed house at the Metropolitan Opera house for the first talk on November 11, did, however. And in Boston, a special Pullman car with HENRY M. STANLEY painted on it waited to take the party on a tour of the continent. It cost the sponsors a rental fee of three thousand dollars per month and contained a dining salon, a bath, two water closets, a kitchen, a pantry, and an observatory. Highlights of the trip included chatting with Gen. William T. Sherman at a New York Press Club engagement; meeting Thomas Edison; having a look around New Orleans; and in Chicago bumping into one of the men from *Handels-Vennootschap*, who paid Stanley seventy-five pounds for fifty borrowed in 1879. A stop in Omaha triggered memories of his youthful fling with Annie Ward. He remembered her as "Clever, fascinating, mischievous Annie!"[66]

The speeches usually lasted about two hours. During most, Stanley hammered away at the failures of the rear column's officers, a favorite accusation being "One thing alone was wanting—the spirit to act and to persevere in their work."[67] He also sought to convince audiences of the "white man's burden" in Africa. While plying the theme of its inhabitants being children in need of European governance for "their own welfare," Stanley portrayed them as "robust courageous men," compared to "timid Hindoos or puny Australians," in an endeavor to show that the effort would yield substantial rewards. For their part, he emphasized that Europeans must show "moral superiority" and rule "in precisely the same spirit, with the same absence of caprice and anger, the same essential respect" as with their own citizens.[68] In general, he shied away from emphasizing the dramatic and sensational. As a reviewer in Chicago put it,

> The talk was a strong, steady flow of plain English, with few gestures and no striving after descriptive language. So plain and even was the speaker's voice that only the closest observers could detect any show of personal feeling in the whole narrative.[69]

It seems that only when Emin Pasha entered the discussion did Stanley let his feelings come to the fore. He would then become more aggressive and let his "cold disdain" for the man be known.[70]

Leopold asked for a favor during the trip. The Free State was costing

Stanley and Dolly together. *Courtesy of the Royal Museum of Central Africa.*

money rather than producing it, and he wanted Stanley to influence American opinion about the need to charge export duties. Only those on imports were allowed under the Berlin agreements. He put forth two arguments: that "Africa must pay some part of the expenses incurred to effect her deliverance from barbarians" (slave traders), and very high import duties the U.S. charged.[71] Stanley now knew for sure that the Free State wouldn't be run as free.

By the time the tour reached California, in mid-March 1891, Stanley had grown weary from the pace and the constant public gaze. He felt he couldn't go for a walk without people bothering him for interviews and autographs. At one point, he considered giving Sali a "switching" for having the audacity to order one hundred greeting cards with Saleh bin Othman (his proper name) printed on them, but he didn't since "this would be telegraphed to the world as 'Another Barbarity of Stanley.'"[72] As the following newspaper ad illustrates, parody and attempts by others to capitalize on his name also had to be endured:

> Stanley Finds His Shoes. The great African Explorer is fortunate as well as courageous. He not only discovered Emin Pasha and his lost rear guard, but he also discovered his lost pair of shoes which he bought of McBride & Garrett. The pair had all the good qualities of the shoes that are sold at our store, they are cheap, durable and perfect as to fit.[73]

The last lecture, in Nashville on April 5, brought the number to 110, for a tidy profit of thirteen thousand pounds. In Pond's mind, the tour "grew into the most successful lecture engagement ever made in the United States."[74] The houses were almost always packed. In Syracuse, New York, for example, three thousand people jammed a downtown theater on a chilly December night, making it the largest gathering the city had seen. A farewell banquet at the Lotos Club in New York City on April 11 marked the formal end, and four days later the party left for England.

One of the first things Stanley did after getting home was arrange for Sali's return to Zanzibar. This "closes the last experience," he remarked. "I shall have with black men in England" because "they all became spoiled by indiscriminate friends."[75] Stairs, then on his way to take up command of the Katanga Company expedition, looked after him. In return for guarantees such as putting two steamers on waterways, building several stations, establishing a police force, and working to end the slave trade, Leopold granted the company a twenty-year concession on mineral rights. Its international backers included Mackinnon, Kirk, and Cameron, among others. By this time, the king realized that the Congo Free State could no longer be a one-man show. Others were needed to ensure control of the huge territory and provide funds.

Some have attempted to question Stanley's regular employment of young boys, suggesting it had sexual connotations. As with the accusation about a slave mistress, there is no evidence to support it. Many travelers and explorers took boys along as personal servants, and, in most instances, it's probably not necessary to dig much deeper to explain the practice than that boys were more easily controlled than older males. They usually did as told.

Stanley took only a few weeks off before beginning a lecture tour of England, Scotland, and Wales. The fifty-five engagements that lasted through June didn't bring in much money, which he attributed to English promoters being less familiar with the business than their American counterparts. He did, though, enjoy the opportunity to speak freely without the likes of Bennett or Leopold looking over his shoulder. Before the tour ended, the Emin Pasha Relief Committee sent him a draft of its official report of the expedition. It cleared Barttelot of all charges and concluded that the evidence showed "fidelity to his orders as he and his officers understood them."[76] Stanley was furious and called the report "a condemnation of us who lived, & a defense of those who are dead."[77] After receiving his comments, the committee decided not to release it.

Badly in need of a rest, the Stanleys set off for Interlaken, Switzerland. He caught a cold almost immediately, while she developed a painful gum abscess. A cool, rainy spell made the start of their vacation even less pleasant, as did the arrival of a Paris *Herald* reporter who'd been sent to inquire into rumors about their marital troubles. Bennett could well have been the source. Each independently said that they were happy together, and the reporter went off relieved that Stanley didn't explode at the questioning.[78] Gradually, health and weather improved to the point that on July 25 they went hiking. During an episode of so-called skylarking with a ten-year-old local boy Leo, Stanley fell and broke his fibula. Back at the hotel, the town doctor set the bone, put a cast on, and told Stanley to stay in bed for three weeks. Stanley later referred to the time as "a blessing in disguise." His health improved under the tender loving care provided by Dolly, and so did his state of mind, for he felt "morally bettered by absence from all bitterness" regarding past events.[79] Letting go was never easy for him.

They left Switzerland for home on August 24, with another speaking tour, this time to Australia and New Zealand, on the horizon. The week before the scheduled departure, Stanley and Mounteney-Jephson went to see Leopold. At one point, the king asked Stanley if he wanted to go back to the

Congo after returning from Australia and fully regaining his health. Stanley replied, "We shall see Your Majesty," to which Leopold reportedly said, " 'I have a big task on hand for you when you are ready.' "[80] He doesn't seem to have revealed precisely what this was. It may have been Stanley's hoped-for military campaign against the Arabs, which began the next year and by 1894 had removed them as serious contenders for Congo supremacy.[81] Tippu Tip never returned to the Congo, preferring a comfortable retirement in Zanzibar. He died in June 1905.

Dolly and her mother accompanied Stanley to Australia. An accident on the train taking them to Brindisi got the trip off to an inauspicious start. Fortunately, no one was injured, and they arrived in time to catch the October 12 sailing of the *Acadia.* Stanley hated the nearly monthlong voyage aboard a ship packed with seven hundred passengers, including a rowdy cricket team. On several occasions, valuables mysteriously disappeared, never to be found. The sight of Melbourne on November 10 brought a sigh of relief. Stanley gave thirty-one lectures in various cities, with Emin, the forest, pygmies, and the importance of railways to Africa's development the major topics. When trains came to Africa, it would, he predicted, "Then be goodbye to the old fetishes, which have kept its population in bondage."[82]

In Brisbane, Stanley wrote to Mackinnon cautioning once again about getting involved in Uganda before the government agreed to help finance a railway. He advised prudence because "Everyday an accident might occur making everything collapse."[83] More lectures followed in New Zealand, before Stanley returned to Melbourne via Hobart, Tasmania, for appearances that brought the total to eighty.

In many ways the most interesting thing about the trip for Stanley involved chance encounters with acquaintances or people who knew them. They included Mackay's brother, who'd served as a pallbearer at Livingstone's funeral; a fellow student of Parke's; a woman acquainted with Mounteney-Jephson; someone Stanley had met in Constantinople in 1866; Captain Webb and his two daughters; and even William Warren, the telegraph operator from Suez. A difficult moment came during a meeting with Edward Owens's widow and children. Stanley described the event as cold

> because the horrible craze of rushing to print with everything that affects me, compels me to cultivate a repression of self so rigid that no one should know of a certain what I feel. Yet what a number of questions almost forced themselves out of me. Poor cousins. I stretch my hands to you all the same, and were we anywhere beyond reach of newspapers my heart would go out to you with all affection.[84]

On the other hand, a get-together with George Grey, the former governor of New Zealand and the Cape Colony, proved an uplifting experience. Grey allowed him to read some private letters from Livingstone. For Stanley, they "breathed of work, loyalty of soul, human duties, imperial objects, & moral obligations." Grey was also impressed. "It is so elevating," Stanley said, "to see a man who is not tainted with meanness & pettiness with whom one can talk as to a father confessor without fear of finding it in the newspapers of the next day. . . . There are many such as he in the world no doubt, but it is only by a rare chance we meet them."[85]

Counting the time at sea, the antipodean trip consumed 191 days and covered thirty thousand miles before the ship docked at Brindisi on April 15. Anxious to get home, the threesome reached London just in time for Easter Sunday two days later. In May Stanley became a British citizen again in order to stand for Parliament in North Lambeth as a Liberal-Unionist strongly opposed to Irish home rule. It was Dorothy's idea: She thought the House of Commons would be "an outlet for his pent-up energy."[86] He however had his doubts and campaigned half-heartedly. Despite this, the July election resulted in a 2,524- to 2,394-vote loss.

Social engagements and speaking and writing about Africa took up much of the rest of the summer. Uganda and the necessity of the British government's support for the activities of the IBEAC continued to be Stanley's favorite themes. Peters had gotten a protection agreement out of Mwanga, but the Treaty of Heligoland agreed to by Britain and Germany on July 1, 1890, made it null and void, leaving the area open for company action.[87] He pressed on with his efforts to get British support for the railway project, stressing that without it the IBEAC wouldn't be able to operate in the country. At stake were the lives of thousands of Christians and the fates of weaker peoples, who might fall victim to slavers again. Furthermore, the railway would require iron and steel from Wales and the opportunity to export numerous other manufactured items like hoes and knives. Stanley said Uganda could supply cotton, sugar, tea, and meat in exchange for products imported from elsewhere. Finally, he warned that the French might eventually step in if the British failed to.[88] Still, when Mackinnon approached him about becoming the company's administrator in Mombasa, he said no, citing a pledge to run for Parliament in the next election.[89]

Stanley also continued to plug for Leopold and the Free State when the chance arose. In one venue he observed that "In time to come the regenerated peoples of central Africa will point to the acts of the Berlin Conference as their charters of freedom from the civilized world."[90] That time has yet to come, and it's doubtful Central Africans will ever view the charters in this light.

On January 1, 1893, Stanley started writing his autobiography. He also produced a preface to Parke's *Guide to Health in Africa*, praising the doctor as "the cleverest of his profession that has been in Equatorial Africa." Because the government ignored him, justice required that he be given "something distinctive."[91] Parke appreciated Stanley's effort, remarking that the preface was "the very thing I wanted, and it should make the book pay if anything would."[92] It never did pay much, as Stanley would soon discover.

At the end of March, Stanley, Dolly, and her brother Charlie went to Italy for some sightseeing. The return trip involved the customary visit with Leopold. The king was worried about British reactions to the Free State's advances toward the Nile and wanted Stanley to disabuse the government of any underhanded intentions. Stanley however could do little to help. His contacts in high places were few and not always friendly. With no new journeys to speak about, he lacked a platform from which to rouse the public. To keep busy and feel useful, he put together a series of tales to create a book called *My Dark Companions and Their Strange Stories*. All the tales contained moral lessons, and several were reprinted in the magazine *Boys*. Just as with *My Kalulu*, Stanley sought to influence the thoughts and behaviors of the next generation. As Pond noted, he displayed "great fondness for children" and always had time for them. He would take the opportunity to advise them about "the importance of honesty and character as essential to success in life" and conclude "with some incident in his experience that is sure to make a lasting impression."[93]

Mackinnon's death in June came as a terrible shock. Reportedly caused by a lingering cold, Stanley credited it to "a depression of spirits created by a sense that his labors, great expenditures, & exercise of his influence on his friends in behalf of British East Africa were not appreciated."[94] Without Mackinnon, there could be no IBEAC. Although George Mackenzie and the board of directors tried to keep it afloat, the company came to an end in July of 1895, having accomplished almost nothing in its seven years of operation.[95]

Then during a tour of Ireland, Stanley learned of Parke's sudden death at only thirty-five years of age on September 10. A visit to the grave in Dromond made his passing even more tragic, because it had happened in such a remote place. More troubling was learning that Parke had nearly gone broke supporting his mother, sisters, and brothers. Only enough remained to afford a hundred-pound insurance policy.[96] The many letters from the doctor carried no mention of financial needs, something Stanley regretted, as he and others, like Mackinnon, could have helped. The atmosphere caused him to note that "Except at Livingstone's funeral I do not think I have ever felt so depressed as I did in this house." He reflected that maybe Parke should have died in Africa, for there they "could have raised something to remind every traveller what a good soul had departed at the spot."[97] A little later, a committee formed to raise money for a monument to honor the "good soul." Stanley contributed the most and convinced others to subscribe. Leinster Lawn in Dublin was chosen as the site, and the unveiling took place on December 19, 1896.

Of the Emin expedition officers, only Mounteney-Jephson, Bonny, and Ward remained. Earlier, Africa had claimed Nelson and Stairs, the former succumbing to yellow fever in Kenya, and Stairs dying from black water fever at a small village near Lake Nyasa.

Stanley led a mostly sedentary life for the rest of the year. A seaside visit to Cromer in October proved especially pleasant. He loved the peace and quiet and remarked, "No Africa for me, if I can get such solitude in England!!"[98] It's clear from reading his diaries and notebooks that Stanley preferred being alone with his thoughts, which is why Africa appealed to him so much. The tent at night provided sanctuary, something hard to find in Europe and America. When informed of yet another death, that of Alexander Low Bruce, a member of the EPRC married to Agnes Livingstone, Stanley, clearly in a melancholy mood, lamented,

> I wonder, indeed, that I am still here—I, who, during thirty-five years, have been subjected to the evils of almost every climate, racked by over three hundred fevers, dosed with inconceivable quantity of medicine, shaken through every nerve by awful experiences, yet here I am! and Bruce, and Parke, and Mackinnon are gone; I write this today as sound, apparently, as when I started on my wanderings; but then a week hence, where shall I be?[99]

Most of 1894 was spent resting, giving an occasional speech, and writing a couple of articles for the magazine *The Youth's Companion*. One, called "Out of the Jaws of Death," recounted the adventure surrounding the canoe capsizing and rescue in 1876 and a second, "Blue-Coat Boy in Africa," dealt with a disagreement at Kinshasa and Swinburne's good work in smoothing things over. Overall, he still felt optimistic about tropical Africa's suitability for European settlers. They just had to get past the coastal lowlands:

> You all know that before you can suck the juice of an orange you must pierce the rind, that before you can get at the kernel of a filbert you must crack the nut, and before you can drink the milk of a coconut you must bore through the thick fibrous husk. It is just the same way with Africa. Before the ordinary

colonist will be able to reach the breezy and healthy highlands we must bridge over the moist and heated maritime region with a railway. It is these hot low-lands which encircle like a zone the heart of the continent that has caused the white man to be shy of Africa.[100]

And he continued to extol the virtues of Livingstone, claiming,

I know no hero with a nobler character that that which distinguished this man who brought to our notice & sympathy the great interior of Africa. Both mor-ally and physically he towered far above the average white traveller who goes to a new country to exploit it for its resources. He was exceptionally great in all those qualities we esteem as highest.[101]

Leopold once again sought Stanley's services. This time he wanted him to help find British officers to staff an expected lease from Britain of all of Bahr al Ghazal.[102] Stanley sent along a few names, including Bonny's, who was denied service due to poor health. French objections to the lease reduced the territory to a small muddy piece of land called the Lado Enclave, and later efforts to occupy a larger area along the Nile within Equatoria ended in disas-ter for Leopold's forces.

By now, Stanley's enthusiasm for the autobiography seems to have waned. There's little to go on to say why. In his journal he commented that the few pages he had written from time to time were "naturally detrimental to the style," and on a couple of occasions he told Marston that other requirements just didn't leave him enough time.[103] That seems doubtful in light of the fact that he found time to write a number of articles and speeches. A couple of other possibilities might come closer to the truth: All the recent deaths could have made the past more difficult for him to bear, and Stanley may have become tired of fabricating so much. There's an interesting notation in a file labeled as a "manuscript" of the autobiography, which reads,

To lie is considered mean, and it is no doubt a habit to be avoided by every self-respecting person. But the best of men & women are sometimes com-pelled to resort to lying to avoid a worse offense. On certain occasions I have had to lie to escape brutality, to prevent the sudden rupture of a pleasant inter-course, to defend myself against inquisitiveness, & stop impertinence.[104]

All that remains of Stanley's autobiographical efforts after 1862 are numerous typescripts and jottings regarding such topics as newspapers, religion, self, learning, love, and illusions, and various individuals.[105] Some of these Doro-thy appended to the *Autobiography*.

In comparison, 1895 turned out to be a much busier year. Marston convinced Stanley to put together his earlier news releases in a book titled *My Early Travels in America and Asia*. Being old news, it didn't generate much interest. Parliamentary elections were slated for July. Stanley would keep his promise to run again. He declared, however, his

> strict resolve never to ask for a vote, never to do any silly personal canvassing in high streets or in by-streets, never to address open air meetings . . . or put myself in any position where I can be baited like a bull in the ring. The honour of M. P. is not worth it.[106]

Nonetheless, he did campaign more enthusiastically and had a flier printed that, as last time, made preserving the union with Ireland his first priority. As for Africa, the flier echoed familiar themes—the suppression of slavery and the extension of legitimate trade. If Britain saw to its duties on the continent, then "that long day of her world-ingathering Empire" was not near completion but "only just begun."[107] This time Stanley came out a winner, garnering 2,878 votes to his opponent's 2,473.

Swearing-in ceremonies took place on August 12, and right from the start Stanley detested the stuffy atmosphere and innumerable speeches that had a tendency to go on past midnight. They explained to him "the pasty, House-of-Commons complexion" most members wore.[108] He also grew to dislike the many meetings with constituents the job required. Feeling the need for a vacation to do "a little civilized exploring," Stanley left on September 4 for a two-and-a-half-month-long cross-continent train trip of the United States and Canada. Dolly didn't go with him. She wanted a rest and the thought of many days of travel seemed unappealing. Besides, there was no one else to accompany Gertrude on her annual visit to St. Moritz. Being separated from Stanley didn't sit well with her, however. "I have a kind of feeling," she said, "that I alone can properly care for him—that he is safe whilst I am with him—then again, I don't *want* him to be happy and get on without me."[109] His sole traveling companion would be Hoffman, by now returned from stints with IBEAC and the Free State.

Stanley tried to keep his presence unknown by using S. M. Henry as an alias. He didn't want to be interviewed or asked to speak or attend social functions.[110] Given how many times his face had appeared in public, it was hard not to be spotted, and reports of his arrival were often carried in newspapers and journalists sometimes sought him out. He gave only one formal interview, to Julian Ralph of the New York *Journal*.[111] It was mostly about his impressions of America.

On the way back from the west coast, Stanley visited Little Rock and with the place where the Grays had crossed the Mississippi on their way to battlefields. Several days of walking around familiar grounds in New Orleans came next, and a stop at the farm in Maryland where he'd been given shelter provided another trip down memory lane. Time in Philadelphia and New York City consisted mostly of attending teas and dinners with American friends and acquaintances. Such an itinerary suggests that Stanley was trying to recall events to include in the autobiography, but his journal covering the period contains only a scattering of mostly fragmentary entries.

During the trip Stanley started collecting newspaper reports about U.S. and U.K. disagreements over the disputed border between Venezuela and British Guyana. In England, he passed them on to the manager of the London *Times* to demonstrate how strongly Americans felt about Venezuela's rightness in the matter. He hoped the press could do something to cool tempers, as it was not good to have such "irritants" come between the two countries that shared so much. Furthermore, he saw prosperity for both as dependent on maintaining the closest possible relationship, with the United Kingdom standing to lose more if anything should come between them. As he put it, "With the growth of the United States we shall grow, with their enrichment we shall also thrive. A reverse to them would be felt as a calamity to us."[112] Tensions escalated when President Grover Cleveland invoked the Monroe Doctrine in a presidential message on December 17, but cooler heads prevailed, and a treaty signed in June 1897 satisfied politicians on both sides of the Atlantic. It didn't, however, solve the issue of the border, which remains contested even now.[113]

Sometime earlier that year, Stanley signed on to be associate editor of *Illustrated Africa*, a United States–based Protestant missionary monthly that began publication in 1890 as *Africa News*. The brainchild of Reverend William Taylor, the "Bishop of Africa" to his followers, it had two basic objectives—to provide missionary news from around the continent and to raise money for Taylor's Africa Industrial Missions. Through them Taylor hoped to train young children in manual skills so that each mission station could be made self-sufficient. He described Stanley as "the highest authority on all African affairs" and clearly saw adding his name to the masthead as way to boost the publication's image and circulation.[114] Upon accepting the position, Stanley remarked,

> While I am not now thinking of making another journey to Africa, my heart is enlisted in the development of that continent, a work which I can help much better now than if I were on the ground. Africa is practically explored,

and the intelligence of its inhabitants is demonstrated. I think that Africa will never be another North American continent, but we must remember that it is only a short time since it has been penetrated by civilizing forces. When I was at Lake Victoria, eighteen years ago, there was not a missionary there; now there are forty thousand native Christians and two hundred churches. The natives are enthusiastic converts and would spend their last penny to acquire a bible. What we want now is to develop the country, not so much for the white man, but for the natives themselves.[115]

For the December 1895 edition Stanley wrote a short editorial called "How to Conquer the Continent" that emphasized the themes he'd been plugging for years—the importance of railways and Uganda's significance. As he told readers, trade would be enhanced if railways connected the continent's many rivers and lakes, while Uganda's value resided largely in its intelligent population, plus being a "strategic position for commerce and for the spread of Christianity."[116] Stanley produced only four more short pieces for Taylor, although he remained an associate editor through the publication's demise in 1898 under another title, *Illustrated Christian World*. In addition Stanley wrote an introduction to Taylor's *The Flaming Torch in Darkest Africa,* recommending the book "for the variety and fullness of information it contains, and the large hope it gives that preserving Christian labor is not in vain even in darkest Africa."[117] Flaming Torch was a widely used nickname for Taylor.

As the New Year approached, another part of Africa caught Stanley's attention, the south. The so-called Jameson Raid into the Transvaal from Rhodesia, purportedly to lift the yoke from British citizens living under Boer rule, provided the catalyst. Begun on December 27, 1895, the raid came to an ignominious end when its members surrendered less than a week later. When first apprised of Jameson's move, Stanley told a reporter, "it is our duty to drive him back quicker than he went in." A little later he remarked to Henry James that "under no circumstances could we profit by this raid however successful it might have been. . . . We are not yet fallen so low as to receive stolen property from a thief."[118]

The first months of 1896 went by slowly, with dinners and a few speeches, some in the House in support of imperialism, being Stanley's main activities.[119] Two days after leaving on May 22 for a vacation in Spain, he literally doubled over from severe stomach pains that a doctor diagnosed as resulting from liver congestion and gallstones. A few days' rest and a diet of milk and soda seemed to work, but a relapse occurred in Paris and Stanley returned to London on June 8 and went immediately to bed.

Just before he took sick, the Stanleys had begun talking about adopting a child. Dolly initially opposed the idea; however, his arguments in favor eventually won her over. According to accounts, while Stanley was still bedridden, a thirteen-month-old son of a former household governess whose husband had just died was brought to his side. Stanley said he looked into the boys eyes and "saw a soul which when matured will . . . fully repay by its development, all care and trouble on its account."[120] They'd found a son, and on October 21 he became Denzil Morton Stanley, the Denzil coming from a friend of Oliver Cromwell, to whom Dolly traced her ancestry. It would have been her name if she'd been a boy.

Recuperation went slowly, and Stanley did little for the rest of the year. He improved enough, however, to attend the opening of Parliament on January 19, 1897. Spring saw him visit Leopold twice to discuss matters in the Congo. Reports had been circulating about atrocities there, with one in particular drawing public ire. It involved a Belgian officer who supposedly flogged two women with a chicotte and then cut off their breasts. Stanley responded to inquiries from the press by saying he'd keep an open mind because "There is no more gossipy place in the world than a Congo trading station." Furthermore, he doubted Leopold was capable of employing such "a cruel villain."[121] Elsewhere Stanley praised the king, noting that without his efforts it might have taken half a century more before Europe awoke "to the value of Africa." As proof of progress, he listed forty-five steamers on the rivers, a rise in exports, growth of the European population, the building of a railway from Matadi to Stanley Pool, an end of intertribal wars, and no more Arab slavery.[122] Whatever problems existed resulted from the Congo's administration:

> The King of the Belgians has often desired me to go back to the Congo; but to go back, would be to see mistakes consummated, to be tortured daily by seeing the effects of an erring and ignorant policy. I would be tempted to re-constitute a great part of the governmental machine, and this would be to disturb a moral malaria injurious to the re-organizer. We have become used to call vast, deep layers of filth, "Augean stables": what shall we call years of stupid government, mischievous encroachment on the executive, years of unnecessary, unqualified officers, years of cumbersome administration, years of neglect at every station, years of confusion and waste in every office? These evils have become habitual, and to remove them would entail much worry and dislike, to hear them would set my nerves on edge, and cause illness.[123]

Many Congolese now referred to the state as Bula Matari, lending support to the contention that the name wasn't meant as a compliment to Stanley.

In better health than he had been for quite some time and feeling restless as a result, Stanley wanted something to do after Parliament adjourned. South Africa caught his attention again. It seemed "interesting politically" and from all accounts had a "divine climate." The chance for a visit came with an invitation from the Bulawayo Festivities Committee to join the celebration for the arrival of the Great Peninsular Railway. When Leopold heard about it, he asked Stanley to see if several hundred native troops could be recruited "to train as soldiers for the suppression of disorders in the state."[124] The so-called disorders were becoming ever more numerous in the face of forced labor for rubber extraction.[125] Stanley seems not to have bothered writing a reply.

With Hoffman along as traveling companion, he set off on October 9, 1897, aboard the SS *Norman*. The noise and cramped quarters aboard ship made Cape Town a welcome sight, even though he felt the city could be given lessons in accommodating visitors by "a third rate American town."[126] The suburbs, however, seemed "simply lovely" because of being situated at the base Table Mountain, and the climate didn't disappoint Stanley. It had, he said, "the quality of making old men young, and the consumptive strong."[127]

The train ride to Bulawayo lasted from October 31 to November 4 and provided Stanley with opportunities to make a number of observations about the land and peoples he saw en route. The Crown Colony of Bechuanaland struck him as having vast economic potential, more than the prairies of Nebraska, Kansas, and Colorado, once an abundant supply of water was made available. Then "lucky colonists" would be able to "enrich themselves faster than by labouring at gold mines."[128] At independence, Bechuanaland became Botswana, with most of its riches coming from mines, not colonists.

Bulawayo didn't make much of an impression on Stanley. He described it as a "straggling nondescript place . . . the skeleton of a town."[129] Nonetheless, the possibilities seemed considerable. Nearby lay coal fields, plus "stone, granite, sandstone, trachyte, the woods, minerals, gold, copper, lead, and iron, the enormous agricultural area."[130] Victoria Falls on the Zambezi River could provide power someday. The colonists produced mixed reactions from him. That they had accomplished much in a short amount of time, and without the violence of the American West, deserved praise. Yet Stanley thought most of them "dandies," and felt that "Honest blacks would be far preferable" for the country's future.[131]

The ceremonies concluded, Stanley went to Johannesburg to see the Transvaal's president, Paul Kruger. Their meeting lasted only 25 minutes, but this was long enough for Stanley to form a highly unfavorable opinion of the old man. He described him as a "Boer Machiavelli, astute and bigoted, obstinate as a mule, and remarkably opinionated, vain, and puffed up with power conferred on him, vindictive, covetous, and always a boer, which means a narrow-minded and obtuse provincial of the illiterate type."[132] Continuing this line of thought, he told Dolly, "There is no room in that brain for one grain of common-sense to be injected into it."[133] The *uitlanders*, as non-Afrikaners were called in the Transvaal, appeared to have little hope for equality while he remained in power. Stanley put at least part of the blame on them for disunity and lack of a plan to force Kruger's hand. If they could get him to react in some obviously hostile way, then maybe Britain would intervene on their behalf. Stanley admitted that he hadn't appreciated the gravity of the situation and concluded that the current "peace-at-any-price" approach must be abandoned. A commission should be tried first, but Britain must be prepared to fight. And if it should come to that, he concluded, "there will be much killing done, and *this will be entirely due to sentimentalists at home,*" if they didn't change their tune.[134]

Back in Cape Town, Stanley told a representative of *South Africa* that Cape Colony needed more English speakers to counter the Boers, who stayed on their farms and multiplied in vast numbers. He suggested making land allotments available to lure settlers. Australia might be a good place to find them, and better advertising could be done in Britain. Stanley definitely viewed Cape Colony as "white man's country." Natives would be "wanted" but in the capacities of "hewers of wood and the drawers of water."[135] That, of course, is pretty much what happened.

Stanley returned home just in time to celebrate the New Year, and with the holidays over, he continued pushing the southern Africa theme. Unless some balance of numbers was attained and British protection provided, he predicted the area would become a "Federated Republic of Boers, or a United South Africa of Dutchmen." It needed companies to encourage immigration and his feeling was that Cape Colony, Natal, Rhodesia, and Bechuanaland together had enough room for a half million new settlers at two hundred acres per family. And with them, commercial people and artisans were bound to follow. Although forty thousand troops might be enough to secure a British military victory, Stanley stressed that the country must first use "patient and wise diplomacy" to seek a solution to the crisis.[136] Regarding those currently on the ground in southern Africa, he singled out Cecil Rhodes for his "munificence" and "bold and successful projects for aggrandizing the empire."[137] Stanley didn't know him personally, and although they shared imperial visions, he clearly wouldn't have approved of Rhodes's lavish lifestyle or his later racist policies.

Stanley's long dreamed railway to Stanley Pool finally became a reality. As he told de Borchgrave,

> Looking back to 1878 all concerned or interested in the development of the region have great reason to rejoice that so much has been accomplished, but personally, I am more possessed with gratitude because of the greater courage the arrival of the railway at the Pool will give to every white worker within the State, and the greater stimulus which will be given to every capitalist in Belgium. It is a guarantee that the Belgians will not tire of the state which his Majesty has created, & that they will turn their efforts toward it—with faith & with affection.[138]

No mention was made of the nearly two thousand lives that were lost during construction. Assuming the Belgians remained active, he projected the country would support a quarter million Europeans and forty million Africans one hundred years hence.[139] The emigration of Europeans after 1960 meant a serious overestimation of their number, and he had underestimated the number of Africans by about ten million.

On August 15, 1898, during a trip to France, Stanley experienced the onset of another bout of gastritis that sent him to bed for six weeks. During his recovery, he concluded that the time had come "to seek my long desired rest" and decided to abandon "the asphyxiating atmosphere of the House of Commons" for retirement and the fresh air of the countryside.[140] Denzil also needed a better place to grow up, and the Stanleys started house hunting. They looked at more than fifty houses before putting down ten thousand pounds on the fifty-six-acre Furze Hill estate in Pirbright, Surrey. Moving day took place on June 7, 1899, after Stanley had paid the remaining nine thousand pounds due. In a reversal of his former practice of putting European names on African soil, Stanley gave African names to various parts of the property. A wood became the Aruwimi Forest, a stream the Congo, one field Wanyamwezi, and another Mazamboni.[141]

In spite of his poor health and all the activities associated with moving, Stanley found time and strength to write two more short articles about Africa for *The Youth's Companion* and a longer piece for the *North American Review* titled "The Origins of the Negro Race."[142] Mirroring his earlier thinking, he wrote that all people come from the same "Father."

Rather out of the blue, Queen Victoria bestowed the Knight Grand Cross of the Order of the Bath on Stanley, and Salisbury personally wrote to tell him the news. Election to the Athenaeum, London's most prestigious private club, followed. The bastard from a small town in Wales who once considered himself an American had made it into the top circles of the world's greatest city, he as Sir, and Dolly as Lady, Henry M. Stanley. Not everyone agreed, as illustrated by a letter reading, "One with you in Africa congratulates in reward of treachery, fraud & dents doing! That with a rich silly woman, is the price of the Yankee adventurer & years of lying, toadying & petting. Humbug and fraud!"[143] It was unsigned, although judging from the language, the writer must have been English.

Shortly afterward William Bonny died. Life after Emin Pasha had gone badly for him. His health had deteriorated, aided no doubt by an addiction to opium, and, as a result, he couldn't hold a job. Both Stanley and Mounteney-Jephson had tried to help him out but to no avail. Although angry at the world, Bonny continued to write Stanley to the last. He seemingly held no grudges against him.

Parliament reassembled on October 17 to debate the Boer War that had broken out a few days earlier. A correspondent from the London *Times* asked Stanley when he thought it would be over. Since the writer was expecting Stanley to predict a short conflict, his estimate of April or May came as a shock.[144] A greater shock was that the war didn't end until 1902. Stanley took the side of the war's supporters, and during a speech in November he lauded troops of the empire for fighting side by side and putting their lives on the line so "that Englishmen may be considered the equals of any other white men in the Transvaal."[145]

Pond suggested another U.S. tour to address the war. Stanley didn't respond directly, which, in essence, meant no. He did, however, say to Pond,

> The war itself and the small disasters we have met with are the penalties we pay for the belief we profess that all men can be persuaded by reason or soothed by sentiment. By all means profess as loudly as you may the very best of sentiments toward people with whom you desire to be on amicable terms, but don't forget that human beings are not angels or children, to be restrained by sentiment alone. If you have interests, no amount of sentiment will protect them, especially when they lie so temptingly close to another race. That is a paraphrase of the old saying: "pray to God, but keep your powder dry." We have prayed to God and the Boer, but in most reprehensible fashion we have forgotten all about the powder.[146]

Stanley's gastritis flared up again on February 2, 1900, for the tenth time since 1882. Seventeen doctors, including, again, William Jenner, tried their hands at treating him, but with little success. Only heavy doses of morphine kept the pain from being unbearable. At the urgings of her sister and Mark

Twain, a longtime friend of Stanley's, Dolly sought to relieve her husband's suffering through application of the famous Kellgren manual vibration, or massage therapy. The standard milk diet gave way to more substantial fare like bacon and eggs. By the end of the month, Stanley felt well enough to leave the bedroom for the first time since the gastritis struck.

When Parliament dissolved on November 5, 1900, Stanley heaved a sigh of relief, exclaiming that he had gained "liberty." In looking back at his brief political career, he claimed to have had "less influence than the man in the street" and lamented Parliament's way of doing things had not allowed him "to serve the Empire" and "advance Africa's interests" in ways he would have liked.[147] He had no heart for the job, so an admirer's earlier statement that should Stanley "enter the House of Commons, he would speedily be recognized as one of the first debaters of his time" never came to pass.[148]

For a while, Stanley continued to improve under Dolly's daily administration of the Kellgren massages. When told after a physical exam in July 1901 about having "a slight chance of living for 10 years," he thought his chances more than slight, noting, "My grandfathers both lived to over four score years."[149] The comment is further proof that he believed Rowlands to have been his father.

Stanley's last journal entry is dated December 19, 1901, and his final publication appeared in the 1902 edition of *The Fortnightly Review*. Titled "The New Aspirants for African Fame and What They Must Be," it proclaimed that "we have seen the last of the old style of pathfinders" and advocated the study of ethnography, anthropology, geology, geomorphology, and biology as ways of making noteworthy contributions. Henceforth, "He who has brought back the greatest store of knowledge and the richest fruits of his study" would win the "most favor from a discerning public." The coronation of Edward VII on August 9, 1902, turned out to be Stanley's final public appearance. For the most part, tasks at Furze Hill filled his days.

A happy Easter 1903 was followed by a stroke on April 17. Dolly said a cry awakened her, and hurrying to Stanley's room, she discovered him "without speech, his face drawn, and his body paralyzed on the left side."[150] The effects kept him bedridden for several months, during which time his speech slowly returned. By summer he was able to spend warm days sitting outdoors in a lawn chair, and in September he could stand and walk short distances with support.

The Stanleys spent most of the winter in London before returning home in time for Easter. Once again, April 17 turned out to be a bad day, as Stanley suffered an attack of pleurisy. Henry Wellcome, the American pharmaceutical magnate, visited regularly, just as he had the previous year. Stanley had taken along the new Burroughs Wellcome Medical Chest on the Emin Pasha expedition, and after meeting in 1890, the two men had formed a fast friendship.[151] Although unwell, Mounteney-Jephson stopped by one day for a visit. On occasion, Stanley felt somewhat better, but time and repeated illness had taken their tolls, and at 6 A.M. on May 10, 1904, Henry Morton Stanley's life came to an end.

Those sending condolences to Dolly included Mark Twain, Edward VII, George Goldie, Henry James, Auguste Rodin, Garnett Wolseley, Joseph Chamberlain, and King Leopold. One letter even came from de Brazza, via the Royal Geographical Society. Dolly assumed Stanley would be buried next to Livingstone in Westminster Abbey. The Abbey's Dean, Joseph Armitage Robinson, however, refused to allow it, without ever publicly explaining why. Dolly's pleadings and appeals from explorer E. H. Shackleton representing the Scottish Royal Geographical Society, Mounteney-Jephson on behalf of himself and the Livingstone family, and the American ambassador produced no more than a memorial service at the Abbey. Both Leopold and King Edward sent representatives to the service, with Mounteney-Jephson, Livingstone Bruce (the doctor's grandson), the Duke of Abercorn, Charles Lyell, George Goldie, Harry Johnston, J. Scott Keltie, and Henry Wellcome, who arranged the funeral, acting as pallbearers. Stanley's body was trans-

Stanley's funeral cortege. *Courtesy of the Royal Museum of Central Africa.*

ported to Pirbright for internment in the churchyard. The huge granite monolith marking the grave bears the simple inscription

HENRY MORTON
STANLEY
BULA MATARI
1841–1904
AFRICA.

Including Furze Hill, Stanley left an estate valued at 145,865 pounds, a tidy sum but not a fortune. His will stipulated that Jephson be given five hundred pounds and Hoffman three hundred.[152] He didn't forget loyalty.

In 1907 Dolly married Dr. Henry Curtis, sixteen years her junior. She lived until 1926, always calling herself Lady Stanley. Per request, Dolly was interred with Stanley in the Pirbright cemetery. Denzil died in 1959. He had no children by birth and adopted Richard to keep the Stanley name alive. Richard passed in 1986. His wife, Jane, survives along with their children, Jonathan, Henrietta, and William. Furze Hill was put up for sale in 2002, and the remaining memorabilia auctioned in September of that year putting the final seal on the life of John Rowlands cum Henry Morton Stanley.

CHAPTER 9

Summing Up

The Stanley Legacy

During the nineteenth century, especially the latter half, Africa was awash with travelers from Europe and America. They came in many stripes, ranging from serious explorers, to fortune hunters, thrill seekers, and big game hunters, to missionaries and others hell-bent on doing their ideas of good for God, country, and Africans. Most of them had little impact on the continent and its peoples beyond being part of the imperial process that culminated in colonial occupation. Even Livingstone left precious little behind, converts included. For the most part, he just wandered from place to place, jotted down observations and thoughts in notebooks, and sent letters to friends and the press. He wrote only two books. *Missionary Travels and Researches in South Africa* (1857) was widely read and played an important role in shaping ideas about Africa. Only later would the book's inaccuracies and omissions be revealed, leading one biographer to characterize it as "essentially a propaganda vehicle and a *tour de force* in the art of covering up."[1] *Narrative of an Expedition to the Zambezi and Its Tributaries; and the Discovery of Lakes Shirwa and Nyasa 1858–1864,* coauthored with his brother Charles, proved far less successful and mostly disappeared from view after its publication in 1865. As for the discovery of the two lakes, it's likely that several Portuguese travelers had seen them earlier, perhaps as early as 1846, and that Livingstone knew this.[2]

Stanley was quite different. In terms of exploration and discovery as defined in nineteenth-century Europe, he clearly stands at the top. Establishing the connection between the Lualaba and Congo Rivers and locating the source of the Victoria Nile would have been enough to put him there. Of greater importance, however, is that things happened because of Stanley, and in more than one instance profound and lasting consequences for Africa followed his actions. Furthermore, Stanley wrote and spoke about Africa constantly. No one at the time, and really no one since, produced as many words on the subject for the public to consume. All of Stanley's books went through multiple editions and were translated into many languages. His other writings and lectures number in the hundreds. That Stanley became a controversial figure worked to further his African connection. As a *Spectator* editorial put it, "attention to Stanley is attention to Africa."[3]

It didn't start out that way. His Abyssinian journey involved nothing more than writing entertaining stories about a British military action in a remote and exotic part of the world in order to enhance his career in journalism. Reporting remained Stanley's main objective in undertaking the journey to find Livingstone. In retrospect, not much of note for Africa happened along his way in or out. The consequences were more general, in that had the journey been unsuccessful, his subsequent ones would have never taken place. Furthermore, the time Stanley spent with Livingstone began a change in his thinking about the continent's need for civilizing influences—in other words, commerce and Christianity. There are two ironies here. First, Stanley's frequent eulogies contributed to the doctor's saintly aura, one that many used as a yardstick to criticize Stanley. Second, Livingstone's most significant legacy may well have been Stanley.

Africa coming to dominate the rest of Stanley's life and, in turn, his becoming a major shaper of events there took a little more time. Covering the Asante campaign was just another journalistic assignment. The story of Stanley's conversion that reportedly took place when he heard of Livingstone's death on the return from the Gold Coast doesn't quite ring true. The doctor's influences notwithstanding, Stanley's meeting with Edwin Arnold seems a better explanation for his undertaking the 1874–1877 expedition. Stanley remained a reporter at heart, and he most likely viewed the opportunity to return to Africa as a way to enhance his career prospects and achieve the kind of recognition and "master" status he expressed a desire for in Spain in 1869. His commitment to Africa's betterment, as he defined it, developed during 1874–1877. From then on, the continent would be at the center of his life, and, ultimately, the cause of his death.

Locally, Stanley's arrival usually didn't have immediate consequences. The major exceptions were the battles fought during 1874–1877 and the Emin Pasha expedition. No matter who instigated the fights, Africans died and families and communities suffered. Nonetheless, when the battles ended, life resumed, even for the Wanyaturu and Bumbire islanders. Of course, they and others who engaged Stanley and his men then knew about the white man's weapons. Thus, at the end of the day, the superiority demonstrated during the journey was of a military, not a moral, kind. All Stanley's efforts aimed at appearance, both in dress and demeanor, counted for little.

It might not be stretching things too far to say that nothing in the annals of European involvement in Africa quite matches Stanley's work for King Leopold. When a station appeared, people's lives in the vicinity began changing almost from the outset, and they changed even more with the economic and cultural forces that soon followed. The consequences, however, didn't stop there. Although a partitioning of the continent by the European powers was a likely eventuality, the location of the king's holding in the center of the continent quickened the process. Perhaps more important, it also served as the fulcrum for the map of colonial possessions that began to take shape during the Berlin Conference of 1884–1885. The Free State sat in the center of the continent. In an almost collage-like fashion, other possessions soon took shape. And on the map of these possessions hung the fates of generation after generation of Africans. Sensing the momentous nature of Stanley's work, one obituary writer noted that his "place is among those who have set the landmarks of nations and moulded their destinies."[4]

That the Free State would become the disaster described by Adam Hochschild in *King Leopold's Ghost* can only indirectly be attributed to Stanley. He had no hand in running it, and he did not, as one commentator recently remarked, "set the standard for cruelty for which the Congo became notorious."[5] As documented in Chapter 6, the stations were, for the most part, established peacefully. Stanley knew it had to be done this way, since African cooperation was needed to achieve the free trade he saw as essential to the state's and, by extension, Congolese success. Even if Stanley had wanted to use force, he couldn't have, given the few men and limited firepower at his disposal. The rubber concessions granted by Leopold that generated the exploitation and brutality were made well after Stanley had left. Where he did fail was in continuing to speak on the king's behalf, even when it became clear that a monster in the heart of Africa had been created. Stanley knew this from reports and personal contacts with Edmund Morel and Roger Casement, two men instrumental in telling the world about the Congo atrocities. Yet as late as 1898, he could still say,

King Leopold found the Congo region "stained by wasteful deformities, tears, and hearts' blood of myriads," cursed by cannibalism, savagery, and despair;

and he has been trying with a patience, which I can never sufficiently admire, to relieve it of its horrors, rescue it from its oppressors, and save it from perdition. . . . It cannot be abandoned to revert to a wilderness, it cannot belong to England, and it would scarcely suit the English to have it transferred to France, Germany, or Portugal. Why do our writers, then, object to hear of steady progress being made under Belgian administration, and prefer to publish malignant letters from some dismissed official or splenetic missionary on which they may base their prognostications of speedy dissolution, rather than on facts which cannot be disproved and which point to opposite conclusions.[6]

Stanley could be loyal to a fault, and he was to Leopold.

Stanley's connection with Buganda had major implications, both in the short and the long run. His amicable relationship with Mutesa helped open the country to European influences, especially those brought by missionaries. At first these almost devastated the country, as Christianity confronted Islam, and each became linked to struggles to control the throne. Rivalries between Protestants and Catholics fanned the flames of an era known for the "wars of religion."[7] Even though Stanley never returned to Buganda after 1875, he continued to champion its cause almost until his death, stressing the area's richness and strategic location. Certainly no voice boomed louder and longer than his in support of building a railway to connect it to the east coast, just as he had earlier argued for the Congo railway. Eventually it was built.

Despite beginning on a hostile note, the friendship Stanley developed with the Bahima peoples during the Emin Pasha expedition also seems to have paved the way for entry by future Europeans. Interestingly, with them and the Baganda, this eventually served to swing regional balances of power further in their favors. They became integral parts of colonial governance, which brought them many advantages, especially with regard to educational opportunities.

By going down the Congo River and up the Aruwimi River, Stanley unintentionally showed slavers the way to new hunting grounds. The consequences were devastating. Predatory raids and the introduction of new diseases, notably smallpox and syphilis, decimated many communities. Some disappeared completely, and, demographically, sections along the Aruwimi carry the scars today.[8]

In summarizing the Stanley and Africa connection, a few more matters are worth noting. His words, whether written or spoken, carried a strong imperial message about the need for Europe, and especially Great Britain, to become more deeply involved in the continent's affairs. He saw it as both a duty and a need. How many converts to the cause these words won can't be determined. At they very least, they joined others in the chorus justifying, and thus preparing the public for, Africa's partitioning.[9] As the *Spectator* editorial cited above put it,

> Whether we like it or not, there is but one way of civilizing East Africa, and that is to govern it regularly, resolutely, and avowedly for at least a century, exercising all taxing powers, distributing all justice, and in all ways, the military way included, training its savages to become orderly men, and therefore men capable of civilization.

The only other option, it declared, was to hand the area over to Arab slavers.

With regard to the suppression of slavery, there's no evidence that Stanley's words mattered very much. His greatest influence in this regard probably came in finding Livingstone and seeing the doctor's letter detailing the Nyangwe massacre into safe hands. As noted in Chapter 5, this helped spur formation of the Bartle Frere mission and an earlier rather than later banning of the slave trade by Zanzibar. As a result, some Africans were spared captivity. The weakened sultanate resulting from the ban helped facilitate later German and British advances in the region.

One area where Stanley's writings and speeches made a difference was in dispelling widely held notions about equatorial Africa's interior being nothing but a vast disease-ridden jungle. He waxed enthusiastically over the resources waiting to be exploited, something Leopold clearly took to heart, and identified many portions suitable for European settlement. It's noteworthy that in no instance did Stanley argue for Europeans displacing Africans. Indeed, he viewed Africans as preferable occupants whenever possible. Stanley did, however, make a frequent mistake by assuming that the lack of villages and farmsteads meant open land for settlers. Later investigations would reveal that few spaces didn't have at least one claimant.

Unfortunately, Stanley contributed to Africa's "dark" image, most directly by using *dark* and *darkest* in the titles of two highly popular books. His many references to cannibals and cannibalism also played a part in developing an imagery so powerful that it remains with us today.[10]

The abuses and failures of imperialism and colonialism mean that anyone associated with them comes out tarnished. That Stanley's tarnish is especially deep hued reflects his many associations, both directly and indirectly. The acts of violence he committed upon Africans are just grounds for condemnation. That many of these were in self-defense doesn't serve to mitigate them. He was an intruder in lands where such people often spelled trouble.

Although softer than that of many of his contemporaries, his paternalism also deserves criticism. At the same time, an argument can be made that history has treated Stanley too harshly, at least in a comparative sense. That he harbored notions about race common to the late nineteenth century is true. Calling him a racist, though, is more difficult. As Norman Bennett pointed out many years ago, unlike Baker and Burton, Stanley didn't despise Africans or view them as innately inferior.[11] In his mind, culture counted more than biology. Whatever requisites they lacked to qualify for higher standing could be achieved in time. This sense of Africans as worthy humans is revealed by the prominent roles they played in Stanley's books. Individuals appear time and again, usually with names and often with praise and occasionally even admiration. His feelings for the Zanzibaris were especially deep. Stanley knew that everything he accomplished in Africa from Livingstone on was due to their efforts on his behalf.

I said I wouldn't try to psychoanalyze Stanley beyond exploring his motives at crucial times. Nonetheless, a few personal characteristics that others deemed deficiencies are worthy of comment. That he lied about his early years is true. The fact is that many people did and still do tell untruths when they're trying to build new lives. America, in particular, has been known for bringing out this trait in immigrants, and for fostering hustlers and con artists, roles Stanley played from time to time. Africa changed him in many ways, including his propensity to lie. The months he spent with Livingstone were the beginning, and his further experiences with Africans continued that transition. As he noted in 1876, Africa allowed him to escape from mundane cares, which allowed for

> independence of mind, which elevates one's thoughts to purer, higher atmospheres. It is not repressed by fear, nor depressed by ridicule and insults. It is not weighed down by sordid thoughts, or petty interests, but now preens itself, and soars free and unrestrained; which liberty, to a vivid mind, imperceptibly changes the whole man after a while.[12]

That Stanley continued to display a penchant for exaggeration and hyperbole can be explained by a combination of self-promotional efforts and a long stint with the *New York Herald.* Such flaws aren't usually considered fatal ones.

The charge of being brutal is more serious and also more directly pertinent to Stanley's role in Africa. There's no doubt that he had a temper and could explode at the presumed failures of people, especially those under him. His use of lashes and chains as means of discipline supports the cruelty charge. And there are the several instances in which he oversaw the execution of his own men and left others to certain death. These are all facts that can't be denied. On the other hand, there's the rather remarkable loyalty Stanley generated among Africans, especially his men from Zanzibar. Many who worked with him once did so again. During his visit to the island in 1891, Stairs wrote Stanley about men from the Emin Pasha expedition wanting to know when he would be coming to "*funga saffari ngini*" (lead a safari again).[13] And in Stanley's obituary, Harry Johnston, who had many contacts with Africans, asserted that he'd "never known any African explorer more universally praised by *black* men than Stanley."[14] To say they expected cruel treatment because of its commonness in caravans would be to insult their intelligence. Judgments depend on where one stands, which is conditioned by time and place. His actions wouldn't be condoned today by the majority. They were then. Beyond this, whether to do with force of character, loyalty, generosity, strength, or whatever, Stanley seems more often than not to have earned the respect of Africans who worked for him and survived.

Charges about Stanley having been paranoid, swaggering, hypocritical, and sadomasochistic are belied by the lasting friendships he formed with so many people of different backgrounds, most of whom wouldn't have put up with such a person. Once again, this is in marked contrast to Livingstone, who wound up alienating virtually everyone he dealt with. Two statements made by two very different people familiar with Stanley in very different circumstances are worth quoting in detail. Together they probably say as much as can be said with any certainty about the kind of man he was. First, Mounteney-Jephson:

> He had many faults, and some of them even were grave ones, but they were, I think, chiefly the faults of his qualities, and without those faults he would not probably have been possessed of some of the great qualities which made him so successful in almost everything that he undertook. His faults were never of a mean or petty kind, and were easily forgiven when one saw the greatness and nobility of his nature beyond. That untiring energy and indomitable resolve to overcome all difficulties; that apparently ruthless determination to sweep away all opposition; his seeming hardness and callousness in working to achieve what he had undertaken, if he felt that the end was a good one; the curiously hard and unsympathetic attitude he had toward failure of any kind, no matter how blameless the failure might be; all these and many others are not the qualities that are usually found in gentle and aimiable natures, and they do not as a rule attract sympathy and affection.[15]

The second comes from Maj. Pond:

> Henry M. Stanley was never fond of company. He appreciates friends, and those who knew him intimately are very fond of him. He is generally cautious

and sparing of words, especially when strangers are about. Receptions and dinners worry him, as he cannot bear being on exhibition under showers of forced
compliments. His manners and habits are those of a gentleman. . . . Altogether, I have never parted with a client with greater regret, or found one
holding me in bonds of friendship and respect to so great a degree. Sir Henry
Stanley does me the honor to regard me as a friend.[16]

In the end, though, the more one studies Stanley through his writings
and those of others about him, the more complicated and undecipherable he
becomes. Time and circumstances seem to have brought forth several different men, often at odds with one another. A major reason for this is that he
played so many roles—newspaper reporter, explorer, advocate of causes,
point man for others, and commander of men, to name the most prominent.
No one yardstick will do. This, in itself, justifies a re-examination of Stanley
every so often. There's another compelling reason to not let him become just
a footnote to the history of Africa. For better or worse, he left his mark on
the continent. Opinions about this mark will change, just as all historical
evaluations do with the coming of new information and different lenses
through which to view the past. Final words are never written, which is why
history and those who helped shape it are so fascinating.

Notes

Notes to Preface

1. E. A. Macdonald, *The Story of Stanley, the Hero of Africa* (Edinburgh: Oliphant, Anderson & Ferrier, 1891), 160.

2. Joseph Joûbert, *Stanley, le Roi des Exporateurs* (Anvers: G. and G. Grassin, 1905)

3. Henry W. Little, *Henry M. Stanley: His Life, Travels, and Explorations* (London: Chapman and Hall Limited, 1890), v.

4. Quoted in James B. Pond, *Eccentricities of Genius* (New York: G. W. Dillingham Company, 1900), 266.

5. David J. Nicoll, *Stanley's Exploits or, Civilizing Africa*, 2nd edition (Aberdeen: J. Leatham, 1891), 29–30.

6. Harry H. Johnston, "The Results of Stanley's Work," *Good Words* 45, 1904, 533–543.

7. See John L. Brom, *Sur les Traces de Stanley* (Paris: Presses de la Cité, 1958); Blaine Littell, *South of the Moon: On Stanley's Trail through the Dark Continent* (London: Weidenfeld and Nicholson, 1966); and John Batchelor and Julie Batchelor, *In Stanley's Footsteps: Across Africa from West to East* (London: Blandford, 1990).

8. Patrice Lumumba, "Un Explorateur Incomparable," *La Voix du Congolais* X, 1954, 516–522.

9. Norman R. Bennett, ed., *Stanley's Despatches to the New York Herald 1871–1872, 1874–1877* (Boston: Boston University Press, 1970), fn., xiii.

10. Cadwaladar Rowlands, *Henry M. Stanley: The Story of His Life from Birth in 1841 to His Discovery of Livingstone, 1871* (London: John Camden Hotten, 1872).

11. See James J. Ellis, *H. M. Stanley* (London: James Nisbet & Co., 1890); Little, *HMS*; and Thomas George, *The Birth, Boyhood and Younger Days of Henry M. Stanley* (London: The Roxburghe Press, 1895)

12. John Bierman, *Dark Safari: The Life Behind the Legend of Henry Morton Stanley* (New York: Alfred A. Knopf, 1990), 3, 356.

13. Frank McLynn, *Stanley: The Making of an African Explorer* (London: Constable, 1989), 14, 17, 30.

14. H. Alan C. Cairns, *Prelude to Imperialism: British Reactions to Central African Society, 1840–1890,* (London, Routledge & Kegan Paul, 1965).

15. Readers interested in all the diplomatic maneuverings associated with the "scramble" are referred to Thomas Pakenham, *The Scramble for Africa: The White Man's Conquest of the Dark Continent from 1876 to 1912* (New York: Random House, 1991).

16. Bennett, *SDNYH*.

17. Albert Maurice, ed., *H. M. Stanley: Unpublished Letters* (New York: Philosophical

Library, Inc., 1957). The critique of the French edition is contained in Jean Stengers, "Quelques Observations sur la Correspondence de Stanley," *Zaire* 9, 1955, 899–926.

18. Richard Stanley and Alan Neame, *The Exploration Diaries of H. M. Stanley* (London: William Kimber, 1961).

19. For details of the people and politics involved see Ian R. Smith, *The Emin Pasha Expedition 1886–1890* (Oxford: The Clarendon Press, 1972). Less thoroughly researched but easier to read is Roger Jones, *The Rescue of Emin Pasha* (New York: St. Martin's Press, 1972). Neither makes use of the Stanley Archive.

20. James A. Casada, *Dr. David Livingstone and Sir Henry Morton Stanley: An Annotated Bibliography* (New York: Garland Publishing, Inc., 1976).

Notes to Chapter 1

1. Emir W. Jones, "Stanley: the Mystery of Three Fathers," *National Library of Wales Journal* XXVIII, 1993–94, 39–56, 127–151.

2. Stanley to Katie Roberts, March 22, 1869, SA.

3. 82, SA.

4. Jones, SMTF.

5. 84, SA.

6. Lucy M. Jones and Ivor W. Jones, *H. M. Stanley and Wales* (Denbigh Wales: Gee and Son, 1972)

7. Emir W. Jones, "Sir Henry Morton Stanley's Schoolmaster: the Vindication of James Francis," *Flintshire Historical Society* 33, 1992, 103–118.

8. Jones and Jones, *HMS W*.

9. Jones and Jones, *HMS W*, 9.

10. Dorothy Stanley, ed., *The Autobiography of Sir Henry Morton Stanley* (New York: Greenwood Press, 1969), 65.

11. D. Stanley, *ASHMS,* 87.

12. D. Stanley, *ASHMS,* 112.

13. Nathaniel C. Hughes, *Sir Henry Morton Stanley, Confederate* (Baton Rouge: Louisiana State University Press, 2000).

14. D. Stanley, *ASHMS,* 99.

15. Mary W. Shuey, "Stanley in Arkansas," *Southwest Review* 27, 1941–42, 197–206.

16. D. Stanley, *ASHMS,* 167.

17. Nearly one-quarter of the Confederate Army's 44,000 men were killed during the battle. Among the dead was the commander, Albert Sydney Johnston. Union deaths were even greater in number.

18. 84, SA.

19. 84, SA.

20. Hughes, *SHMSC,* fn., 149.

21. Hughes, *SHMSC,* fn., 151.

22. Hughes, *SHMSC,* fn., 152.

23. Stanley to Katie Roberts, March 22, 1869, SA.

24. "Mother," SA.

25. Curtis to Elliot, January 18, 1907, SA.

26. The *Sun,* August 24, 1872, in Bennett *SDNYH,* 406–416.

27. Stegman to Stanley, November 30, 1886, SA.

28. Harlow W. Cook, "Résumé of Stanley's Early Manhood," RGS 1/7.

29. Cook to Dorothy Tennant, May 10, 1910, SA.

30. 1, SA.

31. 1, SA.

32. Morris to U.S. Legation in Constantinople, February 18, 1870, SA.

33. Fragment of letter from Stanley to Katie Roberts, in Ramón J. Fraile, "Transcript of Documents Concerning Stanley's Assignments in Spain," n.d., SA.

34. 1, SA.

35. The *Sun,* August 29, 1872, in Bennett, *SDNYH,* 416–424.

36. "Adventures of an American Traveller in Turkey," SA.

37. Henry M. Stanley, *My Early Travel and Adventures in America and Asia,* Vol. 1 (New York: Charles Scribner's Sons, 1895), 11–18.

38. Stanley, *METAAA1,* 41–47.

39. Stanley, *METAAA1,* 104–113.

40. 64B, SA.

41. Stanley to Bennett, September 13, 1872, in Bennett, *SDNYH,* 447–452 and Alfred Sorenson, *The Story of Omaha from the Pioneer Days to the Present,* third edition, (Omaha: National Printing Company, 1923), 242–243.

42. Douglas L. Wheeler, "Henry M. Stanley's Letters to the Missouri Democrat," *Missouri Historical Society Bulletin,* XVII, 1961, 277.

43. Stanley, *ETAAA1,* 274–291.

44. 2, SA.

45. D. Stanley, *ASHMS,* 228.

NOTES TO CHAPTER 2

1. For overviews of Abyssinia in the nineteenth century see Sven Rubenson, "Ethiopia and the Horn," in *Cambridge History of Africa, 5, c. 1790–c. 1870,* ed. John E. Flint (Cambridge: Cambridge University Press, 1976), 51–98, and Richard Pankhurst,"Ethiopia and Somalia," in *UNESCO General History of Africa VI, Africa in the Nineteenth Century until the 1880s,* ed. J. F. Ade Ajayi (Oxford: Heinemann, 1989), 376–411.

2. The letter reads: In the name of the Father, of the Son, and of the Holy Ghost, one God in Trinity, the chosen by God, King of Kings, Teôdros of Ethiopia to her Majesty Victoria, Queen of England. I hope your Majesty is in good health. By the power of God I am well. My fathers the Emperors had forgotten our Creator. He handed over their kingdom to the Gallas and Turks. But God created me, lifted me out of the dust, and restored this Empire to my rule. He endowed me with power, and enabled me to stand in the place of my fathers. By His power I drove away the Gallas. But for the Turks, I have told them to leave the land of my ancestors. They refuse. I am now going to wrestle with them. Mr Plowden, and my late Grand Chamberlain, the Englishman Bell, used to tell me that there is a great Christian Queen who loves all Christians. When they said to me this, 'We are able to make you known to her, and to establish friendship between you,' then in those times I was very glad. I gave them my love, thinking that I had found your Majesty's good will. All men are subject to death, and my enemies, thinking to injure me, killed these my friends. But by the power of

God I have exterminated those enemies, not leaving one alive, though they were of my own family, that I may get, by the power of God your friendship.

I was prevented by the Turks occupying the sea-coast from sending you an Embassy when I was in difficulty. Consul Cameron arrived with a letter and presents of friendship. By the power of God I was very glad hearing of your welfare, and being assured of your amity. I have received your presents, and thank you much.

I fear that if I send ambassadors with presents of amity by Consul Cameron, they may be arrested by the Turks.

And now I wish that you may arrange for the safe passage of my ambassadors everywhere on the road.

I wish to have an answer to this letter by Consul Cameron, and that he may go with my Embassy to England. See how Islam oppresses the Christian. In Clement Markham, *A History of the Abyssinian Expedition* (London: Macmillan and Co., 1869), footnote, 76–77.

3. Maureen J. Tayal. "The Abyssinian Expedition 1867–1868," M. A. Thesis, University of Calgary, Department of History, 1975.

4. Henry M. Stanley, *Coomassie and Magdala: the Story of Two British Campaigns in Africa* (Freeport, NY: Books for Libraries Press, 1971), 281.

5. Pankhurst, "E and S," 400.

6. Byron Farwell, *Queen Victoria's Little Wars* (London: Allen Lane, 1973), 166–167. A more extensive account of the war can be found in Frederick Myatt, *The March to Magdala: The Abyssinian War of 1868* (London: Leo Copper, 1970).

7. Tayal, "AE," 111.

8. 2, SA.

9. Unless otherwise indicated, Stanley's observations come from his *C and M.* They are not noted separately.

10. 2, SA.

11. 2, SA.

12. Farwell, *QVLW*, 169.

13. Sorenson, "E and H," 80.

14. Pankhurst, "E and S," 401.

15. Letter fragment, Stanley to Katie Roberts, July or August 1869, in Fraile, "TDCSAS."

16. Edward Marston, in Stanley, *METAAA*, v. 1, xiii.

17. D. Stanley, *ASHMS*, 230.

18. 2, SA.

19. 2 and 73, SA.

20. 2, SA.

21. The *New York Herald*, November 8, 1868.

22. 2 and 73, SA.

23. Ambella to Stanley, March 15, 1877, SA.

24. "In Memoriam," Livingstoniana, SA.

25. Anderson to Stanley, October 20, 1868, "In Memoriam," Livingstonia, SA.

26. 2, SA.

27. 2, SA.

28. 4, SA.

29. 4, SA.

30. Edwin Balch, "American Explorers of Africa," *Geographical Review* 45, 1918, 274–281.

31. 2, SA.

32. 2, SA and Stanley to Roberts, June 27, 1869, fragment in Fraile, "TDCSAS."
33. Stanley to Katie Roberts, March 22, 1869, SA.
34. D. Stanley, ASHMS, 243–244.
35. A detailed accounting of Stanley's activities in Spain is found in Ramón J. Fraile, *Stanley De Madrid a las Fuentes del Nilo* (Barcelona: Mondadori, 2000).
36. The *New York Herald,* July 26, 1869.
37. 4, SA.
38. Stanley to Roberts, May 3, 1869, Fraile, "TDCSAS."
39. Stanley to Roberts, September 16, 1869, SA.
40. Edward King, "An Expedition with Stanley," *Scribner's Monthly* 5, 1872, 105–112.
41. The *New York Herald,* November 3 and 6, 1869.
42. Henry M. Stanley, *How I Found Livingstone* (New York: Scribner, Armstrong & Co., 1872), xv.
43. Stanley, *HIFL,* xvii.
44. According to Don C. Seitz, *The James Gordon Bennetts: Father and Son* (Indianapolis: The Bobbs-Merrill Company, 1928), 303, there's a good chance that Bennett's agent in London, Finlay Anderson, first broached the idea.
45. Stanley, *HIFL,* xviii–xix.
46. Levien to Stanley, Nov. 29, 1869, SA.
47. 7, 73, SA.
48. Balch, "AEA."
49. King, AES, 12.
50. Stanley, *METAAA*2, 45, 51–52.
51. 73, 3, SA.
52. 73, SA.
53. Stanley, *METAAA*2, 411.
54. Stanley to Katie Roberts, October 7, 1870, SA.
55. "In Memoriam," Livingstoniana, SA.

Notes to Chapter 3

1. Stanley, *HIFL,* 1
2. See Abdul Sheriff, *Slaves, Spices & Ivory in Zanzibar* (London: James Currey, 1987) for the evolution of the Zanzibar economy from 1770 to 1873.
3. Bantu languages have noun classes that are designated by prefixes. For example, Swahili is the root. A single person is Mswahili, whereas Waswahili denotes the people in general. Some Bantu languages use Ba instead of Wa. The language is Kiswahili, alternatively Li, and the country would be Uswahili if there were one. In this case there isn't a place identified as such. Bu is also seen, as in Buganda, the land of the Ganda. It's useful to use these forms to clarify what's being talked about. The prefixes will not be used for non-Bantu peoples, such as the Maasai.
4. Stanley, *HIFL,* 15
5. Francis Galton, *Memories of My Life* (London: Methuen & Co., 1908), 205.
6. 7, SA.
7. Webb to Ropes, July 1, 1871, in Norman Bennett, "Stanley and the American Consuls at Zanzibar," *Essex Institute Historical Collections* 100, 1964, 42.

8. Webb to State Department, February 6, 1871, in Bennett "SACZ," 43.

9. Contract dated February 1, 1871, SA.

10. Reprinted in the *New York Herald*, October 24, 1872.

11. The *New York Herald*, December 22, 1871, in Bennett, *SDNYH*, 11.

12. 73, SA.

13. Stanley, *HIFL*, 83.

14. Stanley, *HIFL*, 102.

15. Stanley, *HIFL*, 104.

16. Stanley, *HIFL*, 114.

17. Stanley, *HIFL*, 124.

18. Stanley, *HIFL*, 115.

19. Stanley, *HIFL*, 147.

20. Stanley, *HIFL*, 153–156.

21. Stanley, *HIFL*, 157–161.

22. 7, SA

23. 73, SA.

24. *New York Herald*, December 22, 1871, in Bennett, *SDNYH*, 19.

25. Stanley, *HIFL*, 176.

26. Stanley, *HIFL*, 187.

27. Stanley, *HIFL*, 204.

28. Stanley, *HIFL*, 211–212.

29. Stanley, *HIFL*, 219.

30. 7 and 73, SA; the *New York Herald*, December 22, 1871, in Bennett, *SDNYH*, 22–23.

31. Stanley, *HIFL*, 221.

32. See Andrew M. Watson, *Agricultural Innovation in the Early Islamic World: The Diffusion of Crops and Farming Techniques, 700–1100* (Cambridge, MA: Cambridge University Press, 1983) for examples of earlier Arab agricultural innovations.

33. Norman R. Bennett, *Miramo of Tanzania, 1840?–1884* (New York: Oxford University Press, 1971), 37.

34. Undated document by an unknown *New York Herald* employee, SA.

35. Stanley, *HIFL*, 283–284.

36. The *New York Herald*, August 9, 1872, in Bennett, *SDNYH*, 47.

37. 7, SA.

38. The *New York Herald*, August 9, 1872, in Bennett, *SDNYH*, 44.

39. Stanley, *HIFL*, 308.

40. 7, SA.

41. 73, SA.

42. 7, SA.

43. Stanley, *HIFL*, 311.

44. The *New York Herald*, August 10, 1872, in Bennett, *SDNYH*, 63.

45. 73, SA.

46. The *New York Herald*, August 10, 1872, in Bennett, *SDNYH*, 64.

47. The *New York Herald*, August 10, 1872, in Bennett, *SDNYH*, 66.

48. Stanley, *HIFL*, 361–362.

49. The *New York Herald*, August 10, 1872, in Bennett, *SDHYH*, 75.

50. Stanley, *HIFL*, 367.

51. Stanley, *HIFL*, 377.

52. Stanley, *HIFL*, 378.

53. The *New York Herald*, August 10, 1872, in Bennett, *SDHYH*, 79–80.

54. The *New York Herald*, August 10, 1872, in Bennett, *SDNYH*, 82.

55. Stanley, *HIFL*, 395.

56. Peggy H. Jackson, *Meteor Out of Africa* (London: Cassell & Company, Ltd., 1962).

57. The *New York Herald*, July 15, 1872, in Bennett, *SDNYH*, 51.

58. Horace Waller, *The Last Journals of David Livingstone in Central Africa* (New York: Harper & Brothers Publishers, 1875), 400.

59. Waller, *LJDL*, 400.

60. Cited in W. Garden Blakie, *The Personal Life of David Livingstone* (New York: Layman's Missionary Movement, 1880), 444–445, and George Seaver, *David Livingstone: His Life and Letters* (London: Lutterworth Press, 1957), 582.

61. Waller, *LJDL*, 382–385.

62. 11, SA.

63. 11, SA.

64. 11, SA.

65. Stanley to Shaw, November 14, 1871, SA.

66. Stanley, *HIFL*, 483–484.

67. 11, SA

68. 7, SA.

69. Stanley, HIFL, 566.

70. Stanley, *HIFL*, 579.

71. 11, SA.

72. 11, SA.

73. Waller, *LJDL*, 410.

74. Waller, *LJDL*, 410.

75. Oliver Ransford, *David Livingstone: The Dark Interior* (New York: St. Martin's Press, 1978), 103–117; Tim Jeal, *Livingstone* (New Haven: Yale University Press, 2001), 348–349.

76. 11, SA.

77. 11, SA.

78. 10, SA.

79. T. Griffith-Jones, "Stanley's First and Second Expeditions through Mpwapwa and W. L. Farquhar's Grave," *Tanganyika Notes and Records* 25, 1948, 28–33.

80. Stanley, *HIFL*, 641.

81. Stanley, *HIFL*, 647.

82. Stanley, *HIFL*, 647–648.

83. 73, SA.

84. Journal fragment in Peabody Museum, Salem, MA, cited in Bennett, *SDNYH*, 126.

NOTES TO CHAPTER 4

1. Galton, *MML*, 204–206.

2. The *New York Herald*, September 3, 1872, in Bennett, *SDNYH*, 403.

3. Stanley, *HIFL*, 660.

4. Stanley to Livingstone, May 25, 1872, Scottish National Library, in McLynn, *SMAE*, 195.

5. Original cable, SA.

6. Stanley to Bennett, May 18, 1872, in Hall, *SAE*, 206.

7. 12, SA.

8. 12, SA.

9. Lurton D. Ingersoll, *Explorations in Africa by Dr. David Livingstone and Others.* (Chicago: Union Publishing Company, 1872), 343.

10. Scrapbooks and newspaper clippings, SA.

11. The *New Haven Palladium*, May 4, 1872.

12. *Proceedings of the Royal Geographical Society* 16, 1871–72, 241.

13. The *Sun*, July 26, 1872.

14. The *Spectator*, July 27, 1872.

15. The *New York Herald*, August 9, 1872, in Bennett, *SDNYH*, 35.

16. The *Daily Telegraph*, July 25, 1872.

17. The *Times* (London), August 3, 1872.

18. 12, SA.

19. Waller Papers, in Seaver, *DLHLL*, 598.

20. Livingstone to Kirk, Kirk Papers, in Reginald Coupland, *Livingstone's Last Journey* (London: Collins, 1945), 187.

21. The *Daily Telegraph*, July 29, 1872.

22. The *Standard*, August 2, 1872.

23. The *Saturday Review*, August 3, 1872.

24. The *Pall Mall Gazette*, August 3, 1872.

25. The *Echo*, August 10, 1872.

26. 12, SA.

27. Roy Bridges, "Towards the Prelude to the Partition of East Africa," in *Imperialism, Decolonization and Africa*, ed. Roy Bridges (New York: St. Martin's Press, 2000), 91.

28. *PRGS* 16, 1871–72, 266, 371.

29. Hugh R. Mill, *The Record of the Royal Geographical Society 1830–1930* (London: Royal Geographical Society, 1930), 114.

30. *PRGS* 16, 1871–72, 429–430.

31. 12, SA.

32. The *Scotsman*, August 17, 1872.

33. The *Standard*, August 17, 1872.

34. The *Echo*, August 17, 1872.

35. The *Daily Telegraph*, August 17, 1872.

36. The *Daily Telegraph*, August 20, 1872. (From the *Brighton Daily News*, August 19, 1872.)

37. Arnold to Helps, August 6, 1872, in Edmund A. Helps, *Correspondence of Sir Arthur Helps* (London: John Lane, 1917), 325.

38. The *Pall Mall Gazette*, August 26, 1872.

39. The *Daily Telegraph*, August 31, 1872.

40. 9, SA and Ian Anstruther, *I Presume: Stanley's Triumph and Disaster* (London: Geoffrey Bless, 1956), 163.

41. Clemens ("Mark Twain") to Stanley, September 1, 1872, SA.

42. Fragment contained in autobiography file, SA.

43. Galton, *EG*, 117–119.

44. Stanley to Markham, October 8, 1872, WLHUM.

45. Vernay L. Cameron, *Across Africa*. 2 vols. (London: Dalby, Isbister & Co, 1877).

46. Cameron to Stanley, October 25, 1872, SA.

47. Clement Markham, "Unpublished History of the Royal Geographical Society" (London: Royal Geographical Society, n.d.), 399.

48. Grant to Rawlinson, October 15 and 17, 1872, RGS.

49. S. O. Beeton and Roland Smith, *Livingstone and Stanley: a Narrative of the Exploration of the English Discoverer and of the Adventures of the American Journalist* (London: Ward Lock, and Tyler, 1872), 95.

50. Stanley to Markham, September 5, 1872, in Derek W. Francis, *Francis Galton: the Life and Work of a Victorian Genius* (London: Paul Elek, 1974), 117–118.

51. *The Spectator*, November 23, 1872; the *Manchester Guardian*, November 13, 1872.

52. Shuey, "SIA."

53. 4, SA.

54. Anstruther, *IP*, 171.

55. 12, SA.

56. The *Sun*, August 24, 1872, in Bennett, *SDNYH*, 406–416.

57. The *Sun*, August 29, 1872, in Bennett, *SDNYH*, 416–424.

58. Cook to Stanley, August 29, 1872, SA.

59. Stanley to Bennett, the *New York Herald*, September 26, 1872, in Bennett, *SDNYH*, 447–452.

60. The *Sun*, September 5, 1872, in Bennett, *SDNYH*, 440–447.

61. Cook to Stanley, October 5, 1872, SA.

62. The *New York Evening Mail*, November 21, 1872.

63. The *New York Tribune*, November 21, 1872.

64. The *New York Tribune*, December 13, 1872; the *New York Times*, December 9, 1872.

65. The *New York Herald*, November 23, 1872.

66. The *New York Herald*, December 5, 1872.

67. Office of the *Herald* to Stanley, December 5, 1872, SA.

68. Rowlands, *HMS*, 178–179.

69. Jennings to Stanley, January 9, 1873, SA.

70. Henry M. Stanley, *My Kalulu, Prince, King, and Slave: A Story of Central Africa* (London: Sampson Low, Marston, Searle & Rivington, 1890), v–vi.

71. Stanley, *MK*, viii.

72. 73, SA.

73. See Ivor Wilks, *Asante in the Nineteenth Century: The Structure and Evolution of a Political Order* (London: Cambridge University Press, 1975), for the details of Asante history, culture, and politics.

74. A. Adu Boahen, "Politics in Ghana, 1899–1874," in *History of West Africa*, Vol. 2, eds. J. F. Ade Ajayi and Michael Crowder (London: Longman, 1974), 202.

75. Unless otherwise indicated, Stanley's observations come from his *C and M*. They are not noted separately.

76. Farwell, *QVLW*, 194.

77. Robert B. Edgerton, *The Fall of the Asante Empire: the Hundred-Year War for Africa's Gold Coast* (New York: The Free Press, 1995), 106.

78. Garnet W. Wolseley, *The Story of a Soldier's Life*, Vol. 2 (Westminster: Archibald Constable & Co., Ltd., 1903), 295.

79. Edgerton, *FAE*, 135.

80. Wolseley, *SSL2*, 342.

81. Wolseley, *SSL2*, 359.

82. G. E. Metcalfe, *Great Britain and Ghana: Documents of Ghana History* (London: Thomas Nelson & sons, Ltd, 1964), 356–357.

83. Richard F. Burton, *Two Trips to Gorilla Land and the Cataracts of the Congo*, Vol. 1 (London: Sampson Low, Marston, Low, and Searle, 1876), x.

84. 73, SA.

85. Henry M. Stanley, *Through the Dark Continent*, Vol. 1 (New York: Harper & Brothers Publishers, 1878), 2.

86. Stanley, *TDC1*, 3.

87. Seitz, *JGBFS*, 300.

88. 14, SA.

89. The *New York Herald*, July 26, 1874.

90. The *New York Herald*, December 24, 1874, in Bennett, *SDNYH*, 154.

91. The *New York Herald*, December 24, 1874, in Bennett, *SDNYH*, 155.

92. 14, SA.

93. Copy of marriage pledge in SA.

94. 14, SA.

Notes to Chapter 5

1. The text of the treaty can be found in Reginald Coupland, *The Exploitation of East Africa, 1865–1890* (Evanston: Northwestern University Press, 1967), 212–213.

2. Coupland, *EEA*, 214.

3. The *New York Herald*, December, 24, 1874, in Bennett, *SDNYH*, 166.

4. Stanley to Levy, December 13, 1874, 29, SA.

5. The *New York Herald*, December 2, 1874, in Bennett, *SDNYH*, 130.

6. The *New York Herald*, December 3, 1874, in Bennett, *SDNYH*, 142.

7. The *New York Herald*, December 4, 1874, in Bennett, *SDNYH*, 151–53.

8. F. Pocock to Parents, the *New York Herald*, August 14, 1876, in Bennett, *SDNYH*, 468.

9. The *New York Herald*, December 24, 1874, in Bennett, *SDNYH*, 167.

10. Stanley to Levy, October 22 and 23, 1874, in 28, SA.

11. The *New York Herald*, December 24, 1874, in Bennett, *SDNYH*, 166.

12. Stanley, *TDC1*, 64–67; the *New York Herald*, December 24, 1874, in Bennett, *SDNYH*, 159.

13. Stanley, *TDC1*, 89.

14. Stanley, *TDC1*, 91.

15. The *New York Herald*, December 24, 1874, in Bennett, *SDNYH*, 162.

16. Stanley and Neame, *EDHMS*, 31.

17. Stanley and Neame, *EDHMS*, 119.

18. Stanley to Levy, December 13, 1874, 29, SA.

19. 16, SA.

20. 16, SA.

21. Stanley, *TDC1*, 100–102.

22. The *New York Herald*, October 11, 1875, in Bennett, *SDNYH*, 193.

23. Stanley and Neame, *EDHMS*, 37.
24. Stanley, *TDC*1, 104.
25. Stanley, *TDC*1, 106.
26. Stanley and Neame, *EDHMS*, 40.
27. 14, SA.
28. 14, SA.
29. Stanley, *TDC*1, 116.
30. 14, SA.
31. Stanley to Alice Pike, March 4, 1875, 29, SA.
32. 14 SA.
33. Stanley to Pike, March 4, 1875, 29, SA.
34. Stanley and Neame, *EDHMS*, 51.
35. The *New York Herald*, October 11, 1875, in Bennett, *SDNYH*, 202.
36. Stanley to E. J. Webb, October 1, 1875, 31, SA.
37. F. Pocock to Brother, The *New York Herald*, May 7, 1877, in Bennett, *SDNYH*, 478.
38. Stanley, *TDC*1, 134.
39. Stanley, *TDC*1, 137–38.
40. Stanley and Neame, *EDHMS*, 60.
41. Stanley, *TDC*1, 153.
42. The *New York Herald*, November 29, 1875, in Bennett, *SDNYH*, 217.
43. Stanley, *TDC*1, 193, 401.
44. Stanley, *TDC*1, 198.
45. The *New York Herald*, August 10, 1876, in Bennett, *SDNYH*, 252.
46. Harold B. Thomas, "Ernest Linant de Bellefonds and Stanley's Letter to the 'Daily Telegraph,'" *Uganda Journal* 2, 1934–35, 7–13.
47. The *New York Herald*, November 29, 1875, in Bennett, *SDNYH*, 227.
48. D. Anthony Low, "The Northern Interior 1840–84," Roland Oliver and Gervase Mathew, eds., *History of East Africa*, Vol. 1, (London: Oxford University Press, 1963), 346.
49. "M. Linant De Bellefond's Account of Stanley's Visit to King M'tse's Capital," the *New York Herald*, January 26, 1876, reprinted in *Journal of the American Geographical* Society 7, 1875, 283–289.
50. Stanley to Alice Pike, May 15, 1875, 30, SA.
51. Bennett, *SDNYH*, fn., 243.
52. Compiled from Stanley to R. Smith, 31, SA, Stanley and Neame, *EDHMS*, 75–76, and the *New York Herald*, August 9, 1876, in Bennett, *SDNYH*, 244–247.
53. *PRGS* 20, 1875–76, 11.
54. Stanley, *TDC*1, 241, and S. Napier Bax, "The Grave of Fred Barker, One of Stanley's Followers," *Tanganyika Notes and Records* 7, 1939, 56–58.
55. The *New York Herald*, August 10, 1876, in Bennett, *SDNYH*, 257.
56. Stanley and Neame, *EDHMS*, 92.
57. The *New York Herald*, August 10, 1876, in Bennett, *SDNYH*, 260.
58. Stanley to Levy, August 15, 1875, SA.
59. Stanley *TDC*1, 303–304 and 16, SA.
60. Stanley and Neame, *EDHMS*, 101.
61. Stanley to E. Marston, September 29, 1875, in Edward Marston, *After Work: Fragments from the Workshop of an Old Publisher* (New York: Charles Scribner's Sons, 1904), 217–218.

62. Stanley, *TDC*1, 325.

63. Stanley, *TDC*1, 326–41; 16, SA.

64. Stanley, *TDC*1, 343.

65. Stanley and Neame, *EDHMS*, 108–109.

66. Stanley, *TDC*1, 430.

67. F. Pocock to Parents, the *New York Herald*, August 14, 1876, in Bennett, *SDNYH*, 475.

68. Stanley, *TDC*1, 434.

69. Harold B. Thomas and I. R. Dale, "Uganda Place Names: Some European Eponyms," *Uganda Journal* 17, 1953, 101–123.

70. Stanley, *TDC*1, 436.

71. Stanley, *TDC*1, 448.

72. 16, SA.

73. Stanley, *TDC*1, 459.

74. 17, SA.

75. Stanley, *TDC*1, 486.

76. Stanley, *HIFL*, 296; 13, SA.

77. Stanley, *TDC*1 492–494.

78. Stanley, *TDC*1, 509.

79. Stanley to Levy, May 31, 1876, 31, SA.

80. Stanley, *TDC*2, 26.

81. Joseph Thomson, *To the Central African Lakes and Back*, Vol. 2 (London Frank Cass & co., Ltd., 2nd ed., 1968), 57.

82. The *New York Herald*, March 26, 1877, in Bennett, *SDNYH*, 284.

83. Stanley to Pike, August 14, 1876, 33, SA.

84. Stanley, *TDC*2, 64.

85. 18, SA.

86. 18, SA.

87. Stanley, *TDC*2, 78.

88. 18, SA.

89. Stanley, *TDC*2, 93.

90. For the life of Tippu Tip see Heinrich Brode, *Tippoo Tib* (London: Edward Arnold, 1907), and Francois Bontinck, *L'Autoboiraphie de Hamed ben Mohammed el-Murjebi Tippu Tip (ca. 1840–1905)* (Bruxelles: Academie Royale des Sciences d'Outre Mer, 1974).

91. Stanley, *TDC*2, 95–96.

92. Stanley, *TDC*2, 107–08.

93. Stanley, *TDC*2, 124.

94. 18, SA.

95. 18, SA.

96. The *New York Herald*, October 10, 1877, in Bennett, *SDNYH*, 317–327.

97. 18, SA.

98. The *New York Herald*, October 9, 1877, in Bennett, *SDNYH*, 331–332.

99. Stanley, *TDC*2, 133.

100. 18, SA.

101. Stanley, *TDC*2, 138.

102. 18, SA.

103. 18, SA; Stanley, *TDC*2, 152.

104. 18, SA.

105. Stanley, *TDC*2, 170.

106. Stanley, *TDC*2, 178–184.

107. 18, SA.

108. Stanley, *TDC*2, 205.

109. Stanley and Neame, *EDHMS*, 148.

110. Stanley, *TDC*2, 241.

111. Stanley, *TDC*2, 250.

112. Stanley and Neame, *EDHMS*, 157.

113. Stanley, *TDC*2, 272.

114. Stanley, *TDC*2, 278.

115. Stanley, *TDC*2, 283.

116. Stanley and Neame, *EDHMS*, 163–164.

117. Stanley and Neame, *EDHMS*, 164.

118. Stanley, *TDC*2, 318–19.

119. Stanley, *TDC*2, 334.

120. Stanley, *TDC*2, 336.

121. Stanley, *TDC*2, 351.

122. 18, SA.

123. A good summary of the Tuckey expedition is contained in Roger Anstey, *Britain and the Congo in the Nineteenth Century* (Oxford: Clarendon Press, 1962), 3–9.

124. Laszlo Magyar, *Explorations of the Zaire Delta* (Pest: Hungarian Academy of Science, 1857).

125. Stanley, *TDC*2, 360–362.

126. Stanley and Neame, *EDHMS*, 187.

127. Stanley and Neame, *EDHMS*, 195.

128. Stanley and Neame, *EDHMS*, 189.

129. Stanley and Neame, *EDHMS*, 193.

130. Stanley, *TDC*2, 426.

131. Stanley and Neame, *EDHMS*, 199.

132. Stanley, *TDC*2, 435.

133. Stanley, *TDC*2, 443.

134. Stanley, *TDC*2, 449.

135. The *New York Herald*, October 12, 1877, in Bennett, *SDNYH*, 341.

136. The *New York Herald*, October 9, 1877, in Bennett *SDNYH*, 341–46.

137. The *New York Herald*, November 14, 1877, in Bennett, *SDNYH*, 371.

138. 20, SA.

139. Marston to Stanley, September 25, 1877, SA.

140. Barney to Stanley, November 17, 1877, SA.

NOTES TO CHAPTER 6

1. John R. Young, *Around the World with General Grant* (New York: American News Company, 1879), 232–233.

2. The *New York Herald*, November 14, 1877, in Bennett, *SDNYH*, 371.

3. *PRGS* 22, 1877–78, 453–55.

4. Kirk to Derby, May 1, 1878, in Bennett, "SACZ," 48–49.

5. Hall, *SAE*, 245–246; McLynn, *SSA*, 12–13.

6. *PRGS* 21, 1876–77, 34.

7. The *Pall Mall Gazette*, December 2, 1875.

8. Coupland, *EEA*, 327.

9. Hyndman to Bates, October 23, 1876, RGS.

10. Hyndman to Bates, October 28, 1876, RGS.

11. Alcock to Bates, October 26, 1876, RGS.

12. Henry Yule and Henry M. Hyndman, *Mr. Henry M. Stanley and the Royal Geographical Society: a Record of Protest* (London: Bickers & Son 1878), 21.

13. The *Pall Mall Gazette*, November 19, 1876.

14. *PRGS*, 22, 1877–78, 166.

15. The *Pall Mall Gazette*, January 30, 1878.

16. Hyndman to Bates, February 11, 1878, RGS, and the *Pall Mall Gazette*, February 11, 1878.

17. The *Pall Mall Gazette*, February 11, 1878.

18. The *Standard*, February 9, 1878.

19. *PRGS*, 22, 1877–78, 151.

20. *PRGS*, 22, 1877–78, 299.

21. Charles P. Daly, "Geographical Work of the World in 1877," *Journal of the American Geographical Society* 10, 1878, 68.

22. *PRGS*, 22, 1877–78, 410.

23. The *Edinburgh Review* CXLVII, 1878, 166–91.

24. Lewis H. Gann and Peter Duignan, *The Rulers of Belgian Africa 1884–1914* (Princeton NJ: Princeton University Press, 1979), 32.

25. Discussions of Leopold's early years and activities can be found in L. Le Febve de Vivy, *Documants d'Histoire Précolonial Belge (1861–1865) Les Idées Coloniales de Léopold Duc de Brabant* (Bruxelles: Acadamie Royale des Sciences d'Outre Mer, 1955), Auguste Roeykens, *Léopold II et l'Afrique 1855–1880, Essai de Synthèse et de Mise au Point* (Bruxelles: Academie Royale des Sciences d'Outre Mer, 1958), and Leopold Greindl, *A la Recherche d'un Etat Indépendent Léopold II et les Philippines (1869–1875)* (Bruxelles: Academie Royale des Sciences d'Outre Mer, 1962).

26. The text of Leopold's remarks is available in Gustave L. Oppelt, *Léopold II* (Bruxelles: F. Heyez, 1885). Also see Auguste Roeykens, *Léopold II et la Conference Geographique de Bruxelles (1876)* (Bruxelles: Academie Royal des Sciences d'Outre Mer, 1956) and Sanford H. Bederman, "The 1876 Brussels Geographical Conference and the Charade of European Cooperation in African Exploration," *Terrae Incognitae* 21, 1989, 63–73.

27. Jean Stengers, *Congo Mythes et Réalitiés* (Paris: Ducult, 1989); Leopold to G. von Bleichröder, May 4, 1883, in Sabine Cornelis, "Stanley au Service de Leopold II in Sabine Cornelis, et al. eds., *H. M. Stanley Exploateur au Service du Roi* (Tervuren: Musée Royal de l'Afrique Centrale, 1991), 53.

28. Maurice, *HMSUL*, 8.

29. J. Scott Keltie, *The Partition of Africa* (London: Edward Sanford, 1895), 122.

30. Mill, *RRGS*, 122.

31. Leopold to Baron Solvyns, November 17, 1877, in Pierre van Zuylen, *L'Echiquier Congolais ou Le Secret du Roi* (Bruxelles: Charles Dessart, 1959), 43–44.

32. Henry M. Stanley, *The Congo and the Founding of Its Free State*, v. 1 (New York: Harper & Brothers, 1885), 21.

33. Greindl to Sanford, June 11, 1877, in Francois Bontinck, *Aux Origines de l'Etat Indépendent du Congo* (Louvain: Editions Nauwelaerts, 1966), 36.

34. Greindl to Stanley, June 26, 1878, Congo Letters, SA.

35. The *Scotsman*, June 17, 1878, the *Manchester Guardian*, June 19, 1878, the *Pall Mall Gazette*, July 11, 1878.

36. 16, 14, SA.

37. Bontinck, *OEIC*, 37–38.

38. Greindl to Stanley, October 5 and 13, 1878, Congo Letters, SA.

39. Original copy, SA.

40. Strauch to Stanley, December 9, 1878, SA.

41. 34, SA.

42. Stanley to Sanford, December 20, 187, in Bontinck, *OEIC*, 51–52.

43. Sanford to Latrobe, July 30, 1877, in Bontinck, *OEIC*, 8–16.

44. Leo T. Molloy, *Henry Shelton Sanford 1823–1891* (Derby, CT: The Bacon Printing Company, 1952), 27.

45. Swinburne to Stanley, December 29, 1877, SA.

46. 34, SA.

47. Kirk to Mackinnon, May 25, 1879, MP 88/30).

48. Stanley to Cambier, in Stanley, *CFFS1*, 39–44.

49. Bennett, *MT*.

50. Maurice, *HMSUL*, 21–22.

51. 34, SA.

52. Pere Ceulemans, "Le Sejour de Stanley a Zanzibat" (18 mars-fnn mai 1879), *Zaire* 11, 1957, 657–685.

53. 34, SA.

54. Stanley to Strauch, July 8, 1879, in Stanley, *CFFS1*, 52–54.

55. Sanford to Leopold, June 1, 1879, in Lysle E. Meyer, "Henry Sanford and the Congo: a Reassessment," *African Historical Studies* 4, 1971, fn., 24.

56. Jean Stengers, "Leopold II and the Association Internationale du Congo, in Stig Förster, Wolfgang J. Mommsen, and Ronald Robinson, eds., *Bismarck, Europe, and Africa* (Oxford: Oxford University Press, 1988), 229–244.

57. Stanley to Governor Rowe, SA.

58. 34, SA.

59. Stanley to Strauch, August 20, 1879, SA.

60. Stanley, *CFFS1*, 96–99.

61. Stanley, *CFFS1*, 95.

62. 34, SA.

63. Stanley, *CFFS1*, 142.

64. 34, SA.

65. Tracy Phillips, "Etymology of Some African Names," *Geographical Journal* 110, 1947, 142–144; Francois Bontinck, "Les Deux Bula Matari," *Etudes Congolaises* 162, 1969, 83–97.

66. Stanley to Sanford, December 8, 1879, in Bontinck, *OEIC*, 1966, 105–109.

67. Stanley, *CFFS1*, 168.

68. 34, SA.

69. Stanley to Strauch, March 14, 1880, in Stanley, *CFFS1*, 189–194.

70. Stanley, *CFFS1*, 190.

71. 34, SA.

72. 34, SA.

73. 34, SA.

74. 34, SA.

75. 34, SA.

76. See Richard West, *Brazza of the Congo* (London: Jonathan Cape, 1972).

77. 34, SA.

78. Stanley, *CFFS*I, 241.

79. 34, SA.

80. Stanley, *CFFS*I, 248.

81. 34, SA.

82. 34, SA

83. Similar, but slightly different accounts can be found in 16, SA, and Stanley, *CFFS*I, 274–275.

84. Strauch to Stanley, March 23, 1881, SA.

85. Stanley to Strauch, June 12, 1881, in Maurice, *HMSUL*, 49.

86. Stanley to Strauch, June 23, 1881, in Maurice, *HMSUL*, 60.

87. Maurice, *HMSUL*, 39.

88. 34, SA.

89. Stanley to Strauch, September 9, 1881, in Maurice, *HMSUL*, 79–80.

90. Stanley to Strauch, November 1881, in Maurice, *HMSUL*, 84–89.

91. Stanley, CFFSI, 324–325.

92. 34, SA.

93. Stanley, *CFFS*I, 335–344. An account also exists in 34, SA.

94. Stanley to Strauch, November 1881, in Maurice, *HMSUL*, 84–89.

95. 34, SA.

96. 34, SA.

97. 34, SA.

98. Stanley, *CFFS*I, 393.

99. 34, SA.

100. Stanley to Strauch, April 7, 1882, in Maurice, *HMSUL*, 117–123.

101. Stanley to Bracconier, July 6, 1881, in Maurice, *HMSUL*, 64–66.

102. 34, SA.

103. Charles Liebrechts, *Léopold II Fondateur d'Empire* (Bruxelles: Office de Publicité, 1932), 47.

104. Stanley, *CFFS*I, 425.

105. Marcel Storme, *NGANKABE, la Prétendue Reine des Baboma* (Bruxelles: Academie Royale des Sciences d'Outre-Mer, 1955).

106. Stanley, *CFFS*I, 463–464.

107. 34, SA.

108. 35, SA.

109. 35, SA.

110. 35, SA; West, *BC*, 122.

111. Henry M. Stanley, "The Comte Savorgnan de Brazza and His Pretensions" (London: J. Miles & Co. 1882).

112. 35, SA.

113. 35, SA.

114. 35, SA.

115. Stanley to Strauch, March 21, 1883, in 17, SA.
116. Stanley to Leopold, April 16, 1883, in 17, SA.
117. 35, SA.
118. 40, SA.
119. 40, SA.
120. Stanley, *CFFS*2, 16.
121. 40, SA.
122. For changing politics along the Congo River, see Robert W. Harms, *River of Wealth, River of Sorrow: The Central Zaire Basin in the Era of the Slave and Ivory Trade, 1500–1891* (New Haven: Yale University Press, 1981).
123. 35, SA.
124. 40, SA.
125. Stanley, *CFFS*2, 45.
126. Stanley to Marston, published in the *Times* (London), September 25, 1883.
127. 40, SA.
128. 35, SA.
129. Strauch to Stanley, April 2, 1883, in 35, SA.
130. Strauch to Stanley, April 30, 1883, in 35, SA.
131. Stanley to Strauch, July 12, 1883, in 35, SA.
132. 35, SA.
133. Stanley to Strauch, July 20, in 35, SA.
134. Stanley to Strauch, July 27 1883, in 35, SA.
135. Leopold to Stanley, May 27, 1883, in 35, SA.
136. De Borchgrave to Stanley, November 25, 1885, SA. Although the U.S. Oriental Exclusion Act didn't help Leopold recruit workers, in 1892, 540 Chinese came to work on the railway from Matadi to Stanley Pool. Some three hundred died or fled, one managing to make it all the way to Zanzibar. Others faded from history. See René Cornet, *La Bataille du Rail: La Construction du Chemin Fer de Matadi au Stanley Pool* (Bruxelles: Editions L. Cuypers, 1947), 230–31.
137. Stanley to Leopold, August 1883, in 35, SA.
138. 35, SA.
139. Stanley, *CFFS*2, 85–86.
140. Stanley, *CFFS*2, 91–94.
141. 35, SA.
142. 35, SA.
143. Stanley, *CFFS*2, 140.
144. 35, SA.
145. Stanley, *CFFS*2, 164–166.
146. Stanley, *CFFS*2, 152.
147. 35, SA.
148. Stanley, *CFFS*2, 164–166.
149. 35, SA.
150. 35, SA.
151. 35, SA.
152. 35, SA.
153. Stanley, *CFFA*2, 182. See Camile Colquihat, *Sur Le Haut-Congo* (Paris: J. Lebégue et Cie, 1888), 168–174, for a fuller version of the story.

154. Leopold to Stanley, September 30, 1883, in 35, SA.

155. Stanley to Johnston, July 23, 1883, in Roland Oliver, "Six Unpublished Letters of H. M. Stanley, *Bulletin de l'Academie Royale des Sciences Coloniales,* 58, New Series, 1957, 344–358.

156. Leopold to Stanley, September 20, 1883, in 35, SA.

157. 35, SA.

158. Stanley to Leopold, January 30, 1884, in 35, SA.

159. Leopold to Stanley, January 7, 1884, translation, SA.

160. The classic history of the Mahdist period is Peter M. Holt, *The Mahdist State in the Sudan 1881–1889* (Oxford: Clarendon Press, 2nd ed., 1970).

161. 35, SA.

162. 35, SA.

163. Stanley, *CFFA*2, 218–219.

164. Stanley, *CFFS*2, 212–213.

165. Stanley to Strauch, May 11, 1884, SA.

166. Stanley to Strauch, June 2, 1884, in 35, SA.

167. 39, SA.

168. 35, SA.

169. Strauch to Stanley, July 31, 1884, SA.

170. The *Times* (London), August 2, 1884.

171. Department of State, Papers Relating to the Foreign Relations of the United States, 1883, GPO 1886, ix, in Bontinck, *OEIC,* 144–45.

172. The Statutes at Large of the United States from December 1883 to March 1886, v. XXIII, GPO, 1885, 781, in Bontinck, *OEIC,* 200–01.

173. Anstey, BCNC.

174. The *Banner,* June 13, 1884.

175. Stanley to Sanford, September 20, 1884, in Bontinck, *OEIC,* 222.

176. Anstey, *BCNC.*

177. Drafts can be found in the British Library.

178. Count de Lalaing to Stanley, October 12, 1884, SA.

179. The *Times* (London), October 22, 1884.

180. William R. Louis, "Great Britain and German Expansion in Africa, 1884–1919," in Prosser Gifford and William R. Louis, eds., *Britain and Germany in Africa* (New Haven: Yale University Press, 1967), 3–46.

181. De Borchgrave to Stanley, November 10, 1884, SA.

182. 35, SA and Stanley, *CFFS*2, 409–414.

183. De Courcel to Ferry, November 22, 1884, in R. J. Gavin and J. A. Betley, *The Scramble for Africa: Documents on the Berlin West African Conference and Related Subjects 1884/1885* (Ibadan: Ibadan University Press, 1973), 353.

184. Bontinck, *OEIC,* 245.

185. Henry M. Stanley, "Inaugural Address," *Scottish Geographical Magazine*1, 1885, 1–16.

186. De Borchgrave to Stanley, December 4, 1884, in 35, SA.

187. John S. Galbraith, "Gordon, Mackinnon, and Leopold: the Scramble for Africa, 1876–84," *Victorian Studies,* 14, 369–388.

188. De Borchgrave to Stanley, January 1, 1885, in Bontinck, *OEIC,* 267, and 36, SA.

189. 36, SA.

190. See Oppelt, *LII,* for the articles and protocols.

191. Jean Stengers, "The Congo Free State and the Belgian Congo before 1914," in Lewis

H. Gann and Peter Duignan, eds., *Colonialism in Africa, Vol. 1, The History and Politics of Colonialism 1870–1914* (Cambridge: Cambridge University Press, 1969), 261–292.

192. John D. Hargreaves, "The Berlin Conference, West African Boundaries, and the Eventual Partition," in Förster, Mommsen, and Robinson, *BEABC,* 313–320.

193. De Borchgrave to Stanley February 23, 1885, in 36, SA.

194. De Borchgrave to Stanley, March 2, 1885, in 36, SA.

195. Stanley, *CFFS*2, 330.

196. Stanley, *CFFS*2, 407–408.

197. Document entitled "House of Harper," SA.

198. Stanley to de Borchgrave, May 26, 1885, SA.

199. De Borchrave to Stanley, May 31, 1885, in 36, SA.

200. Leopold to Strauch, June 27, 1885, in Bontinck, *OEIC,* 323.

201. Stanley to de Borchgrave, June 9, 1885, in 36, SA.

202. De Borchgrave to Stanley, June 28, 1885, SA.

203. Leopold to Stanley, July 19, 1885, SA.

204. Stanley to Sanford, July 15, 1885, in Bontinck, *OEIC,* 324–327.

205. Stanley to Sanford, September 15, 1885, in Bontinck, *OEIC,* 337–338.

206. Van Eetvelde to Stanley, September 24, 1885, SA.

207. Anstey, *BCNC,* 191–201.

208. Stanley to Makinnon, November 4, 1889, MP 55/217; L. van de Velde to Stanley, September 11, 1885, MP 55/217.

209. Stanley to Leopold, January 16, 1886, in 36, SA.

210. 36, SA.

211. Gann and Duignan, *RBE,* 85.

212. De Borchgrave to Stanley, March 10, 1886, in 36, SA.

213. Strauch to Stanley, January 12, 1884, SA.

214. Stanley to de Borchgrave, March 18, 1886, in 36, SA.

215. Tennant to Stanley, June 25, 1885, SA.

216. Stanley to Tennant, June 26, 1885, SA.

217. Stanley to Mackinnon, April 6, 1886, MP 55/218.

218. Contract in SA.

219. Stanley to Tennant, August 11, 1886, SA.

220. Stanley to Sanford, August 20, 1886, in Bontinck , *OEIL,* 358–359.

221. De Borchgrave to Stanley, September 12, 1886, SA.

222. Stanley to Mackinnon, September 23, 1886, MP 55/218.

223. Pond, *EG,* 265.

224. Henry M. Stanley, *In Darkest Africa,* v. 1 (New York: Charles Scribner, 1890), 34.

225. Stanley to Mackinnon, November 15, 1886, "Correspondence Respecting the Expedition for the Relief of Emin Pasha," 1886–87, 8, MP; Stanley to Mackinnon, December 13, 1889, *CREREP,* 1886–87, 17, MP.

Notes to Chapter 7

1. Stanhope White, *Lost Empire on the Nile: H. M. Stanley, Emin Pasha, and the Imperialists* (London: Robert Hale, Limited, 1969).

2. Baker's account is contained in Samuel W. Baker, *Ismailïa* (New York: Harper & Brothers, 1875).

3. Holt, *MSS*, 36.

4. J. Scott Keltie, *The Story of Emin's Rescue as Told in Stanley's Letters* (New York: Harper & Brothers, 1890), 6.

5. Robert W. Felkin, "The Position of Dr. Emin Bey," *Scottish Geographical Magazine* 2, 1886, 705–719.

6. A. Silva to the Earl of Iddesleigh, November 23, 1886, in Georg Schweitzer, *Emin Pasha His Life and Work*, Vol. 1 (Westminster: Archibald Constable & Co. 1898), xxiii–xxiv.

7. Joseph Thomson. *Through Masai Land: A Journey of Exploration among the Snowclad Volcanic Mountains and Strange Tribes of Eastern Africa*, 3rd ed. (London: Cass, 1968); Stanley to Mackinnon, November 15, 1886, *CREREP*: 1886–87, 8, MP.

8. Mackinnon to Foreign Office, November 15, 1886, *CREREP*, 8:4, 1888 MP; Iddesleigh to Sir E. Baring, November 25, 1886, *CREREP*, 8:10, 1888 MP.

9. John S. Galbraith, *Mackinnon and East Africa 1878–1895: A Study in the 'New Imperialism'* (Cambridge: Cambridge University Press, 1872).

10. Harold B. Thomas, "The Last Days of Bishop Hannington," *Uganda Journal* 8, 1940, 19–27.

11. The *Glasgow Herald*, December 30, 1886.

12. 64A, SA.

13. 64A, SA.

14. Mackinnon to Stanley, January 6, 1887, SA.

15. Relief Committee to Marquis of Salisbury, January 12, 1887, *CREREP*, 1886–87, 19, MP.

16. J. Pauncefote to the Secretary EPRC, 16 March, 1887, 88:32, MP; Emin to Mackay, July 11, 1886, in Stanley, *TDC1*, 26–28.

17. Edna Healey, *Lady Unknown: the Life of Angela Burdett-Coutts* (New York: Coward, McCann & Geohagen Inc., 1978).

18. Report to the Committee of Subscribers, SA.

19. See Smith, Mackenzie and Company, Ltd., *The History of Smith, Mackenzie and Company, Ltd.* (Nairobi: W. Boyd & Co., Ltd., 1949).

20. To Stanley c/o RGS, January 18, 1887, RGS, 83:15.

21. Walter G. Barttelot, *The Life of Edmund Musgrave Barttelot* (London: Richard Bentley and Son, 1890), 49–50.

22. Mackinnon to Stanley, January 28, 1887, SA.

23. The *Edinburgh Evening Dispatch*, January 14, 1887.

24. John R. Werner, *A Visit to Stanley's Rear-Guard* (Edinburgh: William Blackwood, 1889); Herbert A. Ward, *My Life with Stanley's Rear Guard* (London: Chatto & Windus, 1891), 196–216.

25. 64A, SDA.

26. De Borchgrave to Stanley, January 18, 1887, SA.

27. The *Scotsman*, January 20, 1887.

28. Anonymous, *Stanley and Africa: By the Author of "The Life of General Gordon"* (London : Walter Scott, 1890), 308.

29. 64A, SA.

30. Emin to Felkin, October 25, MP 91:48.

31. 64A, SA.

32. *CREREP*, 1888, 27, MP.

33. Roy MacLaren, *African Exploits: the Diaries of William Stairs, 1887–1892* (Montreal: McGill-Queens University Press, 1998), 38–39.

34. 64A, SA.

35. *CREREP*, enclosure 39, MP. Also available in SA.

36. Original of the agreement in SA.

37. Dorothy Middleton, *The Diary of A. J. Mounteney-Jephson* (Cambridge: Cambridge University Press, 1969), 74.

38. 64A, SA.

39. Thomas H. Parke, *My Personal Experiences in Equatorial Africa*, 3rd ed. (London: Sampson Low, Marston & Company, 1891), 21. In *Surgeon-Major Parke's African Journey 1887–89* (Dublin: Lilliput Press, 1994), J. B. Lyons contends that the book was actually put together by a good friend of Parke's, Dr. John Knott.

40. Meyer, *HSCA* and James P. White, "The Sanford Exploring Expedition," *Journal of African History* 8, 1967, 291–302.

41. Lyons, *SMPAJ*, 31.

42. 64A, SA; Herbert Ward, *Five Years with Congo Cannibals*, 3rd ed. (London: Chatto & Windus, 1891), 116.

43. Barttelot, *LEMB*, 82.

44. Middleton, *DAJMJ*, 81–83.

45. James S. Jameson, *The Story of the Rear Column of the Emin Pasha Relief Expedition* (London: R. H. Porter, 1890), 14.

46. Jameson, *SRCEPE*, 25.

47. MacLaren, *AEDWS*, 53.

48. Parke, *MPEEA*, 38–39.

49. Ward, *FYCC*, 32–33; Ward to Stanley, March 9, 1887, SA.

50. Stanley, *IDA1*, 84.

51. Middleton, *DAJMJ*, 92.

52. MacLaren, *AEDWS*, 59.

53. Stanley to Mackinnon, April 26, 1887, MP 55:218.

54. Stanley to Mackinnon, April 26, 1887, MP 55:218.

55. 64A, SA.

56. 64A, SA.

57. E. J. Glave, *Six Years of Adventure in Congo-Land* (London: Sampson Low, Marston & Co., 1893), 209.

58. 64A, SA.

59. Bontinck, *AHMMTT*, 142.

60. MacLaren, *AEDWS*, 75.

61. 64A, SA.

62. 64A, SA.

63. Middleton, *DAJMJ*, 108.

64. Barttelot, *LEMB*, 108–109.

65. Barttelot, *LEMB*, 134–139; Stanley, *IDA1*, 116–119.

66. Stanley to Mackinnon, June 23, 1887, MP 55:218.

67. John R. Troup, *The Story of the Rear Column of the Emin Pasha Relief Expedition* (London: Chapman & Hall, 1890), 114–116.

68. Middleton, *DAJMJ*, 113.

69. Stanley, *IDA*I, 149.

70. Middleton, *DAJMJ*, 118.

71. 36, SA.

72. Parke, *MPEEA*, 78.

73. Stanley, *IDA*I, 157.

74. Stanley, *IDA*I, 163.

75. 64A, SA.

76. 7:83, 3474, MP.

77. Stanley, *IDA*I, 189.

78. 55, SA.

79. MacLaren, *AEDWA*, 100.

80. Middleton, *DAJMJ*, 142.

81. MacLaren, *AEDWS*, 104.

82. 55, SA.

83. Stanley to Barttelot, September 18, 1887, 86:29, MP; copy in Barttelot, *LEMB*, 179–83.

84. 64A, SA.

85. 21, SA; Parke, *MPEEA*, 113.

86. Parke, *MPEEA*, 114–115.

87. MacLaren, *AEDWS*, 113–114.

88. Parke, *MPEEA*, 117.

89. Stanley, *IDA*I, 220.

90. Parke, *MPEEA*, 122.

91. Stanley, *IDA*I, 232.

92. Middleton, *DAJMJ*, 166–167.

93. Stanley, *IDA*I, 234.

94. 64A, SA.

95. 64A, SA.

96. Stairs to Jameson, February 26, 1888, SA.

97. Stanley to Stairs, August 6, 1888, SA.

98. MacLaren, *AEDWS*, 128–129.

99. Parke, *MPEEA*, 128.

100. Parke, *MPEEA*, 129–130.

101. 64A, SA.

102. Parke, *MPEEA*, 133.

103. Stanley, *IDA*I, 281.

104. Stanley to the Chairman of the EPRC, August 28, 1888, in Keltie, *SERTSL* 36–55.

105. Stanley, *IDA*I, 294–295; 64A, SA.

106. Stanley, *IDA*I, 314.

107. 56, SA.

108. Stanley, *IDA*I, 316.

109. Middleton, *DAJMJ*, 207.

110. MacLaren, *AEDWS*, 146.

111. Stanley, *IDA*I, 332.

112. 64A, SA.

113. Stanley, *IDA*I, 337.

114. Stanley, *IDA*I, 344–345.

115. Parke's report in Stanley, *IDA*1, 360–362.

116. Parke, *MPEEA*, 151.

117. Parke, *MPEEA*, 191.

118. Stanley to Barttelot, February 14, 1888, 86:29, MP; copy in Barttelot, *LEMB*. 184–92.

119. MacLaren, *AEDWAS*, 160.

120. Parke, *MPEEA*, 207.

121. Middleton, *DAJMJ*, 233–235.

122. Stanley, *IDA*1, 379.

123. Stanley, *IDA*1, 390–392.

124. 64A, SA.

125. Stanley, *IDA*1, 396.

126. Stanley, *IDA*1, 399.

127. Stanley, *IDA*1, 404.

128. John M. Gray. "The Diaries of Emin Pasha—Extract X," *Uganda Journal* 29, 1965, 204.

129. Cited in Schweitzer *EPHLW*, xxxiv; Emin to Felkin, October 25, 1887, 91:48, MP; Gray, "DEPEX," 203.

130. 64A, SA.

131. 64A, SA.

132. Stanley to Mackinnon, September 3, 1888, 55:218, MP.

133. Gray, "DEPEX," 204; Carl Peters, *New Light on Dark Africa*. Translated by H. W. Dulcken (London: Ward, Lock, and Co., 1891), 545.

134. Stanley, *IDA*1, 427–428. The version provided by Mounteney-Jephson in Arthur J. Mounteney-Jephson, *Emin Pasha and the Rebellion at the Equator* (New York: Charles Scribner's Sons, 1891), 48–50, is worded slightly differently. The meaning, however, is the same.

135. Gray, "DEPEX," 208.

136. Mounteney-Jephson, *EPRE*, 33.

137. Rennie M. Bere, "Exploration of the Ruwenzori, *Uganda Journal* 19, 1955, 121–136.

138. Parke, *MPEEA*, 220.

139. Stanley, *IDA*1, 431–432.

140. Bere, "ER," 124.

141. Stanley to the Chairman of the Emin Pasha Relief Committee, August 28, 1888, in Keltie, *SERTSL*, 36–55.

142. Middleton, *DAJMJ*, 259.

143. Emin to Stanley, May 25 and 26, 1888, SA.

144. 64A, SA.

145. Stanley to Grant, September 8, 1888, in Keltie, *SERTSL*, 148–159.

146. Stanley to Stairs, June 13, 1888, SA.

147. Stanley, *IDA*1, 479–481.

148. Stanley, *IDA*1, 484.

149. 58, SA; WCWL, 6010.

150. 64A, SA.

151. For an account of the rear column's time at Yambuya, especially as regards the relationships among the officers see Tony Gould, *In Limbo: The Story of Stanley's Rear Column* (London: Hamisch Hamilton, 1979).

152. William Bonny, "Diary" 1, SA.

153. Bonny to Stanley, September 1, 1889, SA.

154. Jameson, *SRCEPRE*, 136.

155. Ward, *MLSRG*, 81.

156. Bonny, "Diary" 1.

157. William J. Davy, "The Emin Relief Expedition under the Leadership of Henry M. Stanley," unpublished manuscript, SA.

158. Jameson, *SRCEPRE*, 203.

159. Barttelot to Mackinnon, March 27, 1888, 55:218, MP; Barttelot to Mackinnon, March 28, 1888, 85:17, MP.

160. Barttelot to Ward, June 4, 1888, in Barttelot, *LEMB*, 287–288; Ward, *MLSR*, 115.

161. Bonny, "Diary" 1, SA.

162. Trower to Stanley, November 10, 1890, SA.

163. Barttelot to Mackinnon, June 4, 1888, in Barttelot, *LEMB*, 270–82.

164. Barttelot to Sister, June 7, 1888, in Barttelot, *LEMB*, 295–96.

165. Bonny "Diary" 2, SA.

166. Ward, *MLSRG*, 125–132.

167. William Hoffmann, *With Stanley in Africa* (London: Cassell and Company Limited, 1938), 82. The book appears to be ghostwritten.

168. Stanley to Sheikh Hamed Ben Mahomed, August 17, 1888, in Keltie, *SERTSL*, 35–36.

169. Stanley to the RGS, September 1, 1888, *PRGS* 11, 1889, 264.

170. Werner, *VSRG*, 156.

171. Bonny, "Diary" 3, SA.

172. 59, SA.

173. 59, SA.

174. Stanley, *IDA*2, 49.

175. 64B, SA.

176. Stanley, *IDA*2, 65.

177. Bonny, "Diary" 3, SA.

178. 25, SA; Parke, *MPEEA*, 345.

179. Parke, *MPEEA*, 336.

180. Lyons, *SMPAJ*, 124.

181. Stanley, *IDA*2, 119; 64B, SA.

182. Jephson to Stanley, December 18, 1888, SA.

183. A good overview of conditions in Equatoria is contained in Smith, *E PRE*.

184. Mounteney-Jephson, *EPRE*, 213–214.

185. Mounteney-Jephson, *EPRE*, 291.

186. Stanley to Mounteney-Jephson, January 17 & 18, 1889, in Middleton, *DAJMJ*, 321–327.

187. Stanley to Emin, n.d. in Middleton, *DAJMJ*. 327–329.

188. 64B, SA.

189. Emin to Stanley, January 27, 1889, in Stanley, *IDA*2, 137–138.

190. Emin to Stanley, February 13, 1889, in Stanley, *IDA*2, 144–145.

191. Gray, "DEPEXIII," 69.

192. MacLaren, *AEDWS*, 247.

193. Stanley to the Chairman, Emin Pasha Relief Committee, August 17, 1889, 86:29, MP.

194. Parke, *MPEEA*, 381.

195. Stanley to the Chairman, Emin Pasha Relief Committee, August 17, 1889, in Keltie, *SERTSL*, 99–120.

196. Gaetano Casati, *Ten Years in Equatoria and the Return with Emin Pasha*, Vol. 2 London: Frederick Warne and Co., 1891, 249–250.

197. Mounteney-Jephson, *EPRE*, 303.

198. 60, SA.

199. 64B, SA.

200. Gray, "DEPEXIII," 76–77.

201. Casati, *TYEAREP2*, 255.

202. Stanley, *IDA2*, 254–255.

203. Stanley, *IDA2*, 262, 265.

204. Stanley, *IDA2*, 268–269.

205. Stanley, *IDA2*, 332.

206. MacLaren, *AEDWS*, 405–409; original in SA.

207. Casati, *TYEAREP2*, 268.

208. Middleton, *DAJMJ*, 362.

209. Stanley to the Chairman of the Emin Pasha Relief Committee, August 17, 1889, 86:29, MP.

210. 64B, SA.

211. Stanley, *IDA2*, 379.

212. 64B, SA.

213. 64B and William Hoffman, "Letters," SA.

214. Stanley, IDA2, 417; Stanley to de Winton, August 31, 1889, in Keltie, *SERTSL*, 160–69.

215. 64B, SA.

216. Stanley, *IDA2*, 428.

217. Stanley, *IDA2*, 434; 64B, SA.

218. Middleton, *DAJMJ*, 398.

219. Marston to Stanley, June 21, 1888, SA.

220. Stanley to Mackinnon, August 31, 1889, 55:218, MP.

221. 29B, SA; Gray, "DEPEXIV," 194.

222. Emin to Relief Committee, August 23, 1889, in Keltie, *SERTSL*, 159–160.

223. Middleton, *DAJMJ*, 399.

224. Middleton, *DAJMJ*, 404.

225. Auguste W. Schynse, *A Travers l'Afrique avec Stanley et Emin-Pasha*. Published by Charles Hespers. (Paris: W. Hinrichsen, 1890).

226. Stanley, *IDA2*, 443.

227. 64B, SA.

228. Stanley, *IDA2*, 446.

229. Casati, *TYEREP*, v. 2, 310.

230. Schynse, *TASEP*.

231. Thomas Stevens, *Scouting for Stanley in East Africa* (London: Cassell & Company, 1890), 254.

232. Parke to Stanley, December 9, 1889, SA.

233. The *Times* (London), November 25, 1889.

234. The *St. James's Gazette*, November 25, 1889.

235. See "Appendix A," Stanley, *IDA2*.

236. Original in *WCWL*, 7635:34.

237. Stanley to Colonel E. Smith, December 19, 1889, *CREREP*, MP.

238. E. Smith to Sir H. Ponsonby, December 28, 1889, George E. Buckle, *The Letters of Queen Victoria*, Third Series v. 1 (London: John Murray, 1930), 546–48.

239. Stanley to P. L. McDermott, January 25, 1891, 84:11, MP.

240. John M. Gray, "Stanley versus Tippoo Tib," *Tanganyika Notes and Records* 18, 1944, 11–27.

241. Smith to Ponsonby, December 28, 1889, in Buckle, *LQV*, 546–48.

242. Hoffman to Mrs. Shelton, June 28, 1890, Hoffman, "Letters," SA.

243. 64B, SA.

244. E. M. Merrick, *With a Palette in Eastern Palaces*. (London: Sampson Low, Marston & Company, 1899), 57.

245. 36, SA.

246. Stanley to Mackinnon, February 25, 1890, 55:219, MP.

247. Edward Marston, *How Stanley Wrote In Darkest Africa* (London: Sampson Low, Marston, Searle & Rivington, Ltd., 1890), 65–66.

Notes to Chapter 8

1. 36, SA.

2. Stanley to Mackinnon, January 19, 1890, 55:218, MP.

3. The specifics of the agreement can be found in Robert O. Collins, "Origins of the Nile Struggle: Anglo-German Negotiations and the Mackinnon Agreement of 1890." In Britain and Germany in Africa, ed. P. Gifford and William R. Lewis (New Haven: Yale University Press, 1967), 119–151.

4. The *Times* (London), May 6, 1890; *PRGS* 12, 1890, 313–331.

5. John M. Gray, "Early Treaties in Uganda, 1888–1891," *Uganda Journal* 12, 25–42; Louis, "GBGEA."

6. *PRGS* 12, 1890, 287.

7. Buckle, *LQVi*, 601.

8. "Report of the Committee to the Subscribers of the Emin Pasha Relief Fund," SA.

9. Pond, *EG*, 270.

10. The *New York Herald* (London), December 22, 1889.

11. Annie E. Coombes, *Reinventing Africa: Museums, Material Culture and Popular Imagination in Late Victorian and Edwardian England* (New Haven: Yale University Press, 1994); Felix Driver, *Geography Militant: Cultures of Exploration and Empire* (Oxford: Blackwell Publisher Ltd., 2001), 117–145.

12. D. Tennant to Stanley, April 26, 1890, SA.

13. D. Tennant to Stanley, April 28, 1890, SA.

14. D. Tennant to Stanley, May 4, 1890, SA.

15. Stanley to D. Tennant, May 4, 1890, SA.

16. D. Tennant to Stanley, May 6, 1890, SA.

17. D. Tennant to Stanley, May 7, 1890, SA.

18. D. Tennant to Mackinnon, May 15, 1890, 55:221, MP.

19. "Love," SA.

20. The *Times* (London), May 14, 1890.

21. "Religion," SA.

22. *PRGS* 12 1890, 489–91.

23. The *Edinburgh Review* 172, 1890, 372–88.

24. The *Saturday Review*, July 5, 1890.

25. The *Table*, May 24, 1890.

26. Harry H. Johnston, *The Story of My Life* (Indianapolis: The Bobbs-Merill Company, 1923), 266.

27. Stanley to Mackinnon, August 6, 1890, 55:219, MP.

28. Mackenzie to F. Lugard, 17 December 1889, in Margery Perham, *The Diaries of Lord Lugard*, v. 1 (Evanston: Northwestern University Press, 1959), 51.

29. Mounteney-Jephson, *EPRE*, x.

30. 81, SA.

31. 81, SA.

32. Stanley to Mackinnon, September 7, 1890, 55:219, MP.

33. 81, SA.

34. The *St. James's Gazette*, March 26, 1889.

35. A. M. Symington, "The New Found World and Its Hero," *Blackwood's Edinburgh Magazine* CXLVIII, 1890, 235.

36. Stanley to the chairman of the Emin Pasha Relief Committee, August 28, 1888, 86:29, MP.

37. Stanley to Colonel E. Smith, December 19, 1889, MP.

38. The *Times* (London), February 11, 1890.

39. Stanley to W. Barttelot, April 1890, in Barttelot, *LEMB*, 363–371.

40. The *New York Herald*, October 26, 1890

41. The *Times* (London), weekly edition, November 3, 1890.

42. Jameson, *SRGEPRE*, xvi.

43. The *Saturday Review*, November 8, 1890; the *Daily Telegraph*, November 10, 1890.

44. 81, SA.

45. Troup, *SRGEPRE*, 145–146.

46. The *Times* (London), November 12, 1890.

46. Troup, *SRGEPRE*, 260.

48. The *Times* (London), November 10, 1890.

49. Bonny, "Diary" 3; 29A, SA.

50. The *Speaker*, November 15, 1890.

51. The *Speaker*, November 22, 1890.

52. Assad Farran, SA.

53. Jameson to Mackinnon, August 3, 1888, the *Times* (London), November 15, 1889.

54. Jameson, *SRGEPRE*, 291.

55. Manuscript, SA.

56. "Report of the Committee to the Subscribers of the Emin Pasha Relief Fund," SA.

57. Farran to Stanley, January 15, 1890, SA; Assad Farran, "Stanley's Expedition Our Life at Yambuya Camp in Africa from 22nd June 1887 to June 8th 1888," SA; reprinted in Supplement to the *Daily Graphic*, November 27, 1890.

58. Stanley to de Winton, August 31, 1889, SA; reprinted in many newspapers, December 21, 1889.

59. Stanley to de Winton, March 5, 1890, SA.

60. Ward, *MLSRG*.

61. The *Times* (London), December 24, 1890.

62. W. Harcourt to Gladstone, January 7, 1891, in A. G. Gardiner, *The Life of Sir William Harcourt*, Vol. 2 (New York: George H. Doran Company, 1923), 94.

63. Henry R. Fox-Bourne, *The Other Side of the Emin Pasha Relief Expedition* (London: Chatto & Windus, 1891), 201.

64. E. L. Godkin, "Was the Emin Pasha Expedition Piratical?" *The Forum* 10, 1891, 633–644.

65. Francis C. Burnand, *A New Light Thrown Across the Keep It Quite Darkest Africa* (London: Trischlin & Co., 1891); *Some Old Friends . . . With Illustrations from "Punch"* (London: Bradbury, Agnew & Co., 1892).

66. 64B, SA.

67. Speech in New York City, reported in the *New York Times*, December 3, 1890.

68. Speech in Washington, D.C., December 8, 1890, reported in the *New York Times*, December 9, 1890.

69. The *Chicago Tribune*, January 3, 1891.

70. The *Syracuse Standard*, December 2, 1890.

71. 36, SA.

72. 81, SA.

73. The *Syracuse Standard*, December 1, 1890.

74. Pond, *EG*, 270.

75. 81, SA.

76. Report of the Emin Pasha Relief Committee, SA.

77. Stanley to Mackinnon, June 6, 1891, 55:219 MP.

78. Aubrey Stanhope, *On the Track of the Great: Recollections of a "Special Correspondent"* (London: Eveleigh Nash, 1914), 151–155.

79. 81, SA.

80. 81, SA.

81. The fullest history is contained in R. P. Ceulemans, *La Question Arabe et le Congo (1883–1892)*, Academie Royale des Sciences Coloniales, Classe des Sciences Morales et Politiques XII, 1959. A good English summary exists in Norman R. Bennett, *Arab Versus European: Diplomacy and War in Nineteenth Century East Central Africa* (New York: Africana Publishing Company, 1986), 233–244. For a firsthand account of the war, see Samuel L. Hinde, *The Fall of the Congo Arabs* (New York: Thomas Whittaker, 1897).

82. The *New Zealand Herald*, December 24, 1891.

83. Stanley to Mackinnon, December 22, 1891, 55:219, MP.

84. 81, SA.

85. 81, SA; reprinted in D. Stanley, *ASHMS*, 435–436.

86. D. Stanley, *ASHMS*, 439.

87. For the basics of the treaty see Pakenham, *SFA*, 350–351.

88. Speech in Swansea, reported in the *Times* (London), October 4, 1892.

89. 81, SA.

90. Henry M. Stanley, "Slavery and the Slave Trade in Africa," *Harper's New Monthly Magazine* 86, 1893, 623.

91. Thomas H. Parke, *Guide to Health in Africa* (London: Sampson Low, Marston & Company, 1893), viii–ix.

92. Parke to Stanley, March 21, 1893, SA.

93. Pond, *EG*, 279.

94. 81, SA.

95. Galbraith, *MEA*.

96. W. Parke to Stanley, November 20, 1893, SA.

97. 81, SA.

98. D. Stanley, *ASHMS*, 454.

99. D. Stanley, *ASHMS*, 461.

100. Lecture given at the Canterbury Theatre, January 20, 1894, manuscript, SA.

101. "A Memorial to Livingstone," presented at Dartford, April 21, 1894, manuscript, SA.

102. De Borchgrave to Stanley, June 10, 1894, 18, SA.

103. 31, SA; D. Stanley, *ASHMS*, 465; Marston, *AW*, 243–244.

104. "Manuscript" of autobiography, SA.

105. SA. Some of these, plus a few notebook extracts, can be found in D. Stanley, *ASHMS*, 517–538.

106. D. Stanley, *ASHMS*, 443–444.

107. Henry M. Stanley, "To the Electors of North Lambeth" (flier), SA.

108. D. Stanley, *ASHMS*, 480.

109. "Diary" of Dorothy Tennant, SA.

110. The *San Francisco Examiner*, October 4, 1895.

111. The *Journal*, New York City, November 10, 1895.

112. Untitled hand-written manuscript, SA.

113. Robert H. Humphreys, "Anglo-American Rivalries and the Venezuela Crisis of 1895," *Transactions of the Royal Historical Society* 15, 131–164.

114. William Taylor, *Illustrated Africa* 84, December 1885.

115. Henry Morton Stanley, *Illustrated Africa* 82, October 1895.

116. Henry M. Stanley, "How to Conquer a Continent," *Illustrated Africa* 84, December 1895.

117. William Taylor, *The Flaming Torch in Darkest Africa* (New York: Eaton & Mains, 1898), 22.

118. 81, SA.

119. Examples can be found in the *Times* (London), January 30, February 24, and December 4, 1896.

120. 81, SA.

121. The *Saturday Review*, September 19, 1896.

122. Henry M. Stanley, "Twenty-Five Years' Progress in Equatorial Africa," *Atlantic Monthly* 80, October 1897, 471–484.

123. D. Stanley, *ASHMS*, 536.

124. Leopold to Stanley, September 18, 1897, in 18, SA.

125. See Roger Anstey, "The Congo Rubber Atrocities—A Case Study," *African Historical Studies* IV, 1971, 59–76.

126. 81, SA.

127. Henry M. Stanley, *Through South Africa* (London: Samson Low, Marston and Company, 1898), xii, xiv.

128. Stanley, *TSA*, 10.

129. 81, SA.

130. Stanley, *TSA*, 26.

131. 81, SA.

132. Stanley, *TSA*, 104.

133. D. Tennant, *ASHMS*, 491.

134. D. Tennant, *ASHMS*, 486–489.

135. Stanley, *TSA*, 126–140.

136. Henry M. Stanley, "The South African Problem," address at Lowesloft, February 23, 1898, SA.

137. Lionel Decle, *Three Years in Savage Africa* (London: Methuen & Co., 1900), x.

138. Stanley to de Borchgrave, March 28, 1898, in 18, SA.

139. Henry M. Stanley, "Africa in the Twentieth Century," in Henry M. Stanley, et al., *Africa Its Partition and Its Future* (New York: Dodd, Mead and Company, 1898), 3–22.

140. 31, SA; D. Stanley, *ASHMS*, 502.

141. D. Stanley, *ASHMS*, fn., 507.

142. Henry M. Stanley, "For Life and Liberty," *The Youth's Companion* LXXIII, 1899, 645–646; "How I Acted the Missionary and What Came of It," *The Youth's Companion* LXXIV, 1900, 669–670; "The Origin of the Negro Race," *North American Review* CLXX, 1900, 656–665.

143. Anonymous to Stanley, June 10, 1899, SA.

144. 81, SA.

145. Speech at Hercules Road School Rooms, November 30, 1899, manuscript, SA.

146. Pond, *EG*, 286–287.

147. 81, SA.

148. W. T. Stead, "Character Sketch: 1. Mr. H. M. Stanley," *Review of Reviews*, January 1890, 26.

149. 81, SA.

150. D. Stanley, *ASHMS*, 513.

151. Robert R. James, *Henry Wellcome* (London: Hodder & Staughton Ltd., 1994).

152. Copies of Affidavit or Affirmation for Inland Revenue and Will, SA.

Notes to Chapter 9

1. Oliver Ransford, *David Livingstone: The Dark Interior* (New York: St. Martin's Press, 1978), 270.

2. Judith Listowell, *The Other Livingstone* (Cape Town: David Philip, 1974).

3. The *Spectator*, May 8, 1890.

4. Sidney Low, "Henry Morton Stanley," *Cornhill Magazine*, New Series 17, 1904, 30.

5. D. Colwell, "The Complete Mr. Stanley, We Presume," *The Bulletin*, December 13, 2001, 32.

6. "Introduction" to Guy Burrows, *The Land of the Pigmies* (New York: Thomas Y. Crowell & Company, 1898), xii–xiii.

7. Jean Brierley and Thomas Spear, "Mutesa, the Missionaries, and Christian Conversion in Buganda," *International Journal of African Historical Studies* 21, 1988, 601–618.

8. Roger E. De Smet, *Carte de la Densité et de la Localisation de la Population de la Province Orientale (Congo).* (Bruxelles: CEMUBAC, 1962.)

9. Roy C. Bridges, "The Historical Role of British Explorers in East Africa," *Terrae Incognitae* 14, 1982, 1–21.

10. For this and other prevailing images of Africa, see Dorothy Hammond and Alta Jablow, *The Africa That Never Was* (Prospect Heights, IL: Waveland Press, Inc., 1992).

11. Bennett, *SDNYH*, xxxiv–xxxv.

12. D. Stanley, *ASHMS*, 532–533.

13. Stairs to Stanley, June 21, 1891, in 18, SA.

14. Johnston, *RSW*, 535.

15. Arthur J. Mounteney-Jephson, "Reminiscences of Sir Henry Morton Stanley," *Scribners Magazine* 36, 1904, 286.

16. Pond, *EG*, 280.

Bibliography

ARCHIVES

MP   Mackinnon Papers, School of Oriental and African Studies Library, London, England.
RGS   Royal Geographical Society, London, England.
SA   Stanley Archive, Koninklijk Museum voor Midden-Afrika (Musée Royal d'Afrique Centrale), Tervuren, Belgium.
WCWL   Western Collection, Wellcome Library for the History and Understanding of Medicine, London, England.

PUBLICATIONS OF HENRY MORTON STANLEY

Books

Coomassie and Magdala: The Story of Two British Campaigns in Africa. Freeport, NY: Books for Libraries Press, 1971.
Through South Africa. London: Sampson Low, Marston and Company, 1898.
My Early Travels and Adventures in America and Asia. 2 Vols. New York: Charles Scribner's Sons, 1895. Volume 1 reprinted as *My Early Travels and Adventures in America.* Lincoln: University of Nebraska Press, 1982.
My Dark Companions and Their Strange Stories. London: Sampson Low, Marston & Company, 1893.
My Kalulu, Prince, King, and Slave: A Story of Central Africa. London: Sampson Low, Marston, Searle & Rivington, 1890.
In Darkest Africa. 2 Vols. New York: Charles Scribner's Sons, 1890.
The Congo and the Founding of Its Free State. 2 Vols. New York: Harper & Brothers, 1885.
The Comte Savorgnan de Brazza and His Pretensions. London: J. Miles & Co., 1882.
Through the Dark Continent. 2 Vols. New York: Harper & Brothers Publishers, 1878.
How I Found Livingstone. New York: Scribner, Armstrong & Co, 1872.

Articles and Other Writings

"The New Aspirants for African Fame and What They Must Be." *The Fortnightly Review* 77, 1902, 738–746.
"How I Acted a Missionary and What Came of It," *The Youth's Companion* LXXIV, 1900, 669–670.

"The Origin of the Negro Race," *North American Review* CLXX, 1900, 656–665.

"For Life and Liberty," *The Youth's Companion* LXXIII, 1899, 645–646.

"Africa in the Twentieth Century." In *Africa Its Partition and Its Future*, edited by Henry M. Stanley et al. New York: Dodd, Mead and Company, 1898, 3–22.

"Developments in Congo State." *Illustrated Christian World* 112, April 1898.

"Twenty-Five Years' Progress in Equatorial Africa." *Atlantic Monthly* 80, 1897, 471–484.

"Gospel Victories in Uganda." *Illustrated Christian World* 96, December 1896.

"Civilization in the Congo," *Illustrated Christian World* 95, November 1896.

"Zanzibar's Mart," *Illustrated Christian World* 94, October 1896.

"How to Conquer a Continent," *Illustrated Africa* 84, December 1895.

"A Blue Coat Boy in Africa," *The Youth's Companion* LXVIII, 1894, 242–243.

"Out of the Jaws of Death," *The Youth's Companion* LXVIII, 1894, 118–119.

"Slavery and the Slave Trade in Africa," *Harper's New Monthly Magazine* 86, 1893, 613–632.

Henry M. Stanley, "Inaugural Address," *Scottish Geographical Magazine*, 1885, 1–16.

OTHER PUBLICATIONS

Books and Monographs

Anonymous. *Stanley and Africa. By the Author of "The Life of General Gordon."* London: Walter Scott, 1890.

Anstey, Roger. *Britain and the Congo in the Nineteenth Century.* Oxford: Clarendon Press, 1962.

Anstruther, Ian. *I Presume: Stanley's Triumph and Disaster.* London: Geoffrey Bless, 1956.

Baker, Samuel W. *Ismailïa.* New York: Harper & Brothers, 1875.

Barttelot, Walter. G. *The Life of Edmund Musgrave Barttelot.* London: Richard Bentley and Son, 1890.

Batchelor, John, and Julie Batchelor. *In Stanley's Footsteps: Across Africa from West to East.* London: Blandford, 1990.

Beeton, S. O., and Ronald Smith. *Livingstone and Stanley: A Narrative of the Exploration of the English Discoverer and of the Adventures of the American Journalist.* London: Ward Lock, and Tyler, 1872.

Bennett, Norman R. *Arab versus European: Diplomacy and War in Nineteenth Century East Central Africa.* New York: Africana Publishing Company, 1986.

Bennett, Norman R. *Mirambo of Tanzania 1840?–1884.* New York: Oxford University Press, 1971.

Bennett, Norman R., ed. *Stanley's Dispatches to the New York Herald 1871–1872, 1874–1877.* Boston: Boston University Press, 1970.

Bierman, John. *Dark Safari: The Life Behind the Legend of Henry Morton Stanley.* New York: Alfred A. Knopf, 1990.

Blaikie, W. Garden. *The Personal Life of David Livingstone.* New York: Laymen's Missionary Movement, 1890.

Bontinck, Francois. *L'Autobiographie de Hamed ben Mohammed el-Murjebi Tippu Tip (ca. 1840–1905).* Bruxelles: Académie Royale des Sciences d'Outre-Mer, 1974.

Bontinck, Francois. *Aux Origines de l'Etat Indépendent du Congo.* Louvain: Editions Nauwelaerts, 1966.

Brode, Heinrich. *Tippoo Tib.* London: Edward Arnold, 1907.

Brom, John. L. *Sur les Traces de Stanley*. Paris: Presses de la Cité, 1958.

Buckle, George. E. *The Letters of Queen Victoria*. Third Series. 3 Vols. London: John Murray, 1930.

Burnand, Francis C. *Some Old Friends . . . with Illustrations from "Punch."* London: Bradbury, Agnew & Co., 1892.

Burnand, Francis C. *A New Light Thrown Across the Keep It Quite Darkest Africa*. London: Trischlin & Co., 1891.

Burrows, Guy. *The Land of Pygmies*. New York: Thomas Y. Crowell & Company, 1898.

Burton, Richard F. *Two Trips to Gorilla Land and the Cataracts of the Congo*, 2 vols. London: Sampson Low, Marston, Low, and Searle, 1876.

Cairns, H. Alan C. *Prelude to Imperialism: British Reactions to Central African Society 1840–1890*. London: Routledge & Kegan Paul, 1965.

Cameron, Vernay L. *Across Africa*. 2 Vols. London: Dalby, Isbister & Co., 1877.

Casada, James A. *Dr. David Livingstone and Sir Henry Morton Stanley: An Annotated Bibliography*. New York: Garland Publishing, Inc., 1976.

Casati, Gaetano. *Ten Years in Equatoria and the Return with Emin Pasha*. 2 Vols. London: Frederick Warne and Co., 1891.

Ceulemans, Père. *La Question Arabe et le Congo 1883–1892*. Bruxelles: Acadamie Royale des Sciences d'Outre-Mer, 1959.

Colquilhat, Camille. *Sur Le Haut-Congo*. Paris: J. Lebégue et Cie, 1888.

Coombes, Annie E. *Reinventing Africa: Museums, Material Culture in Late Victorian and Edwardian England*. New Haven: Yale University Press, 1994.

Cornet, René. J. *La Bataille du Rail: La Construction du Chemin Fer de Matadi au Stanley Pool*. Bruxelles: Editions L. Cuypers, 1947.

Coupland, Reginald. *The Exploitation of East Africa 1856–1890*. Evanston: Northwestern University Press, 1967.

Coupland, Reginald. *Livingstone's Last Journey*. London: Collins, 1945.

Crowe, Sybil E. *The Berlin West Africa Conference 1884–1885*. London: Longman's Green and Co., 1942

Decle, Lionel. *Three Years in Savage Africa*. London: Methuen & Co., 1900.

Driver, Felix. *Geography Militant: Cultures of Exploration and Empire*. Oxford: Blackwell Publisher, Ltd., 2001.

Edgerton, Robert B. *The Fall of the Asante Empire: The Hundred-Year War for Africa's Gold Coast*. New York: The Free Press, 1995.

Ellis, James J. *H. M. Stanley*. London: James Nisbet & Co., 1890.

Farwell, Byron. *Queen Victoria's Little Wars*. London: Allen Lane, 1973.

Forrest, Derrick W. *Francis Galton: The Life and Work of a Victorian Genius*. London: Paul Elek, 1974.

Fox-Bourne, Henry R. *The Other Side of the Emin Pasha Relief Expedition*. London: Chatto & Windus, 1891.

Fraile, Ramón J. *Stanley De Madrid a las Fuentes del Nilo*. Barcelona: Mondadori, 2000.

Francis, Derek W. *Francis Galton: The Life and Work of a Victorian Genius*. London: Paul Elek, 1974.

Galbraith, John S. *Mackinnon and East Africa 1878–1895: A Study in the "New Imperialism."* Cambridge: Cambridge University Press, 1972.

Galton, Francis. *Memories of My Life*. London: Methuen & Co., 1908.

Gann, Lewis H., and Peter Duignan. *The Rulers of Belgian Africa 1884–1914*. Princeton: Princeton University Press, 1979.

Gardiner, A. G. *The Life of Sir William Harcourt*. 2 Vols. New York: George H. Doran Company, 1923.

Gavin, R. J., and J. A. Betley. *The Scramble for Africa. Documents on the Berlin West African Conference and Related Subjects 1884/1885*. Ibadan, Nigeria: Ibadan University Press, 1973.

George, Thomas. *The Birth, Boyhood and Younger Days of Henry M. Stanley*. London: The Roxburghe Press, 1895.

Glave, E. J. *Six Years of Adventure in Congo-Land*. London: Sampson Low, Marston & Co., 1893.

Gould, Tony. *In Limbo: the Story of Stanley's Rear Column*. London: Hamish Hamilton, 1979.

Greindl, Léopold. *A la Recherche d'un Etat Indépendent Léopold II et les Phillipines (1869–1875)*. Bruxelles: Academie Royale des Sciences d'Outre Mer, 1962.

Hall, Richard. *Stanley: An Adventurer Explored*. Boston: Houghton Mifflin Company, 1975.

Hammond, Dorothy, and Alta Jablow. *The Africa that Never Was*. Prospect Heights, IL: Waveland Press, Inc., 1992.

Harms, Robert W. *River of Wealth, River of Sorrow: The Central Zaire Basin in the Era of the Slave and Ivory Trade, 1500–1891*. New Haven: Yale University Press, 1981.

Healey, Edna. *Lady Unknown: The Life of Angela Burdett-Coutts*. New York: Coward, McCann & Geoghagen Inc., 1978.

Helps, Edmund A., ed. *Correspondence of Sir Arthur Helps*. London: John Lane, 1917.

Hinde, Samuel L. *The Fall of the Congo Arabs*. New York: Thomas Whittaker, 1897.

Hird, Frank. *H. M. Stanley: The Authorized Life*. London: Stanley Paul & Co. Ltd., 1935.

Hoffmann, William. *With Stanley in Africa*. London: Cassell and Company Limited, 1938.

Hochschild, Adam. *King Leopold's Ghost*. Boston: Houghton Mifflin Company, 1998.

Holt, Peter M. *The Mahdist State in the Sudan 1881–1889*. 2nd edition. Oxford: Clarendon Press, 1970.

Hughes, Nathaniel. C. Jr. *Sir Henry Morton Stanley, Confederate*. Baton Rouge: Louisiana State University Press, 2000.

Ingersoll, Lurton D. *Explorations in Africa by Dr. David Livingstone and Others*. Chicago: Union Publishing Company, 1872.

Jackson, Peggy. H. *Meteor Out of Africa*. London: Cassell & Company, Ltd., 1962.

James, Robert R. *Henry Wellcome*. London: Hodder & Staughton Ltd., 1994.

Jameson, James S. *The Story of the Rear Column of the Emin Pasha Relief Expedition*. London: R. H. Porter, 1890.

Jeal, Tim. *Livingstone*. New Haven: Yale University Press, 2001.

Johnston, Harry H. *The Story of My Life*. Indianapolis: The Bobbs-Merrill Company, 1923.

Jones, Emir W. *Sir Henry M. Stanley: The Enigma Review of the Early Years*. Denbigh, Wales: Gee & Son Limited, 1989.

Jones, Lucy. M., and Ivor W. Jones. *H. M. Stanley and Wales*. Denbigh, Wales: Gee and Son, 1972.

Jones, Roger. *The Rescue of Emin Pasha*. New York: St. Martin's Press, 1972.

Joûbert, Joseph. *Stanley, le Roi des Explorateurs*. Anvers, Belgium: G. and G. Grassin, 1905.

Keltie, J. Scott. *The Partition of Africa*. London: Edward Stanford, 1895.

Keltie, J. Scott. ed. 1890. *The Story of Emin's Rescue as Told in Stanley's Letters*. New York: Harper & Brothers, 1890.

Liebrechts, Charles. *Léopold II Fondateur d'Empire*. Bruxelles: Office de Publicité, 1932.

Listowel, Judith. *The Other Livingstone*. Cape Town: David Philip, 1974.

Littell, Blaine. *South of the Moon: On Stanley's Trail through the Dark Continent*. London: Weidenfeld and Nicolson, 1966.

Little, Henry W. *Henry M. Stanley His Life, Travels, and Explorations*. London: Chapman and Hall, Limited, 1890.

Livingstone, David. *Missionary Travels and Researches in South Africa*. London: John Murray, 1857.

Livingstone, David. *Narrative of an Expedition to the Zambezi and Its Tributaries: And the Discovery of Lakes Shirwa and Nyasa 1858–1864*. London: John Murray, 1865.

Lyons, J. B. *Surgeon-Major Parke's African Journey 1887–89*. Dublin: The Lilliput Press, 1994.

Macdonald, E. A. *The Story of Stanley, the Hero of Africa*. Edinburgh: Oliphant, Anderson & Ferrier, 1891.

MacLaren, Roy. ed. *African Exploits: The Diaries of William Stairs, 1887–1892*. Montreal: McGill-Queens University Press, 1998.

Magyar, Laszlo. *Explorations of the Zaire Delta*. Pest: Hungarian Academy of Sciences, 1857.

Markham, Clement. R. *A History of the Abyssinian Expedition*. London: Macmillan and Co., 1869.

Marston, Edward. *After Work: Fragments from the Workshop of an Old Publisher*. London: Heineman, 1904.

Marston, Edward. *How Stanley Wrote in Darkest Africa*. London: Sampson, Low, Marston, Searle, & Rivington, Ltd., 1890.

Maurice, Albert, ed. *H. M. Stanley: Unpublished Letters*. New York: Philosophical Library, Inc., 1957.

McLynn, Frank J. *Stanley Sorcerer's Apprentice*. London: Constable, 1991.

McLynn, Frank J. *Stanley: The Making of African Explorer*. London: Constable, 1989.

Merrick, E. M. *With a Palette in Eastern Palaces*. London: Sampson Low, Marston & Company, 1899.

Metcalfe, G. E. *Great Britain and Ghana. Documents of Ghana History*. London: Thomas Nelson & Sons Ltd., 1964.

Middleton, Dorothy, ed. *The Diary of A. J. Mounteney-Jephson*. Cambridge: Cambridge University Press, 1969.

Mill, Hugh R. *The Record of the Royal Geographical Society 1830–1930*. London: The Royal Geographical Society, 1930.

Molloy, Leo T. *Henry Shelton Sanford 1823–1891*. Derby, CT: The Bacon Printing Company, 1952.

Mounteney-Jephson, Arthur J. *Emin Pasha and the Rebellion at the Equator*. New York: Charles Scribner's Sons, 1891.

Myatt, Frederick. *The March to Magdala: The Abyssinian War of 1868*. London: Leo Cooper, 1970.

Nicoll, David J. *Stanley's Exploits, or Civilizing Africa*. 2nd edition. Aberdeen: J. Leatham, 1891.

Oppelt, Gustave L. *Léopold II*. Bruxelles: F. Heyez, 1885.

Pakenham, Thomas. *The Scramble for Africa: the White Man's Conquest of the Dark Continent from 1876 to 1912*. New York: Random House, 1991.

Parke, Thomas H. *Guide to Health in Africa*. London: Sampson Low, Marston & Company, 1893.

Parke, Thomas H. *My Personal Experiences in Equatorial Africa*. 3rd edition. London: Sampson Low, Marston & Company, 1891.

Perham, Margery, ed. *The Diaries of Lord Lugard*. 3 Vols. Evanston: Northwestern University Press, 1959.

Peters, Carl. K. *New Light on Dark Africa*. Translated by H. W. Dulcken. London: Ward, Lock, and Co, 1891.

Pond, James B. *Eccentricities of Genius*. New York: G. W. Dillingham Company, 1900.

Ransford, Oliver. *David Livingstone: The Dark Interior*. New York: St. Martin's Press, 1978.

Riffenburgh, Beau. *The Myth of the Explorer*. Oxford: Oxford University Press, 1994.

Roeykens. Auguste. *Léopold II et l'Afrique 1855–1880 Essai de Synthèse et de Mise au Point*. Bruxelles: Academie Royale des Sciences d'Outre Mer, 1958.

Roeykens, Auguste. *Léopold II et la Conférence Géographique de Bruxelles (1876)*. Bruxelles: Academie Royale des Sciences d'Outre Mer, 1956.

Rowlands, Cadwaladar. *Henry M. Stanley: The Story of His Life from His Birth in 1841 to His Discovery of Livingstone, 1871*. London: John Camden Hotten, 1872.

Schweitzer, Georg, ed. *Emin Pasha: His Life and Work*. Westminster: Archibald Constable and Co., 1898.

Schynse, Auguste W. *A Travers l'Afrique avec Stanley et Emin-Pasha*. Published by Charles Hespers. Paris: W. Hinrichsen, 1890.

Seaver, George. *David Livingstone: His Life and Letters*. London: Lutterworth Press, 1957.

Seitz, Don C. *The James Gordon Bennetts: Father and Son*. Indianapolis: The Bobbs-Merrill Company, 1928.

Sheriff, Abdul. *Slaves, Spices & Ivory in Zanzibar*. London: James Curry, 1987.

Smet, Roger E. De. *Carte de la Densité et de la Localisation de la Population de la Province Orientale* (Congo). Bruxelles: CEMUBAC, 1962.

Smith, Iain R. *The Emin Pasha Relief Expedition 1886–1890*. Oxford: Clarendon Press., 1972.

Smith, Mackenzie & Company, Ltd. *The History of Smith, Mackenzie and Company, Ltd.* Nairobi: W. Boyd & Co. Ltd., 1949.

Sorenson, Alfred. *The Story of Omaha from the Pioneer Days to the Present Time*. 3rd edition. Omaha: National Printing Company, 1923.

Stanhope, Aubrey. *On the Track of the Great: Recollections of a "Special Correspondent."* London: Eveleigh Nash, 1914.

Stanley, Dorothy, ed. *The Autobiography of Sir Henry Morton Stanley*. New York: Greenwood Press, 1969.

Stanley, Richard, and Alan Neame, eds. *The Exploration Diaries of H. M. Stanley*. London: William Kimber, 1961.

Stengers, Jean. *Congo Mythes et Réalités*. Paris: Ducult, 1989.

Stevens, Thomas. *Scouting for Stanley in East Africa*. London: Cassell & Company, Limited, 1890.

Storme, Marcel. *NGANKABE, la Prétendue Reine des Baboma*. Bruxelles: Academie Royale des Sciences d'Outre-Mer, 1956.

Taylor, William. *The Flaming Torch in Darkest Africa*. New York: Eaton & Mains, 1898.

Thomson, Joseph. *To the Central African Lakes and Back*. 2 Vols. 2nd edition. London: Frank Cass & Co. Ltd, 1968.

Thomson, Joseph. *Through Masai Land: A Journey of Exploration among the Snowclad Volcanic Mountains and Strange Tribes of Eastern Equatorial Africa*. 3rd edition. London: Cass, 1968.

Troup, John. R. *The Story of the Rear Column of the Emin Pasha Relief Expedition*. London: Chapman & Hall, 1890.

Vivy, L. Le Febve de. *Documents d'Histoire Précoloniale Belge (1861–1865) Les Idées Coloniales de Léopold Duc de Brabant*. Bruxelles: Academie Royale des Sciences d'Outre Mer, 1955.

Waller, Horace, ed. *The Last Journals of David Livingstone in Central Africa*. New York: Harper & Brothers Publisher, 1875.

Ward. Herbert. *Five Years with the Congo Cannibals*. 3rd edition. London: Chatto & Windus, 1891.

Ward, Herbert. *My Life with Stanley's Rear Guard*. London: Chatto & Windus, 1891.

Wassremann, Jacob. *Bula Matari: Stanley Conqueror of a Continent*, translated from German by Eden and Cedar Paul. New York: Liveright Publishers, 1933.

Watson, Andrew M. *Agricultural Innovation in the Early Islamic World: The Diffusion of Crops and Farming Techniques, 700–1100*. Cambridge: Cambridge University Press, 1893.

Werner, John R. 1889. *A Visit to Stanley's Rear-Guard*. Edinburgh: William Blackwood and Sons, 1889.

West, Richard. *Brazza of the Congo*. London: Jonathan Cape, 1972.

White, Stanhope. *Lost Empire on the Nile: H. M. Stanley, Emin Pasha, and the Imperialists*. London: Robert Hale Limited, 1969.

Wilks, Ivor. *Asante in the Nineteenth Century: The Structure and Evolution of a Political Order*. London: Cambridge University Press, 1975.

Wolseley, Garnet W. *The Story of a Soldier's Life*. 2 Vols. Westminster: Archibald Constable & Co., Ltd., 1903.

Young, John R. *Around the World with General Grant*. New York: American News Company, 1879.

Yule, Henry and Henry M. Hyndman. *Mr. Henry M. Stanley and the Royal Geographical Society; Being a Record of a Protest*. London: Bickers & Son, 1878.

Zuylen, Pierre van. *L'echiquier Congolais ou Le Secret du Roi*. Bruxelles: Charles Dessart, 1959.

Articles, Book Chapters, and Miscellaneous Publications

Roger Anstey. "The Congo Rubber Atrocities—A Case Study," *African Historical Studies* IV, 1971, 59–76.

Balch, Edwin. S. "American Explorers of Africa," *Geographical Review* 45, 1918, 274–281.

Bax. S. Napier. "The Grave of Fred Barker, One of Stanley's Followers," *Tanganyika Notes and Records* 7, 1939, 56–58.

Bederman, Sanford H. "The 1876 Brussels Geographical Conference and the Charade of European Cooperation in African Exploration," *Terrae Incognitae* 21, 1989, 63–73.

Bennett, Norman R. "Stanley and the American Consuls at Zanzibar," *Essex Institute Historical Collections* 100, 1964, 41–58.

Bere, Rennie M. "Exploration of the Ruwenzori," *Uganda Journal* 19, 1955, 121–136.

Boahen, A. Adu. 1974. "Politics in Ghana, 1800–1874." In *History of West Africa*, Vol 1, edited by J. F. Ade Ajayi and Michael Crowder. London: Longman, 167–261.

Bontinck, Francois. "La Date de la Rencontre Stanley-Livingstone, Africa," *Revista Timestrale di Studie Documentazione dell'Insituto Italo-Africano* 24, 1979, 225–241.

Bontinck, Francois. "Les Deux Bula Matari," *Etudes Congolaises* 12, 1969, 83–97.

Bridges, Roy. "Towards the Prelude to the Partition of East Africa." In *Imperialism, Decolonization and Africa*, edited by Roy Bridges. New York: St. Martin's Press, 2000, 65–113.

Bridges Roy, C. "The Historical Role of British Explorers in East Africa," *Terrae Incognitae* 14, 1982, 1–21.

Brierley, Jean, and Thomas Spear. "Mutesa, the Missionaries, and Christian Conversion in Buganda," *International Journal of African Historical Studies* 21, 1988, 601–618.

Ceulemans, Père. "Le Sejour de Stanley a Zanzibar (18 Mars-fin Mai 1879)," *Zaire* 11, 1957, 675–685.

Collins, Robert O. "Origins of the Nile Struggle: Anglo-German Negotiations and the Mackinnon Agreement of 1890." In *Britain and Germany in Africa*, edited by P. Gifford and William R. Louis. New Haven: Yale University Press, 1967, 119–151.

Colwell, D. "The Complete Mr. Stanley, We Presume," *The Bulletin*, December 13, 2001, 32–34.

Cornelis, Sabine. "Stanley au Service de Leopold II." In *H. M. Stanley, Explorateur au Service du Roi*, edited by Sabine Cornelis, et al. Tervuren: Musée Royal de l'Afrique Centrale, 1991, 41–57.

Davy, William J. "The Emin Relief Expedition under the Leadership of Henry M. Stanley," unpublished manuscript, Tervuren, SA.

Daly, Charles P. "Geographical Work of the World in 1877," *Journal of the American Geographical Society* 10, 1878, 1–76.

Felkin, Robert. W. "The Position of Dr. Emin Bey," *Scottish Geographical Magazine* 2, 1886, 705–719.

Fraile, Ramón J. Transcript of Documents Concerning Stanley's Assignments in Spain, n.d. Tervuren, SA.

Galbraith, John S. "Gordon, Mackinnon, and Leopold: the Scramble for Africa, 1876–84," *Victorian Studies* 14, 1971, 369–388.

Godkin, E. L. "Was the Emin Pasha Expedition Piratical?" *The Forum* 10, 1891, 633–644.

Gray, John M. "The Diaries of Emin Pasha—Extracts," X, XIII, XIV, *Uganda Journal* 29, 1965, 201–204, and 32 1968, 65–80, 189–198.

Gray, John M. "Early Treaties in Uganda, 1888–1891." *Uganda Journal* 12, 1968, 25–42.

Gray, John M. "Stanley versus Tippoo Tib," *Tanganyika Notes and Records* 18, 1944, 11–27.

Griffith-Jones, T. "Stanley's First and Second Expeditions Through Mpwapwa and W. L. Farquhar's Grave," *Tanganyika Notes and Records* 25, 1948, 28–33.

Hargreaves, John D. "The Berlin Conference, West African Boundaries, and the Eventual Partition." In *Bismarck, Europe, and Africa. The Berlin Conference 1884–1885 and the Onset of Partition,* edited by Stig Förster, Wolfgang J. Mommsen, and Ronald Robinson. Oxford: Oxford University Press, 1988, 313–320.

Humphreys, Robert A. "Anglo-American Rivalries and the Venezuela Crisis of 1895," *Transactions of the Royal Historical Society,* 5th series 17, 1967, 131–164.

Johnston, Harry H. "The Results of Stanley's Work," *Good Words* 45 1904, 533–543.

Jones, Emir W. "Stanley: The Mystery of Three Fathers," *The National Library of Wales Journal* XXVIII, 1993–94, 39–56, 127–151.

Jones, Emir W. "Sir Henry M. Stanley's Schoolmaster: The Vindication of James Francis," *Flintshire Historical Society* 33, 1992, 103–118.

King, Edward. "An Expedition with Stanley," *Scribner's Monthly* 5, 1872, 105–112.

Louis, William R. "Great Britain and German Expansion in Africa, 1884–1919." In *Britain and Germany in Africa*, edited by Prosser Gifford and William R. Louis. New Haven: Yale University Press, 1967, 3–46.

Low, D. Anthony. "The Northern Interior 1840–84." In *History of East Africa*, edited by Roland Oliver and Gervase Mathew, Vol. 1. London: Oxford University Press, 1963, 297–351.

Low, Sidney. "Henry Morton Stanley," *Cornhill Magazine*, New Series 17, 1904, 26–42.

Lumumba, Patrice. "Un Explorateur Incomparable," *La Voix du Congolais* X, 1954, 516–522.

Markham, Clement R. "Unpublished History of the Royal Geographical Society." London: Royal Geographical Society, n.d.

Meyer, Lysle. E. "Henry S. Sanford and the Congo: A Reassessment," *African Historical Studies* 4, 1971, 19–39.

Mounteney-Jephson, Arthur J. "Reminiscences of Sir Henry Stanley," *Scribner's Magazine* 36, 1904, 284–289.

Oliver, Roland. "Six Unpublished Letters of H. M. Stanley," *Bulletin de l'Académie Royale des Sciences Coloniales,* Nouvelle Series 58, 1957, 344–358.

Pankhurst, Richard. "Ethiopia and Somalia." In *Africa in the Nineteenth Century until the 1880s,* Vol. VI, edited by J. F. Ade Ajayi, UNESCO General History of Africa. Oxford: Heinemann, 1989, 376–411.

Phillipps, Tracy. "Etymology of Some African Names," *Geographical Journal* 110, 1947, 142–144.

Rubenson, Sven. "Ethiopia and the Horn." In *The Cambridge History of Africa, c. 1790–c. 1870,* Vol. 5, edited by John E. Flint, Cambridge: Cambridge University Press, 1976, 51–98.

Shuey, Mary W. "Stanley in Arkansas," *Southwest Review* 27, 1941–42, 197–206.

Stead, W. T. "Character Sketch: 1. Mr. H. M. Stanley," *Review of Reviews,* January 1890, 20–27.

Stengers, Jean. "Leopold II and the Association Internationale du Congo." In *Bismarck, Europe, and Africa,* edited by S. Förster, W. J. Mommsen, and R. Robinson. Oxford: Oxford University Press, 1988, 229–244.

Stengers, Jean. "The Congo Free State and the Belgian Congo before 1914." In *Colonialism in Africa, V.1, The History and Politics of Colonialism 1870–1914,* edited by Lewis. H. Gann and Peter Duignan. Cambridge: Cambridge University Press, 1969, 261–92.

Stengers, Jean, "Quelques Observations sur la Correspondance de Stanley," *Zaïre* 9, 1955, 899–926.

Symington, A. M. "The New Found World and Its Hero," *Blackwood's Edinburgh Magazine* CXLVIII, 1890, 233–250.

Tayal, Maureen J. " The Abyssinian Expedition 1867–1868," M. A. Thesis, University of Calgary, Department of History, 1975.

Thomas, Harold B. "The Last Days of Bishop Hannington," *Uganda Journal* 8, 1940, 19–27.

Thomas, Harold B. "Ernest Linant de Bellefonds and Stanley's Letter to the 'Daily Telegraph,'" *Uganda Journal* 2, 1934–35, 7–13.

Thomas, Harold B., and I. R. Dale. "Uganda Place Names: Some European Eponyms," *Uganda Journal* 17, 1953, 101–123.

Wheeler, Douglas L. "Henry M. Stanley's Letters to the Missouri Democrat," *Missouri Historical Society Bulletin* XVII, 1961, 269–286.

White, James P. "The Sanford Exploring Expedition," *Journal of African History* 8, 1967, 291–302.

Index

About the Author

JAMES L. NEWMAN is a professor of geography in the Maxwell School of Syracuse University. He has served as a consultant for the *National Geographic Society Atlas* and an originator of its National Geography Bee, a consultant for the *Encyclopedia of Cultures and Everyday Life*, an Africa consultant for the *Columbia Encyclopedia*, and an editorial board member for the *Cambridge History and Culture of Human Nutrition*. His previous books include *The Peopling of Africa: A Geographical Interpretation*; *Eliminating Hunger in Africa: Technical and Human Perspectives*, with Daniel Griffith; *Population: Patterns, Dynamics, and Prospects*, with Gordon Matzke; *Contemporary Africa: Geography and Change*, with C. Gregory Knight; and *The Ecological Basis for Subsistence Change among the Sandawe of Tanzania*. He served as the editor of *Drought, Famine and Population Movements in Africa*. In addition, he has authored numerous articles and book chapters relating to Africa. Professor Newman holds a Ph.D. from the University of Minnesota. He resides in Syracuse, New York.